Higher Education in India

About the Editor

Dr. Mujibul Hasan Siddiqui, M.A. (Economics), B.Ed., M.Ed., M.Phill. (Education), Ph.D. (Education) PGDHE, PGDDE, MADE, CCCA, CCPALA is working as Associate Professor in the Department of Education, Aligarh Muslim University, Aligarh. He has authored and edited several books, encyclopaedias in the area education, research and innovative teaching, published more than fifty research papers, reviewed eighty national and international research papers.

He is a member of editorial board of several national and international journal of research. He has guided several Ph.D. research scholars and research projects of M.Ed. students. He has received several academic and research excellence awards in India like Life Time Education Achievement Award, Bharat Gaurav Ratan Award, Best Educationist Award, Bharat Shiksha Ratan Award, Eminent Educationist Award, Rashtriya Vidya Saraswati Purashkar.

His area of interest in Curriculum, Evaluation, Management of Education, Planning and Finance of Education, ICT, Models of Teaching, Guidance and Counselling, Value Education, Higher Education, Distance Education, Pedagogy of Economics, Social Studies, Indian Education and Problems, Educational Technology, Education of Children with Special Needs.

Higher Education in India

Concepts, History Problems and Suggestions

Edited by
Mujibul Hasan Siddiqui

CONCEPT PUBLISHING COMPANY PVT. LTD.
NEW DELHI-110059

ISBN-13: 93-86682-51-2

First Published 2019

Published and Printed by

Concept
Since 1974

Concept Publishing Company Pvt. Ltd.
A/15-16, Commercial Block, Mohan Garden,
New Delhi-110059 (India)
T : 91 11 25351460, 91 11 25351794
E : publishing@conceptpub.com, *W*: www.conceptpub.com

Cataloging in Publication Data--Courtesy: D.K. Agencies (P) Ltd. <docinfo@dkagencies.com>

Higher education in India / edited by Mujibul Hasan Siddiqui.
pages cm
Contributed articles.
Includes bibliographical references and index.
ISBN 9789386682512

1. Education, Higher--India. I. Siddiqui, Mujibul Hasan, editor.

LCC LA1153.H54 2019 DDC 378.54 23

Preface

Higher education plays significant role in enhancing knowledge, understanding application, skills, attitudes, values, among the people of the whole world. Higher education makes knowledge and innovative and research society. The book entitled "Higher Education in India" highlights conceptual meaning, objectives, history, management, some of the issues of equity, equality excellence, employability, suggestions, total quality management of teacher education (TQM). In higher education, ICT is a scientific, technological and engineering discipline and management technique used in handling information, its application and associate with social, economic and cultural matters [UNESCO (2002)]. Higher education makes development in information and communication technology day by day in our country. Recent development in distance mode of education is massive open online courses (MOOCs) around world. E-learning and blended learning makes a real speed in the area of Higher Education. Overall development of Higher Education in India considers human development, social development, economic, industrial, cultural, science and technological development. This book is very useful for teachers, research scholars and other person who have interests, in higher education and also useful specifically in B.Ed., M.Ed. and M.A. (Education) courses.

Editor

Acknowledgements

I would like to express my sincere gratitude to my contributors of this book who sent book chapters with their great efforts. I am also very grateful to my wife Professor (Dr.) Mrs. Nasreen, Department of Education, Aligarh Muslim University, Aligarh for her best cooperation and encouragements for the completion of this book.

I am also thankful to my colleagues and friends who cooperated me to complete this work.

I am very thankful to the Concept Publishing Co. Pvt. Ltd., New Delhi to publish my book within short time.

Editor

Contents

Section-III
Status and Relevance

Section-IV
Technology and Distance Learning

Section-V
Problems and Challenges Ahead

List of Contributors

Dr. Afshan Anees, Ex-Assistant Professor, Department of Education, Kishanganj Centre, Aligarh Muslim University, Aligarh-202002, Uttar Pradesh, India.
E-mail: *anees1@gmail.com*

Miss Amrutajyoti Mohanty, Lecturer, Department of Education, North Orissa University, Takatpur, Mayurbhanj, Odisha, India.
E-mail: *amrutamadam92@gmail.com*

Dr. Annie Kavitha, L., Assistant Professor of Mathematics, Meston College of Education, Chennai-14, Tamil Nadu, India.
E-mail: *annielkavitha@gmail.com*

Deepti Sharma, Research Scholar, Department of Education, Aligarh Muslim University, Aligarh-202002, Uttar Pradesh, India.
E-mail: *deeptisharma.amu@gmail.com*

Dr. Farida Siddiqui, Professor, Department of Economics, Maulana Azad National Urdu University (MANUU), Hyderabad, Andhra Pradesh, India.
E-mail: *farida.siddiqui@yahoo.com*

Dr. Haseena V.A., Post-Doctoral Fellow (ICSSR), Women Studies Centre, Cochin University of Science and Technology, Cochin-22, Kerela.
E-mail: *economicsasmabi@gmail.com*

Dr. Ismail Thamarasseri, Assistant Professor, Department of Education, Central University of Kashmir, Wanabal, Nowgam Bypass, Srinagar-190015, Jammu & Kashmir, India.
E-mail: *ismailktkl@gmail.com*

Prof. Jahitha Begum, A., Professor & Head, Department of Education, Gandhigram Rural University, Dindigul, Tamil Nadu, India.
E-mail: *jahee_j@yahoo.co.in*

Jaspal Singh, Research Scholar (Ph.D.), Department of Education, Jaipur National University, Jaipur, Rajasthan.
E-mail: *jass.gill85@gmail.com.*

Dr. Jayanta Mete, Professor, Department of Education, University of Kalyani, Nadia, West Bengal.
E-mail: *jayanta_135@yahoo.co.in*

Ms. Julie Chhetri, Research Scholar, Vinaya-Bhavana, Visva-Bharati, Santiniketan, West Bengal.
E-mail : *julekha.chhetri@gmail.com*

Mohmmad Suhail, Doctoral Fellow, Department of Social Work, Aligarh Muslim University, Aligarh.

Dr. Mohd. Uzair, Assistant Professor, Department of Social Work, Aligarh Muslim University, Aligarh-202002, Uttar Pradesh, India.
E-mail : *ms13153@gmail.com*

Dr. Mona Mehta, Assistant Professor, Department of FCRM, Faculty of Family and Community Sciences, The M.S. University of Baroda, Vadodara, Gujarat.
E-mail: *mona.mehta.map@gmail.com*

Dr. Mujibul Hasan Siddiqui, Associate Professor, Department of Education, Aligarh Muslim University, Aligarh-202002, Uttar Pradesh, India.
E-mail: *mhsiddiqui50@gmail.com*

Dr. Nimmi Maria Oommen, Assistant Professor of Education, Titus II Teachers College, Tiruvalla, Kerala.
E-mail : *drnimmioommen@gmail.com*

N. Vivek, MBA, MISTE, UGC-NET, RBP, Teaching Fellow, Department of Management Studies, Anna University Regional Campus, Madurai-19, Tamil Nadu, India.
E-mail : *vjpraj1971@yahoo.com*

Dr. P. Bhaskar, Lecturer in History, S.V. Arts College, Tirupati-517502, Andhra Pradesh, India.
E-mail: *pbrsvac@gmail.com*

Dr. Poonam Singh Kharwar, Assistant Professor, Faculty of Education, B.H.U., Kamachha, Varanasi, Uttar Pradesh, India.
E-mail: *poonam.kharwar3@gmail.com*

Dr. Rajiv Kumar Agarwal, Assistant Professor, Department of Commerce, Vardhman College, Bijnor, Uttar Pradesh, India.
E-mail: *dr.rajivkagarwal@gmail.com*

Rakesh Manna, Assistant Teacher, Santipur Municipal High School (H.S.), Santipur, Nadia, West Bengal.
E-mail: *srijanrkm@gmail.com*

Dr. Sakhawliana, Assistant Professor, Department of Public Administration, Government Kamalanagar College, Chawngte, Mizoram, India.
E-mail: *ska_hlawndo@yahoo.com*

Dr. Sandhya Jain, Assistant Professor, MATEI, Sulakhedi, Indore, Madhya Pradesh, India. E-mail: *sandhyajaincll@gmail.com*

Sarika Sharma, Research Scholar, Department of Education, and Aligarh Muslim University, Aligarh-202002, Uttar Pradesh, India.
E-mail : *sarikasharma2010@rediffmail.com*

Miss Sayeeda Wajal, Research Scholar, Ph.D., Department of Arabic, Baba Ghulam Shah Badshah University, Rajouri, Jammu & Kashmir, PIN. 185234, India.
E-mail: *sayeedawajalmir@yahoo.com*

Dr. Sewali Borah, Lecturer, Deptartment of Education, College of Education, Nagaon, Assam, India.
E-mail: *sewaliborah10@gmail.com*

Dr. Sunita Srivastava, Assistant Professor, MATEI, Sulakhedi, Indore, Madhya Pradesh, India.
E-mail: *sandhyajaincll@gmail.com*

Dr. Swaleha Zubair, Assistant Professor, Computer Science, Women's College, Aligarh Muslim University, Aligarh-202002, Uttar Pradesh, India.
E-mail : *swalehazubair@yahoo.com*

Dr. V. Joseph Paul Raj, M.Com., B.Ed., MBA, M.Phil., Ph.D. Associate Professor, Department of Management Studies, Anna University Regional Campus Madurai-19, Tamil Nadu, India.

Dr. VSV Laxmi Ramana, Professor, Department of English, Majmaah University, Kingdom of Saudi Arab.
E-mail : *vlaxmiramana@gmail.com*

Mr. Zaffar Ahmad Nadaf, Research Scholar, Aligarh Muslim University, Aligarh-202002, Uttar Pradesh, India.
E-mail: *ali.zafar000324@gmail.com*

Introduction

Higher Education is a final stage of formal learning that occurs after completion of secondary education. Higher education includes teaching, research, exacting applied work and social services, activities of universities. The right access to higher education is mentioned in number of international human rights instruments. The UN International Covenant on Economic, Social, Cultural Rights of 1966, declares in Article 13, that higher education shall be made equally accessible to all, on the basis of capacity, by energy appropriate means and in particular by the progressive introduction of free education.With the realm of teaching, it includes both the undergraduate level and beyond that graduate level (or post-graduate level). In addition to the skills, that are specific to any particular degree, potential employers in any profession are looking for evidence of critical thinking and analytical reasoning skills, team working skills, information literacy ethical judgement, decision-making skills, language skills, problem-solving skills and wide knowledge liberal arts and sciences. Higher education aims at the comprehensive development of new generation. Higher education is a tool for social progress. It can be viewed as an end in itself. The Government cannot promote a throw back to diehard attitude of obscurantism and to many stagnant concepts. Society has to change positively as the world changes and adopt itself. Higher education help nation building at all layers. In India, the Department of Higher Education, MHRD, is responsible for the overall development of the basic infrastructure of higher education sector, both in terms of policy and planning. Under a planned development process, the Department looks after expansion of access and qualitative improvement in higher education, through world class universities, colleges and other institutions. In constitution of India, the people have Fundamental Right to Education, inserted by the 86th Constitutional Amendment in December 2002 and passed by the Parliament in July 2009. The provision of the Act came into force from 1 April, 2010.

The text is broadly divided into five sections—each section intends to provide an insight into some aspect of higher education such as conceptual issues, history and development, status and relevance, technology and distance learning and various problems and challenges of higher education of India.

Section-I: Conceptual Issues

The first chapter is on "Aims and Objectives of Higher Education" by *Mujibul Hasan Siddiqui* and *Deepti Sharma*. This chapter highlights the important aims and objectives of higher education such as to provide knowledge and wisdom, to inculcate the value of democracy, justice, liberty, equality and fraternity among the students, to disseminate knowledge and skills, to promote global excellence, to encourage researches and ensure high level of researches, to produce and quality teachers, to enhance self-learning among students of higher education. In this section, chapter second indicates "Higher Education for Social and National Development". This chapter explores that the system of higher education of India is the third largest in the world. In India the Apex body of higher education is the University Grants Commission. This further highlights the brief development of higher education as given in earlier chapters larger. It focuses on international scenario on higher education. The chapter third in this section incorporates "Higher Education in India: A Need for Formalised Monitoring". This chapter reveals the significance of mentoring in higher education with reference to formal monitoring programmes in National and International universities. This chapter further gives the importance of the review of literature of monitoring useful for quantitative and qualitative research. Social work education gives more emphasis on practical exposure along with classroom teaching. Fourth chapter is on "Inclusive Growth, Knowledge, Economy and Neo-Liberal Model of Development for Higher Education". The study in this chapter shows that inclusive growth is a concept which advances access to equal opportunities, productive resources and benefits of development to every segment of the society during the development process. This study shows the global approach to the development of education in the light of Neo-Liberal Model of Development for Higher Education which is higher levels of competition among educational institutions, less government intervention, increased non-governmental sources of funding, decentralisation away from the state and in favour of individual institutions and introduction of performance indicators to analyse the production of institutions. The main aim of Neo-liberal model is to produce more cost-effective flexible institutions that are better able to supply the needs of the labour market. In this section chapter fifth is on "Inclusive Education in Higher Education: Issues and Prospects". This chapter demonstrates about marginalised groups and education, enrolment in higher education and professional education, enrolment of Muslims, public higher education institutions, academic performance, financial and non-financial barriers, and research implications.

Section-II: History and Development

In this section chapter six is on "History of Education System in Ancient India." It deals with the gradual development of higher education in ancient period. The higher education was based on the *Vedas* given the name of Vedic education system which reflects glitters some fundamentals such as developing the wholesome personality, making formal and informal educations, responsible, starting academic sessions solemnly, adjusting school hours, close contact between the teacher and taught, emphasising discipline, providing free education, development of civic responsibilities, and social values. The root of higher education is the development of Indian civilization in all respects. The seventh chapter is about "History of Higher Education in India: A Comparison between Pre- and Post-British Period". This chapter describes that in ancient time, India was known by the oldest having formal university in the world such as Taxila (now in Pakistan), Nalanda (in Bihar), and Ujjaini (in Madhya Pradesh). Around 460 A.D. White Huns (Ephthalites) destroyed Taxila University. Bakhtiyar Khilji destroyed Nalanda University in 1193. Due to this, a rapid decline in the practices of Buddhism took place in India. Ujjaini a major centre for mathematics, literature, philosophy and astronomy was destroyed by Sultan Iltutmish in 1235. An establishment of three universities at Bombay, Calcutta and Madras in 1857 under the British rule started modern higher education system in India. Colleges, imparting higher education, were affiliated with these universities. There were only 25 universities in India by 1947. Rapid expansion of higher education emerged came into existence in post-Independence. The number of universities increased from 25 in 1947 to 348 in 2005 and at present time, 777 universities are in our country. The chapter covers many aspects for the historical development of higher education of our country under different heads: Education in India—Ancient and Modern, Education and the Masses, Education in Ancient

India, Education and Women, Educational Institutions of Repute, Revival of Ancient Knowledge, Modern Education System, Reasons for Introducing Modern Education, Outcomes of Modern Education, Brahmins Ahead of Others, Reasons for Masses Deprived of Modern Education, Reasons for not Succeeding in "Educating All", Impoverished Group, Importance of English Language in Modern World, Alienation of the Masses, Influence of West, Education Policy of the British, Endeavour of the Christian Missionaries, European Era, The Mode of Instruction, Grassroots School System and Education Open to All. The chapter eighth in this section focuses on "Higher Education in Punjab". It has been seen from this chapter that Punjab is land of five rivers. There were three universities during 1966-67 and four universities during 1970-71; now there are 15 private universities, 11 Government universities and deemed universities and other groups of institutes providing much-diversified courses of higher education. The Punjab government is undertaking multiple initiatives to improve the quality of higher education and employability in the state. This chapter gives some important suggestions to raise the quality of higher education such as more investment in learning society, maintaining connections between educational institution and industries, provision of incentives for teachers and researchers, innovative practices, mobilization of resources, development of ICT in Universities and Colleges, learner-centred education and dynamic methods, public private partnership, introducing more vocational courses, maintaining international cooperation, action plan for improving quality etc. The chapter nineth in this section studied "Secondary Teacher Education System in India with Special Emphasis on Respect of Administration, Supervision and Finance". The objectives of the study are to find out the administrational and supervisional role of secondary teacher education in India. The findings are: (i) at the national level NCTE mandate the norms and standard of teacher education, NCERT along with its 6 RIEs and SCERs prepare training modules and undertake specific programmes for training of teachers, and teacher educators and institutional support is provided by the NUEPA. At the District level, in service training is provided by the District Institute of Education and Training (DIETs). Financial support is provided by the Central Government through the SSA and UGC plays great role to maintain standard of quality in teacher training institutions. In this section chapter tenth is on "Value Oriented Education: Issues of Concern". The chapter shows that value comes from the Latin word '*vatere*', which means to be worth, to be strong. The main objective of value oriented education is to develop integrated personality of the students. This chapter includes functions, needs, strategies of value oriented education, recommendations of various commissions and committees for value education, and approaches of imparting value education, and the role of the teacher in enhancing value education in society in general.The chapter eleventh in this section is on "Paulo Freire's Concept on Trivialization of Conscientization". It is concluded from this chapter that education is used to domesticate transfer of knowledge. We can observe a certain incipient conscientization in the way the students react, because the natural intentionality of human awareness cannot be thwarted by any educator's domesticating purpose.

Section-III: Status and Relevance

The chapter twelfth in this section deals with "Higher Education in India: A Study of Educational Development in Mizoram". This chapter tells that education is the backbone of human development in every society of the world. In starting, education was treated as the means to the highest end of life (*Mukti* or Emancipation). The Western society began to interfere into the subcontinent since 1498 and the traditional Indian education cannot withstand with them and rapidly sway to their system. In India, higher education was *ab initio* at the behest of the Buddhist teaching because they gave free education into their monastic institutions and had attracted students from India and abroad. Taxila and Nalanda Universities were pioneering institutions for higher education in India. Kautilya, the famous author of *Arthashastra* had received higher education from Taxila University. In the 5th century A.D., the Chinese traveller Fa-Hien came in India and found no remains of this University. The main aim of the establishment of three universities in 1857 at Bombay, Calcutta and Madras was to prepare youth for civil services, legal profession and medicine. University Education Commission was established under the Chairmanship of Dr. S. Radhakrishnan in 1948 layed the foundation of the future of Higher Education in India. There was a great increase in number of universities in India during the year 1950 to 2015. There were only 30 universities in 1950-51 enhanced to 55 in 1960-61 (83% increase during 1950-1960) and has reached 740 universities and 38856 colleges in 2014-15. This chapter further highlighted the development of higher education in Mizoram. Mizoram made of two words 'Mizo' and 'Ram'. The word Ram means country or land while Mizo is the generalized name of the inhabitants, 'Hillman'. In 1958 Pachunga University College (PUC) was established in Mizoram, and Mizoram University in 2001. By 2010 in

Mizoram 30 colleges were established—21 colleges were meant for Arts, 5 for Science and 11 colleges gives professional degree in different subjects, *viz.* Law, Veterinary Science, Computer, Nursing, Laboratories, and Technologies. The chapter thirteenth in this section is on "Status of Arabic Language in Higher Education in Jammu & Kashmir". In early fourteenth century a large number of Kashmiris began converting to Islam with quaranic language "Arabic". Arabic is studied in Islamic schools including Darul-uloom-Rahimiyah and Darul-Bilal at Srinagar, and Islamic Darul-uloom-Shopian and Darul-uloom University Srinagar for Girls. The Government Colleges of higher education in Jammu & Kashmir focused on teaching the Arabic language at all levels of education. Arabic language at P.G. level was started in Kashmir University in 1980 and later on research at M.Phil. and Ph.D. level was started to make in-depth and higher study in Arabic since 2004, Baba Ghulam Shah Badshah University, started department of Arabic Language. The fourteenth chapter deals with "Indian Higher Educational System: Challenges and Suggestions". In this chapter the words of Swami Vivekananda were quoted that "Education is the manifestation of perfection already in man. Like fire in a piece of flint, knowledge exists in the mind. Suggestion is the friction; which brings it out". It focuses on meaning and Aims of Education in Age-old India, Medieval, British and India and in Independent India. Over past seven decades India has impressive progress in the field of higher education. However, the quality of the bulk of our graduates is extremely bad because many university graduates do not have even rudimentary knowledge conceptual understanding or problem, solving skills in their own discipline. Unemployment is rising day by day due to lack of practical approach of higher education. Still, there is a crisis in higher education due to hourglass human resources structure, outdated Indian examination system, inflexible curriculum without electives, universities exist from undergraduate education, poor teaching quality, inbreeding and lack of appraisal, vested interests, absence of regulatory framework, lack of leadership, the gap between counting needs and provision of system. There are many challenges in reforming higher education system in India. Further, this chapter suggests some of the new reforms proposals like non-monetary inputs, encourage unorthodox education and humanities creative education and humanities, creative examination system, along with continuous, evaluation, faculty recruitment appraisal, problem-solving research, monetary inputs structural reforms differentiation of Indian higher education institutions, public private and non-profit providers, politics, governance and education privation, extending and legitimizing the contribution of non-formal educators. The chapter fifteenth in this section deals with "Instructional Strategies for Creating a Positive Classroom Climate". This chapter presents many things to create a positive classroom climate such as organizing classroom and supplies, checklist room preparation, establishment of classroom norms and expectation, individual work and teacher led activities transition into and out of the classroom, procedure for small group instruction and co-operational group activities, general procedures fostering students accountability, getting off to good start planning and conducting instruction, managing cooperative learning groups, maintaining appropriate students behaviour communication skills for teaching, managing problem, behaviours and managing special groups etc. The chapter sixteenth in this section presents "Relevance of Higher Education in the context of Women Empowerment". This chapter made a study on the importance of higher education in context of women empowerment. The objectives of the study are to know the attitude of parents regarding girls' higher education and the problems of girls' higher education. The sample of the study constitutes 100 parents of Nagoan district of Assam. It was found that 77 per cent of parents expressed that higher education for girls is only wastage of time, for 75 per cent, parents higher education for girls has no practical value in their life, 80 per cent of parents show their maximum hope on boys for their old age life, and for 80 per cent parents, cultural stereotyping is an obstacle in way of girl's higher education and 50 per cent of the parents agreed that early marriage of the girls is always affect the girls higher education. Due to tremendous value crisis in India, values are needed for the development of human life. On the other hand the chapter seventeenth in this section is on "Quality in Teacher Education". This chapter specifically focuses on Total Quality Management (TQM) in teacher education. Quality covers many dimensions such as performance features, reliability, conformance, durability, serviceability, aesthetics, and perceived quality. The chapter eighteenth in this section is on "Quality in Education for Higher Education in India". It is observed from this chapter that the all-round development of a nation depends greatly on the overall quality of education consists of (1) serious concern for improving quality at all levels; (2) giving utmost importance for the customers' demands, treating the customers; (3) as sovereign and trying to satisfying customer fully; (4) management of total commitment for enhancing the quality of products; (5) setting up goals and planning in advance for upgrading quality; and (6) removing the defects in the process of production and improving the process at all levels.

Section- IV: Technology and Distance Learning

The chapter nineteenth in this section explores "Distance Education in 21st Century in Reference to Personal Contact Programme (PCP)". The concept PCP in Open and Distance Learning is completely different from the formal classroom teaching. PCPs are used to organise at the particular and approved study centres or regional centres of the University. The sessions under PCPs basically facilitate face to face interaction between the students and the subject-experts as to be appointed or managed by the University for this specific purpose. The time and duration of the PCP sessions may vary from course to course depending upon the particular need of individual courses and the Distant Learners. The Distant Learners are intimated before hand to make them able to attend the PCP properly and each Distant-learner is expected to attend at least 60 per cent of the total PCPs held. The PCP has certain merits such as development of harmonious relationships between DE system and students, psychological motivation, better understanding of DE students and development of loyalty to the DE system and institutes. PCPs are very helpful for enhancing learning level of the Distant Learners.The chapter twentieth of this section is on "ICT in Higher Education: A Switch over to Learner-Contric-Learning". This chapter explores that the introduction of ICTs in the higher education has profound consequences for the whole education process especially in dealing with strategic issues of access equity, management, efficiency, pedagogy and quality. The Government of India has launched several programmes for the development of ICT specifically for Distance Education. These programmes are NMEICT, the UGC scheme "ICT for Teaching and Learning Process", ERNET, UGC, INFONET, INFLIBNET. These programmes and schemes are very helpful for distant and regular students and teachers in formal system of education. Considering ICT, learning would be classified into three categories: e-Learning, Blended Learning and Distance Learning. In our country there are certain initiatives of use of ICT in Education. IGNOU uses radio, TV and internet technologies. NPTEL is similar to the open courseware initiative of MIT. It uses Internet and TV Eklavya initiative uses internet and TV to raise distance learning. IIT Kanpur has developed 'Brihaspati' for virtual classroom. Calcutta have entered into a strategic alliance with NHT for providing programmes through virtual classroom. Jadavpur University is using a mobile learning centre. IIT Bombay has started the programme of CDEEP-Centre for Distance Engineering Education Programme.The chapter twenty first in this section deals with "E-Learning : A Disruptive Approach in Higher Education System". This chapter presents that the journey of education in India has been dotted with numerous milestones – the most modern among these is e-Learning highlights: the reform push, line interaction, video content, delivery video-conferencing, remote test administration, up-to-date materials, self-learning. The VSAT advantage and business opportunities. The development of technologies makes e-learning revolution like big data storage, application programme interfaces (API), Tin Can API, HTML5, responsive e-learning design, Wearable Technology, Video-conferencing, digital text books, 3D printing, mobile learning, cloud computing and MOOC.The chapter twenty second in this section is on "Institutional Benefits of E-Governance in Higher Education". This chapter shows that Electronic Governance (e-Governance) is the use of ICTs for the planning, implementation, and monitoring of government programmes, projects and activities. E-Governance helps to deliver cost-effective easy to access citizens services, and improve processing of transactions both within the government and between the government and other agencies. It is an urgent necessity to promote e-governance in higher education. In May 2006, Government of India made 27 Mission Mode Projects (MMPs) at the Central, State and Local Government level. Under the National e-Governance Plan (NeGP), the MMPs are Land Records, Road Transport, Property Registration, Agriculture, Treasuries, Municipalities, Gram Panchayat, Commercial Taxes, Police, Employment Exchanges, WCD and SW, Cooperation. Some e-governance solutions are suitable for higher education institution such as biometric and digital signature system, Barcode scanners for everyday library applications skype for interviews. The chapter twenty third focuses on "Information Communication Technology in Teacher Education". This chapter presents the role of ICT in the area of teacher education such as helping teachers for organisational pre-conditions, their personal support, technical preconditions, designing learning situations for both the vocational training, and the training of future teachers.

Section-V: Problems and Challenges Ahead

The chapter twenty fourth in this section indicates "Problems and Challenges of Higher Education in India for 21st Century". This chapter reveals present scenario of higher education, problems and challenges of higher education, measures for promotion of excellence in higher education. It also tells about strategic planning for development of colleges through Rashtriya Uchchatar Shiksha Abhiyan (RUSA). This is the right time when we can take more steps to make India into world's major hub for quality higher education in the 21st century. In this direction, the then honourable President of India, his Excellency Shri Pranab Mukherjee, called for concrete steps to create a "Culture of Excellence" in higher education of our country. The chapter twenty fifth in this section focuses "Students Unrest on Higher Education". Alarming situation of unrest and indiscipline among the youth of university stage is a matter of great concern in our country. However, more or less, it is a worldwide problem. According to UNESCO (2009) students' unrest and violence is not a new problem. It occurs between two or more individuals as inter-personal violence or it involves identifiable group in the society and ".... as intergroup violence between two or more different religions or ethnic group. For centuries, violence has been a commonplace feature of school life with its causes embedded in the social, cultural, historical, and economic contexts of its time." This twenty sixth chapter includes Student's Unrest in India, nature of students' unrest, role of education in students' unrest, main causes of student unrest in India and student's unrest or reflection of society. The chapter twenty fifth this section is on "Challenges and New Trends in Higher Education". It focuses on learning in higher education: natural and systematic, the operations of the internal process of learning and the faculties; the external process of learning: philosophy of education, internal and external challenges of higher education.

Section-I
Conceptual Issues

1
Aims and Objectives of Higher Education

Mujibul Hasan Siddiqui and *Deepti Sharma*

Education is the most important tool that ensures the growth of any nation and it strengthens the nation in every aspect. Education makes people stronger, enables them to cope with normal stresses of life and able to respond to the changing needs of the society. Thus, education is the backbone of any nation, if it is strong then growth and prosperity of any nation is sure, but, if it is weak then the nation would not be able to walk with the pace of other countries and left behind in race of progress.

Education has the power to turn humans into human resources inculcate in them essential abilities and skills that make a workforce productive. For a sustainable and prosperous nation, people with accumulated knowledge and skills that enhance their potential day by day are necessary which mainly depends upon the health and vitality of higher education. Higher education is the most important instrument for development and transformation.

Higher education can also be called tertiary or post-school education. All under-graduate colleges, post-graduate colleges, universities and centres of advanced studies come under the scope of higher education. Thus, higher education includes all post-secondary education, all the training and research guidance at university level that are recognised by the State and Central authorities. All the training courses and all those short-term courses that are provided by the universities or other equivalent institutions either through regular classes or by correspondence using information technology come under the umbrella of higher education.

Higher education means high level of education that usually comes after completing the school education. Education, higher in nature includes a range of diplomas, bachelor degree, and post-graduate programmes such as master degree, doctorates and all the advanced research activities. Duration of the courses depends upon the curriculum and depth of the programme and it may vary from state-to-state and country to country. All the programmes of higher education recognised throughout the world as representing specialist expertise in various skills necessary for a person to live a quality life. Thus, there is hierarchy in the higher education which attributes to the depth of knowledge about the subject and enables a person to become a specialist and expertise in it. Here are some most frequently used terms related to higher education—bachelor's degree, it is an undergraduate academic degree takes three to four years. Post-graduate or master degree, it is a higher level course in some subject a major research project is also attached with it such as in Science, Education, Economics, Psychology etc.; length of this programme is about two years. Master degree comes in various categories such as Master of Arts, Master of Science (specialised in any branch of it), and Master of Theology and so on. Doctorates, it is an academic degree of the highest level. It is a professional degree such as—Doctor of Medicine or academic degree such as—Doctor of Philosophy. After completing the doctorate one accumulated the title of Doctor. The amount of time one must study for achieving such degrees varies greatly by field and institution.

Aims and Objectives of Higher Education

Higher education is one of the important aspects in the rising knowledge society. Youth are considered as nation builders thus the future of a country depends upon them, therefore, a massive expansion of education, particularly at the level of higher education is necessary.

The world is constantly changing and in order to keep pace with the changes we need effective human resources with higher education such as—doctors, politicians, teachers, who not only perform their duties well, but, also able to increase their efficiency day by day through the continue education making use of information technology and all this can only be possible through the higher education. As the world changes, it significantly influences the system of education too. Thus, society becomes knowledge based in every aspect whether it is social, economic, political etc. and so there is a rise in the demand of higher education. Due to these rapid changes in the world risk of unemployment increases in the modern society, because getting hired through connections are long gone. Now-a-days, there is a demand of skilled and efficient manpower who have the most to offer and this requirement can only be possible through quality higher education. Following are the various aims and objectives of higher education:

- The aim of higher education is to provide knowledge and wisdom. It tries not only to impart factual information, but, also awakens pupils towards their responsibilities and duties. Thus, it aims to reduce social, cultural differences and enable pupils to respect all beliefs in the society through the right kind of knowledge and wisdom.
- Higher education aims to inculcate the value of democracy, justice, liberty, equality and fraternity among pupils to develop a healthy civil society and reform the social system through the cultivation of social cohesion. Thus it emphases on the higher values of life and social justice.
- Higher education aims to preserve and interpret the existing knowledge, culture and belief in the light of new wants and discoveries and it also aims to cultivate new knowledge.
- The most important aim of higher education is to provide training of leadership among students in different walks of life, namely—social, political, economical, cultural, scientific and technological. So, they can lead in professional and public life too. Leadership is important for a positive change in the society thus higher education encourages pupils to become good leaders not to control and rule others; but trains them to direct and go along with human resources and increase their productivity. Higher education provides opportunities to youth to find out qualities among them and develop their potential to fullest with positive attitude.
- The role of higher education in the contemporary knowledge society is pivotal because it directly or indirectly contributes to the welfare of the nation and strengthens the nation in terms of economy. It provides competent and skilled man power flourished with current knowledge force, to the society and to the various professions.
- Being at the top of educational hierarchy, higher education aims to inculcate and promote critical and reflective thinking among pupils. Thus makes them capable enough to reflect over social,

economical, cultural, moral and spiritual values in a broad perspective which is very important for the social change rather than following the beaten path.

- The aim of higher education is to disseminate the specialised knowledge and skills. Its aim is to impart T graph among students means to make them able to understand any subject with full of its breadth and depth. Thus, the focus of higher education is to produce expertise and specialist in every walks of life whether teacher, doctor, engineer, technician and so on.
- The aim of higher education is to promote global excellence by providing all types of support including faculty development and facilitating other development initiatives.
- The intension of higher education is to develop employability needs of cooperate and other sectors by promoting continuing discoveries and researches and on the other hand aims to produce efficient people to create a balance between the need and supply of human resources in the society.
- The most important aim of higher education is to encourage researches that ensure high level of education and in turn education develops human resources to do research. Its aim is to promote research and publication on contemporary and relevant issues and make pupils able to critically evaluate information, increase their capability to identify various problems of the society and formulate possible solution to them and tries to aware the whole population towards it. Thus, higher education contributes in the welfare of a society not only by creating knowledge, but also by transmitting it to the younger generation.
- Aim of higher education is to prepare the youth power to collaborate with various organisations in the other parts of the world. So, they can contribute in the success of a nation on the path of globalisation and increase international cooperation.
- The aim of higher education is to provide high quality of education and skills in order to give more choices and possibilities and improve various career opportunities. Thus, higher education must provide miscellaneous formats of education to respond to varying needs.
- Higher education is a great way to enter in various respectable jobs. It aims to provide equal opportunities to everyone for upward social mobility by providing various courses and degrees.

- The aim of higher education is to produce efficient and quality teachers with the effective knowledge of pedagogy so that they can understand the needs and problems of the children and have ability to solve them and pass their knowledge for generation to come. This is the most important aim of higher education because rest of the aims depends upon it, teacher is the architect they knows how to make a strong building out of the raw-material, but if the architect himself is not efficient enough how can we think about a strong building.
- The aim of higher education is to stimulate students to learn, to seek information and make them able to critically synthesize information and knowledge and also offer possibilities for applying their acquired skills. Thus, it aims not only to provide subjective knowledge, but also the practical knowledge and skills.
- The important aim of higher education is to promote self-learning among students, a tool for lifelong learning, by make them understand how to learn and gather knowledge. Higher education gives their students a training of information and communication technology essential for continuing education which is important for the success of a nation as well as for the individual.
- The aim of higher education is to implement various policies and programmes that foster among students a spirit of free inquiry, independent and critical thinking and make them able to render important services to the society thus assist them in the fulfilment of social and economic objectives.

All these are the objectives of higher education that leads towards the success of a nation and ensures quality of life and growth among people in their lives.

REFERENCES

Higher Education Forum. Retrieved from: *http://www.highereduforum.org/objectives.html*

Messy, W., (2009). Objectives and success measures for higher education. Retrieved from: *https://net.educause.edu/ir/library/pdf/ff0910s.pdf*

Yeravdekar, R.V. (2012). Internationalization of Higher Education in India.

D.Phil., Management, Symbosis International University, Pune. Retrieved from: *http://shodhganga.inflibnet.ac.in/handle/10603/15087*

Powar, B.K. (2002). *Indian Higher Education: A Conglomerate of Concept, Facts and Practices*. New Delhi: Concept Publishing Company.

Approaches for Systematic Planning of Development Projects: Higher Education. Institute for International Cooperation and Japan International Cooperation Agency (March 2004). Retrieved from: *https://www.jica.go.jp/jica- ri/IFIC_and_JBICI- Studies/english/publications/reports/study/topical/approaches/pdf/higher_01.pdf*

2
Higher Education for Social and National Development

Sarika Sharma

"Education is the single best investment in prosperous, healthy and equitable societies."

—*UN Food and Agriculture Organisation*

"Spread education, uplift India!
Education, the basic building block for every society."

Education is not a mere process to comprehend the highest levels of knowledge attained by humanity at a given point of time, but a continuous activity that creates new knowledge to sustain life across temporal and spatial barriers. Therefore, from having been a static inquiry into the high points of classical civilisations and their concepts it has become a dynamic movement in shaping life in the present for the future on this planet. It has not, however, ceased to be a process: it is an ever refined and progressively sharpened tool of academic inquiry tempered by the rigour and objectivity of science.

Concept of Higher Education in India

The ancient education offered through *Gurukul* was religious and it was exclusively offered to the privileged classes of society. With the expansion and institutionalisation of higher education in universities such as Nalanda and Taxila, specialised knowledge, primarily religious knowledge, was pursued by Buddhist monks. Similarly, Sanskrit schools, and later *madrasah*, Muslim schools, were devoted to Vedic and Muslim religious education respectively. Later oriental education in language, astronomy, performing arts and mathematics was imparted.

Today, India's higher education system is the third largest in the world, next to the United States and China. The main governing body at the tertiary level is the University Grants Commission, which enforces its standards, advises the government, and helps coordinate between the Centre and the State. Accreditation for higher learning is overseen by 12 autonomous institutions established by the University Grants Commission.

Indian higher education system has expanded at a fast pace by adding nearly 20,000 colleges and more than 8 million students in a decade from 2000-01 to 2010-11. As of 2011, India has 42 Central Universities, 275 State Universities, 130 deemed universities, 90 private universities, 5 institutions established and functioning under the State Act, and 33 Institutes of National Importance. Other institutions include 33,000 colleges as Government Degree Colleges and Private Degree Colleges, including 1800 exclusive women's colleges, functioning under these universities and institutions as reported by the UGC in 2012. The emphasis in the tertiary level of education lies on science and technology. Indian educational institutions by 2004 consisted of a large number of technology institutes. Distance learning and open education is also a feature of the Indian higher education system, and is looked after by the Distance Education Council. Indira Gandhi National Open University is the largest university in the world by number of students, having approximately 3.5 million students across the globe.

Some institutions of India, such as the Indian Institutes of Technology (IITs), National Institute of Technology (NITs), Indian Institutes of Information Technology (IIITs), Indian Institutes of Management (IIMs), International Institute of Information Technology (IIIT-H), University of Mumbai and Jawaharlal Nehru University have been globally acclaimed for their standard of education. The IITs enroll about 8000 students annually and the alumni have contributed to both the growth of the private sector and the public sectors of India. However, India still lacks internationally prestigious universities such as Harward, Cambridge, and Oxford.

Role of Higher Education Institutions

The role of higher education institutions is today's world immense, complex and vital. A wide range of challenges and opportunities is emerging, with many political, economic and social implications. Perhaps most significant are the challenges associated with shifting perspectives of knowledge itself, which are strongly influencing the role and the responsibility of universities in society. Universities are well positioned to link the local and the global and this gives them considerable access to and influence over change process in may societies. It may enhance their potential to contribute to human and social development through the promotion and facilitation of citizen participation and involvement in these processes.

Quality in Higher Education

Quality is often considered to be a standard or norm with which to compare two similar things in order to assess the worth of the thing compared. It is a 'benchmark' arrived at after reckoning the best features of the things compared. If an under-graduate, for instance, has the abilities to self-manage the advancement of his learning, to remain at the frontiers of knowledge in his discipline and to present and defend his ideas before general and specialist audiences, he benchmarks the standard of undergraduate education which alone is acceptable for employment anywhere in the world. Similar benchmarks exist for different qualifications. Quality is context and needspecific. Rural institutions may require a set of skills which may not be indispensable for urban institutions. Similarly, teaching may be considered more important in an under-graduate college and research may take precedence over teaching in a university. Identical bench-marks may not be compatible for rating performers in context diversity. This does not mean that the degree of excellence in performance in different contexts can be different. For instance, a student of agriculture interested in researching into maize cropping needs a set of skills and competencies which are not the same in the case of a researcher in paddy cropping. Nevertheless, the degree of efficiency they manifest in sustaining and improving the quality of the yield as well as the impact of the outcome cannot differ for purposes of standardising performance for judgement. Quality in higher education is a holistic concept.

National Assessment and Accreditation Council (NAAC)

National Assessment and Accreditation Council (NAAC) has brought about awakening among more than a thousand higher institutions of learning in our country which have reset their goals, diversified curricula and improved methods of teaching and learning after the first round of institutional assessments made. Never perhaps in the history of higher education in the country was there such an extensive revision of curricula, in the best among them, which has resulted in a wide range of core, elective and vocational options now made available to learners. Institutional assessment has worked. It responds to the need for quality assurance while maintaining values of self-assessment and self-governance in higher education.

Rashtriya Ucchattar Shiksha Abhiyan (RUSA)

A total of 316 state public universities and 13,024 colleges will be covered under the Rashtriya Ucchattar Shiksha Abhiyan, a plan to manage funding for higher education. This is scheme to develop state universities by Central Government funding (65%).

Higher Education is a Continuous Process

The average age of the learners is also rising as a substantial proportion of them now come from the workforce looking to re-learn. The rapidly changing workplace has made lifelong learning more important than ever. Higher education, therefore, needs to enable individual learning pathways that can help prepare individuals to lead productive lives and equip them with 21st century skills.

Globalisation of Higher Education

Globalisation presents a particularly challenging context for re-examining the educative purpose of higher education for human, community and social development. In the very first place, development itself is rarely explicitly claimed as a deliberate focus of most institutions of higher education. Given that the fundamental purpose of higher education is intellectual and moral development, this is not only a very strange stance, but also one that is increasingly problematic and indeed ethically indefensible. In the face of the complexities of this late modern age, where 'bads' as well as 'goods' are circulating the globe with ever increasing frequency and causing ever-more destructive impacts on nature and society alike, it is becoming glaringly obvious that new ways of 'seeing' the world and 'dealing' with issues in it are urgently needed if sustainable futures for societies are to be achieved across the globe. If, as the substantive argument in this chapter holds, we humans have become victims of our own paradigmatic inadequacies in a manner that now threatens the very sustainability of life on earth, then higher education is duty bound to do all it can to transform prevailing epistemic assumptions and to liberate human and social development in the further pursuit of the considered and inclusively responsible life.

International Scenario on Higher Education

UNESCO has identified higher education as being critical to addressing the sustainable development goals that the UN and other global and local organisations are setting for post-2015. It may seem obvious on one level how education in general and higher education in particular, benefits people. It equips individuals with competencies and skills that are needed in the labour market. But consider this, from the World Bank, in its Education Strategy 2020. Not only do "investments in quality education lead to more rapid and sustainable economic growth and development", but, "Educated individuals are more employable, able to earn higher wages, cope better with economic shocks, and raise healthier children." So, the value of higher education goes beyond skills and competencies needed for a livelihood, it also contributes to the health and well-being of society. "Expanding and improving education is key to adapting to change and confronting these challenges." Besides the basic nature of the higher education sector driving costs higher, the fact is *the demand* for higher education is exploding.

Education and Development

A literate nation is a marching nation; no country can progress if its population is illiterate. The world is seeing fast moving technology changes everyday. Inventions are now a part of everyday life. If the men are uneducated then things will have no meaning. To understand, to acquire skills, to decide between a right or a wrong—education is a must. Education brings maturity, it helps in polishing skills, it makes the person more responsible. It brings development and the country moves ahead. Education plays a pivotal role in the progress of a country.

Education is something that is very helpful in developing a country. There are a lot of positive aspects that help with the relationship betweeen education and national development. Having an educated country can help to keep the society under control, which then helps contribute to the national development. Development in a country is something that is very important and is a goal in many places. There are many different aspects of education that are present in many developing countries. These aspects include, demographic, economic, resource, violence, health, and culture. There are also two goals that are set which help in developing a country. These goals are economic and social. Economic growth plays a big role in the environment. When seeing how developed a country is, you would measure how much communication, technology, industrialisation, and urbanisation is being used. Having social development in a country refers to health, laws, stability and social cohesion. A healthy population is one that is filled with more educated women. Having educated women teachers helps to set good goals for girls that they are teaching. More educated women also have smaller families because they know more about ways to not get pregnant. Education is something that not only effects a society, but also an individual and their behaviours. Education helps to shape people in the workforce that help to make our future national development even better. I think that education is the most important part of a person's life, that will help them develop as a person. Getting an education also helps to develop a country in a big way, because when you have smarter people in the workforce then things may run smoother and develop better. Overall for national development to happen, education must be apart of every citizens life.

Higher Education for Social Development

- As a basis for considering the types of third level education and research activity that are required, research into the quality of life, social and civic attitudes, the components of competence, and the effectiveness of the educational system is first summarized.
- It is concluded that there is no shortage of jobs to be done by hands which are currently idle in our society, but, if the necessary work is to be undertaken, new understandings of society, economics, wealth, public policy and democracy are required. Both the managers of our society, and citizens in general, need to develop new perceptions, expectations, understandings and patterns of competence. It is concluded that the role of the university must change radically. One possibility would be for

it to come to see itself, first and foremost, as a producer of new concepts and understandings and new tools to administer, and provide accountability within, modern society. If this were to happen, it would function only secondarily, in a very much reduced role, as a provider of highly specialised knowledge. Other institutions would take over the competence promoting functions which second and third level educational institutions currently neglect. Although, there is an urgent need for a major programme of adult education, that need might best be met by other educational agencies.

- The changes are inevitable and therefore, it is important to understand how to turn the challenges into opportunities. This requires gathering data, doing careful analysis and developing strategies.
- Higher-education institutions have unique opportunities to engage in partnerships with industry, government, NGOs and other bodies to better understand the needs of learners within the economy and society.
- Technology offers many ways to improve research, teaching, increase independent learning by students, and widen access to global resources (*via* MOOCs, OER etc.). Perhaps, most important of all, though, it offers a means for a greater number of people wherever they are in the world to gain the skills and knowledge they need to live productive and meaningful lives.

Higher education has been a hall-mark of the education landscape and is a vital requirement for economic and social development of countries.

Education for National Development

Education and learning are the most important processes in today's society. Today's youth are tomorrow's teachers. In the "banking method" or education by memorisation, the students are not being taught; they are only expected to memorize the material, which is not actually a learning process. Although, there are a lot of misconceptions about the "banking method", I think that there is also a lot of good in this method as well. The foundation of the society is based on education since it brings economic and social prosperity. Gaining education enhances an individual to live a respectful life in the society. This is because education offers a setting in which culture and values of a society are developed. In this respect, education in modern society provides a forum where the society examines its issues and identifies solutions. The advancement of a society both economically and socially is by gaining education, which consequently enables them to run a modern society.

Education is a Key to Progress of a Developing Country

Education and learning are the most important processes in today's society. Today's youth are tomorrow's teachers. Education plays the most important role in the development of any country. It is the backbone of any country. It is the birth right for every citizen of the country. In any country, it is necessary to invest a big part of the profit in the education field, but in many countries, government prefers to invest in arms not thinking of diverting the resources from the military where war and win is everything. Another reason why government should invest in the education field more is because of increase in child labour.

Illiteracy is a major obstacle. If you notice in the past few years, India has transformed in a lot of fields. This is because people are slowly understanding the importance of education. Education is made compulsory for all kids up to 14 years of age because, "*Padhega India tabhi toh badhega India*". Today, the youth of India, the educated youth of India is taking steps to make India a developed nation. Education is a power to change the mindset of people.

For many developing and developed countries, education is the root of achievement. Education produces a skilful and intelligent generation that will be the future ruler of the country. Moreover, if civilians have been trained with efficient education, they will have a adequate life. Therefore, education is fundamental for development within a country due to the brilliant generation that is bred by it. Students are the most important resource—if we educate them, we indirectly educate and develop our country. Students are expected leaders of a nation. Students absorb basic knowledge and develop skills in school and then university. They are the ones, who will inevitably become a future doctor, an ulterior architect and also President of a nation. Moreover, education arms students with fundamental wisdom and perception of world.

Education plays an important role in the development of any country. In my opinion education is the backbone of any country or you can say that now it is the basic need of the entire world. Education is the birth right of every citizen of the country, so, the government of the country should run the programmes through which every citizen of the country becomes educated and after the government, it is the responsibility of the people to educate their family members.

Education is not only the factor that affects the development of any country, but it affects the surroundings or the person himself also. Education increases the personality of a person in many ways like education changes the behaviour, life style, the way of dressing, sitting and talking also. Education is the most important factor for our freedom or democracy.

Developing country literally means, a poor agricultural country that is seeking to become more advanced economically and socially. Education can be the major factor, in the development of a country. It not only benefits the country's people economically, but also socially among other countries, which can be helpful. It not only civilizes people and makes them gain more and more job opportunities, but also helps in personality development of each and every person which tremendously affects the growth of a developing country.

However, still it cannot be considered as the 'single' most important factor as there are other factors too such as politics. Education is one of the significant factors to build a modern country. First of all, a country needs societies that have knowledge that is useful. When societies have much awareness that is usable, they can help government to build a perfect country that is appreciated by other countries. For instance, some societies can take part in the administration to distribute their ideas about developing country easily. If societies do not have some important abilities, they find it difficult to share their information, and especially if they do not play a useful part in government, people will find it hard to accept them. After all, a country can be recognised by the other countries when it has societies that it can boast of. It is education that will help the country move forward and be recognised.

Education, without a doubt, can affect a person's future. Every individual needs to be educated to the right level before they can join the workforce; especially when it is becoming more knowledge-based. These people will directly determine the quality and gains a country can make.

Another important point is that without education, people have to turn to jobs which are usually low-paid, or they even hardly find a job. These people will rely on unemployment or low-income support from the government. Also, companies with low quality employers will hardly compete with others overseas. Impact of people's investment in education is profound: education results in raising income, improving health, promoting gender equality, mitigating climate change, and reducing poverty. In short, education has the power to make the world a better place. Education has an impact in the development of the country, it is still an instrument of destroying peace and endangering lives. If you look at the broader picture, we have seen many inventions in these last 100 years, but we have destroyed greenery of the whole world by 50 per cent, paving way for modernisation. This has led to some unwanted happenings such as global warming and uncertain weather changes which are ignored even after effective warnings. This irresponsibility has led to melting of poles and mountains, leading to floods!

Developing a country needs awareness and practicality. Even people with high grades are not able to answer a simple question like "Who is the President of India?". People get educated to develop themselves. If you remember people like Aristotle, Albert Einstein, they were not much educated...but were still capable of giving a huge hand to develop THE WORLD!!

Awareness and usage of person's brain brings about 85 per cent of development ...education brings the rest!

Education is most important in the development of a country. Education plays a crucial role in the advancement of technologies. Education means obtaining knowledge. A person who has knowledge of his surroundings can survive happily in this society. Education not only helps us in surviving, but also makes people aware of their rights and duties towards the nation. Education itself is a right everybody is born with.

Every person born in this country should at least be educated till XII standard. Education provides many opportunities in various fields for the development of the country. Education makes people independent, builds confidence and self-esteem, which is very important for the development of a country. Development of the country includes development in fields such as IT, medical sciences, agriculture, economy etc. All this development comes about only when people are educated in these fields. When people have enough knowledge about a certain field it is easy to bring about new reforms for the development of the society. If a country has education by its side then no one can stop it from developing itself.

Role of Youth in Social and National Development

India can become a developed nation only if everyone contributes to the best of his or her capacity and ability. Youth is wholly experimental and with the full utilisation of the talents of the youth, India will become a complete Nation. The youth of today is the driving force of tomorrow. It has some responsibility towards its country, which it must acknowledge and practice. Instead of blaming the system, youth should come together and mould the nation for a better tomorrow. Youth have some responsibility towards their country. We need to learn from yesterday and live with hope for a better tomorrow. We can learn from our past how the young warriors shed their blood for the country.

Conclusion

For thousands of years, education has been an integral part of society. India can become a developed nation only if everyone contributes to the best of his or her capacity and ability. Youth is wholly experimental and with the full utilisation of the talents of the youth, India will become a complete Nation. It is true that youth have got energy, skill, hopes, and dreams and along with those the determination and exuberance, but they also lack proper and critical thinking. Thus, here lies the role of a nation and its government in guiding the youth to the correct way of living and in utilizing their vital energy and desire for the betterment of the nation. For this, proper education system and good political situation is required. Moral education is a must for this as well. If youth can be motivated and educated the right way, they surely can spearhead the progress of a nation and make the world a better place to live. Hence, all the citizens are to be involved in building or developing a nation.

REFERENCES

Higher Education and Development *www.ghfp.org/Portals/ghfp/publications/thomson_hei_role_dev.pd*

The role of higher education for human and social development | Guni... *www.guninetwork.org › GUNi Topics*

Higher education in India—Wikipedia, the free encyclopedia *https://en.wikipedia.org/wiki/Higher_education_in_India*

Literature Review on Social Responsibility in Higher Education *unescochair-cbrsr.org/unesco/pdf/Occaisional_paper.pdf*

Raven John,(1984). *Quality of Life, the Development of Competence and Higher Education,* Volume 13, Issue 4, pp. 393-404.

Drivers for Change in Higher Education, COL *https://www.col.org/news/speeches-presentations/drivers-change-higher-education*

Quest: Education Key to Progress of any Country, *The Indian Express*
indianexpress.com › cities › mumbai

Improving Education in Developing Countries | Canadian Feed The...
www.canadianfeedthechildren.ca ›

Role of Youth in India's Development—Merinews
www.merinews.com/article/role-of-youth-in-indias-development/140606.shtml

Role of Youth in National Development—A Level General...
www.markedbyteachers.com/as-and-a./role-of-youth-in-national-development.html

Role of Youth in National Development—The Point Newspaper, Banjul...
thepoint.gm › africa › gambia

3

Higher Education in India

A Need for Formalised Mentoring

Mohmmad Suhail and *Mohd. Uzair*

Introduction

It is often said, the future of a nation is shaped inside the classroom. With the introduction of new teaching pedagogical approaches, the student's learning level has been enhanced. However, to ensure the student's all-round development, the need for additional attention outside the classroom has been recognised. This attention and care can be provided to the students in the form of mentorship. Mentors provide support, direction, and essential resources to the mentees. It is a professional activity, a trusted relationship, and a meaningful commitment. The origins of mentoring can be traced back to ancient Greece as a technique to impart young men important social, spiritual, and personal values (Metros & Yang, 2006). The meaningful relationship between mentor and mentee is seen advantageous for a productive academic life. It has a various developmental phases of the mentoring relationship, the dynamics of the mentoring relationship itself, and the application of cognitive developmental theory to the mentoring process (Bey & Holmes, 1992). It is an interpersonal relationship that fosters support between a mentor and mentee. In education, mentoring is a multifaceted and multi-dimensional process of guiding, teaching, influencing and supporting students to their development. According to Koki (1998), a mentor teacher leads, guides and advises another teacher more junior in experience in a work situation characterised by mutual trust and belief. The focus on launching formal mentoring in higher education is visible in Western countries, where they also launch formal mentoring programmes. In India, the term mentoring is often used interchangeable with student adviser and supervisor. However, there is a fine difference between a mentor and a student adviser/counsellor. A mentor is more than an adviser while a good adviser assists students in learning about their discipline and the skills needed to conduct research or practice their profession, a mentor develops a relationship with her or his mentee on several levels. A mentor is a trusted guide. A mentor can offer support in difficult times. A mentor socialises her or his mentee, the values, norms, practices and attitudes of a discipline (Yaher & Lynne, 2016). The mentorship can be provided to student or a newly recruited faculty by an experienced faculty. Similarly, various disciplines like Medical, Social Work, Management etc. do focus on integrating theory and practice. The graduation and post-graduation in social work is designed in such a way to provide classroom teaching and field exposure among student. A faculty supervisor is assigned for every student in graduation and post-graduation for guidance and supervision. These faculty supervisors provide each student ample time to discuss issues regarding fieldwork, classroom learning and other learning requirements of the course curriculum. Individual conferences are designed in such a way that every student can get ample time with the supervisor. Student spend time with supervisor also helps to seek professional and carrier advice. And, therefore, the supervisor apart from routine fieldwork activities also helps students in their carrier and personality development. It focuses on academic writing skill, group discussions in the form on tutorials and group conferences. Similarly, professions like medical, management and engineering also focuses on imparting practical aspect of learning to students. However, what seems to be missing is the formal component of mentoring in Indian higher education system. Therefore, the need for introducing formal mentoring system in higher education in India is imperative for the over all development of students and for better training and skills. Through this effort, the Indian higher education system can ensure quality education and inculcation of required skill set for employability.

Concept of Mentoring

The concept of mentoring goes beyond supervision and advising. It is a part of a larger thrust to build a knowledge producing and sharing community, as well as an integral part of critical pedagogy. It is much concerned about building relationships, which involves knowledge sharing, being available, approachable, and proactive in building skills among students and colleagues. Mentoring is an interpersonal relationship that fosters support between a mentor and mentee. Students need mentors, facilitators and advisers. They require, according to Carl Rogers (1980), authentic professional human beings who are worthy of emulation. They need models who exhibit professional behaviour, a sense of commitment and purposefulness. Students cannot be divulged for work without showing them practical aspect of it. However, mentoring is not easy; it needs time and commitment, professionally and personally. In spite of shortage of time in academic life, the need for mentoring to develop students based on the requirements of current job market and sense of active citizenry is important (Terrion & Leonard, 2007). Yaher & Lynne (2016) listed some essential qualities for a mentor, In essence a mentor is:

1. An adviser, who has career interests similar to the student and shares their knowledge with the student informally or in the classroom.
2. A supporter, who gives the necessary level of emotional and moral encouragement, as for example, prior to the final oral examination.
3. A sponsor, who provides sources of information about research, grant, internship, employment, or other opportunities.
4. A tutor, who gives specific, timely, and constructive feedback on performance.
5. A model, who is a professional with integrity, thereby serving as a good role model.

The essential qualities of a mentor as discussed by Yaher & Lynne (2016) shows the mentor needs professional expertise in the subject as well as commitment to give time, effort and courage to students. Wunsch (1994), and Darwin (2000), stated that there is no universally accepted definition of mentoring. Johnson (1989), give working definition of mentoring as "a way of individualizing a student's education by allowing or encouraging the student to connect with a college staff Member who is experienced in a particular field or set of skills" (Johnson, cited in Cuseo, J., 2002). Campbell & Campbell (1997), also proposed definition of mentoring as "a situation in which a more experienced member of an organisation maintains a relationship with a less experienced, often new member to the organisation and provides information, support, and guidance so as to enhance the less experienced member's chances of success in the organisation and beyond." This form of mentorship assumes a hierarchical approach where the mentor is doing the majority of the teaching and instructing and often includes more academic or career related guidance. A similar yet different approach is the peer mentoring, which "matches mentors and mentees who are roughly equal in age, experience, and power to provide task and psychosocial support". There are various types of mentoring discussed by authors. Informal mentoring, formal mentoring, peer mentoring are such types of mentoring. A formal relationship is established when protégés are assigned to mentors by the organisation. Informal mentoring is not assigned by the instituion, but are based on mutal collboration.

Review of Literature

Research on mentoring indicates that it has a positive impact on the personal and professional development of young adults (Levinson *et al.*, cited in Knippelmeyer, S. and Torraco, R., 2007). There is also a growing body of research in higher education that suggests an empirical link between student mentoring and student retention (Campbell & Campbell, 1997). For instance Miller *et al.* (1988) used an experimental research design in which students were randomly assigned to either an experimental group—who received mentoring, or a control group—who did not (Miller *et al.*, cited in Cuseo, J., 2002). It was found that students who received mentoring evinced higher retention rates than non-mentored students with similar pre-enrolment characteristics. Many studies on mentoring in higher education prove its positive impact on students as well as faculty. It has been found that in order to flourish mentoring and the faculty-student relationship, it is important that the interaction between faculty and students must benefit both participants. Sorcinelli and Yun (2007) and Lumpkin (2011), defined how mentoring programmes can help smooth the shift of faculty into new roles. There is support for the value of mentoring in higher education (Luna and Cullen, 1995), even though the academy has been slow to formalize faculty-mentoring programmes. Baldwin, cited in Lumpkin, (2011), suggested the cause can be of higher education's failure to acknowledge the developmental nature of faculty careers. Hudson (2013), conducted a study which emphasis on the strategies of how to teaching effectively with pedagogical knowledge. The study includes 27 mentor teachers who were involved in a professional development programme titled *Mentoring for Effective Teaching* (MET).

The study found that mentors ability to effective planning and teaching directly affects the mentees development. Horenstein *et al.* (2010), also explored the impact of mentoring, the study on mentoring undergraduate students reveals that the students described their gains in cognitive skill sets and abilities including interpreting data on their own, making frequent presentations, questioning existing protocol, or getting published. This finding is consistent with the literature and supports the research belief that mentors provide to the students, they did better in their presentation and publication experiences. Sultana (2015), in his research study on "*Knowledge and Psychological Skills Training for Faculty to Mentor Students Having Learning Disabilities in Higher Education*" found the positive and significant relation between the mentoring and students learning outcome. Parylo *et al.* (2012), in their qualitative study on principal's mentorship, which includes 16 principals of State Georgia, USA, found the mentoring was generally described as the best system of supports. Almost all studies on mentoring reveal a positive outcome, which support the mentees in their career development.

The review of literature suggests the concept of mentoring is an important area in research. Many authors and researchers have conducted quantitative and qualitative research on the needs and importance of mentoring in different countries. However, what seems to be missing is the research on mentoring in India. Very few writers and scholars are talking about the importance of mentoring in India. The need for formalised mentoring in Indian higher education system is the gap in review of literature and need to focus by Indian writers and researchers.

Status of Higher Education in India

Indian Higher Education System is currently the third largest in the world, next only to China and the United States (World Bank, 2007). It is likely to surpass the US in the next five years and China in the next 15 years to be the largest system of higher education in the world (*ToI*, 2014). India is having 46 Central Universities, 350 State Public Universities, 122 Deemed Universities, 228 Private Universities and 74 Institute of National Importance (UGC, 2016). The highest numbers of students are enrolled at Under-Graduate level across India. Out of the total enrolment of 342, 11,637 students, a vast majority of 2,71,72,346 students are enrolled at Under-Graduate level. On the other hand, 11.3 per cent students are enrolled in Post-Graduation. There are 1,41,870 students enrolled in Integrated course in addition to 1,17,301 students enrolled at Ph.D. Level.

There are small share of 7.3 per cent students enrolled at Diploma level in India that amounts to 25,07,694. Similarly, a small share of 1,70,245 students is enrolled in Certificate courses and 2,15,372 in PG Diplomas respectively (AISHE, 2014-15).

By 2030, India will be amongst the youngest nations in the world. With nearly 140 million people in the college-going age group, one in every four graduates in the world will be a product of the Indian education system (Ernst & Young Global Limited, 2016). Higher education in India has recorded impressive growth since Independence. University Grants Commission (UGC, GoI) designing programmes and implementing various schemes through academic, administrative and financial support, has contributed in the growth and development of Indian Higher Education. Many new institutions of medicine, science, technology and others have been introduced. The immediate need for transforming governance and leadership in higher education institutions are reported (*ToI*, 2014). It is also desirable that a certain optimum degree of standardisation in the examination system and in the assessment of students is put in place before grades are awarded to them. Lately, a chorus of criticism is heard from various well-meaning quarters about the deteriorating quality of higher education in India. Therefore, with Indian higher education massive structure, the need for more focused quality level intervention is imperative, in which mentoring can be seen as an aid in ensuring quality education.

Need for Mentoring Higher Education

The concept of mentoring is not a new it has found purpose in practically all forms of learning. Dating back to Homer, Mentor has been described as a wise and trusted counsellor (Daloz, cited in Rice, 2007). In academics, the term is often referred to a "faculty adviser". But there is an essential difference between a mentor and an adviser. The role of adviser is to give advice; however mentor is more personal, as it focuses on the professional as well as on the personal relationship. Thus, we can say that, a mentoring is a bond that develops over a period of time. It is considered a process of influencing and fostering the intellectual development of students (Daloz, cited in Rice, 2007). The need of mentoring in higher education has been widely accepted, many researcher emphasise its need in their studies. The academic decor is far diverse today than it was three decades ago (Belar, cited in Darwin, 2000). As proposed by Lumpkin (2011), first, mentors socialize mentee into the culture of academic units and emphasize interactions and connections with mentee to help reduce feelings of isolation while mentors benefit by helping initiate the next generation into the professoriate. Second, mentors provide emotional support, facilitate networking, and encourage open communications with the mentees. Third, mentors can provide disciplinary and role-specific assistance that helps to increase job performance as mentee gain confidence in their abilities. Reciprocally, mentee may share with their mentors disciplinary and technological insights brought from their doctoral studies. These outcomes directly contribute to mentee and mentors enjoying mutually beneficial relationships.

In the present competitive environment, where skills ranged from networking, collaboration, communication, documentation is pertinent; writers are focusing on the importance of mentoring. Similarly, various studies conducted by researchers uncovered the benefits of Mentoring. The research conducted by Campbell & Campbell (1997), reports that those students who had a faculty mentor "attained a higher grade-point average equivalent to between .2 and .3 of a grade point" when compared to students who did not have a faculty mentor. Another study done by Fox and Connelly (2010), showed that the mentees who participated in a peer-mentor programme "achieved higher deep, strategic and surface apathetic scores after their involvement". Compared to students not engaged in the peer-mentor programme, the mentees in this study scored significantly higher not only on grades but also in how they were studying (Fox and Connelly cited in Hatfield, 2011). The effects of mentors have been unanimously positive on the overall development of student. Feminist educators have also seen mentoring as essential for the development and success of adult learners (Mullen *et al.*, 2010). Biehl (1996) advocates that mentoring relationships be considered lifelong relationships. By definition one of the contributions of a mentor is to offer the mentee helpful information, suggestions, and even introduction to others who can be helpful to the person. While initially one cannot expect friendship, it may well be an outcome and long-term benefit (Penner, 2001). Another major benefit of mentoring for the student mentee is the psycho-social encouragement received. Stress is often listed as one of the major reasons for student attrition yet Terrion and Leonard (2010), point out that a peer mentor can serve as one source of support to reduce the stress experienced by a younger and less experienced student which, in turn, has the potential to reduce the attrition rate of universities. The research of Shotton *et al.* (2007), listed three ways that peer mentors helped their mentees: (a) connecting students to the community, (b) providing support, and (c) providing guidance. Colvin and Ashman (2010), provide a similar list of benefits for the mentees who described their mentors as being a "connecting link, peer leader, teach coach, student advocate, and trusted friend". If students are mentored during graduation years, they will become self-determining architects of knowledge or users of research. It will assist them to move on to the next phase of professional life (Jimenez, 2015). Many programmes and course curriculum are designed and adopted by International Universities to foster students with required skill set through mentoring. For instance, The Xavier University, Ohio Mentor Programme links students with leading executives and career professionals to offer an innovative approach. Providing students practical application of networking skills, personal and professional growth is the focus of the programme. Indiana University South East, Centre for Mentoring connects students through various programmes that engage the institution and local community to enhance student's ability to succeed in college. University of Iowa also have student-mentoring programmes designed for different courses and based on the student's requirements. Similarly, non-residential Learning Community at the University of Michigan is also designed to help fresh year graduates become more familiarise to campus life. University of Minnesota, the College of Design facilitates an annual programme that helps students grow professionally by matching them with a mentor in their field of study. Together, they discuss the goals of the students and help them with career exploration, networking, and professional skill building.

In India, Social work education also focuses on practical exposure along with classroom teaching. The model of social work education in India can be applied to other streams of higher education. The mere focus on classroom teaching will not help students learn the practicality of a subject. Thus, they are not able be equipped with the current demands of employability. Social work education in Indian universities follows mostly similar pattern. The focus is on integration of theory and practice. Graduate and Undergraduate level social work education in India provides 60:40 theory and practical exposure. Every student has to attend three to four days of lectures followed by two days of concurrent fieldwork. The concurrent fieldwork serves as a practical laboratory, where they learn working with individuals, families, communities and groups. Through, fieldwork students of social work learn social problems, implementation status of policies, programmes and schemes. The fieldwork is usually conducted in slums, rural communities, and urban areas or with Governmental and Non-Governmental Organisations, hospitals, aganwadis, schools etc. Every student of social work is attached with a faculty supervisor, who not only helps them to work in the community, they also assists them in report writing and presentations. These faculty supervisors closely monitors the professional development of student with the focus of developing required skill set for being a responsible citizen and employable. As the faculty supervisor and student spend time together, they sometime become mentor and mentee. This relationship helps mentee to learn more from the mentor, and mentor also guides, helps them professionally, socially and emotionally. The model of social work education is seen as an illustration of mentoring provided to students. However, the formal mentoring structure is also missing in Indian social work education. The model of social work education in India should also be followed to all the professional disciplines. This will be the initiation of developing sense of mentoring in Indian higher education system. In the future, this will also help in developing and launching formal mentoring programmes for student and newly recruited teachers.

Conclusion

According to Industry reports supported by NASSCOM, only 25 per cent of technical graduates and about 15 per cent of other graduates are considered employable by IT/ITES industry (Mehra, 2016). Another survey conducted on 800 MBA students across different cities in India reveals only 23 per cent of them were considered employable (*ToI*, 2014). Hence, the need for providing necessary skill set is being recognised over the years to generate more employability. The students should be mentored to make their careers in the areas of their strength and abilities. There are many advantages of having Mentors over those who do not have the same. The prime advantage of having a mentor is the academic benefit that helps them to perform better in academics and industry world. Mentors socialise mentee into the culture of academic units. They also emphasize interactions and connections with mentee to help reduce feelings of isolation and provide them a positive direction in life. At the graduate and post-graduate level, mentors are desirable to offer advice and guidance in academic matters. In addition, they become a valued support for the mentee. The actual role of the faculty mentor is one of nurturing and providing support for a student during the difficult transition period. The mentor also serves as a resource that answers many questions, small or complex, that the student might enquire. Most important, the mentor must serve as a positive role model.

With the recognition of mentoring by many international universities, formal mentoring programmes in their curriculum are being included. This formalized mentoring should also be included in Indian higher education system. A faculty or staff should be attached with student to mentor them for necessary skill development and help them in difficult times and transition period. This will not only boost the academic performance and skill development among students, it will also help them to development a sense of commitment and attachment for the university and the organisation. The social work education structure in India is however, focusing on individual supervision to students; other streams of higher education can adopt the similar. This will create a system of formalised mentoring in Indian higher education, and will ensure the effective education which incudes inculcation of required skill set for employability.

REFERENCES

Bey, T. and Holmes, C. (1992). Mentoring: Contemporary Principles and Issues. Retrieved from: *http://files.eric.ed.gov/fulltext/ED351327.pdf*

Campbell, T. and Campbell, D. (1997). Faculty/Student Mentor Programme: Effects on Academic Performance and Retention. Retrieved from: *http://www.jstor.org/stable/40196285*

Colvin, J. and Ashman, M. (2010). Roles, Risks, and Benefits of Peer Mentoring Relationships in Higher Education. Retrieved from: *https://www.researchgate.net/publication/233052034_Roles_Risks_and_Benefits_of_Peer_Mentoring_Relationships_in_Higher_Education*

Cuseo, J. (2005). The case for faculty student mentoring. Retrieved from: *http://uwc.edu/sites/uwc.edu/files/imceuploads/employees/academicresources/esfy/_files/case_for_faculty-student_mentoring*

Cuseo, J. (2002). The Case for Faculty-Student Mentoring. Retrieved from *http://uwc.edu/sites/uwc.edu/files/imce-uploads/employees/academic-resources/esfy/_files/case_for_faculty-student_mentoring.pdf*

Darwin, A. (2000). Critical reflections on mentoring in work settings. *Adult Education Quarterly* 50(3): 197–211. Retrieved from *https://www.researchgate.net/publication/240703334_Critical_Reflections_on_Mentoring_in_Work_Settings*

EY (2016). Higher Education in India—Vision 2030. Retrieved from *http://www.ey.com/in/en/industries/india-sectors/education/ey-higher-education-in-india-vision-2030*

GoI, UGC (2013) *Higher Education in India: Issues, Concerns and New Directions*. Retrieved: *http://www.ugc.ac.in/oldpdf/pub/he/heindia.pdf*

Hatfield, T. (2011). Mentoring in Higher Education and Student Development. Retrieved from: *http://www.acsd.org/article/mentoring-in-higher-education-and-student-development*

Horenstein, L., *et. al.*, (2010). Mentoring undergraduate Researchers: An explorative study of students and Professors perception. *Mentoring and Tutoring: Partnership in Learning*, 18:3, 269-291, retrieved from: *http://dx.doi.org/10.1080/13611267.2010.492945*

Hudson, P. (2013). Strategies for mentoring pedagogical knowledge. *Teachers and Teaching: Theory and Practice*, 19:4, 363-381, retrieved from: *http://dx.doi.org/10.1080/13540602.2013.770226*

Indiana University South East (2016). https://www.ius.edu/mentoring/

Jaipuria, S. (2014) *Higher Education in India: An Introspection* retrieved from *http://timesofindia.indiatimes.com/home/education/news/Higher-Education-in-India-An-introspection/articleshow/38776482.cms*

Jimenez, M. (2015). *How to mentor Graduate students: a guide for faculty.* Retrieved from *http://www.rackham.umich.edu/downloads/publications*

Knippelmeyer, S. and Torraco, R. (2007). *Mentoring as a Developmental Tool for Higher Education.* Retrieved from *http://research.utah.edu/_documents/mentoring/Knippelmeyer2007.pdf*

Kogan, L., Schoenfeld, R. and Hellyer, P. (2010) Student evaluations of teaching: perceptions of faculty based on gender, position, and rank, *Teaching in Higher Education*, 15:6, 623-636, DOI: 10.1080/13562517.2010.491911 retrieved from: *http://dx.doi.org/10.1080/13562517.2010.491911*

Koki, S. (1998). *The Role of Teacher Mentoring in Educational Reform.* Retrieved from: *http://www.charlesfrodeauthor.com/f/mentoring8.pdf*

Long, C., J. *et. al.*, (2010). *Mentoring Undergraduates: Professors Strategically Guiding the Next Generation of Professionals*, retrieved from: *http://hdl.hadle.net/2027/spo.4919087.0014.104*

Lumpkin, A. (2011). A Model for Mentoring University Faculty, *The Educational Forum*, 75:4, 357-368, retrieved from: *http://dx.doi.org/10.1080/00131725.2011.602466*

Mehra, L. (2016). Enhancing employability of India's IT workforce. Retreived from: *http://www.cisco.com/c/en_in/about/knowledge-network/enhancing-employability.html*

Metros, S. and Yang. C. (2006). The importance of Mentors. Retrieved from: *http://www.educause.edu/research-publications/books/cultivating-careers-professional-development-campus-it/chapter-5-importance-mentors*

Ministry of Human Resource Development, Government of India. (2016). *All India Survey on Higher Education 2014-15*. New Delhi: India.

Mullen, C., Valorie, L. and Hutinger (2010) Mentoring doctoral students through scholastic engagement: adult learning principles in action, *Journal of Further and Higher Education*, 34:2, 179-197, DOI: *http://www.tandfonline.com/action/showCitFormats?doi=10.1080/03098771003695452*

Parylo, Sally and Zepeda, (2012). "The different faces of principal mentorship", *International Journal of Mentoring and Coaching in Education*, Vol. 1, Iss: 2, pp. 120–135 retrieved from: *http://dx.doi.org/10.1108/20466851211262 860*

Penner, R. (2001). *Mentoring in Higher Education*, 30:1, 45-52. Education and Theology, retrieved from: *http://www.directionjournal.org/30/1/mentoring-in-higher-education.html*

Rice, R. (2007). The Mentor's use of Adult Learning Theories: are theory and practice co-extensive? Retrieved from: *http://www.leeds.ac.uk/educol/documents/166216.html*

Sorcinelli, M. and Yun, Y. (2007). *From Mentor to Mentoring Networks: Mentoring in the New Academy*. Retrieved from: *https://works.bepress.com/marydeane_sorcinelli/7/*

Sultana, N. (2015). Knowledge and psychological Skills Training for Faculty to Mentor Students Having Learning Disabilities in Higher Education. Unpublished. retrieved from: *http://shodhganga.inflibnet.ac.in/handle/10603/34305*

Terrion, J. and Leonard, D. (2007). A taxonomy of the characteristics of student peer mentors in higher education: Findings from a literature review. Retrieved from *https://www.ruor.uottawa.ca/bitstream/10393/22769/1/Lennox_ Terrion_Taxonomy_Characteristics_Student_Peer_Mentoring.pdf*

The University of Iowa (2016). *https://provost.uiowa.edu/mentoring/students.html*

ToI (2014). Higher Education in India: An introspection. Retrieved from: *http://timesofindia.indiatimes.com/home/education/news/Higher-Education-in-India-An-introspection/articleshow/38776482.cms*

University of Michigan (2016). *http://onsp.umich.edu/mentorship*

University of Minnesota (2016). *http://design.umn.edu/alumni_friends/mentor/*

World Bank (2007). Higher Education in India. Retrieved from: *http://www.worldbank.org/en/search?q=higher+education+india*

Wunsch, M.A. (1994) Developing mentoring programmes: Major themes and issues. New Directions for Teaching and Learning 57: 27–34. Retrieved from: *http://onlinelibrary.wiley.com/doi/10.1002/tl.37219945705/full#references*

Xavier University (2016). *https://www.xavier.edu/career/mentor/*

Yahner, R. and Goodstein, L. (2016). Graduate Student Mentoring: Be More Than an Adviser. Retrieved from: *http://www.gradschool.psu.edu/faculty-and-staff/practices/mentoring/*

4
Inclusive Growth, Knowledge, Economy and Neo-Liberal Model of Development for Higher Education

Farida Siddiqui

Introduction

Higher Education plays a dynamic role in a country's development. The expansion in higher education took place in the world economies as human capital arguments were beginning to make an impact on economic planners which also coincided with the perspective of inclusive growth. In many developing countries education has been seen as a means of promoting inclusion by uniting different ethnic and linguistic groups within countries. In many countries such as Indonesia and Malaysia, Education is seen as a means of countering perceived colonial hegemony in a post-colonial world (Nguyen, A., 1996). A substantial education system in both developed as well as developing economies always offers a highly visible way of meeting demands for social equality, social justice and inclusive growth.

Inclusive Growth: Definition and Approach

According to the World Bank (2006), inclusive growth is "the only sure means for correcting the deeply ingrained regional imbalances, inequities and for consolidating economic gains", as inclusive growth is the growth "with emphasis not only on the distribution of economic gains, but also on the security, vulnerability, empowerment, and sense of full participation that people may enjoy in social life".

Inclusive growth allows people to *contribute to* and *benefit from* economic growth.[1] This growth should be sustainable in the long run, *broad-based* across sectors,[2] and *inclusive* of the large part of the country's labour force.[3] Inclusive growth refers *both* to the pace and pattern of growth, which are considered interlinked, and therefore, in need to be addressed together. The idea that both the pace and pattern of growth are critical for achieving a high growth, sustainable growth record, as well as poverty reduction, is consistent with the findings in the *Growth Report: Strategies for Sustained Growth and Inclusive Development* (Commission on Growth and Development, 2008). The Commission notes that inclusiveness—a concept that encompasses equity, equality of opportunity, and protection in market and employment transitions—is an essential ingredient of any successful growth strategy. Here we emphasize the idea of equality of opportunity in terms of access to markets, resources, and unbiased regulatory environment for businesses and individuals.[4]

The inclusive growth approach takes a longer term perspective as the focus is on productive employment rather than on direct income redistribution, as a means of increasing incomes for excluded groups. In the short run, governments could use income distribution schemes to attenuate negative impacts on the poor.[5] In poor countries such schemes can impose significant burdens on already stretched budgets, and it is theoretically impossible to reduce poverty through redistribution in countries where average income falls below US$ 700 per year. According to a recent OECD study, even in developed countries, redistribution schemes cannot be the only response to rising poverty rates in certain segments of the population.[6]

Inclusive growth is about raising the pace of growth and enlarging the size of the economy, while levelling the playing field for investment and increasing productive employment opportunities. Inclusive growth focuses on *ex-ante* analysis of sources of, and constraints to sustained, high growth, and not only on one group—the poor. The analysis focuses on ways to raise the pace of growth by utilizing more fully parts of the labour force trapped in low-productivity activities or completely excluded from the growth process.

According to Asia Development Bank Strategy 2020 Inclusive growth is based on 3 pillars:

- High Growth and sustainable growth to create and expand economic opportunities;
- Broader access to economic opportunities to ensure that members

of society can participate and benefit from growth; and
- Social safety nets to prevent extreme deprivation.

The main instrument for a sustainable and inclusive growth is assumed to be *productive* employment.[7] *Employment growth* generates new jobs and income for the individuals especially in micro-firms, while *productivity growth* has the potential to lift the wages of those employed and the returns to the self-employed. Hence, inclusive growth is not only about employment growth, but also about productivity growth[8] which may be achieved only through education based on knowledge.

Knowledge-Based Economies

The most important economic development of our lifetime has been the rise of a new system for creating wealth, based no longer on muscle but on mind (Toffler,1990). The last decade of the 20th century saw greater emphasis than ever before placed on higher education. In both developed and developing nations, higher education was believed to be the key to the continuing growth of national economies. Alvin Toffler was writing in 1990, when the knowledge economy was only a concept and before statistics had been developed to quantify the contribution of knowledge to an economy. However, even in 1990, the effects of globalisation could no longer be ignored. Toffler was prescient in noting the now well-recognised international trend in employment from blue-collar low-skilled jobs, to white-collar highly-skilled employment, and the importance of widely diffused and ever expanding knowledge that contributes significantly to current economic growth.

The Organisation for Economic Co-operation and Development (OECD) defines a country with a knowledge-based economy as one where "the production, diffusion and use of technology and information are key to economic activity and sustainable growth" (OECD,1999). Investment in knowledge refers to investment in areas that generate knowledge, such as research and development, software, education and basic science. It also refers to 'innovation' and the machinery, equipment and infrastructure to support it. While the relationship between increasing levels of knowledge and economic growth is not yet clear, what is clear, is that most industrialised countries have been investing heavily in new knowledge, its creation, dissemination and adaptation to production, on a par with their investment in machinery and equipment (8%), particularly since the mid-1990s (OECD, 1999).

Education based on knowledge has now become an important subject of discussion in international economic fora. The Uruguay Round of the General Agreement on Tariffs and Trade (GATT) and the General Agreement on Trade in Services (GATS), classified education as a service and sought to ensure the gradual reduction of restrictions on educational services such as technology transfer, consultancy, distance education and so on. The eventual aim was to create an international marketplace in education (Kelsey, 1998).

In a knowledge-based global economy the emphasis must be not only on the structure of educational institutions, but also on the quality of education that they provide. This is particularly important in a global economy, because the effect of globalisation "has been to create patterns of employment, expectations, and demands for skills and products which cannot be met solely within national boundaries, not solely through national policies" (Riddell, 1996). This is why the highest performing economies of the last several decades are from Asia. As the public investment in education grew faster in Asia than in any other region in the world, both as a per centage of total expenditure and on a per capita basis (Tilak,1994), the idea of an "Asian model" of education inspired by the success of Japan in gaining an economic parity with the West, became a driver of economic growth.

The Neo Liberal Model of Development for Education

The International Perspective of Variations in Public Expenditure for Higher Education

Development is guided by the neo-liberal economic policies almost all over the world. The term 'neo-liberal' is taken from Christopher, C. (1996) who uses it to refer exclusively to financial policies of education. The basic characteristics ascribe to this model have also been called 'neo-Fordist' (Brown and Lauder, 1996), 'new order' (Riddell, 1996), or less accurately, 'marketisation' (Qiping and White, 1994) and 'privatisation' (Kelsey,1998) by those who highlight the economic aspects of the model.

The World Bank, from a neo-liberal perspective, stresses three key factors to support *knowledge-driven development*, while ensuring quality, efficiency and equity in tertiary education (World Bank, 2002):

- a coherent policy framework;
- an enabling regulatory environment; and
- appropriate financial incentives.

These factors are indicative of a "new managerialism" approach to public administration, and to managing higher education in particular. This approach consists of "The package of reforms put forward and promoted by the core of the OECD countries enrolled under the banner of the new model of public management whose order of the day was "steering at a distance" (Braun,1999). Some of the key aspects of new managerialism include decentralisation, deregulation, accountability and quality control through the monitoring of medium and long term plans that specify clearly defined objectives (Braun, 1999).

Higher education is passing through a phase of internationalisation. Almost all countries in the world are experiencing difficulty in financing higher education. As development is guided by the neo-liberal economic policies almost all over the world and, therefore, higher education is increasingly being viewed as a private good. It is important to understand how different countries are responding to the neo liberal challenges in financing higher education (Bhushan, S., 2008). With regard to neo-liberal model of development for higher education, the present section briefly reviews the recent trends in cost sharing and how education planners are developing newer ways of finding the resources and searching for appropriate alternatives for higher education.

The Status of State Funding of Higher Education

The international trend of the State funding of Higher Education gives a mixed trend. Among the 94 developing countries; 62 countries increased their share in public expenditure as a proportion of GNP, whereas 32 countries decreased their share in public expenditure as a proportion of GNP. In the case of developed countries, however, out of 36 countries, 16 countries have decreased public expenditure on education as a proportion of GNP (Bhushan, S., 2008*)*. Thus, an overall trend shows that over 40 per cent of the countries in the world are experiencing constraints in the public financing of education (Table 27.1).

Table 4.1: Countries Showing Variations in Public Expenditure as a Proportion of GNP (1990-91 and 2001-02)

Countries	*Increased*	*Decreased*	*Stationary*	*Total*
Countries in Transition	1	7	1	9
Developed Countries	20	16	0	36
Developing Countries	62	32	0	94
World	93	57	1	139

Source: Bhushan, S. (2008), p. 257.

It is important to note that not only the share of public expenditure in education has been falling, share of public expenditure on higher education as a proportion of total public expenditure in education during the period 1991 and 2001-02 have also shown a decline in many developing countries (34 out of 72) whereas it has increased in most of the developed countries (28 out of 34). It clearly shows that developed countries have prioritised their resources for higher education (Bhushan, S., 2008). However, most of the developing countries have not been able to devote greater resources for higher education (Table 4.2).

Table 4.2: Countries Showing Variations in Public Expenditure in Higher Education as a Proportion to Total Public Expenditure in Education (1990-91 and 2001-02)

Countries	*Increased*	*Decreased*	*Stationary*	*Total*
Countries in Transition	4	1	0	5
Developed Countries	28	6	0	34
Developing Countries	38	34	0	72
World	70	41	0	111

Source: Bhushan, S. (2008), p. 257.

Privatisation

The declining trend in state support for higher education gave a fillip to the growth of private sector in the field of higher education. Sanyal and Martin (2006) note that privatisation has taken the following forms in different countries:

- Privatisation of public institutions encouraging government institutions to tap private sources of financing through fees and other sources.
- New private institutions have been encouraged to establish institutions with government support. This is followed in India in the form of government aided private colleges and government aided private deemed universities. Latin American countries, such as Chile, Columbia, Paraguay and Peru, have much larger share of private institutions with government support. Tunisia devotes 2 per cent of GNP to higher education; still it has set-up a legal framework to encourage investment in higher education through the creation of large number of private institutions.

- There are self-financed non-profit private institutions in both developing and developed countries established by religious and philanthropic foundations.
- Lastly, there has been a recent move to establish profit-making private institutions all over the world. They offer onsite and offsite programmes spread over many countries in Latin America, Europe and Asia. Tuition fee is the main source of income of these companies.

The important point to note here is that if cost sharing is not managed properly there are chances that public institutions will suffer from quality gaps as well as equity gaps and will not be able to respond to increasing demand for higher education. On the other hand, privatisation will promote increasing profit-seeking activities and will turn out to be creating educational inequalities particularly in developing countries.

The Cost Sharing with Students

Bruce Johnston (2006b), an authority in the financing of higher education system has analysed cost sharing in international perspective. He argues that rising costs, limited public revenues, increasing enrolment and the quest for quality have led to the need for increasing reliance on revenue supplementation. World-wide this has led to the sharing of costs with parents and students. There are three important reasons for increasing sharing of costs:

(i) The benefits of subsidy to the higher education are cornered by the rich.
(ii) Cost sharing can be equity based both in high tuition as well as loan scheme. Cost sharing will, however, have a tendency to minimize the cost of higher education as price charged will imply the demand for return.
(iii) Efficiency rationale implies that free higher education may have a tendency for wastes that may be manifested in various forms.

The Tuition Fees Trends

Tuition is an important means of cost sharing. The recent trend in tuition fees in some of the countries is analysed in Table 4.3. There seems to be a present phase of higher education where cost sharing with students through hike in tuition fees is being practiced world-wide. Countries who have rationalized the tuition fees structure in favour of efficiency, productivity and equity have met a part of resources for higher education. Countries who have evaded the issue on ideological grounds or merely due to political convenience have lost the resources for higher education and affected the quality rather adversely.

Table 4.3: Public Sector Tuition Fee: First Degree in US Dollars College/ University

Country	*High Tuition ($)*	*Low Tuition ($)*
Austria	746	746
Canada	5000	1366
China	2591	518
Japan	2974	2974
India	85	20
Mexico	1159	178
Russia	12026	0
South Africa	3293	1085
USA	6000	1600
UK	1565	1565

Source: Johnstone B. (2006a).

The time has arisen to face the issue upfront and evolve the fee structure that is rational to meet the part of resources required for higher education. Relatively speaking, India has one of the lowest tuition fee structures, as is evident from Table 4.3. Figure given below demonstrates that the tuition fee is the highest in Russia and the lowest in India.

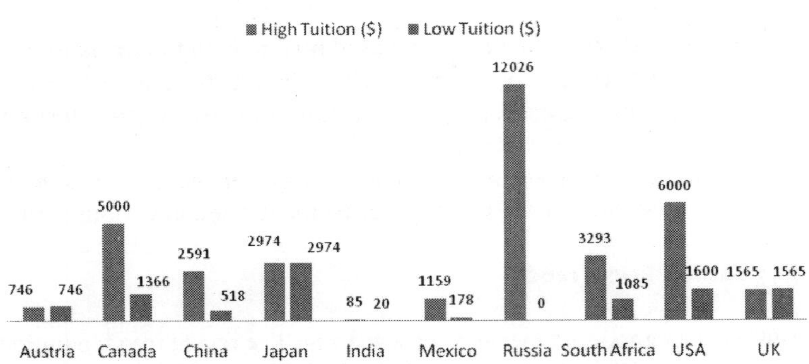

Fig. 4.1: Cross Country Variation in Public Sector Tuition Fee

Source: Johnstone B. (2006a).

UK: Britain in 1997, under the labour government, became the first European country to accept the principle of an increase in tuition fees in higher education. The new system allows English universities to charge fees of up to £ 3000 a year in 2006, provided there is an "access plan" offering bursaries to increase wider access by disadvantaged students. Fees will not be paid upfront by students, but will be paid after graduation, on an income contingent basis. Students will be given a loan to cover the full cost of their fees, and Graduates must repay the loan, after their income reaches a fixed threshold (currently 15,000 £ per annum) by means of deduction, collected through their income tax, of 9 per cent of their income above the threshold. In UK, the experience of the new system is still to be tested on access and equity. In principle, the above scheme of deferred fees is considered to be fairer and less likely to damage access.

Austria: Funding pattern in Austrian higher education system during 1986-98 has undergone radical changes. Government contribution fell from 87 per cent to 52 per cent. During this period, students' fees increased from 5 per cent to 16 per cent (Table 4.4). Decline of government funding has led to innovations in the financing of higher education in Austria. The new system is a combination of tuition plus income contingent loan available to most Austria students. The loan covers the full amount of tuition as established by the university up to limits set by the government within three bands. Up to 20 per cent of the tuition due is discounted for paying upfront. Repayments are income contingent on annual income above US $ 24,898. Rates range from 3 per cent to maximum amount of 8 per cent on annual income in excess of US $ 47,445. Repayments due are collected as income surtax by the employer or are paid along with estimated or year-end taxes due. As the above Table 4.4 shows HECS

Table 4.4: Sources of Funds for Austrian Higher Education (1986-98)

Year	*Governments (per cent)*	*Higher Education Contribution Scheme (%)*	*Students Fees and Charges for Services (%)*	*Donations and Investments*	*Other Sources*	*Total*
1986	87	0	5	8	0	100
1990	68	12	8	7	4	100
1994	62	13	11	3	11	100
1998	52	17	16	5	10	100

Source: Department of Education, Training and Youth Affairs, DETYA (1999). Above table is obtained from Marginson Simon (2003).

scheme has contributed 17 per cent to the higher education finance in 1998. The scheme was necessitated due to fall in funding of the government per student from $ 10,114 in 1995 to $ 7954 in 1999 (Johnstone, B., 2006a).

Another innovation has been the corporatisation and market orientation to the courses in higher education. As a result of export of higher education international fee income reached 8.3 per cent of all institutional income by 1998 (DETYA, 1999).

US: In the US, tuition fee has increased with the tightening of fiscal belt to account for the increase in the cost in quality. However, the access is not adversely affected as there is efficient and diversified grant system for students. Besides the competitive conditions in the market, innovations in financing and use of education technology to save the costs have been important features of higher education. In the US, most major State Universities have increased their non-state funding to around 70 per cent of their total income. Universities are becoming entrepreneurial at a rapid rate.

Japan: In the Japanese higher education system, substantial differences exist in the public expenditure in the national and private universities. The overall ratio of subsidy for expenditure in the two sectors is 4.25:1. Tuition and fees provide an extraordinarily high share of income in private universities, exceeding 70 per cent of the total. The share of Government subsidies to the private universities remains around 12 per cent. Thus, tuition charges and fees are critical to the financing of higher education.

Every student in the private sector pays tuition and fees that are more than double those paid by students in the national sector. Essentially, therefore, students in the national sector enjoy a much more advantageous position than the students in private sector. The challenge for private universities in Japan is to diversify donations as well as funds for scholarship, since the level of tuition charges and fees may already have reached a limit beyond which further increases may be counter-productive (Arimoto, A., 2006).

China: In 1989, China introduced the policy of charging tution and other fees. As a result, government dependence of funds reduced from 96 per cent in 1978 to 82 per cent in 1992. The higher education in the year 1998 made tution fees compulsory for college students while ensuring that the government continues to increase its financial allocation to public institutions. As a result, in 1997, Government share in the higher education funding declined to 63.4 per cent in the country.

Student Loan as a Form of Cost Sharing

In understanding new forms of loan programmes, it is essential to re-examine the conventional wisdom that only government taxes and subsidy to higher education provide the equitable basis of financing. However, increasing indirect taxes are regressive in character and the taxes paid by general public may not benefit them as access to higher education is skewed in favour of households with high per capita consumption expenditure (NSSO, 1999-2000). It leads to the conclusion that government subsidy to higher education may not always be an efficient way of financing. The conventional wisdom, therefore, needs to be modified to include diversified modes of funding which could be linked to equity objective.

NIEPA (2005b) notes that Scope for any further increase in cost recovery is extremely limited and further increases in the same, particularly through student fees, will be highly regressive in effect. It also opposes a differential fee system in higher education on account of practical difficulties. On student programmes it recommends that a body like "Higher Education Finance Corporation" may be set-up with contributions from the government and the corporate sector to coordinate the student loan schemes being operated by several banks to provide on its own scholarship and soft loans to students (*Ibid.,* p. 48). It maintains that "educational loan programmes have to be designed keeping educational considerations, and they cannot be run solely on commercial lines by commercial banks" (*Ibid.*). In view of CABE Committee recommendations, it is important to review the international trends on student loan programme to make it more equity based. It is also necessary because too many student loan programmes have failed due to both poor design and poor execution.

Examples of Cost Sharing in the form of Student Loan Programmes[9]

Austria: In the Higher Education Contribution Scheme (HECS), explained above, repayment due is collected as income surtax by the employer. There is no forgiveness after a certain age or passage of years. It has a low administrative cost of servicing as well as a very low default rate (Chapman and Ryan, 2002).

China: Loan scheme was introduced in 6 cities of China in 1999. There is a government subsidy in students' loan scheme. As a result, students pay rate of interest considerably less than the market rate after graduation with a repayment periods of six years. The loans are disbursed by participating banks, and the risk is shared by the university, the government, and the bank. There is also provision for non-subsidised commercial loan scheme that is available for affluent students (Shen and Li., 2003).

Germany: There is extensive means—tested, or need-based, study assistance in Germany. A portion of the grant—one half of the study assistance—is repayable at a zero nominal rate of interest. Repayment begins after five years of graduation.

Japan: Japan has a unique system. Here, the loan is administered by Japan Student Services Organisation (JASSO). There are two types of student loans. The first is (i) merit, and (ii) need-based. It carries no interest. The second carries 3 per cent interest. It is awarded during school years. Loan repayment is on a fixed monthly basis. Repayment period is 20 years.

Kenya: Kenya launched a new loan programme in 1995 after a loan programme failed in 1970s due to high default. The new loan programme is means tested. Interest is four per cent and capital is provided by the government. Loan programme has the backing of legislation by the government. Legislation mandates employers to deduct amounts due from employees in repayment. Loan programme is managed under a quasi-public Higher Education Board in 1995.

Netherlands: Student loan has two components. First component is basic allowance that is not means tested, the second component is means-tested and is in the form of a grant, if academic progress of the student is shown satisfactory. Interest on the remainder is government borrowing rate plus 1 per cent for administrative cost. Repayment has an income contingent feature for low income groups.

Russia: Russia imposes the obligation to work *in lieu* of tuition fee provided to the students. If admitted to an institution, and agrees to work for a certain period of time then institution is entitled to receive grants or vouchers providing tuition free higher education to students scoring high in national entrance examination. Interest is not charged on such loans. This is strictly speaking not a loan (Protapenko, 2002; Vossenstyne and Salerno, 2002).

South Africa: Tertiary Education Fund of South Africa (TEFSA), a Government sponsored organisation, manages the loan. It is need-based. Interest rate is high however; there is forgiveness, as 40 per cent of loan is converted into grant if student passes in all subjects. Repayment is income-contingent with an element of progression (Jackson, 2002).

Sweden: Since 1960s Sweden and other Scandinavian countries have relieved parents from paying living cost, as loan programme covers living costs of the students. Loan carries the nominal interest and is available to all. Repayment is income contingent and there is hardly any default. The university is tuition free. That's the reason Swedish higher education is heavily subsidised by the government.

Thailand: The Thai Student Loans Scheme (TSLS) was created in 1996. The annual loan budget is sanctioned by the government and allocated to the institutions. Every institution makes its own rules. The loan covers tuition fee and other educational expenditure. The rate of interest on loans is only 1 per cent. Loan awards are based on need. Repayments are spread over 15 years. Repayment is income-contingent.

United Kingdom: In 1989-90, a small conventional loan programme was launched. It was means-tested maintenance grants. In 1998-99, a much expanded programme was announced by the government. The loan programme carries a zero real rate of interest. Repayment is income-contingent to be repaid at 9 per cent of marginal income above £ 15,000 (US$ 16,181) (increased from £ 10,000 in April 2005), which is deducted by the employer as though it were an income surtax and passed to the government treasury (Richards, 2002; Johnstone, 2005).

United States: Loans and parental contributions are the most important features of the United States higher education. The United States provides mainly conventional, fixed-schedule loans, available to all students with some financial need at minimally subsidised rates of interest. The Federal government guarantees all student loans and pays all interest during the 'in-school' years and for a grace period for those with financial need. Unsubsidized loans are also available that do not require the demonstration of financial need and that carry only the implicit (but not insubstantial) subsidy of the governmental guarantee and the benefit of an interest rate near the government's borrowing rate. Much of the capital and loan origination is provided by the private banking sector, which in turn sells much of its student loan portfolio to private secondary markets.

Inclusive Growth and Neo-Liberal Model of Education: The Indian Context

India is recognised as an economy with a "stunning", but "jobless growth" (UNDP-ILO, 2007), and a "booming economy with growing gaps" where the spectacular successes made have not been shared by all equally (World Bank, 2006). The growth of the Indian economy has been exclusive and there is a need to make it inclusive (e.g., K.N. Raj in Mody, 2006; Kannan, 2006). The Planning Commission has also realised that economic growth has failed to be sufficiently inclusive, particularly after the mid-1990s. It noted in the approach to the Eleventh Five Year Plan, "While the performance reflects the strength of the economy in many areas, it is also true that large parts of our population are still to experience a decisive improvement in their standard of living. Far too many people still lack access to basic services such as health, education, clean drinking water and sanitation facilities without which they cannot be empowered to claim their share in the benefits of growth. These problems are more severe in some states than in others, and in general they are especially severe in rural areas" (Planning Commission, 2006).

Inclusive growth is expected to focus on the poor, the marginalised, the neglected, the disadvantaged and deprived sections of the society, and the backward regions of the country. An added dimension of the new development strategy also includes linking growth to the quality of basic services like education and healthcare. Inclusive growth presupposes inclusive education-good quality education that is accessible to all (Jandhyala, B.G. and Tilak, 2007). The role of education in ensuring inclusive growth is very critical. As noted in the Economic Survey 2006-07, "the inclusive nature of the growth itself will be conditioned by the progress that is made in the areas of education".

In a knowledge-based global economy the emphasis is on the structure of educational institutions as well as on their content. This is particularly important in a global economy, because the effect of globalisation "has been to create patterns of employment, expectations, and demands for skills and products which cannot be met solely within national boundaries, not solely through national policies" (Riddell, 1996). It is higher education institutions that are already in the best position to benefit from, and contribute to, the increasing exchange of knowledge and the economic development as recognised by the World Bank. In comparison to many developing as well as developed countries the education in India is very inclusive in nature. Although it is evident from Table 4.3 given above that India has the lowest tuition fee structures but the increasing burden of financing the expansion of higher education by the state has become a matter of concern for the country.

Although crises in financing of higher education is not something unique for India as considerably large number of developing countries are experiencing resource crunch for higher education. In response to neo-liberal model of development for higher education, privatisation and commercialisation was considered as the best solution to the problem. India too opened its doors to private players in the field of higher education. Table 4.5 below highlights the status of higher education in India. It can be seen this Table 4.5 that there are 105 private state universities and 91 private deemed universities in the country. These universities on one hand are filling the gap between demand for and supply of higher education by giving access to higher education to those who have access to economic resources, but on the other hand simultaneously excluding those who suffer from deficit in access to such economic resources. Although, the higher education in India has witnessed many fold increase in its institutional capacity since independence. During 1950-2008, the number of universities has increased from 20 to about 431, colleges from 500 to 20,677 and the teachers from 15,000 to nearly 5.05 lakh. Consequently, the enrolment of students has increased from a mere 1.00 lakh in 1950 to over 116.12 lakhs (Thorat, 2008). Table 4.5 reveals that India has expanded its institutional capacity for higher education in terms of number of State/Open/Central /Technical/Private Universities yet India is confronted with high level of disparities in access to higher education based on region, religion, caste, creed and gender.

Disparities in Access to Higher Education in India

The access to higher education is measured in term of Gross Enrolment Ratio (GER), which is a ratio of persons enrolled in higher education institutions to total population of the persons in age group of 18 to 23 years. The estimate based on Selected Education Statistics (SES) for 2006-07, indicates that the access to higher education measured in term of gross enrolment ratio increased from 0.7 per cent in 1950-51 to 1.4 per cent in 1960-61. By 2006-07 the GER increased to about 11 per cent. While the enrolment rate at aggregate level is about 11 per cent in 2006-07 at overall level, it varies significantly across the states and districts. As against the 11 per cent of all India average, the GER is lower in states of Arunachal Pradesh, Bihar, Madhya Pradesh, Meghalaya, Mizoram, Rajasthan, Sikkim, Tripura and Jharkahnd (Srivastava, R., & Dubey, A., 2008). The Eleventh Five Year Plan recognised that the 11 per cent enrolment rate is too low compared to 23 per cent of world average or 36.5 per cent for countries in transitions or more than 55 per cent for developed countries. Development experience of the developed countries indicates that sustained economic growth requires a minimum of 20 per cent to 25 per cent enrolment in higher education. The basis for the low

Table 4.5: State and Type-wise Number of Universities in India

States	Central University	Central Open University	Institution of National Importance	State Public University	State Open University	State Private University	Institution Established Under State Legislature 1Act	Government Deemed University	Private Deemed University	Others	Grand Total
1	2	3	4	5	6	7	8	9	10	11	12
Andhra Pradesh	3		2	31	1		2	2	5	1	47
Arunachal Pradesh	1		1					1			3
Assam	2		2	3	1	1					9
Bihar	1		2	14	1		1	1			20
Chandigarh			1	1				1			3
Chhattisgarh	1		1	9	1	5					17
Delhi	4	1	3	55				9	2	1	25
Goa	1		1	1							2
Gujarat	1		2	21	1	10			2		37
Haryana	1		1	10		3		2	5		22
Himachal Pradesh	1		2	4		11					18
J & K	2		1	7			1				11
Jharkhand	1		1	7		1		1	1		12
Karnataka	1		1	23		2		4	11		43
Kerala	1		3	11				2			17
Madhya Pradesh	1		3	16		7		3		1	33
Maharashtra	1		3	18	1			7	14		44
Manipur	2		1								3
Meghalaya	1		1			8					10
Mizoram	1		1			1					3
Nagaland	1		1			2					4

(*Contd.*)

1	2	3	4	5	6	7	8	9	10	11	12
Odisha	1		2	12		2			2		19
Puducherry	1		2						1		4
Punjab	1		4	8		4		1	1		19
Rajasthan	1		2	14	11	19			8		45
Sikkim	1		1			4					6
Tamil Nadu	2		4	23	1			1	28		59
Tripura	1		1			1					3
Uttar Pradesh	4		3	21	1	18	1	3	7		58
Uttarakhand	1		2	6	1	6		1	3		20
West Bengal	1		4	19	1				1		26
All India	**42**	**1**	**59**	**284**	**13**	**105**	**5**	**39**	**91**	**3**	**642**

There is no University in UTs of Andaman & Nicobar Islands, Dadra & Nagar Haveli, Daman & Diu and Lakshadweep.

Source: GOI, AISHE, 2013.

enrolment ratio in the country is the inter-group disparities in access to higher education in the country.

For the first time Ravi Srivastava and Sinha (UGC Report, 2008) estimated the gross enrolment rate for various groups and bring out the variation in enrolment rate in 2004-05, between male-female, between SC, ST, OBC and between religious groups, economic groups such as self-employed and wage labourer, between income groups (in term of per capita consumption expenditure) and poor and non-poor. The findings of their study are as under:

Rural-Urban Disparities

The NSS data for 2004-05 indicates significant rural and urban disparities-enrolment rate being 6.73 per cent and 19.80 per cent for the rural and the urban areas respectively—the GER in the urban areas being three times higher compared to rural areas. However, inter-caste/tribe disparities are the most prominent. In 2004-05, the GER was about 11 per cent at overall levels. The GER among the SCs (6.3%), the STs (6.33%), and the OBCs (8.50%) was much lower compared with the Others (16.60%). Thus, the GER for the SC/STs was three times and that of the OBCs about two times less compared with the Others. Between the SC/STs and the OBCs, however, the GER was lower among the former by about two per centage points.

Religion Based Disparities

Another feature about access to higher education is the religion. The SCs, the STs, and the OBCs suffer unequally as religious group. For instance, in 2004-05, the GER of the OBC Muslims was 6 per cent as compared with 7.34 per cent for Non-OBC Muslims. Similar disparities are apparent in the case of SC and the Non-SC/ST Christians. In the case of the SC Sikhs, the GER was only 2 per cent compared with 15 per cent among Non-SC Sikhs. Similarly, the GER of tribal Christians was 6.48 per cent compared to 23.29 per cent for Non-SC/ST Christians. It is, thus, evident that the SCs, the STs, and the OBCs from all religion suffer from lower access to higher education. However, the SCs within the Hindu and the Sikh suffer more acutely than the SCs belonging to other religions. Similarly, the OBCs within the Muslims probably suffer more than the Hindu OBCs. Similarly, the STs within the Hindu fold suffer more than their Christian counterparts. In 2004-05, disparities are also evident in enrolment rate between religious groups. The GER for the Hindus, the Muslims, the Christians, the Sikhs, and the others stood at 11.9, 6.84, 16.68, about 12, and 15.4 per centage points respectively. Thus, the GER was the lowest among the Muslims followed by the Hindus.

Gender Disparities

Also, there are wide gender disparities in terms of access to higher education. Access is generally lower for girls as compared to the boys—the GER being 12.42 per cent for the males and 9.11 per cent for the females. It needs to be recognised that although the enrolment rate are generally lower for the females compared to the males; the females belonging to the lower castes and some religious groups suffer more acutely in accessing higher education than other female. For instance, in 2004-05, as against the overall average of 9.11 per cent, GER among the females was 4.76 per cent, 4.43 per cent, 6.60 per cent, and 19.53 per cent points respectively for the ST, the SC, the OBC, and the Other females. Thus, the GER among the ST/SC females was about five times and that of the OBC females about three times less compared to the higher caste females (Saraswati, R., 2008). In the case of religious groups, the Muslim women seem to be facing the most difficult circumstance. The GER among Muslim females was 5.8 per cent compared to 9.32 per cent for Hindu females, 12.7 per cent for Sikh females, and 16 per cent for Christian females.

Poor and Non-Poor Disparities

There are perceivable differences in enrolment rates among the poor and non-poor (irrespective of their caste, ethnic, religious, or gender backgrounds). The GER for the poor was 2.21 per cent as against 12.36 per cent for the non-poor. Therefore, the GER among the poor was almost twelve times lower compared with the non-poor. In the rural and the urban areas, the GER for the poor stood at 1.40 per cent and 4 per cent respectively, which was evidently quite low compared with 7.12 per cent and 27.15 per cent for non-poor respectively. Within the poor households, however, the GER was the lowest among the poor households belonging to the STs and the SCs, followed by the OBCs and the others. The GER for poor belonging to the STs, the SCs, the OBCs, and the Others stood at 1.55 per cent, 1.89 per cent, 2.30 per cent, and 3.58 per cent respectively. In the rural areas, the GER was the lowest among the STs at a marginal level of 1.11 per cent followed by the SCs at 1.35 per cent, the OBCs at 1.13 per cent, and the Others at 1.66 per cent—the overall GER being 1.30 per cent. In the urban areas, the GER for the urban poor stood at 3.86, 4.78, 5.16, and 7 per centage points respectively for the SCs, the STs, the OBCs, and the Others—the average being 5.51 per cent.

Occupational Disparities

Differences in the GER are also equally evident across occupational groups in the rural and the urban areas. The GER was 3 per cent for non-farm wage labourers and 1.41 per cent for farm wage labourers. Similarly, in the urban areas, the GER was only 3.26 per cent for casual labourers. Thus, both in the rural and the urban areas, the enrolment rates for wage (casual) labourers were the lowest, particularly, for the farm wage labourers. For the wage labourers, the GER was particularly low amongst the SC/STs compared with the Others. For instance, as against 1.41 per cent at overall level for the wage labourers in the rural areas; the ratio was 0.67, 1.63, 1.16, and 1.93 per centage points for the ST, the SC, the OBC, and the Other wage labourers respectively. Similarly, in the urban areas, the GER for casual labourers was 3.26 per cent at overall level as against 1.53 per cent, 2.61 per cent, 3.34 per cent, and 4.30 per cent for the ST, the SC, the OBC, and other wage labourers respectively.

Conclusion

The prerequisite to inclusive growth is to provide equal *access* to and *provision* of higher education to each and every segment of the society. In Indian context the approach and strategies for promoting higher education need to be formulated in such a way that equal access to higher education is provided to SCs, STs, OBCs, disables, women, poor people and minorities so that they become the participant as well as the recipient of the benefits of inclusive growth. In this context the neo-liberal model which calls for reducing government sources of funding for higher education should under no circumstances be blindly followed by developing countries. The developing countries should also not reduce public expenditure on higher education as the reduction in public expenditure will cause ever widening inequalities in higher education which will hamper the very process of inclusive growth in the developing societies.

The neo-liberal model aims to produce more cost-effective flexible institutions that are better able to supply the needs of the labour market. Hence, developing countries in general and India in particular must establish close coordination between the institutions of higher learning and the labour market so that the academic programmes as per the needs of the labour market are designed and the wealth, *based on knowledge*, is createdin the economy.

NOTES

1. This statement is in line with the OECD Development Assistance Committee's policy statement on pro-poor growth. However, a difference between pro-poor and inclusive growth is that the pro-poor approach is mainly interested in the welfare of the poor while inclusive growth is concerned with opportunities for the majority of the labour force, poor and middle-class alike.
2. Imb and Wacziag (2003) show that countries diversify over most of their development path. Countries start specialising quite late in the development process, and the turnaround point occurs at a robust level of income per capita (around constant 1985 $10,000). They conclude that increased sectoral specialisation applies only to high-income economies. It is important to note that some countries may not broaden their economic base as they develop due to their specific economic conditions (e.g. small states).
3. Encouraging broad-based and inclusive growth does not imply a return to government-sponsored industrial policies, but instead puts the emphasis on policies that remove constraints to growth and create a level playing field for investment.
4. According to the report of the Commission on Growth and Development, persistent, determined focus on inclusive long-term growth by governments is one of the ingredients of a successful growth strategy. Yet, there is limited analytic work integrating the literature on growth and productive employment.
5. The term "shared growth" can be misunderstood as implying a focus on income distribution schemes, which is why inclusive growth is preferred.
6. Source Growing Unequal? Income Distribution and Poverty in OECD Countries, OECD (2008).
7. According to the Commission on Growth and Development Report (2008), sustained high growth requires rapid incremental productive employment.
8. There is no preconception or bias in favour of labour-intensive industry policies. Indeed, the self-employed poor need improvements in productivity and levelling of the business environment in order to raise their incomes.
9. This particular section draws heavily Chapman, B. and Greenway, D. (2004).

REFERENCES

Arimoto, A. (2006). Structure and Functions of Financing Higher Education in Higher Education. In The World 2006 in GUN1 (Ed) Financing of Universities, Palgrave, New York.

Bhushan, S. (2008). Universities and Colleges Requirement for 15% target During 11th Plan — An Estimate, In Higher Education in India—Issues

Related to Expansion, Inclusiveness, Quality and Finance, UGC Report, New Delhi.

Braun, D. and Merrien, F.X. (1999). *Towards a New Model of Governance for Universities? A Comparative View*, Jessica Kingsley Publishers, London.

Brown and Lauder (1996). Education, Globalization and Economic Development, *Journal of Education Policy*, 10(3/4): 225-237.

Chapman, B. and D. Greenaway (2006). Learning to Live with Loans? International Policy Transfer and the Funding of Higher Education, *The World Economy*, Volume 29, Issue 8:1057-1075.

Christopher, C. (1996). Education and the Market: Which parts of the Neoliberal Solution are Correct? *World Development*, Elsevier, vol. 24(4), 589-610, April.

Commission on Growth and Development (2008). Growth Report: Strategies for Sustained Growth and Inclusive Development, World Bank.

DETYA (1999a). Selected Higher Education Staff Statistics 1998, Department of Education, Training and Youth Affairs, Australian Government Publishing Service, Canberra.

DFID (2004). What is Pro-Poor Growth and Why Do We Need to Know? Pro-Poor Growth Briefing Note 1, Department for International Development, London.

Imbs and Wacziarg (2003). Stages of Diversification, American Economic Review, *American Economic Association*, vol. 93(1) : 63-86, March.

Jackson, R. (2002). The National Student Financial Aid Scheme of South Africa, *The Welsh Journal of Education,* II (I): 82-94.

Jandhyala B.G. and Tilak (2007). Inclusive Growth and Education: On the Approach to the Eleventh Plan *Economic and Political Weekly*, Vol. 42, No. 38:3872-3877.

Johnston, B. (2005). *Fear and Loathing of Tuition Fees: An American Perspective on Higher Education Finance in the UK Perspectives*, 9(1): 12-16.

Johnstone, B. (2006a) *Financing Higher Education: Cost-Sharing In International Perspective*, Sense Publishers, Rotterdam, Netherland.

Kannan, K.P. (2006). Interrogative Inclusive Growth: Some Reflections on Exclusionary Growth and Prospects for Inclusive Development in India, VB Singh Memorial Lecture Mimeo.

Kelsey, J. (1998). Privatising the Universities, *Journal of Law and Society*, March: 51-70.

Kothari Commission (1966). Report of the Education Commission (1964-66) Education and National Development. Ministry of Education, GOI, New Delhi.

Marginson Simon (2003). Higher Education Reform in Australia — A*n* evaluation, in Eggins, H. (Ed.) *Globalisation and Reform in Higher Education, Society for Research into Higher Education*/Open University Press, Buckingham.

Nguyen, A. 11996) Education in Asia: Features and Prospects, *The Vietnam Review*, 1 (Autumn- Winter): 514-532.

NIEPA (2005b) *Financing of Higher Education in India: With Special Reference to the System of Financial Management*, New Delhi.

NSSO (1999-2000) NSS 55th Round: July 1999-June 2000, National Sample Survey Organisation, Ministry of Statistics and Programme Implementation, Government of India.

Planning Commission (2006). Towards Faster and More Inclusive Growth, Planning Commission, Government of India, New Delhi.

Protapenko, M. (2002). *Student Loans in Russia, University at Buffalo Center for Comparative and Global Studies (In) Education*, Buffalo.

Qiping, Y. and G. White (1994). The 'Marketisation' of Chinese Higher Education: A Critical Assessment, *Comparative Education* 30(8): 1357-1372.

Ravallion, M. (2001). Growth, Inequality and Poverty: Looking Beyond Averages, *World Development 29(11)*:1803-1815.

Richards, K. (2002). Reforming Higher Education Student Finance in The U.K.: The Impact of Recent Changes and Proposals for the Future. *The Welsh Journal of Education*, II (I): 18- 36. UK.

Riddell, A. (1996). Globalisation: Emasculation or Opportunity for Educational Planning? *World Development* 24(8), 1357-1372.

Saraswati, R. (2008). Gender Differentials in Access to Higher Education. In Higher Education in India: Issues Related to Expansion, Inclusiveness, Quality and Finance, University Grants Commission, New Delhi

Shen and Li (2003). *A Review of the Student Loans Scheme in China*. Bangkok: HEPL, UNESCO, Bangkok.

Srivastava, R. and Sinha, S. (2008). Inter-Social Groups Disparities in Access to Higher Education in India in Higher Education In India: Issues Related to Expansion, Inclusiveness. Quality and Finance. University Grants Commission, New Delhi.

Thorat, S. (2008). Emerging Issues In Higher Education—Approach and Strategy of 11th Plan. In Higher Education in India: Issues Related to Expansion. Inclusiveness, Quality and finance. University Grants Commission, New Delhi.

Tilak. J.B.G. (1994). *Education for Development in Asia*, Sage Publications, New Delhi. Toffler, A. (1990). *Power Shift: Knowledge, Wealth and Violence at the edge of the 21st Century*.Bantam Books, New York.

UNDP-1LO (2007). Asian Experiences on Growth. Employment and Poverty: An Overview with special reference to the findings of some recent case studies, Colombo.

Vossensyne, H. and Salerno, C. (2002). State Subsistence in the field of Education; A Commentary and International Reflection to the proposal of State Substance for Education in the Russian Federation, Enscheda, Center for Higher Educational Policy Studies. Netherlands.

Watson, K. (1980). *Education and Development in Thailand*. Heinemann Asia. Hong Kong.

World Bank (1990). World Development Report 1990, World Bank, Washington DC.

World Bank (2002). Constructing Knowledge Societies: New Challenges for Tertiary Education, World Bank, Washington DC .

World Bank (2005). Economic Growth in the 1990s: Learning from a Decade of Reform, World Bank, Washington DC.

World Bank (2006). India: Inclusive Growth and Service Delivery: Building on India's Success-Development Policy Review, Report No. 34580, Washington DC.

World Bank (2007). Mongolia: Sources of Growth Report No. 39009-MN. World Bank, Washington DC.

World Bank (2008). What Are the Constraints to Inclusive Growth in Zambia? Report No. 44286- ZM, World Bank, Washington DC.

5
Inclusive Education in Higher Education

Issues and Prospects

Poonam Singh Kharwar

Introduction

Government of India constituted several commissions and framed policies for achieving the goal education for all; still many children remain out of school indicating lack of inclusion. These commissions have recommended education of deprived and marginalised children with equity, fairness and quality, i.e. inclusion. Equity in education means that personal or social circumstances such as gender, ethnic origin or family background, are not obstacles to achieving educational potential (fairness) and that that all individuals reach at least a basic minimum level of quality education (inclusion). Students from low socio-economic background are likely to be low performers, implying that personal or social circumstances are obstacles to achieving their educational potential indicating lack of fairness. Lack of inclusion and fairness fuels school failure, of which dropout is the most visible manifestation. Educated people contribute to sustainable economy in democratic society; they are best prepared to respond economic downturns. Therefore, investing in early, primary and secondary education for all, and in particular for children from disadvantaged backgrounds, is both fair and economically efficient (OECD, 2012). International legislations also emphasize inclusive education, worth to mention are Universal declaration of human rights (1948), the Convention against Discrimination in Education (1960), Social and Cultural Rights (1966), the UN Convention on the Rights of the Child (1989). Large numbers of children who struggle daily with additional hardships are not getting the chance to improve their lives through education; they are caught in a spiral of low expectation, low esteem and low income (UNICEF, 2015). The major objective of modern society is the development if inclusive processes to provide social equality, qualitative education and culture of open relationship. This task may be solved by the formation of the inclusive policy which makes the basis of inclusive education development, social inclusion, inclusive culture and inclusive practice.

Marginalised Groups and Education

Scheduled Caste (SC) and Scheduled Tribe (ST): SCs form nearly 15 per cent of the population. SCs have the lowest ritual standing and economic position. Majority of them have given up the stigmatised occupations but still do not enjoy a status equal to high castes. The distribution of scarce goods and resources such as income, health and education is relatively low. STs form 7.5 per cent of Indian population. STs of the central India region differs from those of North-Eastern Hill states in many aspects. (1) *STs of Central India* (mainly the states of Madhya Pradesh, Bihar, Orissa, Andhra Pradesh) are characterised by geographical isolation and low economic status. The tribes in central India are impoverished and are the most backward. They have also suffered from the intrusion of the Indian mainstream and of the pan-Indian model of the state, society, economy and culture. The new forces released during the colonial period affected them adversely and led to the denial of their traditional rights to land, forests and its produce and other natural resources. They were also unable to benefit from the impact of new economic and political processes. *(2) The STs of North-Eastern Hill states*, though heterogeneous, are distinctly different since they are not as poor or oppressed as those in central India. They have had more education due to a longer exposure to missionary activity. In these regions, the STs have been a majority. Therefore, the oppression of untouchability did not affect them. These societies were not characterised by extremely hierarchical social divisions of Hinduism and therefore were not as unequal as the 'mainstream' Indian society. However, they share marginalisation with other STs (Chanana, 2004).

Minorities: Muslim, Sikh, Christian, Buddhist, Zoroastrian (Parsi) and Jain are notified as minority communities under Section 2 (c) of the

National Commission for Minorities Act, 1992. According to Census of 2001, the per centage population of minority in India is—Muslims 12.43, Christians 2.34, Sikhs 1.86, Buddhists 0.77, Zoroastrians 0.007 and Jains 0.41 per cent. Percentage of literacy is: Muslims 59.1, Christians 80.3, Sikhs 69.4, Buddhists 72.7 and Zoroastrians 97.9 per cent.

Disabled: UNICEF's *Report on the Status of Disability in India 2000* states that there are around 30 million children in India suffering from some form of disability. The minority of children with disability that do get places are often not sitting in the same classroom as other boys and girls because of a sense that they need to be separated and treated differently. Globally, it is estimated that 70 per cent of children with disabilities, including those with mild mental retardation, can attend regular schools provided the environment is designed to be accessible and the institution is willing to accommodate them (UNICEF, 2015). The Sixth All-India Educational Survey reports that out of India's 200 million school-aged children (6-14 years), 20 million require special education. While the national average for gross enrolment in school is over 90 per cent, less than five per cent of children with disabilities are in school (NCERT, 1998).

In order to eliminate several disadvantages, education was viewed in the Constitution of India as an instrument of social change, individual mobility and social equality for all social groups through social justice and of integration and mainstreaming. While the minorities needed to be brought into the mainstream, SCs and STs required social justice and equality.

Inclusion of marginalised groups in the educational development is important as they constitute a sizable segment of the population of the country. The SCs and STs who have been historically out of the main stream development initiatives, partly due to the still continuing socio-cultural barriers and partly due to the inadequacy of the Government programmes in reaching this disadvantage group, still find themselves in difficult to compete terrains *vis-à-vis* the other sections in the society. In present era of globalisation, equal access to education, is increasingly viewed as a basic duty of a progressive government and mature society. The pressures for change emanating from globalisation came when higher education system was unable to meet the rising social demand for professional education. Marginalised groups gained access to higher education because it was fully government funded and was highly subsidised; however, their participation was characterised by clustering in the non-professional and non-market courses in higher education. Their development in higher education is painted with dull colours. Further, socio-cultural and economic factors acted as barriers to their ability to access to professional education. By examining the socio-demographic fabric it can be understood that disparities at the community, gender and regional levels plague the higher education sector all over the India. Deprivations over time negatively affected the living standards of weaker sections and since such deprivations are based on socio-demographic considerations, in order to formulate effective policies for overall development, the underlying aspects of such deprivation must also be addressed.

Enrolment in Higher Education

Total student enrolment in higher educational institutions in India has been increasing rapidly over the past half-century, but the proportionate representation of SC and ST students in total higher educational enrolment has been slowly rising. From the late 1970s to the late 1990s the SC proportion rose from 7 per cent to 7.8 per cent and the ST proportion rose from 1.6 per cent to 2.7 per cent only (Rao, 2002). The SC proportion of all graduates of Indian higher educational institutions raised from 0.9 per cent in 1961 to 3.3 per cent in 1981, and the corresponding ST proportion raised from 0.1 per cent in 1961 to 0.8 per cent in 1981. No doubt the SC and ST proportions have increased further since then. But SC and ST graduates represented in 1981 only about 3 per cent and 1 per cent of all Indian graduates—far below their shares of the total Indian population (Thomas, 2004). It should be noted that data on SC and ST enrolments in Indian higher educational institutions are probably somewhat overstated, because some non-SC and ST applicants manage to claim SC and ST status and thereby gain admission *via* reserved seats to institutions for which they do not qualify as general entrants (Velaskar, 1986 and Palshikar, 1992).

Enrolment in Higher Professional Education

Though the increase in Gross enrolment rates of SC/ST communities in higher education is quite impressive, but the increase in GER took place more in the traditional arts and science courses rather than in the job oriented technical and professional courses (George, 2011). The per centages of SC and ST students enrolled in the most prestigious programmes such as engineering, law and medicine—are much lower than for students from the rest of the population (Chanana, 1993 and Government of India, 1997). Only about a third of the SC and ST students enrolled in higher educational institutions in the late 1990s were pursuing higher education in a relatively more desirable programme because of the existence of reservation policies in admissions (Thomas, 2004). No data is readily available on the total strength of students in higher and technical education colleges. During 2009 numbers of SC and ST students are disproportionately low in engineering and medical colleges including Ayurveda Colleges in Kerala. In fact, there was no representation for STs in Ayurveda, dental, nursing and pharmacy colleges (Zachariah, 2010). Part of the reason is in the larger increase in the number of self-financing colleges than government owned and aided colleges where the fees are highly subsidized (George, 2011).

The situation of SC and ST students at elite Indian institutions is well illustrated by their experience at the Indian Institutes of Technology (IITs), whose programmes attract many of the best students in India. Admissions data for 1994-95 indicate that only about half of the seats reserved for SC students were filled, while the corresponding figure for ST students was less than one-sixth (Rao, 2002). Velaskar (1986) observed similar in medical colleges in Mumbai, in 1979-80 and 1980-81 only a third of seats reserved for SC and ST were filled—while some had no SC and ST students at all. In more recent times Mumbai medical colleges have most often been filling SC reserved seats; but medical schools across the country have continued to lag in this respect.

Enrolment of Muslims

According to Sachar Committee Report (2006), one-fourth of Muslim children in age group of 6-14 years has either never attended school or is drop-outs. For children above the age of 17 years, the educational attainment of Muslims at matriculation is 17 per cent, as against national average of 26 per cent. Only 50 per cent of Muslims who complete middle school are likely to complete secondary education as against national average 62 per cent. The report has also drawn attention to low level of educational attainment among Muslim women, Muslim in rural areas as well as technical and higher education. NSSS Survey 64th round (2007-08) presents the information of participation in higher education. The Gross Attendance Ratio of Muslim stand at 8.7 per cent as opposed to 16.8 per cent GAR of non-Muslim. This per centage is higher than that of ST (6.60%) and lower than that of SC (10.65%) and much lower than that OBC (13.67%). Recent literature on Muslims reflects a sense of deprivation and their disengagement with the wider civil society and this slow rate of educational progress may well be a constituent of that. Children often face harassment and ridicule, and rising religious tensions lead to children's alienation from school. Since Muslim families are disproportionately urban, access to schools is less likely to be a problem, but discrimination by teachers and a hostile school environment may pose a major impediment (GoI, 2006).

Public Higher Education Institutions: Equity and Quality

The changes spearheaded by economic liberalisation and globalisation are impacting on higher education worldwide. The relationships between the governments and universities are changing all over the world. Some of the features that characterise this change are: reduction in government funding and the pressure on the universities to raise funds from the industry, the market and the individual student; universities have been forced to downsize; and the language of efficiency and accountability associated with corporate management is being used to run and to evaluate universities. All these changes have negative impact on pursuing equity issues within the universities because "a commitment to equity and a commitment to cost-cutting" may not go hand-in-hand (Bacchi, 2001).

After independence, higher education was entrusted with the responsibility of protecting the constitutional provisions for positive discrimination with the responsibility of promoting social change until 1991. Due to the twin concern with equality and excellence higher education in India was fully supported by the federal and provincial governments. However, since 1991 the policies of the government have dramatically changed. The government began to talk remove public support to higher education and make it self-financing while privatising it. The gradual reduction in proportion of plan expenditure as well as capital expenditure in education sector in ratio of growing population prevented the government from expanding capacity of government owned and government aided institutions in the higher education and technical education sectors when the demand for enrolment and funds was growing. This vacuum was filled initially by the self-financing institutions. The under-investment by successive governments in education led to erosion in quality of institutions owned by it, thus increasing the private costs for the students of the institutions (Chanana, 2004).

Academic Performance

Indian reservation policies have no doubt played a major role in increasing the opportunities for SC and ST students to continue their education at the college and university level. While entrance qualifying examination scores cannot be considered a good predictor of performance in higher education, the lower scores characteristic of most SC and ST students—especially at elite institutions—do reflect less adequate academic preparation for the demands of a university level education. Both the lower scores and the less adequate academic preparation are correlated with socio-economic disadvantage, which further heightens the challenge faced by SC/ST student embarking on a higher educational experience.

Kirpal and Gupta (1978) found average graduation rate for all SC and ST students was 84 per cent, as compared with 94 per cent for general-entry students. Mean cumulative performance index figures were 7.88 for general-entry students, 6.23 for SC students and 5.93 for ST students. SC/ST students lag well behind general-entry students in their performance on IIT examinations. Moreover, those who graduate as a rule take more years to do so than their general-entry peers. The average drop-out rate of 16 per cent for reserved-seat students entering in the 1980s compares very favourably with the much higher rates of wastage found among such students in the 1970s (by Kirpal *et al.*, 1985 and Chitnis, 1986). After an initial period in which many SC/ST students admitted *via* reservations were found to be poorly prepared and dropped out, the IITs significantly improved recruitment, preparation and retention efforts—including a year long remedial programme for many SC and ST applicants whose entrance examination scores are less than two-thirds of the general entry cut-off score. These students gain admission to reserved seats only if they successfully complete that preparatory programme. The fact that graduation rates for SC and ST students are now over 80 per cent at the IITs suggests that these beneficiaries of reserved seats—and the institutions that are admitting them—are achieving important successes.

Aikara (1980) concluded from his study of Mumbai colleges that, with the exception of a high-performing minority, the great majority of SC students suffered from high rates of wastage and stagnation and registered lower rates of performance and progress as compared to their non-SC peers. Primary reason for which SC students dropped out of college was failure at examinations; but almost as significant was a need to find employment in order to provide financial support for oneself and one's family. The investigator concluded that considerably higher levels of financial aid would be necessary in order to reduce the high incidence of SC student wastage and stagnation.

Velaskar (1986) found that roughly a quarter of SC students finished their degree programme on time—as compared to roughly three-quarters of non-SC students, a majority of the SC students do eventually manage to graduate from Mumbai's medical colleges, typically requiring some extra years of study; virtually all non-SC students graduate, most often on time. However, she found that they are considerably more likely to persist in and graduate from Mumbai's medical colleges than from engineering colleges—probably because the former have a social environment that is more local in flavour and thus more congenial to SC students, who are less comfortable with national culture in general and the English language in particular.

Patwardhan and Palshikar (1992) observed that SC and ST students were behind other students academically at the time of their admission to Medical College, and tend to fall further behind during the course of their studies.

Financial Barriers

(1) Increasing Private Costs of Education: Monthly Per Capita Consumption Expenditure of STs is the lowest followed by SCs, OBCs and other; they lagged behind 'others' marginally in the case of food expenditure and substantially in the case of non-food expenditure. In rural areas, per centage of poor in the population was the highest among STs followed by SCs and the OBCs. The forward castes and communities have the least share of poor among them. Same trend is among the urban poor except that the SCs have bigger concentration of poor than the STs (NSSO, 2004-05). Though no fee is charged on the SC and ST students as supported by state funding in government institutions, it is not totally free for them as they have to incur costs of several types. Study by Kumar (2008) in government medical colleges report that about 90 per cent of the cost of education incurred by the students is on non-fee expenses. The educational assistance given by way of lump sum grants, stipend and scholarships to SC/ST students is inadequate to cover fully these private costs especially in medical and engineering colleges.

(2) Proliferation of Private and Self-financing Institutions: Since 1991, a large number of private colleges on self-financing basis are being set up and there number has increased rapidly. Most of the increase in higher educational opportunities is taking place in the private sector rather than in the public sector. For example, in 2002, of 977 undergraduate engineering colleges 764 (78.2%); of 1349 medical colleges, 1028 (76.2%); of 505 management institutions, 324 (64.2%); of 1521 teacher education colleges, 1038 (67.4%) were private (Bhattacharya, 2004). One of the recent trends in education system is the starting of a number of self-financing courses in the government owned and government aided colleges. These courses are mostly job oriented and were started avowedly to meet the emerging demands of the job market. Access to education market abroad is also limited due to the high costs for availing education and their lack of social network. Zachariah (2010) observed that the share of SCs and STs in the self-financing stream is considerably lower than in the regular aided streams. What is more, their share has been coming down both at the UG and PG level.

The private technical education system in India is the largest in the world and the growth of higher education in the last 15 years has been mainly in the private sector (Anandkrishnan, 2004). Traditionally, medical colleges in India were largely funded by the government and the contribution of private sector was negligible (Rao *et al.*, 2008). But with the implementation of new economic policy of 1991, broadly known as structural adjustment programme, the trend shifted towards private funding of medical education and the growth of private medical colleges has been phenomenal. The share of private sector in total number of medical colleges has increased from 3.6 per cent in 1950 to 54.3 per cent in 2014 (Choudhary, 2014).

3. Increasing Costs of Private Education: The private institutions levy hefty tuition fees with/without the approval of the State Governments. The State Governments and the judiciary have to intervene in the matter of fixation of fees. Increasingly, these colleges have sought the status of deemed universities in order to be autonomous in matters of curriculum and examination/evaluation. Along with the financial exploitation of the students, the quality of their education is also suspect and so are their motivations (Anandkrishnan, 2004). Another limitation is that since private institutions get land at subsidised rates, they are expected to reserve seats for the SC/STs, but there is little monitoring of these measures and no statistics are publicly known about reservations (Chanana, 2004). The SC/ST students are finding it difficult to get educated in the unaided institutions at all levels. Cost of private education deters these communities to get education beginning from lower level and increasing many folds in higher professional education.

Non-financial Barriers

Meta-analysis by George (2011) points that it is not poverty or other financial barriers alone that stand in the way of the SC/ST students getting enrolled in professional educational institutions. Even among the non-poor households, the enrolment of SC students was much lower than that of others. This suggests the possibility of the SC/ST students facing larger non-financial barriers inherent in their caste/community status and their social and educational background:

1. Socio-economic Background: Many studies have confirmed that high SES is correlated with good academic performance in higher educational institutions both at entry point and during course. This is true within each major category of students as well as across the student body as a whole (Aikara,1980; Palshikar & Patwardhan, 1992; Kirpal and Gupta, 1999).

2. Academic Background: Velaskar (1986) found that SC students enter college with poorer socio-economic and academic backgrounds, which helps to explain why they perform more poorly than other students. SC students tend to go to lower-quality primary and secondary schools than other students; and very few of them can afford the kinds of special tutoring or coaching classes that enable so many other students to prepare themselves well for examinations.

3. Socio-cultural Background: Velaskar (1986) noted that the relatively poor academic performance of most SC students can be explained in terms of differences in their socio-cultural backgrounds, even more than differences in their socio-economic backgrounds. The most significant deficit of SC students' *vis-à-vis* general-entry students is in their 'cultural capital'. The cultural capital deprivation of SC students is evidenced by lower levels of education among family members, lower levels of participation in edifying cultural activities, and in general a home environment less conducive to learning. SC students generally lack the most important source of cultural capital in modern India—good command of the English language. Parmaji (1985) also reported that performance on various examinations was positively and significantly correlated with caste status more due to cultural deprivation than to low socio-economic status.

4. Generation Gap: Palshikar & Patwardhan (1992) concluded that reservations favour urban and male students, and that they disproportionately benefit a small number of sub-castes within the SC group and particular tribes within the ST group. They suggest, further, that the beneficiaries of reserved seats are increasingly second-generation students from the favoured groups. Kirpal and Gupta (1999) found that 40 per cent of the SC and ST students in their sample of IIT B.Tech. students admitted from 1989 through 1992 were second-generation beneficiaries.

5. Social Support: Kirpal and Gupta (1999) reported that social support contributes to confident disposition and linguistic competence among SC students in IITs, which help in interviews and oral examinations. SC students experience considerable social distancing because of disdain from non-SC students, which tends to be compounded by their own feelings of inferiority. Social discrimination against SC students in colleges and universities is a fact of Indian life; what is not so clear is if it is based primarily on caste identity *per se* or on cultural differences. To overcome this kind of handicap requires an especially strong motivation and effort by an SC student, as well as a facilitating environment—including friendship and help from other students.

6. Socio-political Factors: According to George (2011) expanding educational opportunities irrespective of regions, religions, castes and classes, was top most in the agenda of all the government and political parties in the past. State funding of education directly or through liberal grants-in-aid to private agencies helped the process of expanding educational opportunities. But the political parties today do not have any clear strategy of protecting inclusive development from the onslaught of privatisation and marketisation emanating from within and outside the country. There is a growing tendency for the middle class to opt out of the government owned and aided educational system because of its low quality but also due to social reasons, which in turn has led to further deterioration of the system and the expansion of the unaided sector.

Research Implications

Meta-analysis by Thomas (2004) concluded that most SC and ST students enrolled in elite higher educational institutions in India do indeed go on to successful careers despite generally poor prospects for Indian college graduates, in an economy that suffers from a substantial excess supply of educated job-seekers for positions requiring a high level of education. The availability of reserved seats improves the quality of the professional institution that an SC/ST student can enter and hence, the value of a higher educational degree in the job market.

Many factors could be identified for the lag in higher education sectors in India which may be elusive to policy interventions. While such studies have greatly increased the understanding of the area, the inferences derived from these are limited owing to the reach of the indicators used in the studies. These studies tend to discount the dynamic nature of the contexts (like tribal communities, socio-economically backward classes, rural areas etc.) when researching on issues like effectiveness of educational policies. The paucity of hard evidence related to social exclusion points to the great need for more systematic empirical research on this topic. Research for inclusive policy of SC/ST in higher education should incorporate the 'Process-Status-Process' approach, i.e. identify and examine the process that led to social exclusion, evaluate the present status/magnitude and chart out processes to achieve the desired level of social inclusion.

Research on educational stratification suggests that inequality in education between different social strata continues and sometimes even widens in spite of educational growth. The gap between upper caste Hindu/ other religious groups and SC/ST diminished. This decline in inequality accelerated during the 1990s, a period of intensified affirmative action directed at SC/ST. The educational gap declined at the primary school level rather than at the college level. There no improvement in college graduation rates, casting doubt on the effectiveness of government policies. The decline in inequality at the primary level may be associated with affirmative action in employment (Raftery and Hout, 1993).

Conclusion

Enrolment and achievement of marginalised group such as SC/STs, Muslims and disabled is increasing very slowly. Further strengthening of government support is needed to overcome the problem of barriers as they are not reaching to beneficiary to optimum level. Regular monitoring and systematic empirical research is required. Private professional institutions must realise the fact that apart from the projection of welfare view of weaker section of society by providing facility to these marginalised group students, prospect of bright future placement value in present globalised India would certainly improve their reputations and income not only locally but also globally.

REFERENCES

Aikara, J. (1980). *Scheduled Castes and Higher Education: A Study of College Students in Mumbai*, Pune: Dastane.

Anandkrishnan, M. (2004). Private Investments in Technical Education. In K.B. Powar and K.L. Johar (eds.), *Private Initiatives in Higher Education,* Sneh Prakashan and Amity Foundation for Learning, pp. 202-225.

Bachhi, Carol (2001). Managing Equity: Mainstreaming and 'Diversity' in Australian Universities, In A. Brooks and A. McInnon (eds.), pp. 119-135.

Bhattacharya, S. (2004). Organisation of Higher Education: Moving Towards a System of uncorporated Universities. In K.B. Powar and K.L. Johar (eds.) *Private Initiatives in Higher Education.*

Chanana, K. (1993). "Accessing Higher Education—The Dilemma of Schooling: Women, Minorities, Scheduled Castes and Scheduled Tribes in Contemporary India", in S. Chitnis and P. Altbach (eds.), *Higher Education Reform in India*, New Delhi: Sage Publications.

Chanana, K. (2004). Gender and Disciplinary Choice: Women in Higher Education in India, Paper for the UNESCO Colloquium in Paris on Research and Higher Education Policy "Knowledge, Access and Governance: Strategies for Change".

Chitnis, S. (1986). Measuring up to Reserved Admissions in V.P. Shah and B.C. Agrawal (eds.), *Reservation: Policy, Programmes and Issues*, Jaipur: Rawat Publications.

Choudhary, P.K. (2014). Role of private sector in medical education and human resource development for health in India, New Delhi: Institute for Study in Industrial Development.

George, K.K. (2011). *Higher Education in Kerala: How Inclusive is it to Scheduled Castes and Scheduled Tribes?* Education Exclusion and Economic Growth Working Paper Series. 1(4). Cochin: Centre for the Study of Social Exclusion and Inclusive Policy, Cochin University of Science and Technology.

Government of India (1997). *Selected Educational Statistics, 1996-97,* New Delhi: Ministry of Human Resources Development.

Government of India (2006). *Social, Economic and Educational Status of the Muslim Community in India.* New Delhi.

Government of India (2006). *Social, Economic and Educational Status of the Muslim Community in India*, retrieved from : *www.ncbi.nlm.nih.gov/pmc/article/2474466.*

Government of India (2011). Minority Welfare Department retrieved from : *http://mhrd.gov.in/educational-development-minorities.*

Government of India (2014). *Education for all towards Quality with Equity India*, New Delhi: NUEPA.

Government of India (2014). *Selected information on school education 2011-12,* Bureau of Planning, Monitoring and Statistics Division, New Delhi.

Kirpal, V. (1978). Higher Education for the Scheduled Castes and Scheduled Tribes, *Economic and Political Weekly*, Vol. 13, pp. 165-69.

Kirpal, V., Swamidasan, N., Gupta, A. and Gupta, R.K. (1985). Scheduled Caste and Tribe Students in Higher Education: A Study of an IIT, *Economic and Political Weekly*, 20: 1238-48.

Kumar, A. (2008). Private Cost of Medical and Para-Medical Education in Kerala, in K.N. Nair, P.R. Gopinathan Nair (eds.), *Higher Education in Kerala: Micro-Level Perspectives*, pp. 18-48, New Delhi: Danish Books.

National Sample Survey Organisation (2006). *Household Consumer Expenditure among Socio-Economic Groups: 2004-05*, 61st Round, (July 2004-June 2005), Report No. 514, New Delhi: Government of India.

NCERT, (1998). *The Sixth All-India Educational Survey*. New Delhi: NCERT.

OECD (2012). Equity and Quality in Education, Supporting Disadvantaged Students and Schools, OECD Publishing. Retrieved from *http://dx.doi.org/10.1787/9789264130852-en*

Parmaji (1985). *Caste Reservations and Performance: Research Findings*, Warangal, Andhra Pradesh: Mamata Publications.

Patwardhan, V. and Palshikar, V. (1992). Reserved Seats in Medical Education: a Study, *Journal of Education and Social Change*, 5: 1-117.

Raftery, A.E., Hout, M. (1993). Maximally Maintained Inequality: Expansion, Reform, and Opportunity in Irish Education, 1921–75, *Sociology of Education*, 66: 41–62.

Rao, S.S. (2002). Equality in Higher Education: Impact of Affirmative Action Policies in India, in E.F. Beckham (ed.), *Global Collaborations: TheRole of Higher Education in Diverse Democracies*, Washington DC: Association of American Colleges and Universities.

Thomas, E.W. (2004). *Affirmative Action in the United States and India: A Comparative Perspective,* London: Routledge Publications.

Velaskar, P.R. (1986). *Inequality in Higher Education: A Study of Scheduled Caste Students in Medical Colleges of Bombay*, unpublished Ph.D. dissertation, Mumbai: Tata Institute of Social Sciences.

Zachariah, G. (2010). *Changing Enrolment Patterns in Arts and Science Colleges in Kerala*, Cochin: Centre for Socio-Economic and Environmental Studies sponsored by Kerala State Higher Education Council, Government of Kerala.

Section-II
History and Development

6
History of Education System in Ancient India

P. Bhaskar

Introduction

Learning in India through the ages had been prized and pursued not for its own sake, if we may so put it, but for the sake, and as a part, of religion. It was sought as the means of self-realisation, as the means to the highest end of life, *viz. Mukti* or Emancipation. Ancient Indian education is also to be understood as being ultimately the outcome of the Indian theory of knowledge as part of the corresponding scheme of life and values. The scheme takes full account of the fact that Life includes Death and the two forms the whole truth. This gives a particular angle of vision, a sense of perspective and proportion in which the material and the moral, the physical and spiritual, the perishable and permanent interests and values of life are clearly defined and strictly differentiated. Of all the people of the world the Hindu is the most impressed and affected by the fact of death as the central fact of life. The individual's supreme duty is thus to achieve his expansion into the Absolute, his self-fulfilment, for he is a potential God, a spark of the Divine. Education must aid in this self-fulfilment, and not in the acquisition of mere objective knowledge.

The education system which was evolved first in ancient India is known as the Vedic System of Education. In other words, the ancient system of education was based on the *Vedas* and, therefore, it was given the name of Vedic Educational System.

Swadesh Pujyate Raja, Vidwan Sarvatra Pujyate.

This verse widely quoted in India illustrates the significance of education in India. The education system of Vedic period has unique characteristics and qualities which were not found in the ancient education system of any other country of the world. According to Dr. F.E. Key,— To achieve their aim not only did Brahmans develop a system of education which, survived even in the events of the crumbling of empires and the changes of society, but they, also through all those thousands of years, kept a glow of torch of higher learning. In the words of Dr. P.N. Prabhu— Education in ancient India was free from any external control like that of the State and Government or any party politics. It was the king's duties to see that learned *Pandits*, pursued their studies and performed their duty of imparting knowledge without interference from any source what so ever.

Fundamentals of Ancient Indian Education

The ancient education system has been a source of inspiration to all educational systems of the world. The ingredients, which our present system lacks, and which were the predominant facets of our ancient system relate to admission policies (*upanayana*), monitorial system, low teacher-pupil-ratio, healthy teaching surroundings, free schooling and college education, sympathetic treatment, role of punishment in discipline, regulation governing student life (Ghosh, 2007).

1. Developing the Wholesome Personality

The primary aim of any system of education should be development of a wholesome personality. The Brahmanic system of education stood on former grounds of lofty ideals, because its primary aim was development of personality and character. Moral strength and moral excellence were developed to the fullest extent, which we lack so utterly. The moral stature of our educated people is deplorably low. Moral values are at stake— The old values, which held society together are disappearing and as therein no effective programme to replace them by a new sense of responsibility (Jain, 2003). Innumerable signs of social disorganisation are evident everywhere and are continually on the increase. These include strikes increasing lawlessness, and a disregard for public property corruption in public life.

2. Making Formal and Informal Educations Responsible

Imparting and receiving of education was as sacred as anything can be, for example, education started and ended with certain prescribed religious rituals like *upanayana* and *samvartana*. The disciple was to devote himself whole heartedly to the cause of learning while he remained with his teacher. Not every boy was required to enter studentship it was still a custom to receive education at the hands of his father. How many of the parents look after their children now in this respect? The ancient system gave an equal importance to informal education as it did to the formal one (Lall, 2005).

3. Starting Academic Sessions Solemnly

In most cases the boy went to a teacher for studentship. The maximum age of entrance into school was different for different castes. The period of schooling was long, at least 12 years for one *Veda*. The whole session was punctuated with holidays especially on new moon full days of the month.

4. Adjusting School Hours

The school in the Ancient Education System lasted for 7 to 8 hours a day. In fair weather classes were held in the open under shady groves. In the rainy season schools ran in a set of apartment. Temple colleges of the past had been of great renown for having spacious buildings for classroom, hostels and residential quarters for teachers. *Gurukuls* and *Ashrams* were generally situated on the river banks or on the lake. The whole atmosphere was quiet, calm and peaceful. It must be noted that schools and colleges were not kept far away from human habitation (Mookerji, 1990).

5. Close Contact

Never in the history of education will we find such a close contact between the teacher and the taught. The teacher was the spiritual father, he had to nurse, when the pupil fell sick, he had to feed, clothe and teach his student as he fed, clothed and taught his son. The student also regarded the teachers as he regarded his parents, king and god. Both were united by communion of life. In fact they communed together.

6. Emphasizing Discipline

The student had to observe strict regulations. Instruction was important, but was even more significant than teaching was discipline—discipline inculcated through strict obedience to laws and regulations of student life, discipline that was rooted in morality and religion. A student was required to give-up lust, anger, greed, vanity, conceit and over joy. It was ordered to him not to gamble, gossip, lie, backbite, hurt feelings of others, dance, sing, look or talk or touch the other sex and kill animals (Ramchandra and Ramkumar, 2005). It was demanded of every student whether rich of poor that he should lead a simple life in the *Gurukul* or in the *Ashram*.

7. Providing Free Education

It was free because no student was required to pay any fees. It was free also because no outside agency could interfere in the matters of education. There was perfect autonomy. No external authority/no external beneficiary/no politics was permitted to enter the school or college system (Giddens, 1991). A student had to pay nothing in return for education he received in a *Gurukul* or *Ashram*. Access to good education depended not on wealth, but on talent. The student was expected, if desired, but never compelled to offer a field, cow, horse or even vegetables to his teacher according to his financial position in the society. Education could not be bought, one could go up the ladder as his abilities permitted.

8. Development of Civic Responsibilities and Social Values

The inculcation of civic virtues and social values was an equally important objective of education in India. The *Brahmachari* after his education in the *Gurukuls* went back to the society to serve the rich and the poor, to relieve the diseased and the distressed. He was required to be hospitable to the guests and charitable to the needy. After a certain period of studies he was required to become a householder and to perpetuate his race and transmit his culture to his own offsprings (Held, McGrew, Goldblatt & Perraton, 1999).

Acceptable features of Education of Vedic period for Modern Education. There is a wide gap of Education between Ancient Indian Education and Modern Indian Education. Still there are several elements of ancient education which can find room in modern education both in theory and practice (Field, 2000). We are living in modern age, but we feel proud of the civilisation and culture of our ancestors inherited to us. Even now, we give importance to religion, god and desireless deeds. We give more preference to character, spiritualism, philosophy rather than wealth, materialism and science. The present world gives reverence to wealth, power, violence and diplomacy whereas we rely in truth, non-violence and mortification (Rawat, 1956). We still believe in idealism and wish to lead an ideal life. The sense of discipline and the cordial relation between teacher and pupil of Vedic age is well known to the world today, we see the educational environment has become so venomous due to indiscipline, that has become an uncountable problem (Reyhner, 2004). The sense of discipline can be developed if teacher-pupil relationship can be made to adopt the ideal relationship between teacher and pupil.

The main aim was integral and all-round development in ancient India. The same aim is kept in view in modern education. The ancient education never neglected physical development although the main emphasis was given the intellectual and spiritual development. For this a peaceful, calm, clean, attractive and natural environment far away from town and villages was provided to students (Sharma, 2006). Although, we profess to look after physical, moral spiritual emotional and intellectual development of pupil in modern schools yet it is only bookish knowledge which gets the most of an attention. This idea of all-round development of child must be adhered to practically.

The ancient schools followed the principle of education for self-sufficiency. The school was small integrated community self-sufficient in every way. The students used to grow their food products, tended cows, collected firewood's and erected cottages themselves under the guidance of teacher. Modern education also lays stress upon preparing students to prepare themselves for their future life (Vashist, 2005). Vocational subjects have been included in the curriculum in order to vocationalise education, but much is needed to be done in this direction in order to achieve the desired aim.

The ancient Indian education system was successful in preserving and spreading its culture and literature even without the help of art of writing. It was only because of the destruction of temples and monasteries by invaders that literature was lost. The cultural unity that exists even today in the vast subcontinent is due to successful preservation and spread of culture (Giddens, 1990). The education system infused a sense of responsibilities and social values. The ancient education system achieved its aims to the fullest extent. Ancient education emerged from Vedas. The basis of Indian culture lies in the *Vedas*.

Conclusion

The education system in ancient India was very rich in terms of human development and contributed to the growth of Indian civilisation. The idea of Indian civilisation continued to flourish as India transcended its journey from Ancient to Medieval to Modern times. The aims of education were to provide good training to young men and women in the performance of their social, economic and religious duties. Also preservation and enrichment of culture, character and personality development and cultivation of noble ideals were the other aims of education in ancient India. The Vedic system of education has inspired the modern day education system.

REFERENCES

Dash, M. (2000), *Education in India: Problems and Perspectives*, Eastern Book Corporation, Chanderlok Enclave, Pitampura, Delhi.

Field, J. (2000) *Lifelong Learning and the New Educational Order, Stoke of Trent*: Trentham Books Staffordshire, London.

Ghosh, S.C. (2007), *History of Education in India*, Eastern Book Corporation, Chanderlok Enclave, Pitampura, Delhi.

Giddens, A. (1990) *Consequences of Modernity*, Cambridge: Polity Press.

Giddens, A. (1991) *Modernity and Self Identity*, Cambridge: Polity Press.

Held, D., McGrew, A., Goldblatt, D. and Perraton, J. (1999) *Global Transformations: Politics, Economics and Culture*, Cambridge: Polity Press.

Jain, M. (2003), *History in the New NCERT Textbooks Fallacies in the IIIC Report*, Delhi: NCERT.

Lall, M. (2005), *The Challenges for India's Education System*, Chatham House, London.

Mookerji, R.K. (1990), *Ancient Indian Education: Brahmanical and Buddhist* Delhi: Motilal Banarsidass Publishers.

Ramchandra, P. and Ramkumar, V. (2005), *Education in India*. Eastern Book Corporation, Chanderlok Enclave, Pitampura, Delhi.

Rawat, P.L. (1956) *History of Indian Education: Ancient to Modern*, Delhi : Bharat Publication.

Reyhner, J. (2004) *History of Indian Education*, Vohra Publishers, Allahabad Uttar Pradesh, India.

Sharma, R. (2006) *History of Indian Education*, Shubhi Publishers, Gurgaon, Delhi, India.

Vashist, R. (2005), *History of Education in India*, Eastern Book Corporation, Chanderlok Enclave, Pitampura, Delhi.

7
History of Higher Education in India

A Comparison Between Pre- and Post-British Periods

V. Joseph Paul Raj and *N. Vivek*

Introduction

> "Education is more than just reading the sciences and reading biotechnology or specialising in particular sphere. I think, the primary goal of our education has to be the development of the human being to be a better human being. All our aims, whether they are technological or scientific, must be towards the same end. When we are able to achieve and move towards this target we shall really see a betterment coming about in India..."
>
> — *Rajiv Gandhi*

India has a long and venerable history in the field of higher education. In ancient times, the country was known to have been home to the oldest formal universities in the world. The more striking of these ancient universities were Taxila (now in Pakistan), Nalanda (in the modern state of Bihar) and Ujjaini (in modern Madhya Pradesh). These were famous in the prehistoric world and attracted students from all parts of India, Central Asia, China and South-east Asia. The Hindu-Buddhist university of Taxila, the oldest, was probably established in sixth century B.C. Unfortunately, Taxila University was destroyed by the White Huns (Ephthalites) around 460 A.D. In 1193, Nalanda University was sacked and totally destroyed by Bakhtiyar Khilji. This event not only ended the university, but was also followed by a rapid decline in the practice of Buddhism in India. In 1235, Sultan Iltutmish completely destroyed Ujjaini, a major centre for mathematics, literature, philosophy and astronomy. History of higher education in India had thus begun its journey quite with a bang, which had to face temporary hindrance in the form of outside invasion. It is significant that at exactly the same time, half-way across the world, Oxford University was being established.

Indian tradition is steeped in the highest philosophical foundation laid by her ancient sages and seers in the course of their pursuit of the highest knowledge and excellence. Ancient records of this good Indian tradition testify that India had a highly developed system of higher education at par with the modern university system. Historically, the earliest university in India dates back to 6th century BC and was set-up in Taxila, now in Pakistan. Later in fourth and fifth century AD the highly acclaimed universities of Nalanda and Vikramashila came into existence. The modern higher education system is 150 years old with the first three universities being set-up in Bombay, Calcutta, and Madras in 1857 under the British rule. The "*Sutra* Literature" mentions the greatness of a teacher. A unique feature of Indian tradition is the unstained and undiluted respect and devotion towards the Teacher or "*Guru*". *Guru*, literally means "one who deserves and commands "*Gaurava*" or "Honour". *Gu* means darkness and *Ru* means removal and hence *Guru* is the one who removes darkness. Guru leads one from darkness unto light."

The following centuries saw a few centres of Islamic and Hindu learning emerge. However, India did not produce another world-class university for several hundred years. Just like in any other sphere in daily life, it was only during British colonial rule that formal university education was revived. Modern colleges were set-up in Agra, Nagpur, Calcutta, Bombay and Madras in the early nineteenth century. This introduction of Western learning, made accessible through the knowledge of English, was a very important factor that allowed the emergence of India's middle class. And this so termed 'middle class' would go on to produce legends after legends when it came to history of higher education in India. In 1857, three federal examining universities on the pattern of London University were established in the three main British-controlled cities of Calcutta, Bombay and Madras. The existing colleges were affiliated to these universities. Over the next several decades, more universities were founded and by 1947 there were 25 universities in the country.

Post-Independence history of higher education in India went through phases of rapid expansion. The number of universities in the country leapt from 25 in 1947 to 348 in 2005. Enrolment rose from 0.1 million in 1947 to 10.5 million in 2005. In present times, the country's higher educational institutions have an enrolment of 10.5 million students and turn out 2.5 million each year. Approximately 45 per cent of the students pursue degrees in the arts, 20 per cent in sciences and 18 per cent in commerce. The remaining 17 per cent are enroled into professional courses like law and medicine. The sheer numbers may seem enormous, but that appears pretty small for a country of India's size.[1]

EDUCATION IN INDIA—'ANCIENT' AND 'MODERN'

In India, illiteracy of a large number of people has turned the visions of "Education for All" into empty dreams. Especially, population explosion has put a heavy pressure on its available infrastructure. India has the world's largest population of illiterates. According to 2011 Census, literacy rate has gone only up to 74 per cent from 65 per cent. For males it has risen to 82 per cent from 75 per cent, for females to 65 per cent from 54 per cent. In absolute number, the figure of illiterates is alarming. No nation can afford to have a large number of its population to remain illiterate, ignorant and unskilled.

Education and the Masses

In ancient India, education was confined within a very small section of Indian society. It was not so much that common people were debarred or denied access to education because of discrimination, as it was method to educate in the past, because of the method of education, education remained confined within a very small section of the society. In absence of any written material, priestly schools in India had devised a most remarkable and effective system of transferring knowledge to succeeding generations in the form of hymns. They restricted it only to those, who possessed brilliant feats of memory and capability to keep its extreme sanctity. Masses remained away from formal education, even when everything was put together in the epics—'*Vedas*', '*Smritis*', '*Sutras*', and '*Upanishads*', because of the medium being Sanskrit. Masses were busy in their hereditary/traditional occupations. Skills were learnt more on job under the training and guidance of people already on the job/occupation. For attaining more skills or furthering their future prospects masses did not depend on formal education, certificates/degrees/diplomas or on formal centres of education and training, i.e. schools/colleges.

The manner, in which hereditary occupational knowledge and skills were transferred, was through practice and experience; not through formal classroom lectures, which often kills originality and verve of people. The system led society to have more production, economic efficiency and specialisation in various areas of activities like spinning, weaving, pottery making, bead making, seal making, terracotta, handicrafts, brick-laying, metal work etc. But still, illiterate masses got the benefit of the knowledge of learned sages and *munis*. On the basis of their scholarly researches and experiences, the sages prescribed certain guidelines in the form of rituals to be followed by common men.

Education in Ancient India

Knowledge was passed on orally from one generation to another in ancient India. Education involved three basic processes—one, which included '*Shravana*' (stage of acquiring knowledge of '*Shrutis*' by listening); two, '*Manana*' (meaning pupils to think, analyse themselves about what they heard, assimilate the lessons taught by their teacher and make their own inferences; and three '*Nidhyasana*' (meaning comprehension of truth and apply/use it into real life).

Education and Women

In ancient India women were given equal right to education and teaching. Women seers like 'Gargi', 'Gayatri' or 'Maitreyi' were prominent participants in educational debates and proceedings of '*Parishads*' (Assemblies). It was mostly the Brahmins followed by Kshatriyas that received education at the *gurukuls*, while boys from the lower castes learnt their family trade from their fathers.

Educational Institutions of Repute

Few most important universities of ancient India were Taxila (being the first university of world established in Seventh century B.C.), Vikramashila University and Nalanda University (built in 4th and 5th century A.D). Huen Tsang in his records mentioned the University of Taxila to be at par with Nalanda and Vikramashila Universities. These institutions were considered to be the best Universities of that times in the subcontinent and an honour to ancient Indian educational system.

Taxila University was famous for medical studies. Varanasi was famous for religious teachings. In the south, Kanchi was famous for its studies while the Vallabhi University was no less. There was a galaxy of eminent teachers like Panini—well known grammarian, Kautilya—the Prime Minister of Chandragupta Maurya and Charaka—a medical teacher of repute. Nalanda University—it was supposed to be the highest learning centre not just for India, but also for the entire South Asia. Students from foreign countries like China, Japan, Korea used to come here for higher studies. It had eight colleges, one of it having four storied building and around 10,000 students and teachers on its roll card. It was one of the earliest examples of residential-*cum*-learning complex.

No Bar

Individuals from humblest origin were highly educated and were respected in Indian society as great achievers. Vashishtha, the principal of conservative school of Brahmanism, was the son of Urvashi, a prostitute. Vishvamitra, the quintessence of Vedic Brahmanism and maker of *Gayatri Mantra*, was a *Kshatriya. Aitareya*, after whom sacramental part of *Rig-Veda* is named as *Aitareya Brahamana*, was the son from a non-Aryan wife of a Brahman sage. Vyasa of *Mahabharata* fame was the son of a fish-woman. Valmiki, an untouchable according to present standards and the original author of *Ramayana*, is highly respected all over India.

"An Ocean of Knowledge in a Jar"

Ancient Indian philosophy and Vedic literature contained "an ocean of knowledge in a jar." It was supposed to be a magnificent example of scientific division and orderly arrangement of rules, in a few words, in different branches of human knowledge, covering almost all the aspects of life, be it phonetics, arts, literature, medicine, polity, metrics, law, philosophy, astrology or astronomy. It spoke of everything—on staying health, social evils, improving concentration and tenets of behaviour, which are relevant even today.

Rituals

The substance of the knowlegde, learning and research work of *Rishis-Munis* (sages and saints) was put in the form of rituals for the benefit of commonmen. Certain practices/guidelines were shaped in the form of rituals by intellectuals and prescribed for the benefit of common men. These rituals and guidelines inspired people to lead a harmonious and healthy life.

Spot Out Gems

With a rational mind, raising it from ignorance, one can understand the greatness of Vedic literature. A knowledgeable person can spot gems from this ocean of knowledge; pick them up and leave like worthless pebbles the undesired, obsolete elements developed into the system with passage of time.

Revival of Ancient Knowledge

During second half of the nineteenth and beginning of the twentieth century, Swami Vivekananda, Ramakrishna Mission and Theosophical Society of India tried to familiarise the Western World, too, to the charm and graciousness of the ancient gold mine of knowledge, which had inspired not only Indians, but foreigners as well. Intellectuals from various countries have translated it in their own languages and reinterpreted it for a rational mind.

As India progressed from ancient to medieval, its education system deteriorated. Various factors were responsible for the degradation of such an efficient and most ancient education system of the world.

MODERN EDUCATION BEFORE INDEPENDENCE

Modern Education System

Modern education system was implanted by British rulers. Before the advent of British in India, education system was private one. In 1835, Lord Thomas Babington Macauley introduced modern education in India. It was the introduction of Wood's Dispatch of 1854, known as Magna Carta of Indian Education that laid the foundation of present system of education and changed the scenario. The main purpose of it was to prepare Indian Clerks for running local administration. Under it the means of school educations were vernacular languages, while the higher education was granted in English only. British Government started giving funds to indigenous schools in need of help and slowly some of the schools became government aided.

Reasons for Introducing Modern Education

Finding it too costly and perhaps practically impossible to import enough Englishmen to man the large and increasing number of subordinate or lower posts in administration, British rulers planned of educating Indians in such a way that they "should through Western education get Anglicised in terms of both cultural and intellectual attainments". Lord Macauley clearly said that, "we must at present do our best to form a class, who may be interpreters between us and the millions whom we govern; a class of persons, Indians in blood and colour, but English in taste, in opinions, in morals and in intellect."

Welcoming Modern Education

The atmosphere was completely ready for Lord Macauley to lay the foundation of modern education in India by 1835. Missionaries and their supporters as well as National leaders, Intellectuals and Reformers not only welcomed but exerted pressure on the Company to encourage and promote Western education in India. Missionaries believed that modern education would lead the people to adopt Christianity. Humanitarians, intellectuals and nationalist leaders considered modern education "the key to the treasures of scientific and democratic thought of the modern West" and the best remedy for social, political and economic ills of the country.

Outcome of Modern Education

In 1844, through a Declaration knowledge of English was made compulsory for Government employment. The traditional Indian system of education gradually withered away for the lack of official support. The government made English medium schools very popular. English as Official language alienated the masses from the educated Indians. Because of modern education and new employment opportunities, many traditional occupations became obsolete. In near absence of industrial, commercial or social service activity, people in India were forced to depend on modern education and Government jobs for their respectful earning. Modernisation of occupations and industrialisation processes increased role of formal education and training for furthering future prospects of people.

The universities at Calcutta, Bombay and Madras were started in 1837 and higher education spread rapidly thereafter. For scientific and technical education, only three Medical Colleges—one each at Calcutta, Bombay and Madras, was established by 1857. There was only one good engineering college at Roorkee.

National Leaders, Intellectuals and Reformers

Modern education not only produced persons to fill the lower levels of administration, as desired by the rulers, but also produced national leaders, intellectuals and reformers like Raja Ram Mohun Roy, Dadabhai Naoroji, Ferozeshah Mehta, Gopalkrishna Gokhale, Mahatma Gandhi, M.A. Jinnah, B.R. Ambedkar, B.G. Tilak, Lala Lajpat Rai, Motilal Nehru, Jawaharlal Nehru, Subhas Chandra Bose, Sardar Ballabhbhai Patel and many more. They took upon themselves the responsibility to build a modern, open, plural, culturally rich, prosperous and powerful India out of a fragmented, poverty stricken, superstitious, weak, indifferent, backward and inward looking society. In short, they believed that—Western literature and philosophy would give Indians the understanding of liberal, scientific, democratic and humanitarian ideas thought of Western World.

- It would make Indians aware of the real issues hampering the progress of Indian society.
- Modern education would improve the life of common men and conquer ignorance, hunger, poverty and disease.
- It would open the key to the treasures of Scientific and Democratic thought of Western World.
- Principles of Democracy would spread rapidly across the nation and finish imperialism and tyranny.
- It would remedy many social, political and economic ills of the nation.

Brahmins Ahead of Others

Initially, it was an impoverished group of Brahmin and caste Hindus in search of livelihood, who desire to live with dignity and honour opted for modern education. Gradual displacement from their source of income after decline in financial status of their patrons—Princes and Zamindars, appalling poverty of Brahmins compelled them to opt for modern education.

Reason being Their Poverty, not Discrimination

Sir Alfred Croft, Director of Public Instruction in Bengal wrote to Rev. J. Johnston in 1881, "We know well that any considerable increase in the fees paid by college students would compel many to withdraw. It seems not to be fully understood… how poor the middle classes that flock to our colleges really are. Half the students live from hand to mouth…. And yet though, far behind in point of wealth, they correspond to, and are in fact the only representative of our professional classes at home, and the pressure on them for the means of subsistence is so great, that they must either be educated or go to wall."

Their poverty gets confirmed by a study done to examine the annual income of the guarantors of 1271 Brahmin Students enrolled at Ferguson College, Pune from 1885 to 1895. According to it, 76 per cent of the Chitpavan Brahmin guarantors belonged to the low or medium income groups. Similarly, of the 277 Deshastha Brahmin guarantors, 70 per cent came from low or medium groups.

They being natural learners and pursuers of knowledge utilised new type of employment opportunities created with introduction of modern education in 1835. They were quick and far ahead of other communities to grasp almost all the opportunities in these spheres. Their long tradition and undisputed role in the field of knowledge and learning, their intelligence, sincerity and hard work helped them even after independence to secure important places in the modern society.

Reasons for Masses Deprived of Modern Education

Except for a few, masses could not avail the advantage of formal modern education. Relentless effort of missionaries and reformers could educate a very small number of people. Reasons being:

- Modern education was very costly and, therefore, unaffordable by the masses.
- Masses did not see any immediate use of education. It was more important for them to work and arrange two square meals day.
- The emphasis was on English medium education system.
- Served double purpose.

Introduction of modern education had served a double purpose for the British rulers—they got the credit for the amelioration of the Indian society. But at the same time, through it, they devised a unique method of distribution of power, kept balance of power and prolonged their rule in India by keeping the natives busy in their in-fights.

Impact of Modern Education

The second half of the nineteenth century saw the impact of modern education on the minds of Indians as under:—

Christian missionaries brainwashed many people especially the poor by preaching and educating them and developed in their minds a complex about the primitiveness of Indian society, influenced them towards the alien culture and then converted them into Christianity. With the help of British rulers, Christian missionaries and religious minded Westerners, like William Webberforce or Charles Grant, they succeeded in converting many persons into Christianity.

National leaders, social reformers, educated people and intellectuals welcomed rationality and other good features of Modern English education. They also got alarmed at divisive policies of the rulers. It led them to lead the national movement. They understood the real issues hampering the progress of Indian society. These organisations had purely an economic and social thrust. They fought against social evils caused by ignorance, superstitions or irrationality like untouchability and inhuman treatment to women, *Sati*, polygamy, child marriage, and many others prevalent at that time. Emphasis was laid on education and science. They criticized the *mumbo-jumbo* of rituals and superstitions created by some selfish people to entangle the ignorant and poor masses.

Reformers got alarmed at the erosion of Indian Culture. Organisations [like Brahmo Samaj founded by Raja Ram Mohun Roy (1828) in Bengal, Prarthana Samaj in Maharashtra (1867), Arya Samaj (1875) founded by Swami Dayananda in Northern India, Ramakrishna Mission, Theosophical Society of India (1879), Dev Samaj in Lahore and Servants of India Society], interpreted religion rationally and advised people to remain firmly rooted to the Indian Culture and not get swayed away by the glamour and materialism of alien culture.

Back to Vedas

Therefore, they organised people, held conferences, published articles and undertook internal reform efforts through Sanskritisation. They gave a call for "Back to Vedas" and advised people to set free Hinduism from all degenerate features. It was not the Hindu principles, but the practices, which went wrong. Vivekananda said, "It is we, who are responsible for our degeneration."

Swami Vivekananda, who founded the Ramakrishna Mission, "Each nation like each individual has a theme in this life, which is its centre, the principle note, around which every other note comes to form the harmony. If any nation attempts to throw off its national vitality, the direction, which has become its own through the transmission of centuries, nation dies."

Divisible Policies of the Rulers

Many national leaders and intellectuals got alarmed at the divisible policies of the rulers. They realised the impact of British racial discrimination in the areas of education and jobs and their repressive policies elsewhere. They realised the impact of British racial discrimination, Economic loot, political subjugation, assertion of lordly superiority over the subject on the ground of race, assumption of a haughty exclusiveness, persistent insulting and supercilious behaviour towards all Indians, exclusion of Indians from all places of authority and responsibility and denial of their capacity for self-governance united Indians against British rule. The destructive character of repressive policies of British rulers lit the fire and gave birth to national movement.

After Independence

After Independence, even relentless effort of reformers, government and NGOs only a small could educate a very small number of people especially from amongst backwards. Masses could not avail the benefit of modern/formal education. It is not so much because of resistance from caste Hindus, as for other reasons.

Reasons for not Succeeding in "Educating All"

It is falsely accused and propagated by some intellectuals, leaders, reformers and supporters of Reservation/Affirmative Action Policy that privileged upper castes have taken advantage of modern education to establish or reinforce its traditional dominance. They prevented lower castes from getting educated or promoting their status in modern society. However, as modern history points out, on the contrary, it was mainly impoverished group amongst Brahmin and caste Hindus opting for modern education, who were in search of livelihood.

Impoverished Group

Impoverished group of caste Hindus looked upon modern education as means to earn their living respectfully. Therefore, when modern education was introduced, they opted for costly Western Education and devoted their scarce resources on it.

Costly nature—General masses have not still availed the benefit of modern education. Reasons for illiteracy of a large number of people are many. Quality education is still very costly for common men and, therefore, unaffordable for masses. Costly nature has tended to make it a monopoly of the richer classes and city dwellers.

Population explosion—Population explosion has put a heavy pressure on available. There has been insufficient infrastructure. There is lack of quality education and training systems in government or government aided institutions. Masses do not see any immediate use of education. It still is more important for the poor people to work and arrange two square meals a day.

Importance of English Language in Modern World

With the changed scenario due to globalisation, liberalisation and revolution in Information Technology, English has been accepted internationally as a means of communication. Therefore, learning English language has become necessary to get a space in international world. Education through foreign medium is a difficult task. Earlier English medium had already put undue strain upon the nerves of the Indian students.

Alienation of Masses

The language of majority of people is Hindi. However, stress on English medium education and English language is more than it was before Independence. After Hindi, English language is being spoken especially by educated Indians, mostly belonging to upper echelons of the society. Increasing importance of English has alienated further the masses from educated ones.

Shortcomings of Present Education System

There are some deficiencies in the present Education system, some of which have been inherited from the British. There are many internal as well as external many pressures on the system, because of which quality of education suffers.

External pressures—Externally, recent social changes and larger political turmoil have affected adversely the whole atmosphere. Some changes took place in the recent past in the character, role and inter-relationship of the six main constituent of the national elites—the political executive, the legislators, the businessmen, the organised workers, the surplus farmers and the bureaucrats. Narrow loyalties, sectional interests and sub-cultures,, like—favouritism, nepotism and corruption have fast become an accepted way of life.

Result is that communal, regional and caste conflicts and unhealthy competition between different sections for power and pelf are increasing everyday. Powerful lobbies desire to have exclusive hold on scarce resources of the nation. Few persons and groups, who have the power in their hands and who control almost every walk of national life are working to deny justice to common men. The reflection of all these social evils is found in the educational system as well.

Internal pressures—Based on colonised British Grammar School type education has made Indian students crammer, imitators and unfit them for original work and thought. It has not taught them to have pride in their surroundings. The more they get, the farther they are removed from their surroundings and at the end of their education, they become estranged from their surroundings. They are loosing their natural character, because they are getting away from their traditional aspirations and values in preference to the Western materialism. Alienation of modern generations from their roots and culture alarmed Gandhiji and he said,

> "My real education began after I had forgotten all that I had learned at School". Erosion of Indian culture—Modern education has disassociating Indian people from their traditional way of learning, classical roots and knowledge. With it have faded Indian values, philosophies and traditions, which had taught Indians the spirit of tolerance and firm belief in the principle, "Live and let live" has always been the part of Indian ethos. Indians believe in '*Vasudhaiva Kutumbakam*'—the whole world is one family.

C. Rajgopalachari had said, "If there is honesty in India today, any hospitality, any charity—any aversion to evil, any love to be good, it is due to whatever remains of the old faith and the old culture." Tolerance, truth, *Ahimsa*, peace and non-aggression are the hallmark of Indian culture.

What should be the limit of tolerance—The people in India endure injustice and unfairness until they are pushed right up to the wall. Many times in the past, Indians had accepted oppression and exploitation without much protest, while such situations would have led to bloody revolutions elsewhere in the world. Even today, the people are tolerating the corruption, scams, scandals and criminal activities developed in political sphere, as well as inefficiency seeped deeply in administration without much protest. People needs to be taught not to tolerate injustice and raise their voice against it peacefully.

Influence of West

Present education system has given rise to a group of Indian intelligentsia which is influenced in a big way by social, political, economic norms of Western world and their way of living. It vehemently denounce culture, character and social value system of India. It regards the culture of the land as indefensible, responsible for creating many discriminatory social values. The number of such people is increasing. The more its number of such persons grows, especially amongst Indian intelligentsia, the more intolerant, people would become. Influence on modern youth.

A drastic change is visible in the values, behaviour and etiquette of a new educated neo-rich youth of elitist class, which has emerged especially in Metros. Their life style and value system are being gradually replaced by the Western ones. They want to enjoy pleasures of modern life at any cost without any restriction. They are more conscious of their rights and want to enjoy life fully in any possible way without any bondage. They do not like any restriction/comment on their behaviour or way of life. Loosening grip of social bondage and observances have made many of them selfish, self-willed and arrogant. Some of them have become so intolerant and aggressive, that they outrightly discard all social norms and etiquette.

Their thinking and value systems are quite different from the older ones. Most of them generally regard Indian value system as rubbish and its epics as irrelevant. They set their own rules. Their yardstick of smartness is interest in stock exchanges, glamour, pubs, parties, discos or late night culture, which gives rise to many kinds of social problems.

With growing cult of materialism and consumerism, finer values of life are disappearing fast. Lust for material gains, comforts, craze for luxurious and glamorous life style has made them so insensitive that they hardly feel anything about the hardships and agonies of the 'have-nots'. Friendship/relationship prospers only if these cost-effective. Otherwise people do not hesitate in showing their helplessness due to lack of time or energy. The persons, who readily help people in need are considered fools in modern society.

Objective of Education

Gaining mere knowledge is not the purpose of learning. As Khalil Gibran has said, a little knowledge that acts is worth more than much knowledge that is inactive. Also, one whose knowledge is confined to books cannot use his knowledge wealth when the need for them arises. Knowledge, the object of knowledge and application of the knowledge—all the three are equally important for motivating to take a wise action.

Pursuit of material success is super-most objective in the minds of young students. It is making them more-and-more selfish and intolerant to others. They are drifting almost rudderless without sense of direction. Academic background, career and good earning is important in life for happiness and satisfaction, but more important is living a quality of life, humanity, compassion and self-discipline for enjoying life fully.

Once more, India has to be made a hub of knowledge creation. It will be a big blunder, if it fails to do it now. India's massive human resource needs to be cultivated through sound system of education and training to get out of the rut of mediocrity. The system of education and learning should be such that it could the faculties of human beings in proper manner towards proper objectives, channelise the desires and energies of Indian people towards proper objectives and right activities. Discipline and productivity are necessary for education.

DEVELOPMENT OF EDUCATION SYSTEM IN INDIA DURING BRITISH PERIOD

Education Policy of the British

In pre-British days Hindus and Muslims were educated through *Pathshala* and Madrasah respectively. Britishers showed no interest in advancement of learning in the first stage of their rule in India. Some of the Britishers in personal endeavour and for political gain showed some interest in spreading education. Warren Hastings, Governor-General of Bengal showed keen interest in spreading oriental education in which effort Jonathan Duncan, Nathani Halhead, Sir William Jones, joined hands. Sir William Jones, the Justice, Calcutta High Court, established Asiatic Society at Calcutta (1784 A.D.). Here they started research on oriental education and culture. At the time of Lord Wellesley, Fort William College was established (1800 A.D.). Here the British Civilians were taught Indian languages, laws, customs, religion, geography etc. By endeavour of Wilkins Jones, Colebrook, William Carey this oriental education got a foothold.

Endeavour of the Christian Missionaries

British colonial ruler did not show any interest in education. The Christian Missionaries were the first to come forward. The Baptist Missionary William Carey came to India in the year 1793 A.D. He along with his friends established Baptist Mission in Serampore (1800 A.D.). By their enthusiasm many primary schools came up in nearly places. They established a printing press and stilled printing booklets in Bengali. Carry translated the *Ramayana* in English (1800 A.D.). By his inspiration the Bible was translated in different Indian languages and Halhead's Bengali Grammar's new edition was published. By their zeal an English school was established in Serampore in 1818 A.D. That is now known as Serampore College.

Personal Endeavour

At that time by the attempt of few liberal Indians and foreigners non-government schools were founded to spread English education. Out of them most memorable were Raja Ram Mohun Roy, Raja Radhakanta Deb, Tejchandra Rai Bahadur of Burdwan, David Hare, the watchmaker of Scotland. Raja Ram Mohun Roy was the father of modern India. By his own endeavour he established Anglo Hindu School in 1815 A.D. By personal endeavour two English schools were founded in Chinsurah (1800 A.D.) and Bhawanipur (1848 A.D). Few energetic Indians and high-minded English civilians came forward to establish Hindu College in Calcutta in the year 1817 A.D. This is now the famous Presidency College.

Endeavour of the Government

In the Charter Act of 1813, Rs. one lakhs per year was sanctioned for advancement of education in India. Now, there was a debate about the line of expenditure of this amount. Some said that it should go for oriental education; the others said that the sum was to be spent for English education. Raja Ram Mohun Roy was in favour of spending the money in Western education. But that was not done. The General Committee of Public Instruction (1823 A.D.) decided to spend the money on oriental studies. In 1823 A.D. the decision was taken to establish a Sanskrit College at Calcutta. Ram Mohun Roy opposed this decision.

During the rule of Lord William Bentinck (1828-1835 A.D.) there was change in government's education policy. He appointed Thomas Babington Macaulay, a renowned educationist, the chairman of the Committee of Public Instruction. At that time the committee was divided in the issue of Oriental or European education. Princep, Colebrook, Wilson were the supporters of Oriental education. They were known as Orientalists. But people like T.B. Macaulay were the supporters of European education. He had with him Alexander Duff, Sanders, Colvin etc. at his side. They became known as Anglicists. Macaulay presented a proposal of advancement of English education in 1835 A.D. This was known as Macaulay minutes.

1. He expressed his strong opinion in favour of English education, as he thought that oriental culture was defective, unholy and corrupted.
2. He thought that it would be better to give proper teaching to a small number of upper and middle-class students as a law of infiltration it would reach to more number of people. This law was known as infiltration theory.
3. He opined that a shelf of Europeans library was equal to the whole literature of India and Arab. Practically, this opinion was the result of his complete ignorance and blind nationalism.
4. He wanted to create a good number of black Europeans who would support the British government. The government approved the Macaulay proposal and after that by the government the education of English language and science started spreading very quickly. It was in the same year (1835 A.D.) Calcutta Medical College and Elphinstone College at Bombay were established. During the time of Lord Auckland (1836-1842 A.D.) government sanctioned more money for propagating Anglicized education.

In 1842, the Public Instruction Committee was rejected and Council of Education was formed. Few Indian members were taken in this Council. Charles Wood's recommendation in the question of spreading of higher education was very important. He was the Chairman of the Board of Control. His proposal about education was known as Wood's despatch. He gave instruction to regularize the education system from primary stage to University level. He also instructed to educate pupils in both English and Vernacular. By his recommendation Education Department was established. In 1857 A.D. Calcutta, Bombay and Madras Universities were established.[3]

EDUCATIONAL SYSTEM DURING PRE-BRITISH DAYS

Ancient India was celebrated for its learning all over civilized Asia and Europe. Megasthenese (*ca.* 302 B.C.) was struck by the depth of this learning during his mission to the court of Chandragupta. Fa-Hien, the famous Chinese traveller (399-413 A.D.) spent some years at the Pataliputra and Tamralipti monasteries. He also spent two years in Ceylon which too had its monasteries after the India fashion. These monasteries were a big affair, housing and teaching several hundred monks. Two centuries after came Hiuen-Tsang undertaking a hazardous journey across Central Asia and northern parts of India. During the seventeen years he spent in India (629-645 A.D.) he visited many monasteries belonging to the Mahayana and the Hinayana schools. He visited Hiranyaparvata, the Golden Hill (Munghir), a city on the bank of the Ganges, which had 10 Sangharamas with 4,000 priests, and 12 Deva temples. At Tamralipti (at the mouth of Hoogly), there were 10 monasteries with a thousand monks. The same story is told of many other towns he visited.

I-tsing (671-695 A.D.) came to India by sea-route. He spent ten years studying at the Nalanda University, the most dominant at his time. It was supported by a revenue of 200 villages and housed more than 3,000 monks. The building contained eight halls and three hundred apartments. On the way back, he spent seven years in Sribhoja (Sumatra), which was a cultural extension of India.

In the face of continued Muslim onslaught from across the north-west frontier, Hindu Buddhist sciences began to retire into the ineterior. Alberuni tells us how "Mahmud ruined the prosperity of the country (India)", how they (Hindus) were turned into "atoms of dust scattered in all directions", how "this is the reason, too, why Hindu sciences have retired far away from those parts of the country conquered by us, and have fled to places which our hand cannot yet reach, to Kashmir, Benares, and other places." As time passed and the Muslim inroads became deeper, Hindu centres of learning were destroyed in the interior too. Eventually, from there they retired into neighbouring countries like Tibet.

Tibet preserved as best as it could, what India was no longer in a position to do. For example, 4000 books belonging to the Sanskrit, Pali and Prakrit literature were translated into Tibetan language. Today, about 3800 of them are no longer even known in India. They were so completely destroyed. The work of destruction was so complete. Today much of old India is found in neighbouring countries like Tibet, Siam and Cambodia; and India's old past history cannot be reconstructed except with their aid.

The Nalanda University continued its glorious existence for a thousand years till it was destroyed by the Muslims. Bakhtiyar Khilji invaded Bihar in 1193 A.D. and found that at Odantapuri (present-day Bihar-Sharif in Patna District) "most of inhabitants were Brahmins with shaven heads. They were put to death. Large number of books were found there, and, when the Muhammadans saw them, they called for some persons to explain their contents, but all the men had been killed. It was discovered that the whole fort and city was a place of study. In the Hindi language the word Behar (*vihār*) means a college" (Elliot and Dowson, *The History of India*, Vol. 11, p. 306).

After this, India entered an era lasting over several centuries which may be called its dark period. Hindus came under the repeated attacks of the Muslims who destroyed their places of worship and learning. But their hands could not reach everywhere; and even in places where they were more securely established, their rule did not remain undisputed for long. As a result, Hindu India and its institutions, though badly mauled, still survived.

European Era

As we enter the period of European conquest, we find that the European travellers and administrators bear testimony to the great veneration in which the Hindus hold learning and instruction. One of the earliest observations made on the subject of indigenous education was by Fra Paolino Da Bartolomeo. Born in Austria, he spent fourteen years in India (1776-1789). Recalling what Megasthenese wrote, he says that the method of teaching and writing was introduced into India two hundred years before Christ, and that he still found it in practice. "No people, perhaps, on earth have adhered as much to their ancient usage and customs as the Indians," he says. He tells us that the Greek historians represent the Indians as people of greater size, and much more robust than those of other nations. He himself "seldom saw in India a person either lame, crooked, or otherwise deformed". Among many factors, climatic and cultural (like wholesome nourishment, cold bath, oil message etc.), which he recounts, he says that "temperance and education contribute, in an uncommon degree, to the bodily conformation, and to the increase of these people." Then he describes the method and practice of teaching and instruction as he found them in Malabar schools.

We may here also quote the testimony of Brigadier-General Alexander Walker who served in India between 1780 and 1810. He says that "no people probably appreciate more justly the importance of instruction than the Hindus." According to him, "they sacrifice all the feelings of wealth, family pride and caste that their children may have the advantage of good education." He also found that this love of learning was no exclusive characteristic of the Brahmins but "this desire is strongly impressed on the minds of all the Hindus. It is inculcated by their own system, which provided schools in every village." He adds that the "spirit of enquiry and of liberty has most probably been effected by the soodors (*Shudras*) who compose the great body of population, and who were in possession of the principal authority and property of the country."

Even during the early days of the British, when they had not entrenched themselves so well, indigenous education was thriving. Discussing the famous "Nuddeah School" of Bengal, an article (Calcutta Monthly Register, January 1791) has the following to say: "In the college of Nuddeah alone, there are at present 1,100 students and 150 masters. Their numbers, it is true fall very short of those in former days. In Rajah Roodre's time (*Circa* 1680) there were at Nuddeah, no less than 4,000 students and masters in proportion." All, the teachers as well as the pupils, were supported by the revenue of free land, the Rajah's treasury supplying any deficiency.

The fact of widespread education—a school in every village—was uniformly noticed by most early observers. Even writing as late as 1820, Abbe J.A. Dubois says that "there are very few villages in which one or many public schools are not to be found, that the students learn in them all that is necessary to their ranks and wants. namely, reading, writing, and accounts."

The Government Survey

For a hundred years, the hands of the British Government were full with the problems of military conquest and revenue system. But for the consolidation of their power, they had to turn to other more intangible aspects of the country's life. Education, so important an Institution, could not be left out of their vigilant attention. The Raj made a thorough study of the prevailing indigenous educational system before introducing its own. Surveys were made in the Bombay Presidency (1820-1830), and the Madras Presidency (1823-1826). A limited, semi-official survey was also made in the Presidency of Bengal ten years later by W. Adam, an excommunicated Baptist missionary, and the findings were published in 1835 in a Report on the State of Education in Bengal. [His first Report was followed by two more, published in 1836 and 1838.] When Punjab was annexed in 1849, the British Government had already developed its Educational policy which it put into operation immediately in this region. G.W. Leitner, Principal of Government College, Lahore, and for some time also the Director of Public Instruction, Punjab, made his own investigations and published his Report in 1883.

Adam's Reports on Bengal became celebrated and saw several reprints, the last in 1983 with a scholarly introduction by Joseph Dibona, the Associate Professor of Education at the Duke University, Durham.[4] Leitner's Report on Punjab, which has been unavailable for decades, has also been reprinted in 1971 by the Languages Department, Punjab.[5] Madras data was the most comprehensive, but it never came out in print though its conclusions were known and were referred to by several authorities in several occasions. Dharampal has collected this data on its fullness and published it for the first time. With a long, illuminating introduction, and with many appendices including long portion from Adam's Reports and Leitner's History, his "The Beautiful Tree" may be considered as the single, most comprehensive document in the subject.

It turned out that what the Government undertook was not a sample survey, but a veritable census. The Madras study and Adam's study of the Thana of the Nattore in the Rajashahy District of Bengal counted every school, scholar and teacher. These reports described the mode of instruction. They touched many points: curriculum, text-books, the hours of coaching, the tuition fees, the financial support of the system. They also contained information regarding the state of the female education; they collected the caste-composition of the scholars and the teachers and also their religious and linguistic affiliations. In this way, these reports, besides throwing light on the educational state of the period, became a mine of information on many sociological facts.

The Mode of Instruction

There were certain characteristic features of the Hindu mode of instruction. Reading and writing were combined. As a pupil spoke aloud a letter, he also wrote it with his finger on the ground in sand. When he had acquired a little proficiency, he could use an iron style or reed or some other instrument to write on a palm-leaf or plantain-leaf. Wooden-boards and brazen-plates were also used. The writing could be effaced with a wet cloth, and boards and slates used again for writing upon. The method was economical.

The very first lessons which taught a knowledge of letters also provided moral and religious instruction. A letter was learnt by referring to a word beginning with that letter, then by a verse which was also a moral maxim, in order to impress it better in the memory. For example the letter 'k' stood for *kubrā* (hump-backed), and it was accompanied by the verse: *kakkākarkartākīpūjā, wahīnirañjanaurnadūjā* (worship the Creator; He is pure and He has no second). Again, the alphabet 'd' was accompanied by this verse; dosh *nadījekāhū*; *dosh karamapnekā* (do not attribute your failure to others; attribute it to your own destiny). G.W. Leitner gives a whole list of these verses for all the letters. Thus, the very first lessons which taught knowledge of the alphabets also provided moral and religious instruction.

There was also another feature of this mode of learning: the pupils learnt in groups of four or five, generally led by a more advanced student. Describing the method, A.D. Campbell, Collector of Bellary, says: "The economy with which children are taught to write in the native schools, and the system by which the more advanced scholars are caused to teach the less advanced, and at the same time to confirm their own knowledge is certainly admirable, and well deserves the imitation it has received in England." This refers to the well known fact that some of the features of the Indian indigenous education were borrowed by Europe.

Grassroots Schools System

Even though already much decayed when the British undertook the survey, the remains indicated an immense edifice which had its foundations deep in the culture of the country and had penetrated every village. W. Adam's

Report of 1835 showed that in the then states of Bengal and Bihar, there were 1,00,000 indigenous elementary schools, or one school for every 31 or 32 boys of school-going age, as the author calculated. The Madras Report which was the most comprehensive showed that there were 12,498 schools containing 1,88,650 scholars. During the same period, schools of a similar nature were found scattered throughout the Bombay Presidency too. Leitner found that 8,000 pupils still received their education in the indigenous schools of Punjab in spite of "the 26 years of repressive education of the Educational Department."

The data shows that the female education was very much neglected though it was not altogether absent. Certain regions like Malabar and Joypoor in Vizaygapatnam made a better showing then other areas. In these regions, we also find that the *Shudras* did better in the matter of female education than the upper class Hindus including the Brahmins. In the Punjab, according to Leitner, "female education is to be met in all parts." According to him, the Punjabi woman has not only been "always more or less educated herself, but she has been an educator of others". He tells us that even before the annexation of the Punjab, six public schools for girls in Delhi were kept by Punjabi women.

The Reports also show that besides the system of public education, there was also widespread private coaching. The Collector of Canara wrote, that whatever education was there in his district was "entirely private". In Madras, the number of pupils taught privately at home was considered to be "above five times greater than that taught in the schools", according to Sir Thomas Munro, Governor of Madras Presidency. In Malabar District, 1,094 Hindu students of advanced learning, were being coached privately, while only 75 attended the only one public institution financed by the impoverished Raja. The Collector narrates the pathetic story of this ancient institution, first destroyed by the Muslims in 966, and later on ruined by being denied its revenues by the British. According to Adam, in the Nattore Thana, while only 659 pupils were taught in any kind of public schools, 2,382 were taught at home.

Private coaching including self-education remained an impoi tant part of the Indian scene. Edward Thompson writing in the 1930s says: "There are in India poor folk who never went to any sort of school who have learnt to read. There must be more literacy in the sense of reading the vernaculars, than the numbers in schools indicate, or else how every Bengal bazaar swarms with these frightfully printed (but cheap) texts of Ramprasad, Chandidas, Krittibas's *Ramayana* (before the War, according to Dinesh Sen, two hundred thousand sold every year). Sarat Chandra

Chatterjee told me that in 1921 the twelve *annas* edition of his fiction had brought him in twelve thousand rupees in royalties, which I estimate to be on a sale of two hundred thousand."

Higher Education

There was also a well-developed system of specialised education and higher learning. According to the Survey of Indigenous Education in the Province of Bombay (1820-1830), there were 16 schools of higher learning in Ahmednagar and in Poona there was as many as 164 such schools out of a total of 222 educational institutions of all descriptions.

Madras Presidency reported 1101 schools (with 5431 students) of higher learning, Rajahmundry heading the list with 279 such schools. Trichnopoly had 173, Nellore 137 and Tanjore 109. These taught 5431 scholars who learnt here, according to their specialisation, the *Vedas*, or Law, or Astronomy, or Poetics, or Music etc.

Hamilton said in 1801 that within the limits of the 24 Parganas, beyond the limits of Calcutta, there were 190 seminaries, all indigenously maintained where Hindu Law, Grammar and Metaphysics were taught. Ward, who wrote in 1818, enumerated 28 institutions of higher learning in the city of Calcutta alone where *Nyāya* and *Smriti-Shāstras* were taught. There was well organised instruction in the Indian system of medicine and inoculation against small-pox was also taught.

Adam gives much data on the subject. According to his Report, in the Thana of Nattore in the District of Rajashahy alone, there were 38 higher schools of learning with 379 scholars, of whom 261 came from distant places. We have the same story from another corner in India, namely the Punjab. Leitner's Report says: "The Vedas were, comparatively speaking, little taught in the Punjab in Ranjit Singh's time, the teachers chiefly coming from the Dekkan"; but, he adds that in Sanskrit and in Grammar, "Punjab Learning was proverbial throughout India, whilst *Punjabi Pandits* also excelled in *Nyāya* (Logic), *Mimānsā*, the *Dharmashāstras*, *Vedānta* and *Sāmkhya* (six *Shāstras*), *Patidhānta* and *Siddhānta* (Astronomy)."

Subjects

The subjects taught in these schools of higher learning were the *Vedas*, *Sāmkhya* (Philosophy), the Six *Darshanas*, Law, Logic, Poetics, Grammar, Astrology and Astronomy, and Medicine. Fra Paolino Da Bartolomeo, describing education in Malabar also mentions the following subjects: Chess (*ciudarangam*), Fencing (*payatta*), Navigation (*naushantra*) and the use of the spear on foot (*hastiludiun*). Another interesting subject taught was silence or *mauna*. Yes, *mauna* too has to be taught and it is as important a subject as any other. We learn from Leitner's Report that Ranjit Singh also gave grants to architects and gun-makers. It is not clear whether the grants were personal or meant for teaching their arts to other deserving students.

The *Pandits*

Adam praises the teachers for their learning which was equalled only by their modesty. He found them "not only unpretending but also plain and simple." Though "adepts in the subtleties of the profoundest grammar" of a language "probably the most philosophical", and masters of logic, ethical philosophy and of their national laws, they were "discriminating and mild". He found in them "no abjectness to a supposed or official superior". They praised other *Pandits* for their learning, generally in their absence, rather than themselves. Let us salute their memory. What was said about the country's cotton-weavers could as justly be said about its teachers and *Acharyas*—their bones are bleaching the plains of the country.

Text-books

The Collector of Bellary District reports that "the three books which are most common in all the schools, and which are used indiscriminately by all the several castes, are the *Ramayana, Mahabharata*, and *Bhagavata*". Thus, contrary to the current notion, the highest ethical and spiritual literature of the Hindus was open to all irrespective of their caste. Very much unlike the West, where the Bible remained unread and even a prohibited reading for many, many centuries; and, in fact, many times its translators into vernacular were burned at the stake—till the triumph of Protestantism, which gave birth to an opposite movement called bibliolatry.

F.W. Robertson, Collector of Rajahmundry District, names 66 text books including the *Ramayana*, various *Suktams* (*Krishna Suktam, Suryanarayan Suktam, Jankeya Suktam, Narayana Suktams*), and various *Charitams* (like *Vamana Charitam, Mala Charitam* etc.). Some text-books, like the *Visvakarama-Purana*, were special to the manufacturing classes. Adam names 29 text-books taught in elementary schools in Bengal, and 120 books taught in higher Institutes. These related to such subjects as Grammar (20), General Literature (11), Law (17), *Vedanta* (4), Logic (31), Astronomy and Astrology (19), Medicine (4) etc.

In his Report on the Punjab, Leitner names hundreds of textbooks—Sanskrit, Persian, Arabic and *Gurmukhi*—taught in Hindu and Muhammadan schools of different grades in the Punjab. For example, text-books taught to Sikh students of *Gurmukhi* schools are divided into two sections: those taught to the beginners and those taught to advanced students. To the first section belonged *Balopdesha*, *Panj Granthi*, *Janam Sakhi*, the tenth Guru's *Panj Ekadash*, *Bhagavat*, *Tulsi Ramayana*, *Vishnu Purana*, *Pingal* (10 parts), *Ashwa Medha*, *Adhyatma Ramayana*, *Vichara Sagar*, *Moksha Pantha*, *Surya Prakash*, the sixth Guru's *Guru Vilas*, *Vashishtha Purana*, and *Daswanaskandha*. This must be embarrassing to the new-style, collaborationist Sikh intellectuals.

Education Open to All

There is a popular notion that education in India was monopolised by the Brahmins; but the data destroys this myth completely. This interested lie was first spread by the missionaries and the British rulers and the colonised mind of many Indian intellectuals still continue to sing their tune. But the data reveals a different story. It tells us that out of the total number of 1,75,089 students, both male and female, elementary and advanced, only 42,502 were *Brahmins* (24.25%); 19,669 were *Vaishya* students (about 11%); but 85,400 were *Shudras* (about 48.8%); and still 27,516 more were "all other castes", meaning castes even lower than the *Shudras* including the *pariahs* (15.7%). Thus, the higher castes were only about 35 per cent and the *Shudras* and other castes were about 65 per cent of the total Hindu students. If we also include the Muslims who were about 7 per cent of the total Hindu and Muslim students, then the share of the Brahmins was even less.

We have a table showing the caste-wise division of all male school students, both in absolute numbers and in percentage, of all the 20 districts of Madras Presidency. The data shows that the share of the Brahmins in certain areas was indeed very low. For example, in Seringapatam, it was only 7.83 per cent 'in Madura 8.67 per cent, in North Arcot, *Brahmin* boys were 9.57 per cent, while the *Shudras* and "other castes" were 84.46 per cent.

Table 7.1: Caste-wise Division

Caste Division	Area-wise division of all male school students	Percentage	Caste Division	Area-wise division of all male school students	Percentage
Brahmins	Seringapatam	7.83%	Shudras and "other castes"	Seringapatam Madura North Arcot	84.46%
	Madura	8.67%			
	North Arcot	9.57%			
	Total	**26.07%**		**Total**	**84.46%**

Even in higher learning, non-Brahmins were not unrepresented. In Malabar, out of 1,588 scholars of Theology, Law, Astronomy, Metaphysics, Ethics and Medical Science, only 639 were *Brahmins*, 23 *Vaishyas*, 254 *Shudras* and 672 "other castes". Only in the *Vedas* and Theology did the *Brahmins* have a near-monopoly, as the *Shudras* and the "other castes" had in other branches of advanced learning like Astronomy and Medical Science. In Astronomy, out of a total of 806 scholars, *Brahmins* were only 78, *Vaishyas* 23, *Shudras* 195, and other lower castes 510. In Medical Science, the share of the *Brahmin* scholars was only 31 out of a total of 190. The rest belonged to the *Shudras* and "other castes".

According to the Survey of Indigenous Education in the Province of Bombay (1820-1830), *Brahmins* constituted only 30 per cent of the total scholars in that province.

Adam tells the same story about Bengal and Bihar. In the five districts he investigated, the total number of Hindu students was 22,957. Out of these 5,744 were *Brahmins*, or about 25 per cent. *Kayasthas* were about 12 per cent. Students belonging to 95 castes find representation in his Report. It includes 66 *Chandals*, 20 *Muchis*, 84 *Doms*, 102 *Kahars*, and 615 *Kurmis*.

In spite of the claims of the missionaries, they did no better for the Hindu low-castes. According to Adam's findings, Burdwan had 13 missionary schools, yet they had only 1 Chandal student while the native schools had 60. The former had only 3 *Doms* and no *Muchis* while the latter had 58 and 16 respectively. Of the 760 pupils belonging to the lowest 16 castes, "only 86 were found in the missionary schools, and the remaining number in native schools."

As teachers, the *Brahmins* were even less represented. Out of a total of 2,261 teachers in these districts, Brahmins were only 208, or about 11 per cent. In this region *Kayasthas* were the teachers par excellence. They were 1,019 in number, or a little less than half the total. Other teachers belonged to other 32 castes. *Chandals* had six, *Goalas* had five, *Telis* had eleven; while *Rajputs* had only two, and *Chhatri* or *Kshatriya* taken together had only three.

Comparison

It will not be out of place here to compare the state of instruction in India at this period with the one prevalent in the West, and particularly in England, the country with which we have better acquaintance. The West was at this time acquiring monasteries and new-style universities which were gaining fame for teaching theology, but it still had no national system of elementary education for instructing its younger ones.

In England, the attempt to introduce any semblance of wider instruction was first made in mid-fifties in the nineteenth century under factory laws. But the legislation "provided nothing more than that the children shall on certain days of the week, and for a certain number of hours (three) in each day, be inclosed within the four walls of a place called a school, and that the employer of the child shall receive weekly a certificate to that effect signed by a person designated by the subscriber as a school master or school mistress" (Report of the Inspector of Factories, Parliamentary Papers, June 30, 1857).

The level of literacy of these teachers was such that many of them signed the certificate of attendance at school with a cross. As a result, an Act had to be passed in 1844 which required that the "figures in the school certificate must be filled-up in the handwriting of the school master, who must also sign his Christian and surname in full". But that did not improve matters very much. Sir John Kincaid, Factory Inspector for Scotland, tells us how a school teacher, one Mrs. Ann Killin, spelled her name sometimes with letter C, sometimes with K and in various other ways. He also tells us of a "schoolroom 15 feet long, and 10 feet wide, and counted in this space 75 children, who were gabbling something unintelligible" (Parliamentary Papers, 31st October, 1858). About the "cultural" acquirements of these scholars, one may read Karl Marx (*Das Kapital*, Part III, Chapter 10, Section 4), who quotes extensively from the Children's Employment Commission Report.

Punishment in India under the indigenous system of education was mild. Even in the Punjab region where it was more common, it consisted in making a student stand in a corner, or making him pull his own ears by passing his hands through his knees; or making him sit down and stand-up for a number of times; or disallowing him to leave the classroom during the meal time. There were no fines. On the other hand, teachers in England were sadists—at least, this is what the English accounts of the period tell us. For example, Charles Dickens in his Nicholas Nickleby (1838-39) describes these schools and their teachers, particularly in Yorkshire. He says that these "school masters, as a race, were the blockheads and impostures"; that, they "were the lowest and most rotten in the whole ladder"; that they were "ignorant, sordid, brutal men, to whom few considerate men would have entrusted the board and lodging of a horse or dog". He said that these schools were opened by "any man who had proved his unfitness for any other occupation in life".

Sanction in Hinduism

The Indian national education system was no freak. It was grounded in Hindu culture and its system of local self-government. Ludlow's British India says that "in every Hindu village which has retained anything of its form. The rudiments of knowledge are sought to be imparted; there is not a child, who is not able to read, to write, to cipher; in the last branch of learning they are confessedly most proficient." The same source says at another place that "where the village system has been swept away by us, as in Bengal, there the school system has equally disappeared". Leitner quotes a report of a British Inspector of Schools in the Punjab which too brings out the intimate link between indigenous educational system and it underlying system of ideas and polity. It says: "The indigenous education of India was founded on the sanction of the *Shāstras*, which elevated into religious duties and conferred dignity on the commonest transactions of everyday life. The existence of village communities, which left not only their municipal, but also in part their revenue and judicial administrations, in the hands of the people themselves, greatly helped to spread education among all the different members of the community."

British Hostility

The new rulers were understandably hostile to the indigenous system. As soon as the British took over the Punjab, the Education Report of 1858 says: "A village school left to itself is not an institution which we have any great interest in maintaining."

This hostility arose partly from a lack of imagination. To the new rulers, brought up so differently, a school was no school if it did not teach

English. To such preponderant elements among them, the answer of a rare and imaginative administrator like Leitner was this: "If a collegium held, according to Hindu tradition, in the teacher's own house, is not a school; if to read and write *Gurmukhi* and the *naharas* is not to know the three or any r's, then, of course, all discussion is at an end. When, however, by school is meant an indigenous school; by a knowledge of reading and writing that of the indigenous characters; by learning or science, oriental learning and science, then indeed was education far extended when we took the Punjab than it is at present." To these who despised an indigenous school because it taught a small number of students, he answered: "If the Lahore Government College could be called a college when it had only four students, there is no reason why an indigenous school should not be called a school when it has less than ten students."

Financial Support

The teacher of an indigenous school was an idealist, but the system itself was founded on realistic public financial support. Schools were supported by the grant of rent-free lands and monetary assignments. During the British rule, this support was withheld or drastically curtailed. The data for rent-free lands to support local needs like the police, the temples, the education has not been fully worked out but that this portion was very large is beyond doubt. Dharampal shows that it was sometimes as large as 35 per cent of the total land, and sometimes even 50 per cent. Leitner gives the names of many hundreds of scholars who were endowed with such lands, but whose grants were terminated and as a result of which the institutions they ran so well died down within a generation. The Collector of Bellary District wrote: "There is no doubt that in former times especially under the Hindu Government very large grants both in money and in land were issued for the sake of learning."

When the British started studying indigenous education, they had already been in control of the territory for over fifty years; and during these years much harm had already been done. The land grants were already stopped or curtailed. There was a general breakdown in the economy at large. The old classes which supported local institutions were impoverished. These and other causes combined to bring about a fast deterioration in the educational condition. Adam mentions many specific villages in Nattore Thana which at the time of investigation had only two schools where there had been once ten or eleven schools in living memory. The decay was fast.

Increasing Illiteracy

No doubt, indigenous education decayed and illiteracy increased during the British period. According to Sir Henry Lawrence, there was one school for every 1,783 inhabitants of the most backward division of the Punjab at the time of annexation. But thirty years later in 1881, "there is one school of whatever sort, to every 9,028 inhabitants", according the President of the Educational Commission.

Adam estimated that there was 11 per cent literacy in the Thana of Nattore during 1830s. "A century later the British considered this an accomplishment in many parts of India," says Joseph DiBona, the author of One Teacher, One School. This is the charge which Mahatma Gandhi also brought against the British when he said in 1931 that "today India is more illiterate than it was fifty or a hundred years ago". He charged that the British destroyed "the Beautiful Tree", an epithet he used to describe old Indian indigenous education and which Dharampal has also borrowed from him to provide the title to his book on the subject.

Indigenous education served local needs, both economic and cultural and religious. Under the British, it was divorced from both. For example, one Government report says: "If a boy learns arithmetic in our schools, he is of little use for the shop, because he finds there a different system of accounts, and the meanest Banya can cast up the intricacies of the grain-trade accounts by a mental process far more rapidly than if he had taken honours in Mathematics at the Calcuttta University."

Under the indigenous system, primary education was imparted in the local language. But the British Government introduced Urdu as the medium of instruction over a large territory of North India. This "practically excluded from primary instruction" the whole Hindu priestly class, the artisans and the agricultural classes, according to the testimony of the Brahmo Samaj. The common men and women wanted to learn to read in order to be able to study the *Ramayana* and other religious books which were available in their own language. But Urdu which was foreign to them did not help them in that direction. It was meant to make students munshis which was not their aim.

Cultural Self-alienation

While teaching a boy three r's, indigenous education also familiarised him with the nation's epics, religion and literature. This did not suit the white rulers and missionaries. So, they put forward the principles of "secularism" and "religious neutrality"—principles which continue to be pleaded even today by our brown *sahibs* with equal duplicity and equal harm to the deeper life of the nation. Pleading these convenient principles, the then Inspector of a provincial schools reported: "I directed the disuse of all books of a religious character in the schools." The *Ramayana* and the other great indigenous literature still continue to be on the Index of the so-called indigenous Government seventy years after independence.

Thus, the nation's accumulated riches were denied to the new generations and they grew in self-forgetfulness of their rich heritage. The nation's sciences, philosophies, religion and literature were taken out of the life of the growing generations and these merely became the topics or subjects of Indology.

Under the indigenous system, the Hindu schools were closed on *Purnima* of every month and on other Hindu festivals. Under the new dispensation, Sunday became the new holiday. Thus, we were cut off from our calendar too with which so much else in our history and religious discipline and observances is also connected. In due course, came into being a class of Macaulay's dream, a class oblivious of its roots, a class of cultural barbarians, a class Indian in blood and colour but European and missionary in its contempt of everything Indian in general and Hindu in particular.

Deep down, the issue was not English language, or higher learning of the West or modern sciences. Hindu culture had a rich tradition of secular learning and it could easily imbibe whatever the West had to offer. In fact, it could even make its own contribution to the pool and perhaps help in taming the aggressive urges of modern sciences. The problem was deeper. It had to do with a pattern of self-forgetfulness and self-alienation that was imposed on the country. And we were so thoroughly brainwashed that we now delight in it. The imperialist missionary policies of the British have now become the political religion of our own neo-intellectuals and administrators. The attack still continues under the guise of "Tradition *versus* Modernity".

The Indian system of education was so economical, so effective that some of its features were exported to England and Europe. The "monitor", the "slate", the "group-study" were directly borrowed from the old Indian practice. A short account of this practice is available from an eyewitness report of a European named Pietro Della Valle published in 1623. But 200 years later, around 1800, two Britons, Dr. Bell and Mr. Lancaster, who were servants of the East India Company, introduced in England a "New System of Schooling", embodying Indian practices of teaching.

Both claimed originality for themselves. In the controversy that ensued, it was found that both had borrowed from India without acknowledgment, of course. In this connection we have the testimony of Brigadier-General Alexander Walker who served in the East India Company from 1780 to 1810. While reporting on teaching methods in Malabar, he says that the new British "system was borrowed from the Brahmans and brought from India to Europe. It has been made the foundation of the National Schools in every enlightened country. Some gratitude is due to a people from who we have learnt to diffuse among the lower ranks of society instructions by one of the most unerring and economical methods which has ever been invented." According to him, by this method, "the children are instructed without violence, and by a process peculiarly simple."

Conclusion

Eastern part of the world surpasses the West by no small measure on issues of culture-starting from Egypt and moving eastward through Mesopotamia, Indian subcontinent, China and south-east Asia. Indian culture has kept, thousands of years old XYZ alive, despite hit after hit on our successive generations from outsiders.

When it comes to advancement in knowledge and science it is the West that has led the world. Looking at the mechanism of expansionism and spreading out, the West has always had the upper hand. Otherwise how could a nation of a handful travel the world over and thrust its imperialism on it. A segment of this group, by sheer hard work and patience, threw the imperial mechanism overboard and built-up a nation, living in which is a dream of every young person. In short, the above discussion throws up following important issues—

Importance of knowledge in education cannot be denied. Purpose of education has unfortunately been misunderstood to mean acquiring as much academic knowledge as possible, leading towards award of degrees. But equally importance is inculcating skills in all the vocations according to aptitude of different individuals through practical training for overall development of nation. Training in different vocations should be given when minds of individuals are still in formative stage. Training becomes necessary for applying knowledge in real life.

There is no doubt that modern education has given to India the key to the treasures of scientific and modern democratic thought. It is the West that has led the world in advancement in technology and science. It opened up the doors for liberal and rational thinking. It widened the mental horizons of Indian intelligentsia during nineteenth century. However, somewhere it got derailed and now the system of education at all the stages, from preliminary through secondary right up to the college stage makes mind just a store-house of knowledge and discourages creative thinking.

India surpasses the West by no small measure on issues of culture. It is one of the oldest living culture in the whole world, despite hit after hit on it in the past during alien rule.

For building an ideal structure for education, an amalgamation of Eastern Culture and Western methods, liberal thinking and advancement in science and technology of the West would be the best for future generations. would be the best.

The world is now a global village. Thanks to revolution in areas of information, communications technology and travel apparatus. It will be good if the forces of both—culture and systems—could be combined and a charter of an ideal education blueprint could be evolved for future generations. Why not we combine the forces of both these, Culture and Mechanics, and evolve a charter of an ideal education blueprint for our future generations. Technology advances have brought us to a stage where every concept is an option! Why not cash upon it.[6]

NOTES

1. *http://www.indianetzone.com/38/history_higher_education_india.html*
2. *https://latasinha.wordpress.com/2010/06/20/ancient-and-modern-education-system-in- india/*
3. *http://www.importantindia.com/11643/development-of-education-system-in-india- during-british-period/*
4. *One Teacher, One School: The Adam Reports on Indigenous Education in 19th Century India*, by Joseph DiBona, BibliaImpex Pvt. Ltd., New Delhi.
5. *History of Indigenous Education in the Punjab since Annexation and in 1882*, by G.W. Leitner, 1883, Reprinted by Languages Department, Punjab, Patiala, 1971.
6. *The Beautiful Tree: Indigenous Indian Education in the Eighteenth Century*, by Dharampal (BibliaImpex Pvt. Ltd., New Delhi).

8
Higher Education in Punjab

Jaspal Singh

Introduction

The optimum development of a Nation depends upon the Education. Due to same fact, in this era of globalisation, all countries of the world have been paying special attention towards providing quality education to their folk. Education is the only way which takes human being from earth to sky. This alone can sustain culture and civilisation. A balanced development of mind and body in harmony with the spirit is the key to enrichment of human personality and also the key to true education which must, in the ultimate analysis, help humanity to right to a higher level of awareness.

"Punjab is a land of five rivers but in 1966, after the reorganisation of Punjab, due to many social and political pressures the Punjab Government has made many conscientious efforts and policies to develop and expand educational facilities in the state in a planned manner. All these planned efforts, though limited in nature, have led to establishment of large number of colleges either in the public sector or in the aided private sector. Two new universities—Punjabi University, Patiala (1962) and Guru Nanak Dev University, Amritsar (1969)—were also established. These steps have increased and strengthened the access to general higher education in the state. But, now-a-days, there is an urgent need to encourage students to shift from the liberal arts and sciences to paramedical and applied science courses as "this will bridge the gap between technical and professional and arts and sciences courses. The higher education in Punjab—whether formal or non-formal—has a very long historical past with a strong colonial legacy. Its expansion was very limited and its accessibility to the general masses, however, was marred by the poor socio-economic conditions as the British Rule had vested interests in its expansion as well as accessibility. After India's independence in 1947, the Punjab Government, especially after the Reorganisation of Punjab in 1966, has made many conscientious and planned efforts to develop and expand higher educational facilities in the public sector to create a pool of highly skilled manpower to fulfil the anticipated demand of such persons in the state. Under this policy, the government (state) has allocated more funds to open the new higher education institutions. All these state efforts have brought out many significant changes in the expansion of higher education system in the state. The structure of higher education developed in the Punjab state, in fact, has followed the national pattern of imparting higher education generally in the liberal, technical and professional subjects through the universities and their affiliated colleges (Mittar, Singh and Brar, 2002)."[1]

In Punjab, there were three universities during 1966-67, and four universities during 1970-71 imparting the higher education in the whole state and, now, there are 15 Private Universities, 11 Government Universities and Deemed University and other groups of institutes providing much-diversified courses of higher education in the state. Three important State Universities, namely, Panjab University, Chandigarh (1948); Punjabi University, Patiala (1962); and Guru Nanak Dev University, Amritsar (1969) train the students of state in the general as well as professional education. Another important university, i.e. Punjab Agricultural University, Ludhiana (1962) has earned a well-known distinction for its contribution in the field of agricultural and allied sciences related to higher education, research and extension services (research lab-to-field application) that has promoted the agricultural economy of the state.

In the recent years, professional education like business management, education, computer science, and law subjects has also gained importance in the state. Earlier, the respective departments of three universities of Punjab provided such professional education on a limited scale. In fact, there was no college up to 1998 that provided higher education in these courses. Rajiv Gandhi Law University, university constituent colleges impart higher education in these fields.

As expected, with the increase in number of colleges/institutes and available seats in them, the accessibility to higher education, at least theoretically, has increase in the state. In nutshell, the higher education of the state has witnessed two significant trends. One, during the decades of 1970s and 1980s, most of the established colleges were providing the general education. Two, during the 1990s and onwards, the new colleges/ institutes imparting professional and technical education have gained an upper hand, mainly due to the private initiative at the very fast speed.

"Punjab aims to significantly increase access to higher education in Urban and Rural areas by 2022 and is focusing on ensuring employability of its graduates

The Punjab Government is undertaking multiple initiatives to improve the quality of higher education and employability in the state. These include:

- Promoting private participation in higher education; the Private University Bill was passed in 2014 to set-up Rayat-Bahra University and GNA University.
- ***Providing scholarships to talented students***: In 2013-14, the Punjab State Government launched a scheme worth INR 150 m (GBP 1.5 m) in scholarships to support higher education for students scoring 80 per cent and above in their matriculation examinations.
- ***Enhancing employability***: The Punjab Skill Training for Employment Potential (P-STEP) for graduates is an initiative that aims to increase the employability of students in the state with the help of the IT/knowledge industry. The programme includes training on communication and soft skills as well as basic IT skills.
- ***State of privatisation***: No umbrella act exists in the state for the establishment of new private universities. Desh Bhagat University, Mandi Gobindgarh came into existence as a State Private University under Punjab Government. Desh Bhagat University Act, 2012. Similarly, The DAV University Act, 2012 was passed to establish DAV University in 2012. Every new university would have to be established on the basis of a new act passed by the state legislature, making it prone to more regulatory hurdles. While the Punjab Government will continue to expand access and equity of its higher education system, its focus seems to be shifting to ensuring the employability of graduates (given the high unemployment rate in the state) as

well as promoting research that is relevant at the state and national levels. Its main targets and initiatives to realise its goals are as follows:

Higher Education Targets and Initiatives Planned for Punjab

Axis	*Targets*	*Initiatives planned*
Access	To provide access to higher education to 100 per cent of its population in urban and rural areas by 2022	The Punjab Government has proposed setting up of a new medical college in SAS Nagar to the Union Ministry of Health and Family Welfare
Equity	To expand the reach of higher education to rural and tribal areas and to poor students (no specific targets)	It is planning to start a programme to provide free higher education to poor students in collaboration with private universities in the state
Excellence	To make improvement in quality the key imperative for all institutes in the state (no specific targets)	• The government seeks to implement compulsory rating of institutes by independent agencies • It is planning at least one IIM in the state by 2022 • It is developing a concept to establish Chandigarh Region Innovation and Knowledge Cluster (CRIKC) to facilitate innovation, knowledge creation and excellence in the region
Employability	Making graduates globally employable (no specific targets)	• The Government plans to increase the number of vocational education institutions in the state • It will focus on imparting soft and IT skills through finishings schools

Punjab is an Important Market for the Recruitment of Indian Students by Foreign Higher Education Institutions

Outbound student mobility: Punjab is an important market from a student recruitment point of view. This is reflected in the fact that four major destination countries—the US, the UK, Australia and Canada—have their education promotion arm offices in the state. The leading four major education consultants have 10 offices in the state; which represents 12 per cent of their overall number of offices in the country.

Inbound student mobility: Around 235 international students were reported to be enrolled in higher education institutions in Punjab in 2010-11 out of which 8 were enrolled in Ph.D./M. Phil. courses, 44 in Masters' degree/diploma courses and 183 in UG degree/diploma courses.

International collaborations: A number of Punjab universities are active in the collaboration space and have inked agreements covering curricula development, student/faculty exchange and research collaborations. Some of the main MoU's signed by Punjab's universities include the following:

Country	*Collaborations*
UK	• Lovely Professional University (LPU) has tie-ups with UK universities such as the University of Sunderland, the University of East London and Thames Valley University. • Chitkara University has a tie-up with Glasgow Caledonian University. • Panjab University has a tie-up with CERN as part of the ALICE collaboration.
US	• Punjab Technical University (PTU) has signed an MoU with the University of California, Santa Cruz (UCSC) to set up an Institute of Excellence (IoE) at Chandigarh. • LPU has tie-up with Troy University, Washburn and Iowa State University. • Panjab University (PU), Chandigarh has been selected by the Government of India as the nodal agency for Indian Institutional collaboration with US institutions in research on neutrino physics.
CANADA	• The Punjab Government has invited Canadian institutes to establish education and healthcare institutions in the upcoming Educity and Medicity in Chandigarh. • The Government of British Columbia has opened an office in Chandigarh. The aim of the office is to promote joint research and development.
Australia	• The Australian Centre for International Agricultural Research has funded research programmes in Punjab on improving crops, cropping systems and economics. • Australian and Indian Scientists from CSIRO and the Institute of Microbial Technology, Chandigarh have collaborated on developing a tool to diagnose tuberculosis.

Source: The Chopras website; Edwise website; IDP website; Global Opportnities website; Press articles; International collaboration bodies websites.[2]

Suggestions for Improving Quality of Higher Education in Punjab

"There are some Suggestions and Expectations from Government, Industry, Educational Institutions, Parents and Students for improving quality of higher education—

1. ***Invest more in learning society***—As we move towards a learning society, every human activity will require contributions from experts, and this will place the entire sector of higher education in sharp focus. Although the priorities, which are being assigned today to the task of Education for All, will continue to be preponderant, the state will have to prepare itself to invest more-and-more on higher education and, simultaneously, measures will have to be taken to refine, diversify and upgrade higher education and research programmes.

2. ***Connection between educational institution and industries***—Industry and Academia connect necessary to ensure curriculum and skills in line with requirements. Skill building is really very crucial to ensure employability of academia to understand and make sure good jobs (keeping in view knowledge + skills+ global professional skills = good jobs).

3. ***Incentives should be provided to Teachers and Researchers***—Industry and students are expecting specialised courses to be offered so that they get the latest and best in education and they are also industry ready and employable. Vocational and Diploma courses need to be made more attractive to facilitate specialised programmes being offered to students. Incentives should be provided to teachers and researchers to make these professions more attractive for the younger generation.

4. ***Innovative Practices should be there***—The new technologies offer vast opportunities for progress in all walks of life. It offers opportunities for economic growth, improved health, better service delivery, improved learning and socio-cultural advances. Though efforts are required to improve the state's innovative capacity, yet the efforts should be to build on the existing strengths in light of new understanding of the research-innovation-growth linkage.

5. ***To mobilise resources***—The decline in public funding in the last periods has resulted in serious effects on standards due to increasing costs on non-salary items and emoluments of staff, on the one hand, and declining resources, on the other. Effective measures will have to be adopted to mobilise resources for higher education. There is also a need to relate the fee structure to the student's capacity to pay for the cost. So

that, students at lower economic levels can be given highly subsidised and fully subsidised education.

6. *Coming of Information Age*—The world is entering into an Information Age and developments in communication, information and technology will open-up new and cost-effective approaches for providing the reach of higher education to the youth as well as to those who need continuing education for meeting the demands of explosion of information, fast-changing nature of occupations, and lifelong education. Knowledge, which is at the heart of higher education, is a crucial resource in the development of political democracy, the struggle for social justice and progress towards individual enlightenment.

7. *Learner-centred Education and Dynamic Methods*—Methods of higher education also have to be appropriate to the needs of learning to learn, learning to do, learning to be and learning to become. Student-centred education and employment of dynamic methods of education will require from teachers new attitudes and new skills. Methods of teaching through lectures will have to subordinate to the methods that will lay stress on self-study, personal consultation between teachers and pupils, and dynamic sessions of seminars and workshops. Methods of distance education will have to be employed on a vast scale.

8. *Public and Private Partnership*—PPP is most essential to bring in quality in the higher education system. Governments can ensure PPP through an appropriate policy. University Grants Commission and Ministry of HRD should play a major role in developing a purposeful interface between the Universities, Industries and National Research Laboratories (NRLs) as a step towards PPP. Funding to NRLs by the government should ensure the involvement of institutions of higher education engaged in research activities to facilitate availability of latest sophisticated Equipment. There has been some effort both by the government and the private education institutions to develop the teaching staff at various levels. However, this needs to be intensified with appropriate attention to all the aspects related in order to prepare quality and sufficient number of educational staff. Such efforts need a very serious structuring for the research base institutions. We have to be optimistic that private-public-partnership and the Industry interface will take place in the field of education at all levels, and particularly in the backward regions, which is the need of the hour. To achieve excellence, we thus need to create a real partnership between government, educators and industry—Partnerships that can provide our high-tech industries with skilled workers who meet the standards of their industry.

9. *Vocational Courses*—All-round development of personality is the purpose of education. But the present day education is neither imparting true knowledge of life and nor improving the talent of a student by which one can achieve laurels in the field one is interested. So, combination of arts subjects and computer science and science and humanities or literature should be introduced so that such courses could be useful for the students to do jobs after recruitment in some companies which would reduce unnecessary rush to higher education. The programme must be focused on graduate studies and research and developing strategies and mechanisms for the rapid and efficient transfer of knowledge and for its application to specific national and local conditions and needs. Meritorious doctoral students should be recognised through teaching assistantships with stipends over and above the research fellowships. Finally, based on knowledge only vision of the future life and work can be had; based on this vision only a broad ambition can be fixed for oneself; and based on this ambition only one can lead interesting life doing satisfying job to do remarkable achievements in some field in the world.

10. *International Cooperation*—Universities in Punjab have been a primary conduit for the advancement and transmission of knowledge through traditional functions such as research, innovation, teaching, human resource development, and continuing education. International cooperation is gaining importance as yet another function. With the increased development of transport and communication, the global village is witnessing a growing emphasis on international cooperation and action to find satisfactory solutions to problems that have global dimensions and higher education is one of them.

11. *Action Plan for Improving Quality*—Academic and administrative audit should be conducted once in three years in colleges by external experts for ensuring quality in all aspects of academic activities. The self-finance colleges should come forward for accreditation and fulfil the requirements of accreditation. Universities and colleges should realise the need for quality education and come forward with action plan for improving quality in higher educational institutions.

12. *Individuality*—The life of one will not be interesting, but rather boring, monotonous and frustrating. This is mainly due to parental interference in the education of the children. Parental guidance is necessary, but it should not interfere in the creativity or individuality of the students. Also, in spite of the obsolete type of education system, some are achieving wonderful things in Sports, Music, Dance, Painting, Science and Technology in the world. This is only due to the encouragement of the parents and some dedicated teachers in the educational institutions. Higher education is necessary for one to achieve excellence in the line one is best. But one should be selected for higher education on the basis of merit only. Further, fees for education in general should not be high; especially, the fees for higher studies should be within the reach of every class of people in the nation.

13. *Privatisation of Higher Education*—Privatisation of higher education is absolutely necessary because government alone is helpless to do so.

14. *Quality Development*—Quality depends on its all functions and activities: teaching and academic programmes, research and scholarship, staffing, students, building, facilities, equipments, services to the community and the academic environment. It also requires that higher education should be characterised by its international dimensions: exchange of knowledge, interactive networking, mobility of teachers and students and international research projects, while taking into account the national cultural values and circumstances. The level of education and knowledge being imparted by many colleges is not up to the mark. Instead of concentrating on quantity, these institutions should concentrate on quality. The approach of doctoral research in social sciences needs to be more analytical and comparative and be related to society, policy and economy.

15. *World Class Education*—Punjab government is not giving proper priority to the development of Standard in education. Punjab should aspire for the international standard in education. To achieve that goal it should adopt uniform international syllabus in its educational institutions.

16. *Personality Development*—Finally, education should be for the flowering of personality, but not for the suppression of creativity or natural skill. In the globalised world opportunities for the educated people are naturally ample in scope. As a result business process outsourcing (BPO) activities have increased competition in the world trade leading towards the production of quality goods and their easy availability everywhere in the world market. That is the way the world can be developed for peace, prosperity and progress by able and skilful men.

17. *Stipends to Research Fellows*—The number of Ph.Ds. from Universities should increase with proper standards. This should be seen in the context of extremely low fraction of Ph.Ds. in Punjab in relation to M.Sc./B.Tech., as compared to other states.

18. *Fair Quality Assurance System*—Colleges and Private institutes should set-up Internal Quality Assurance Cell and must follow a minimum standard to give degrees. The quality assurance system must be independent of political and institutional interaction and it must have a basis in the legislation. There should be operational, financial and academic autonomy coupled with accountability. There is a need of an independent accreditation agency with a conglomerate of government, industry, academia, society etc. means all stakeholders of the education to ensure that the stakeholders particularly the students are not taken for a ride. They should be able to know whether a particular institution delivers value or not, then things can be under control to some extent. It is also important that all institutes of higher learning must make public the acceptability of their courses and degrees (i.e. the status, recognition and acceptability of their courses by other institutions).

19. *Examination Reforms*—Examination reforms, gradually shifting from the terminal, annual and semester examinations to regular and continuous assessment of student's performance in learning should be implemented.

20. *High-tech Libraries*—Our university libraries have a very good collection of books, but they are all in mess. A library must be online and conducive for serious study. Universities should concentrate more on providing quality education which is comparable to that of international standards.[3]

Conclusion

According to Former Prime Minister of India Dr. Manmohan Singh "The time has come to create a second wave of institution building and of excellence in the fields of education, research and capability building." We need an educational system that is modern, liberal and can adapt to the changing needs of a changing society, a changing economy and a changing world. The thrust of public policy for higher education in Punjab has to be to address these challenges. However, one university cannot make much difference. If the government welcomes more such initiatives, the future will be ours. We will be able to match and compete with other states and countries.

NOTES

1. Ghuman, R.S. and *et al.* (2006). *Rural Students in Universities of Punjab*. Department of Economics, Research Project, Sponsored by Punjabi University, Patiala, Punjab.

2. The Indian states (2015) Opportunities for international higher education collaboration, *www.britishcouncil.org/education/ihe*.
3. Dr. J.D. Singh, *Higher Education in India: Issues, Challenges and Suggestions. www.google.com*

REFERENCES

Census 2011, New Delhi, Government of India.

Ghuman, R.S. and *et al.* (2006). *Rural Students in Universities of Punjab.* Department of Economics, research project, sponsored by Panjabi University, Patiala, Punjab.

Gill, S.S., S. Singh and J.S. Brar (2005). *Financing of Secondary Education: Grants in Aid Policies and Practices in Punjab*, A Report submitted to NIEPA, New Delhi.

Kaur, C. (1992). *Education in Punjab (A Historical Study)*, New Delhi: Intellectual Publishing House.

MHRD (2006). *Annual Report.* Ministry of Human Resource Development, Department of Secondary and Higher Education. Government of India. New Delhi.

Singh, J.D. *Higher Education in India—Issues, Challenges and Suggestions,* www.google.com

The Indian States (2015). Opportunities for international higher education collaboration, *www.britishcouncil.org/education/ihe*.

9

Secondary Teacher Education System in India with Special Emphasis on Respect of Administration, Supervision and Finance

Rakesh Manna and *Jayanta Mete*

Introduction

After independence education was a State subject in this country; the Central Government has neither any direct responsibility nor any Constitutional Right in its administration. The Central Government had responsibilities only for the education of minorities for promoting educational facilities for all parts of society. In 1976, an amendment was added to the Article 42 of the Constitution that transferred education from the State list of responsibilities to the Central Government. However, the Central Government helps the State Governments in the organisation and planning of Teacher Education. According to the recommendation of NPE 1986, education and training of primary teachers are organised in District Institutes of Education and Training (DIETs) and Primary Teachers' Training Institutions (PTTIs) under the supervision of concerned State Governments.

In India there are large number of variations in teacher education programmes including variations in the purpose for which persons join teacher training courses of various levels. There are four types of teacher education institutions: (a) State Government managed; (b) Examining body managed; (c) State Government aided and privately managed and

(d) Self-financed and privately managed. While certain States do not have any private teacher training institution, there are other States that have large numbers of recognised self-financed private teacher training institutions. Many States do not have examining bodies for pre-school teacher education. Though the teacher education institutions of Union Territories are organised and administered directly by the Central Government.

Education is not just to provide comfort to individual citizens, but to sustain society and that can only happen if education supports just a society and teachers student to believe in the possibility of a better future, Therefore, education must create a spirit of enquiry, teaching our children to challenge the status through education that imparts values, but does not indoctrinate. An important purpose of education is to enable an individual to honestly earn his/her live hood through skills that contribute to the national economy. Teacher education should help to improve skills raise aspiration and enable student to improve in life.

So, the governance of teacher education is the overarching framework. For the development of secondary teacher education administration, management, finance will give the highest priority into curriculum development, textbook development and teacher training etc.

In India National Policy of Education (NPE, 1986) formulates the administrative framework in secondary teacher education in whole India. But the State Government in all states partly controls the administration of Secondary teacher education.

Management of teacher education is a difficult task, especially at the present juncture where teacher education programmes are being delivered by a large number of untrained private teacher education institutions. In this chapter, the researcher has tried to examine the role of administrative agencies for supervision and management of elementary/primary and secondary teacher education system in India and specifically in West Bengal as well as the financial support for that.

Objectives of the Study

The study based on the following objectives:

(i) To find out the Administrational role of Secondary Teacher Education in India.
(ii) To find out the Supervisional role of Secondary Teacher Education in India.

Administration, Supervision and Finance of Secondary Teacher Education System in India

Administration and Supervision in Elementary/Primary Teacher Education

Department of Elementary Education and Literacy of Ministry of Human Resource Development of the Government of India is the apex body that looks after policy for teacher education. Its agencies include National Council for Teacher Education (NCTE), National Council of Educational Research and Training (NCERT) and National University for Educational Planning and Administration (NUEPA). At the National Level, the National Council of Educational Research and Training (NCERT), along with its 6 Regional Institutes of Education (RIEs) prepares a host of training modules and undertakes specific programmes for training of teachers and teacher educators. Institutional Support is also provided by the National University on Educational Planning and Administration (NUEPA). Both NCERT and NUEPA are national level autonomous bodies. University Grants Commission (UGC) is also involved with Departments of Teacher education or Departments of Education in the Universities.

At the State level, the apex body that looks after teacher education is the Government Department of Education/State Board of Education. In certain States, it is looked after by the Department of School Education. A few States have independent Directorates for teacher education. In a few others, the Directorate and SCERT function under one Director. In certain States all teacher education institutions are managed by the States Government. In certain other States, majority of teacher training institution are managed by private agencies under self-financed category. There are teacher training institutions being run by the Departments of Tribal Welfare and other administrative departments. Creation of separate cadre for teacher educators has been an important issue to be solved in many States.

The State Councils of Educational Research and Trainings (SCERTs) prepare modules for teacher training and conducts some specialised courses for teacher educators and primary school teachers. The Colleges of Teacher Educations (CTEs) and Institutes for Advanced Learning in Educations (IASEs) provide in-service training to secondary school teachers and teacher educators.

At the district level, in-service training is provided by the District Institutes of Education and Trainings (DIETs). The Block Resource

Centres (BRCs) and Cluster Resource Centres (CRCs) form the lowest rung of institutions for providing in-service training to school teachers.

Role of National Council for Teacher Education (NCTE)

The National Council for Teacher Education was established by an act of Parliament in 1993. NCTE functions through the following Standing Committees:

1. Pre-primary, primary teachers' education committee.
2. Secondary collage-teacher education committee.
3. Special education-teacher education committee.
4. In-service teacher education committee.

According to the Act 1993, NCTE performs the following functions:

1. Undertake survey and studies relating to various aspects of teacher education and publish the results.
2. Making recommendations to the Central and State Government Universities, the U.G.C. and other institutions in the preparation of plans and programmes in the field of teacher education.
3. Coordinating and monitoring teacher education and its development in the country.
4. Preparing a guideline with regard to minimum qualifications for the candidates to be employed as teacher educators at different levels.
5. Developing norms for any specified category of courses or training in teacher-education, including minimum eligibility criterion for admission.
6. Preparing a guideline and specified requirements for starting new courses and programmes under teacher education.
7. Developing a guideline for general teacher-education programme.
8. To advise Central Government on matters like teacher education (in building pre-service/in-service training), evaluation of the curricula for teacher education and periodical review with respect to revision of curricula.
9. To advise State Governments on any matter of their concern.
10. To review the progress of plan of teacher-education, submitted by Central/State Governments.

11. To advise the government on ensuring adequate standards in teacher education.
12. To give approval to teacher education institutions.
13. To lay down norms for maintaining standards of teachers education.
14. Promoting innovations and research studies and organise them periodically or annually.
15. Supervising the teacher education programmes and providing financial assistance.
16. Enforcing accountability of teacher development programmes in the country.
17. Preparing a programme for in-service teacher education for orienting teachers for latest development.

Role of National Council for Educational Research and Training (NCERT)

Ministry of Education of Government of India established NCERT in 1961. The functions of NCERT broadly relate to (a) research and development; (b) in-service and pre-service training; and (c) extension and dissemination work—all these tuned to achieve the main objective of improving the quality of school education.

The NCERT, therefore, performs the following functions regarding teacher education:

1. Develops curriculum, instructional and exemplar materials, methods of teaching, techniques of evaluation, teaching aids, kits and equipments, learning resources etc.
2. To monitor the administration of National Institute of Education/ Regional Institutes of Education.
3. Organizes pre-service and in-service training of teachers, teacher educators and other educational personnel.
4. Disseminates improved educational techniques and practices and research findings.
5. Acts as a cleaning house for ideas and information on all matters relating to school education and teacher education.

Role of National University for Educational Planning and Administration (NUEPA)

As the highest organisation of educational planning and administration NUEPA (formerly known as NIEPA—National University of Educational Planning and Administration) has the following functions to perform:

1. Providing training of educational planning and administration to develop the abilities and competencies in the educational administration as the in-service programme.
2. Providing training facilities in educational planning and administration at state level and regional level to develop efficiency at their level.
3. Integrating educational studies and researches under the area of educational planning and administration and make co-ordinations in these activities.
4. Encouraging the teachers to solve the problems of educational planning and administration by organising seminars and workshops.
5. Arranging extension programmes for new developments and innovations in the area of planning and administration.
6. Establishing contact with other countries to understand the development and innovations of the developed countries.
7. Providing guidance at National and State levels in the area of planning and administration.
8. Multi-dimensional activities under extension programmes, journal on educational planning and administration and other book are published.
9. Review of educational planning and administration of other countries-used to develop our educational system and solve educational problems.
10. Orientation programmes for educational administrators-provide awareness of new developments in this area.
11. Educational research reports are published. The publication unit established the coordination between theory and practice.
12. Seminars and workshops are organised and their discussions and results are published.
13. Training Institutions for special fields for school and collages these provide elementary in special fields, like computers, educational technology and fine arts.

Role of State Council for Educational Research and Training (SCERT)

State Institutes of Education (SIEs) were established in some States in mid-60s to organise in-service training for teacher and supervisory personnel, extension activities, research and publication of instructional materials, and to provide academic support to the school education in areas like science education, educational technology, English language teaching, examination reforms, evaluation, educational and vocational guidance etc. As the support to the school system increased, the then Ministry of Education and Social Welfare recommended in 1973 that all such existing institutions be merged into a single organisation to be called State Council of Educational Research and Training (SCERT).

At present, there are SCERTs in 25 States and State Institutes of Education (SIEs) in Assam, Arunachal Pradesh, Jammu & Kashmir (2), Sikkim, Andaman and Nicobar Islands, Uttar Pradesh and Chandigarh (Report of NCERT, 2009). Now, SCERT is the apex institute of the State. A 'model' structure of the SCERT is proposed taking into account the various functions of the SCERTs.

The Role and Functions of SCERT are primarily concerned with ensuring quality in respect of: Planning, Management, Research, Evaluation and Training. Its functions are as under:

1. Review of existing Teacher Education Institutions in the State like DIETs, CTEs, IASEs, University Departments of Education, Government and Private PTTIs in terms of:
    - Structure
    - Role
    - Recruitment/Placement Policy
    - Intake capacity at various levels
    - Linkage with Schools and BRCs/CRCs
    - Linkage with academic institutions for academic support and nature of support
    - Annual output of teachers by stage and subject
    - Curriculum of various teacher education programmes
    - Evaluation of quality of Teacher Education in the state
2. Review of performance of Teacher Education Institutions related to teacher education and secondary education curriculum and material development, support to schools, DIETs, BRCs, CRCs etc.
3. Review of quality of pre-service education-curriculum and programmes.
4. Review of in-service education about coverage, quality, impact and follow-up.
5. Review of Modalities for teacher education and professional development of teacher educators.

Role of State Board of Teacher Education (SBTE)

Kothari Commission for the first time in 1966 recommended for establishing SBTE, whose main function was to develop teacher education in the State to be administered by the State Board. State Boards were established in Madhya Pradesh in 1967, and Maharashtra, Jammu & Kashmir and Tamil Nadu in 1973. Ministry of Education forced States to established SBTE in almost all States in India.

Functions of SBTE

1. Determining the standards of Teacher Education Institutions (TEIs).
2. Modifying and improving the curriculum, text books and the system of Teacher Education of the State.
3. Developing the criterion for the recognition of the TEIs.
4. Organizing the guidance facility of TEIs.
5. Developing the criteria for admission is TEIs and evaluating the teacher efficiency of student-teachers.
6. Preparing the plan for the qualitative and quantitative and quantitative development of teacher education.
7. Providing guidance to the Universities and State institutes for improving and modifying curriculum, textbooks and examination system of teacher education programmes.
8. Determining the educational and physical conditions of the TEIs for affiliations.
9. Developing the sense of cooperation among university departments and other training institutions.
10. Providing suggestions for the development of state teacher educators.

Role of District Institutes of Education and Training (DIETs)

1. Providing pre-service and in-service education programmes for elementary teachers.
2. Organizing District level and State level Educational Researches on issues pertaining to enrolment, retention, achievement, gender parity, proficiency and drop outs.
3. Providing training and orientation of Heads of institutions in institutional planning in management.

4. Providing academic support to School Complex and District Boards of Education.
5. Facilitating Collaborative Action Researches to enable practicing teachers to address class room processes.
6. Scouting Innovative Practice of Primary/Upper Primary teachers and disseminating them among their colleagues by organizing periodical District Level Seminars and releasing News Bulletins which carry information on innovative class room processes.
7. Providing Resource Support to Non-formal education sector by extending DIET expertise in developing curriculum and supplementary Learning Materials to adult learners.
8. Designing and developing trainer Manuals for *Anganwadi* workers and for addressing social concerns such as Crisis and Disaster Management, Gender Sensitivity, Leadership Manual for School Heads etc.

The NCERT in its Report of August 2009 on Comprehensive Evaluation of the Centrally Sponsored Scheme on Teacher Education has underscored the need to restructure the existing BRCs (Block Resource Centre's) and CRCs (Cluster Resource Centre's) to revamp the present system of in-service training of untrained teachers. Strengthening and streamlining the roles and functions of BRCs need special attention. An important requirement is that BRCs and CRCs work on close coordination with the DIETs.

The revised SSA Implementation Framework of SSA (2011) has recommended strengthening of the BRCs, Urban Resource Centre's (URCs) and CRCs for providing academic support to teachers. BRCs/URCs and CRCs are the most critical units for providing training and on-site support to schools and teachers.

Finance in Elementary/Primary Teacher Education

From two sources funds are allocated for education of primary/elementary teachers, namely, (i) C.S. (Centrally Sponsored) and S.P. (State Plan). Financial support for in-service training of primary and/or elementary teachers is provided by the Central Government through the Sarva Shiksha Abhiyan (SSA) and the Centrally Sponsored Scheme on Teacher Education. In many states State Board of Teacher Education (SBTE) providing financial assistance for teacher education at different levels.

Administration and Management in Secondary Teacher Education

The Fifth All India Educational Survey (1986) indicates that about 87 per cent of primary and upper primary teachers were trained, i.e. they have acquired a primary or elementary teacher training certificate after alone or two year course or a bachelor's degree in education. There were, however, significant regional variations of the total number of teachers working at the secondary and higher secondary levels, approximate 90 per cent are trained, i.e. they have a bachelor's degree in education. The per centage of trained teachers at both the levels is the highest in Chandigarh (99.8% and 100% respectively).

Teachers are autonomous in the management of their own classes. They are encouraged to undertake experimentation and action research and are provided incentives, both at the state and national levels. The National Council of Educational Research and Training (NCERT) is an apex resource organisation set-up in September, 1961 with headquarters at New Delhi, assists and advises the Central and State Governments on academic matters related to school education. The Council is fully funded by the Government of India.

NCERT provides academic and technical support for qualitative improvement of school education through its constituent Departments of National Institute of Education (NIE) at New Delhi, Central Institute of Educational Technology (CIET), at New Delhi, Pandit Sundarlal Sharma Centre Institute of Vocational Education (PSSCIVE) at Bhopal, Bhubaneswar, Mysore and Shillong. The Council conducts, aids, promotes and coordinates research in school education and teacher education, organise pre-service and in-service training of teachers, extension services for institutions; develops and experiments with improved educational techniques, practices and innovations, collects, compiles, processes and disseminates educational information, assists the states/UTs in developing and implementing programmes for qualitative improvement of school education. Collaborates with international organisation serves as the academic secretariat of the National Development Group (NDG) for the Asia and the Pacific Programme of Education Innovation for Development (APEID). UNESCO, Bangkok are develops prints and distributes textual materials etc.

In order to improve the quality of the teacher's education, the following steps have been recommended:

(a) Introduction of reform in the system of selection of teacher.
(b) Improvement in the living and working conditions of teacher.

(c) Creation of effective machinery for removal of grievances.
(d) Involvement of teachers in planning and management of education.
(e) Involvement of teacher's in upholding the dignity professional misconducts.
(f) Perfection of code of professional ethics for teachers and ensuring that teachers perform their duties in accordance with it.
(g) Willingness to take decisions with regard to the observation of an effective machinery and professional ethics.
(h) Creation of opportunities and atmosphere to promote autonomy and innovation among teachers.

The National Council for Teacher Education (NCTE) established by an act of parliament in August 1995 provides for achieving planned and coordinated development of teacher education system and regulation and proper maintenance of norms and standards of teacher education in the country. The NCTE is fully funded by Central Government. As on June 2002, 2578 teacher education institutions were recognised by NCTE.

The mandate of the NCTE is quite wide and includes regulatory as well as developmental functions. Some of the major functions are laying down of norms for various teacher education courses, recognition of teacher education institutions, laying down of guidelines in respect of minimum qualification for appointment of teacher, surveys and studies, research and innovation, prevention of commercialisation of teacher education etc.

The National Council for Teacher Education (NCTE) which is a statutory body responsible for achieving planned and coordinated development of the teacher education system throughout the country. The main functions of National Council of Teacher Education (NCTE) are as follows:

- To advise the Government of India on all matters concerning teacher education, including pre-service and in-service training, evaluation of curriculum for teacher education and periodical review of progress in revising the curriculum.
- To advise the State Government any matters to the Council by them.
- To review the programmes of plan schemes, both Central and State, concerning teacher education.
- To advise the government on ensuring the adequate standard in teacher education.

The educational reforms in education seek to develop pedagogical skills of school teachers, adult and non-formal functionaries and teacher educations in the country. The reforms envisage setting-up of District Institutions of Education and Training (DIETs) in each district to provide academic and resource support to elementary education teachers and Non Formal Education (NFE)/Adult Education (AE) instructions. They also envisages upgradation of Selected Secondary Teacher Education Institutions (STEIs) into Colleges of Teacher Education (CTEs) and Institutes of Advanced Studies in Education (IASEs) to organise pre-service and in-service training for secondary teachers and to provide extension and resource support services to secondary schools.

485 DIETs, 86 CTEs and 38 IASEs have been sanctioned in various states/UTs till now. Financial assistance has also extended for strengthening of 20 States Councils of Education Research and Training (SCERTs). More than 20 lakh teachers have been given orientation training under Special Orientation Programme for School Teachers (SOPT) in the use of Operation Blackboard (OB) material and implementation of Minimum Levels of Training (MLT) strategy with focus on teaching of Language, Mathematics and Environmental studies.

Finance in Secondary Teacher Education

Finance provision for teachers Education is included provisions for Secondary Education as well as University Education, in the departmental plans. In the absence of specific allocations for teacher education, it is difficult to judge adequacy of funds. However, there is currently a glut of trained teachers as certain states in the country; consequently, funding may be considered sufficient for training out the numbers required, but if the aim is to provide quality input teacher training institution. For which financial resources are crucial the funds are inadequate.

Important functions of University Grants Commission (1956) are:

- To maintain standard of quality in teacher training institution.
- Recently teacher education institutions to be assessed.

Important function of NCTE (Act 1987) are:

- Statutory body to develop norms and standards of teacher education.

- Powers to give recognition to teacher education institutions offering various courses.
- Planned and coordinated development of teacher education institutions.

The number of elementary and secondary teacher training institution has also increased. In 1979-1980 there were about 945 (presently above 1000) elementary teacher training institutions in the country with a total enrolment of 87,382. In 1970-80 there were about 338 (presently 600) secondary teacher training institutions is in the country a total enrolment of 56,339.51 academic staff collages for academic training of teachers.

Administration, Supervision and Finance of Secondary Teacher Education System in West Bengal

The West Bengal Board of Primary Education (WBBPE) is the administrative body of primary teacher education system in West Bengal. WBBPE is functioning to manage, control and to conduct the examination at various PTTIs. Similarly, various Universities' Education Department is the administrative body of secondary teacher education system in West Bengal. Both also gives affiliation to all NCTE recognised PTTIs and B.Ed. including Government, Government aided and Self-financed PTTIs and B.Ed. colleges respectively. DIETs are linked to the substructures of SSA, WBBPE and SCERT. SSA provides funding to DIETs for many of their programmes, WBBPE is only administrative body and SCERT extends academic support at times.

The academic and administrative responsibility of the DIETs was delegated to SCERT, West Bengal on 29-01-2013. In West Bengal SCERT was formed in 1980, but the State Government had not envisaged a key role for them till recently.

In West Bengal, SCERT will be designed as academic authority from 2014 and needs to be empowered and strengthened to play this crucial role. In order to strengthen the linkage between SCERT, DIETs, BRCs, CRCs, the West Bengal SCERT has proposed the following initiatives for 2013-14:

- In-service Education of Teachers at the primary, upper-primary and secondary level in the state of West Bengal by which the linkage between the different teacher education institutions (TIEs) is expected to be strengthened.

- *Managing Change*: Capacity Building of SCERT and DIETs personnel proposal under which SCERT will organise a series of residential capacity building workshops for the Academic Officers of SCERT, DIET Officials, SPO and DPO Officials and the PCP coordinators who are *ex-officio* of the schools (SI/S).

In India, State Government partly control the administration of secondary teacher education institutions. But they have to maintain SCERTs (State Councils of Educational Research and Training), 1961 rules and regulation. In India as well as in West Bengal, SCERT and University control the secondary teacher education programme.

Findings

The researcher found that:

(i) At the National level, NCTE mandate the norms and standard of teacher education, NCERT along with its 6 RIEs prepare training modules and undertake specific programmes for training of teachers and teacher educators, and institutional support is provided by the NUEPA.

(ii) At the State Level, the State Council of Educational Research and Training (SCERTs) prepare modules for teacher training and conducts some specialised courses for teacher educators and primary school teachers and universities educational department prepare the syllabus for secondary school teachers (according to NCTE norms).

(iii) At the District level, in-service training is provided by the District Institutes of Education and Training (DIETs).

(iv) Financial support for in-service training of primary and/or elementary teachers is mainly provided by the Central Government through the Sarva Shiksha Abhiyan (SSA) and the Centrally Sponsored Scheme on teacher education. State Government also release fund for that purpose.

(v) University Grants Commission (1956) play a great role to maintain standard of quality in teacher training institution. Recently, teacher education institutions to be assessed by the UGC.

Conclusion

Education and training of secondary teachers are organised and control by NCERT and various Universities under the supervision of concerned State Governments. At the National level, NCTE mandate the norms and standard of teacher education, NCERT along with its 6 RIEs prepare training modules and undertake specific programmes for training of teachers and teacher educators, and institutional support is provided by the NUEPA. At the State level, the State Council of Educational Research and Training (SCERTs) prepare modules for teacher training and conducts some specialised courses for teacher educators and primary school teachers. At the district level, in-service training is provided by the District Institute of Education and Training (DIETs). The Block Resource Centre's (BRCs) and Cluster Resources Centre's (CRCs) are also providing in-service training to school teachers. Financial support for in-service training of primary and/or elementary teachers is mainly provided by the Central Government through the Sarva Shiksha Abhiyan (SSA) and the Centrally Sponsored Scheme on Teacher Education. State Government also release fund for that purpose. In West Bengal, the West Bengal Board of Primary Education (WBBPE) is the administrative body of Primary Teacher Education System, which affiliate, manage, control and conduct examination of various PTTIs. From 29 January, 2013, the academic and administrative responsibility of the DIETs was delegated to SCERT, West Bengal. In India State Government partly control the administration of secondary teacher's education institutions. In India, NCERT and University control the secondary teacher education programme. They have to maintain NCERTs, 1961 rules and regulations.

REFERENCES

A Joint Review Mission on Teacher Education for West Bengal, MHRD, Government of India, 2013, 12, 21-22.

Behera, L. and Basantia, K.T. (2005). Evaluation of the Elementary Level Pre-service Teacher Education Syllabus in Orissa. *Indian Educational Review*, 41.2, 96-117.

Chopra, R.K. (2000). Working Conditions of Primary School Teachers in Rural and Urban Settings: A Comparative Study. *Journal of Educational Research and Extension,* 37.2, 21-35.

Government of India, Ministry of Human Resource Development (2008). *Annual Report, 2007-2008.* New Delhi.

Government of India, Planning Commission (2007). *Working Group Report on Elementary Education and Literacy, XI Five Year Plan*, pp. 187-190. New Delhi.

Guidelines for Implementation, 2012 of Centrally Sponsored Scheme on Teacher Education, MHRD, Government of India, 97, 71 and 10.

N. Venkataiah, *Teacher Education*, 240.

Solachi, T. (2003). *A Study of Training Technology in DIETs in Tamil Nadu: A System Analysis*. Ph.D. Education, Alagappa University, Karaikudi.

Sudarsan, S., (2001). Attitude of Teachers towards Team Teaching at the Primary Level. *Journal of Educational Research and Extension,* 38.1.

The Gazette of India (2009). *Right of Children to Free and Compulsory Education Act*, 2009, p. 9. New Delhi.

10
Value Oriented Education

Issue of Concern

Julie Chhetri

The Context

India has been a land of ethics, spirituality, religious tradition, culture, arts and literature. India is blessed with unity in diversity. Indian education system during the Vedic period had given due importance to the teachings of values to the children. Untiring efforts by some Indian sages and seers of that time had developed priceless heritage of Indian culture. But the continuity of our great cultural and educational tradition has been broken by religious fundamentalism, communalism, caste factors and so on. The social atrocities occurring in Indian society constantly reminds that there has been a substantial erosion of values, the fabric of the society is being torn and age-old ties are breaking-up. Students, the future saviours of the society, are getting increasingly inclined towards violence, social evil and lack of respect towards world around them. Their respect for parents teachers and society in general is vanishing. Most of the problems today in our country are created not by uneducated but by educated youth. The question arises as to why our children are lacking in values today. The answer is loud and clear. Our present education system, our family system and our present society, they all have misguided priorities. Our children are getting deprived of value education in their early life when their hearts are pure and brains are fully receptive. Though value education can be given at any stage, still its efficacy is much more when given in early stages of life. Practically speaking schools in India have no interest in subject like spiritual education. Secondly, parents are responsible. They blindly accept whatever the children do without bothering to correct them. Today, only worry of the parents is to prepare their children for entry into some reputed school. Thirdly, our society is also equally responsible in spoiling its youth. Our media and cinema are always presenting us the stories which show that men with values are suffering in life. Recent crisis in values that our country has been currently facing has revived the concern for value education.

Value-oriented Education—Concept

Value comes from the Latin word 'Valēre' which means to be worth, to be strong. Values are bricks which are used to build the strong wall of character. The term value covers the entire domain of the development of an integrated personality.

Value orientation should be one of the main objectives of education to develop student's integrated personality so that he may contribute his best to the country. The content of education has to be value-oriented. Value-oriented education does not imply only moral education. It has a wider connotation and includes all the subjects as well as all the teachers who can correlate their lessons to higher purpose and meaning in life for their students. It does not merely imply an intellectual discussion on the theme of syllabus in various disciplines but also practice of those values in day-to-day life by the students and teachers. It is, therefore, imperative that value-oriented education should be the core of all stages of education, i.e. from primary to higher education.

Functions of Value education will have the following features:

- It will be integrated with the present syllabi and text.
- It will be handled by the same teachers with the fact and imagination and taught through their subjects.
- It will be demonstrated by the teachers and students through their day-to-day behaviour in educational institution and community.
- It will be taught through various co-curricular activities organised meaningfully in the classroom and outside the classroom.

Need of Value-oriented Education

- Foremost thing is that human behaviour cannot be determined and regularized in the absence of values. Value education is needed in order to guide individuals in the right direction.

- Secondly, values are depreciating not only in our country, but all over the world. We are giving-up the old values and are not able to determine the new ones. Therefore, value education is very essential in our country.
- Trust, love and compassion have been lost and all people look at each other in suspicion. Family relations are breaking down. Lawlessness rules in the society and people are living a stressful life. It appears that if we do not awake in time, we will re-enter the barbarous period. If we want to protect human civilisation and culture, we will have to lay emphasis on the value education.
- All education commissions, committees and policies have stressed on the need of value education and the schools should play a special role in it.
- Value education is required because Indian society is facing tremendous value crisis. There is urgent need to revive and reform the values of human life.

Recommendation of Various Commissions and Committees for Value Education

Values are not inborn in nature. No one is born with set of values relating to events, situations, practices, individuals or institutions. These are shaped, nurtured and developed at home and educational institutions. Various commissions and committees at National and International levels have advocated in favour of giving a value orientation to education. Some of the recommendations of the commissions are as follows:

I. University Education Commission (1948-49)

It strongly advocated for imparting religious education so that our youths are not drifted towards immorality and indiscipline, regionalism and scepticism.

II. Secondary Education Commission (1952-53)

It stressed the need for imparting education for development of personality of the students.

III. Sri Prakash Committee (1959)

This is a committee which was appointed specially for religious and moral education that laid emphasis on inculcation of good manners, social services and love for the country.

IV. National Policy on Education (1986)

The policy document devotes a small section on value education under part-VIII-Reorienting the content and process of education to be "based on our cultural heritage, national goals and universal perceptions".

1.4 Strategies for Value Orientation to Education

The strategies for value education can be discussed under four heads: What, How, When and Who.

I. What Kinds of Values are to be Inculcated?

What values are to be inculcated among the children and youth? Various commissions and committees, experts, spiritual leaders, researchers and scholars have offered various suggestions in this regard. The following value which fosters moral, spiritual, national and human values are to be instilled among the learners:

- Democratic spirit, secularism socialism and Justice (fairness).
- World citizenship.
- Scientific temper.
- Honesty, integrity, courage and cooperation, discipline and conduct.
- Equality of sexes/gender equality.
- Caring for the social, economic and ecological welfare of the society and the Nation.
- Caring for other species (animals and birds).
- Caring for truth, goodness and beauty.

II. How are Values to be Imparted?

Value education can be imparted through following approaches:

- **Direct Approach:** Instruction in values can be given by an experienced and competent teacher of the school, a retired Headmaster or a spiritual leader in a specified period of the school timetable. This may require readjustment in the school time-table and may cause an increase in the workload of the particular teacher.
- **Indirect Approach**: Value based themes can be incorporated at appropriate points in different subjects such as Language, science, history etc. There is no necessity of a separate period or special books for value education. Every teacher has to be a teacher of values.
- **Incidental Approach:** Specific values can be imparted on appropriate occasions. For example, acts of courage, bravery, discipline etc. can be highlighted on various occasions in the school such as morning assembly, sports day etc.
- **Value Clarification Approach:** The value clarification approach may be followed by the teacher to discuss about a problem involving value conflict such as small family norm. In this approach the teacher is not an expert on values. He is to create an atmosphere for the students which will help them to explore values, clarify their doubts, choose appropriate values and behave accordingly.

III. When is the Right Time to Impart Value?

Value orientation to education should begin at the grassroots level such as primary education and continue throughout school, college and university education. The time and duration of such instruction should vary depending upon the school factors, availability of suitable learning materials, availability of guest speakers, interest of students etc.

IV. Who can Impart Value Education?

Value education is the responsibility of any single teacher. In fact every teacher should be a teacher of values. It should not be the sole responsibility of teachers only. In an informal way parents transmit values to their children. Community members also have a major role to play in this regard. However, just as in other cases, the school has a major role to play in giving a value orientation to education. The following personnel can render service to humanity by helping children and youth learn essential values:

- Spiritual leaders,
- NCC cadets,
- Community leaders, and
- Retired teachers.

Role of Teacher

"Destiny of India is being shaped in the classrooms."—Dr. Kothari. This statement puts a huge responsibility upon the teachers. The statement is made with the belief that teachers are the builders of the society. Directly or indirectly they influence their students, hence teachers should present themselves as ideals. They should be honest, sincere, punctual and should follow the professional ethics. They should devote time for discussion with the students. Discussion should be made informal, outside the classrooms also, not on contents but on social problems, individual problems faced by the students and on social values. It is the role of a teacher to make the children realise about the depth, magnitude and significance of values.

A very old saying, "values are caught and not taught", is also not relevant today due to undesirable situations and persons in society. Therefore, values need to be taught as well as caught. The teacher through his thoughts, words and deeds should give an impression of an honest, upright life which can serve as a model for the students to copy, follow and emulate. Teacher must become a model of selfless service. The role of teacher in developing desirable values among students is very significant. The teacher, therefore, needs to be equipped with appropriate value inculcation strategies.

Conclusion

At present when moral and spiritual values are disintegrated, when religion is loosing its hold, when power and knowledge are being misused, it is essential that education for values should be imparted. The political tension at the present times is mainly due to the fact that knowledge has increased but values have lagged behind. The challenge before us is to revive our country and all sections of our society by inculcation of right type of values. The present situation in India demands such a system of education which apart from strengthening national unit must strengthen social solidarity through meaningful and constructive value education by adopting the inter-disciplinary approach. To live in a blissful consciousness let us join our hand to create the value-oriented climate in the school, colleges and the society. Our co-ordinated efforts are bound to give us fruit—the fruit of shining India.

REFERENCES

Chaudhary, A.K. (2013). Value Education: The Need of the Nation. *University News*. April, 2013. Vol. 51, No. 14.

Dash, N. (2003). Strategies for Value Education. *Edutracks*. April, 2003. Vol. 2, No.8.

Hafeez, Q. (2003). Value Education without Moral Science Textbook. *Edutracks*. August, 2003. Vol. 2, No. 12.

Malhotra and Lal (2009). *Education in Emerging Indian Society*. Meerut: Raj Printers.

Mundase, V. (2014). Value Education: A pathway to Global Paradise. *Edutracks*. December, 2014. Vol. 14, No. 4.

Sharma, R.A. (2007). *Human Values and Education*. Meerut: Raj Printers.

Venkataiah, N. (1998). *Value Education*, New Delhi: APH Publishing Corporation.

11
Paulo Freire's Concept on Trivialization of Conscientisation

Nimmi Maria Oommen

Introduction

Education, in the broad sense, is the formation of man as a person and a member of society. It must aim at the enrichment of human personality by building-up a strong character and by developing a sense of responsibility for the future, personal convictions and spirit of service. Education is not only the property of the privileged. Each human being has the right to acquire knowledge to develop his skills and critical thinking and to improve his living with a concern for the society. Education should inculcate the values of social commitment, social justice, promotion of human rights, equality of women and the under privileged classes and instill the thoughts of national integration.

No contemporary writer more persistently explored the many dimensions of critical consciousness than Paulo Freire, a multi-cultural educator with the whole world as his classroom notwithstanding the totally Brazilian flavour of his emotions, his languages and his universe of thought. The idea that education can and should act as a liberating agent has been the inspiration of many leading educators in the past. It is here that Paulo Freire offers a powerful challenge to all those who are committed to the liberation of the masses.

Paulo Freire admits that he has adopted this term (Brazilian form: Conscientizacao process) which he first heard at a round table conference with some professors at the Brazilian Institute of higher studies (ISED) in 1964. But, Bordenave (1977) states that it was the young Catholic university student of Barzil who coined the word in 1961-62 and defined it as, "the discovery of the self and the dignity of the human person together with the realisation that the person in cooperative association with other persons can humanise the world". Helder Camera was the one, according to Freire, who popularised the term and gave it in English.

The literal meaning of the word conscientisation is "to make aware" or "awakening of consciousness" or "critical consciousness". But for Freire, conscientisation is a political educational process which enables the masses to overcome "false consciousness" to realise their real situation in society and to take part in changing society in the capacity of subjects.

Freire refers to the French expression, "prise de conscience", which is often taken as synonymous with conscientisation. But he distinguishes them. For him "prise de conscience" is only the first level of apprehension of reality. Conscientisation is a prise de conscience that goes deeper; it is the critical development of a prise de conscience. Conscientisation implies going beyond the spontaneous phase of apprehension of reality to a critical phase, where reality become a knowable object, where man tries to know it.

According to Freire, the more a person conscientizes himself, the more he unveils reality and gets at the phenomenic essence of the object, he stands in front of, to analyse it. Therefore, conscientisation cannot exist without praxis, i.e. without action-reflection as two paired dialecticised elements permanently constituting that special way of being in the world (or transforming it) that is peculiar to man (Freire, 1970).

The dialectic can be expressed as:

> The four dimensions emerge out of the combination and dialectic of the two levels of critical concern (structural and psychological). They also encompass action and reflection at both levels.

Ideology refers to the presence of critical social awareness. By itself it does not constitute conscientisation because, "To recognise one's oppression is the beginning of the process of liberation" (Freire, 1970). A distortion which stresses only this aspect to the neglect of the other three is mere indoctrination. Transformation of structure occurs when critical knowledge motivates social action. This contributes to further development of ideology in a cyclical fashion. As Engels writes, "The more they (human beings) make their history themselves consciously, the less becomes the influence of unforeseen effects." But, when structural action edges out reflection, the result is "pure activism". This is so because ".... action will constitute authentic praxis only if its consequence becomes the object of critical reflection". When the individual, because of his social action becomes conscious of his historical role and becomes "self-conscious" the result is social identification. When man becomes aware of his own humanness, a behavioural change occurs which qualitatively alters his social functioning and interaction. But action merely to change behaviour without taking structural issues into account becomes 'psychologism'.

Educational programmes can be identified as being more academic (reflective rather than active); as being more person oriented (psychological rather than structural); or as more ideologically oriented. This point to an ongoing debate about the starting point of a conscientisation process aimed at social change. The important thing is that collectively these dimensions form part of a much broader process. And in this conscientisation of people has a vital role to play, in that it encapsulates all the aspects of the person's education so as to make him a more full human being.

Conscientisation is a historical commitment. It is a critical insertion in history. This implies that men and women take the role of the agents, makers, and re-makers of the world. In this process, the first step is to discover oneself as oppressed. In discovering oneself as oppressed, one should know that liberation is in knowing that something can be done and in trying to transform the oppressing situation in which one is. Conscientisation thus implies a critical insertion in the praxis and the process of historical change. It is social process, taking place among men as they unite in common reflection and action upon this world.

For Freire, conscientisation is an invitation to take a utopian attitude to the world. For him utopia is not that which cannot be real, its not idealism. "Utopia is the dialectical process of denouncing and announcing-denouncing the oppressing structure and announcing the humanising structure. It is, therefore, a historical commitment and engagement. Utopia is an act of knowing critically" (Freire, 1970). Freire is convinced that if we are not utopian we will easily become bureaucratic and dehumanising; the typical risk faced by all revolutions. For Freire, revolution must be permanent and it must be cultural revolution—a continuous cultural self-criticism of men in society and word. As he aptly summarises "conscientizacao is a permanent critical approach to reality in order to discover it and discover the myths that deceive us and help to maintain in the oppressing de-humanising structures."

The Process of Conscientisation

The Freirean approach conceives education as a process of 'conscientisation' and seeks practices consonant with this aim. The "how" of conscientisation implies a basic starting point: the distinction between education as an instrument of domination. That is, Banking approach to education and education as an instrument of liberation, i.e. Problem—posing approach to education.

The banking type of education is designed to prevent critical thinking and perpetuate the *status quo*. Here the educator is the guardian of a secret. He teaches and the students are taught. The teacher is the one who know, thinks, talks, disciplines, chooses the content acts and so on. Only he is the subject in the learning process. It is the "digestive or nutritive" concept of education. The teacher just deposits ready-made bits of knowledge in the students which they have to memorise and repeat. The students are passive and encouraged to adapt rather than question. It is in brief, a process of "domestication" an exercise in domination.

"Problem-posing education" on the other hand is an act of knowing together, where the teacher and the learners enter into a "dialogue" through which they investigate the problems together. The basic assumptions are that "no one can teach anyone else", "no one can learn along" and that "people learn together, acting in and on their world". Learning is critical analysis, deepening self-perception and confidence building. The mode of learning is dialogue, in which love, humility, hope and faith prevail. "The approach abolishes authoritarian in the class room, ends irrelevance and encourages critical thinking about society. Hence, it is a process of 'liberation' a practice of freedom" (Youngman, 1986:156). For Freire, problem posing education is the alternate way which leads to conscientisation.

According to Freire, consciousness is determined by the socio-economic and political context, and also by cultural conditioning through one's upbringing, education and religion. In other words, it is an interchange between economic and cultural structures.

Freire distinguishes *three* different levels of consciousness.

Magical Consciousness

Such people adapt themselves defencelessly and passively to the expectation of a superior force: they are not conscious of the socio-economic contradictions within this society; they accept life for what it is and do not question injustices done to their lives. They are silent and docile.

Naïve Consciousness

This involves gaining insight into and becoming aware of one's own problems, but without making connections with the world outside—in other words individualising problems. Problems are more or less seen as coincidences, accidents etc.

Critical Consciousness

Such people stop looking at problem as mostly individual accident, but see them more as structural problems. Critical consciousness involves making connection with the socio-economic contradictions in society. It means looking at reality and recognising such contractions as fact.

Freire suggests three stages in the progression by which critical consciousness is attained (1973). The first of these stages is semi-intransitive consciousness. Verbs which do not act upon an object are intransitive. Consciousness of and action upon reality are two constituents of a critical relationship with the world. Consciousness of and action upon reality are two constituents of a critical relationship with the world. Consciousness which does not challenge the world is, therefore, uncritical and intransitive, for it does not act upon the world as an object. Total intransitivity is not a form of consciousness at all. Therefore, the first phase in the emergence of consciousness is, for Freire, semi-intransitivity. Semi-intransitive consciousness is the state of those whose sphere of perception is limit, whose interests centre almost totally around matters of survival, and who are impermeable to challenges situated outside the demands of biological necessity. Freire observes that when these persons amplify their power to perceive and respond to suggestions and questions arising in their context, and increase their capacity to enter into dialogue not only with others, but with their own world, their consciousness becomes transitive.

The second stage of consciousness is naïve transitivity. Freire characterizes this stage of consciousness by an over simplification of problems, nostalgia for the past, an under estimation of ordinary people, a strong tendency to gregariousness, a disinterest in investigation, a fascination with fanciful explanations of reality; and by the practice of polemics (arguments about doctrines) rather than dialogue. Naïve transitivity is never totally and irrevocably surpassed; for all who enter the learning process, this remains a lifelong task.

The third and final stage is critical transitivity. This stage is characterised by depth in the interpretation of problems, by testing one's own funding and openness to revision and reconstruction, by the attempt to avoid distortion when perceiving problems and to avoid pre conceived notions when analysing them, by rejecting passivity, by the practice of dialogue rather than polemics, by receptivity to the new without rejecting the old, and by permeable, interrogative, restless and dialogical forms of life.

Trivialization of 'Conscientisation'

One of the worst experiences with regard to Freirean theory has been the trivialisation of the concept of conscientisation. The word has come to mean anything from crude publicity to subtle indoctrination. Freire himself explained the philosophical dimensions of this.

> "The word conscientisation in English derives from 'consciousnes'. When we speak about; 'consciousness' we are in danger of falling into two mistakes. The first one is an Hegelian subjectivism in the understanding of consciousness. According to this opinion, the consciousness is the creator of reality, of the world, of objectivity. The other mistake is a Marxian distortion—consciousness as a mechanical objectivism. Objectivity so shapes my consciousness as to make it a reflexion of reality. However, Marx also said that consciousness and the world were in a dialectical unity...." (Freire, 1970).

Conscientisation is a Painful Birth

Freire remarks "Conscientisation is a painful birth". There is no palliative for it like those exercises that women use to avoid birth pangs. Conscientisation also involves an excruciation movement a tremendously upsetting one, in anyone who begins to conscientise himself, the moment when he starts to be reborn. Conscientisation thus demands an Easter. That is, it demands that we die to be born again. Every Christian must live his Easter, and that too is a utopia. The man who does not make his Easter, in the sense of dying in order to be reborn is no real Christian.

That is why Christianity, for me, is such as a marvellous doctrine. People have accused me of being a communist, but no communist could say what I have just said. I never had any temptation to cease being, to cease existing I am not yet completely a Catholic, I just keeping on trying to be one more completely day after day."

Conscientisation could never be an imposition on other or a manipulation of them. One cannot impose his ideas on others, but only discuss on them. To impose on others one's way would be a real contradiction. For loving is not only a free act, it is an act of freedom and love that cannot produce more freedom is not love.

Conclusion

Education that is used to domesticate merely transfers knowledge, as the educator passes on thirst for knowing to his pupils, who passively receive that knowledge. In that sort of relationship, conscientisation is impossible. We can however see a certain incipient conscientisation in the way the students react, because the natural intentionality of human awareness cannot be thwarted by any educator's domesticating purpose.

A conscientising and therefore, liberating education is not that transfer of neatly wrapped knowledge; it is a true act of knowing. Through it, both teacher and pupils simultaneously become knowing subjects, brought together by the object they know. There is no longer one who thinks, who knows, stranding in front of others who admit they do not know, that they have to be taught. Rather, all of them are inquisitive learners, keen to learn.

REFERENCES

Aggarwal, J.C. (1996). *Teacher and Education in a Developing Society*. New Delhi: Vikas Publishing House Pvt. Ltd.

Chitkara, M.G. (2009). *Education and Human Values*. New Delhi: APH Publishing Corporation.

Das, B.C. (2000). *Teacher Education at a Distance*. New Delhi: Kalyani Publishers.

Dash, B.N. (2006). *Principles of Education*. Hyderabad: Neelkamal Publications Pvt. Ltd.

Freire, P. (1973). *Education for Critical Consciousness*. New York: The Seabury Press.

Freire, P. (1974). *Pedagogy of the Oppressed*. New York: The Seabury Press.

Section-III
Status and Relevance

12
Higher Education in India
A Study of Educational Development in Mizoram

Sakhawliana

Introduction

Education is the backbone of human development in every society of the world. Since the Vedic time, all the spheres of human life, in India, were predominantly dominated by spiritual values. Initially, education was open to everybody without any distinction on caste. It was sought as the means of salvation or self-realisation, as the means to the highest end of life, viz. '*Mukti*' or 'Emancipation'. However, as time progressed, education was imparted on the basis of caste and the related duties that one had to perform as a member of a specific case. The Western society began to interfere into the subcontinent since 1498 and the traditional Indian education cannot withstand with them and rapidly sway to their system.

Pre-Colonial

Ancient Indian Education had been evolved strictly on the foundation of Indian epistemological and philosophical traditions. The idea of the ephemerality of life and the world, the concept of ultimate death and the futility of mundane pleasures, had provided them with a special angle of vision. Basically, the pupils kept themselves away from the haunt of din and distractions of the material world in the early education, they rather amid to the beauty of natural surroundings.

In India, higher education was *abinitio* at the behest of the Buddhist teaching, because they give free education into their monastic institutions and had attracted students from India and abroad. As far as higher education is concern, the institutions in Taxila and Nalanda were pioneering University education in India. From time immemorial Taxila University had been an important centre of Brahmanical education, and its fame continued during the Buddhist period in the Northern India. Kautilya, the famous author of *Arthasastra* had received his higher education in this University too. The Chinese traveller Fa Hien found no remains of University when had visited India in the 5th Century A.D. However, Hiuen-Tsang was very much disappointed to see some of the last relics of Taxila University when he visited India in 7th Century A.D.

In the 10th century, Indian subcontinent was invaded from the north-west, which has the emergence of dynastic rule. The dual traditions of Sanskrit and Farsi education were kept alive till the colonisation of India by the British, and Persian became the court language. On the other hand, the British established schools to teach English and Science stream. In 1857, three universities were established in the metropolitan cities, Bombay (now Mumbai), Calcutta (now Kolkata), Madras (now Chennai) and in 1887 Allahabad University was established. All these Universities imparted education in the liberal arts and sciences. Over and above, its main objective was to prepare young aspirants for careers in the Civil Service, Legal profession and in Medicine. The need for technical education was also felt by the Colonial ruler; accordingly the first industrial school was established in Chennai in 1842.

Post-Colonial

There was a radical administrative change in India after independence in 1947. In the meantime, the higher education sector witnesses a tremendous transformation for a couple of years. There are merely 20 Universities and 500 colleges in India at the time of Independence in 1947, while approximately 210,000 students enrolled in different institutions of higher studies. By knowing the quantum of higher institutions and its urgency for scientific development, for socio-economic status of the people, the Government set-up the University Education Commission under the chairmanship of Dr. S. Radhakrishnan in 1948, this Commission lays the foundation of the future of Higher Education in India.

As shown in Table 12.1, there was a splendid increase of Universities in India during the year 1950 to 2015. There are only 30 Universities in 1950-51, but it was enhance to 55 in the next decade (1960-61) or there was an enhancement of 83.3 per cent during 1950-1960. The total number of Universities increase to 256 in the year 2000-01 and has reached 740 in 2014-15.

Table 12.1: Total Universities in India (1950-2015)

Sl: No.	*Year*	*No. of Universities*
1.	1950-51	30
2.	1960-61	55
3.	1970-71	103
4.	1980-81	133
5.	1990-91	190
6.	2000-01	256
7.	2010-11	634
8.	2011-12	659
9.	2012-13	665
10.	2013-14	719
11.	2014-15	740

Source: AISHE (Provisional), 2015.

Corresponding to the University, there was a marvelous increase of colleges after Independence. As portrays in Table 12.2, the total number of college increases to 4722 in 1980, it is to be recapitulated from the previous paragraph that there are only 500 colleges in 1947.

Table 12.2: Growth of Colleges (1980-2015)

Sl. No.	*Year*	*No.*
1.	1980-1981	4,722
2.	1990-1991	7,346
3.	2000-01	12,806
4.	2007-08	21,170
5.	2011-12	33,023
6.	2012-13	35,829
7.	2014-15 (AISHE Provisional)	38,056

Source: AISHE report (Provisional), 2015.

In 2000-01, the number of colleges in India jump to 12,806, and its strength added up without any lapse and climbed to 35,829 in 2012-13. According to the provisional report of AISHE the quantity of colleges in India has reached 38,056 in 2014-15.

Type of Universities (and Number of College)

Subject to the provision of entries 63 to 66 of List I (Union List), higher education in India was incorporated under the Concurrent List (entry 25 of List III) of the Constitution. As far as India's higher education is concern, it is the third largest in the world, next only to the United States of America and China. It was mainly govern by the University Grants Commission (UGC), which enforces its standards, advises the government, and helping the coordination between the Centre and the State. Under the guidance of UGC, accreditation of institution was managed by an autonomous body of 12 independent bureaus.

Different types of Universities in India are : (i) Central University, (ii) State University, (iii) Private University, (iv) Deemed to be University, and (v) Institution of National Importance. Central University means, university established or incorporated by the Central Act through the Parliament, while the State University is established by the State Act through the concern State Assembly. A university established by the Central or State by a sponsoring body is called Private University; the body got registration under the Societies Registration Act, 1860 or any other corresponding law for the time being in force in a State or Public Trust/Company registered under the Companies Act, 1956. There is other type of institution known by the name Deemed University, which was declared, as such, by the Central Government under Section 3 of the UGC Act, 1956, they are high performing institutions. Besides, the Union Parliament established Institution of National Importance by giving the status of University.

Table 12.3 clearly portrays the development of Universities in India. According to Table 12.3, there are 719 Universities in May 2015, but it raise to unexpected high of 740 Universities within the span of just 7 months only.

Table 12.3: Type of Universities (May 2015 to January 2016)

Type of Universities	*May 2015*	*January 2016*
Central Universities	46	46
State Universities	330	342
Deemed to be Universities	128	125
Private Universities	215	227
Total	**719**	**740**

Source: Analyse from UGC Reports and AISHE Reports.

It is obvious from Table 12.3 that Central Universities remain at 46 in number during the given year of 2015-16, but State Universities has boost to 342 from 330. There was a negative growth of Deemed to be Universities from the tune of 128 to 125 in the year 2015 to 2016. But overall increases of University's were very much satisfactory within the given period.

Table 12.4 illustrate the largest and least number of Colleges in different states. Accordingly Uttar Pradesh has 5,922 colleges, which is the biggest in number, preceded by Maharashtra with 4,714, Karnataka 3,416 and Rajasthan 2,786. Small states, basically has marginal number of colleges, while Nagaland has 62, Goa, Tripura and Mizoram has 56, 49 and 29 colleges respectively.

Table 12.4: Top Ten Largest and Least Numbers of Colleges

Sl No.	*State having Largest Number of Colleges*	*No. of Colleges*	*Sl. No.*	*State having Least Number of Colleges*	*No. of Colleges*
1.	Uttar Pradesh	5922	1.	Daman & Diu	7
2.	Maharashtra	4714	2.	Andaman & Nicobar Islands	7
3.	Karnataka	3416	3.	Dadra & Nagar Haveli	10
4.	Rajasthan	2786	4.	Sikkim	13
5.	Andhra Pradesh	2591	5.	Arunachal Pradesh	27
6.	Tamil Nadu	2531	6.	Chandigarh	27
7.	Telengana	2328	7.	Mizoram	29
8.	Madh Phradesh	2218	8.	Tripura	49
9.	Gujarat	2055	9.	Goa	56
10.	Kerala	1240	10.	Nagaland	62
	All India	38056			

Source: www.ugc.ac.in & AISHE Report 2015 (Provisional).

Table 12.4 has depicts that the northeast state of Arunachal Pradesh and the Union Territory of Chandigarh has 27 colleges each, on the other hand the two Centrally administered Islands of Daman & Diu and Andaman & Nicobar has each of 7 colleges. Thus, the gross number of colleges in India is at the tune of 38,056.

Mizoram (A Brief Profile)

Mizoram, the name of the State, is a combination of two words—*'Mizo'* and *'Ram'*. The word, *'Ram'* means Country or Land while *'Mizo'* is the generalised name of the inhabitants. Thus, Mizoram means the Land of the Mizos. The generic term Mizo means 'Hillman' or 'Highlander'. The name of the State otherwise is synonymous with its geographical topography. Situated approximately between 22.12' and 24.9' North Latitude and 92.20' and 93.90' East Longitude, Mizoram occupies the North-Eastern corner of India. It has a Geographical Area of 21,081 Sq. km with north to south length being 277 km and the breadth from East to west being 121 km. State has 722 km International boundary and shares a common boundary of 404 km with Myanmar on the east and South, and 318 km with Bangladesh on the west. The State is bound to the North by 123 km and 95 km by Assam and Manipur and 66 km in the West by Tripura respectively. Due to the British expedition in 1890, Mizoram State fell under the sweeping British Rule. This Imperial Government introduced a variety of Rules and Regulations comprising the Assam Frontier Tract Regulation, 1880, Scheduled District Act, 1870, Chin Hills Regulations, 1896, Government of India Act, 1919 and Inner Lines Regulations (Bengal and Eastern Frontier Act) 1873, till today entry of non-indigenous people are allowed only through permit.

When India was given Independence by the British on 15th August, 1947, Mizoram (erstwhile Lushai Hills) continued to remain under the Assam Government. This Government granted Autonomous District Council to Mizoram (then known as Mizo Hills) in April 1952 and the newly created District Council had 24 Members. This Council was later elevated to the Centrally Administered Union Territory (UT) status in January 1972 and again to Statehood on 20th February, 1987. As for its name, the present State of Mizoram was known as Lushai Hills till the 1951 Census, it was then called Mizo Hills in 1961 and as Mizo District till 1971. The whole Area of Mizoram State was declared a 'Disturbed Area' in 1966 and the Armed Forces (Special Powers) Act, 1958 was enforced to counter insurgency that enveloped Mizoram from March 1966. The State was under Militancy for more than 20 years, from 1st March, 1966 to 30th June, 1986. The Guerrilla War waged between Indian Forces and Mizo National Front (MNF) Militants ended due to the successful 'Peace Accord' signed between the Government of India and MNF Militants on June 1986. Consequently, the 53rd Constitutional Amendment Act, 1986 granted the Status of State to Mizoram, now turns to be one of the most peaceful States in the Country.

Status and Growth of Higher Education (in Mizoram)

The crux of formal education system has started only after the British manipulation of the Chief administration in 1890. Traditionally, young aspirants had to go through rigorous training and discipline at home and in the village community. Besides, the '*Zawlbuk*' is bachelor's dormitory, where young boys are given informal training under the guidance of elders. As far as formal education is concern, it is the Christian missionaries who pioneering the development with the arrival of Rev. J.H. Lorrain (local name Pu Buanga) and Dr. F.W. Savidge (local name Sap Upa) on 11th January, 1894. The two Christian missionaries prepared Mizo Alphabets for the indigenous people, and the first Primary School was started in the year 1898. The early schools established by the missionaries were temporary and experimental, in their functioning, with no clear policy guidelines from the authority.

The first High School started in 1944, and it was only in 1958 that the foremost College, named Pachhunga University College (PUC) was established in Mizoram for undergraduate studies. During the Union Territory Government, the State Council for Educational Research and Training (SCERT) was constituted in 1980. With the passing of Mizoram University Act in the Union Parliament the first and only full-fledged University of the State was established under the nomenclature "Mizoram University" in 2001. Moreover, ICFAI University was also established by the State Assembly in 2005, and followed by the inauguration of District Institute of Education and Training (DIET) in the same year.

Table 12.5 clearly shows the positive development of institution for higher studies in Mizoram. The table clearly demonstrate that, 21 colleges were meant for Arts, while 5 are Science, and 11 institutes/colleges give professional degrees in different subjects, viz. Law, Veterinary Science, Computer, Nursing, Laboratory and Technologies. Besides, Mizoram University, the National Institute of Technology (NIT) is the only institute of the state which have Post-graduate studies, up to doctorate.

Challenges and Prospects

All the above studies clearly depicts the fact that, Indian Higher Education system has expanded at fast pace by adding more than 700 Universities and 30,000 colleges after independence. As of 2015, India has 46 Central Universities, 342 State Universities, 125 deemed universities, 227 private universities respectively. Besides there are 93 Institutes of National Importance established by the Union Parliament, which includes AIIMS, IITs, NITs. Moreover, distance learning and open education is also a feature of the Indian higher education system, and is looked after by the

Table 12.5: Higher Educational Institutions in Mizoram (As on August 2016)

Sl. No.	*College Names*	*Year of establish-ment*	*Course Conducted*
1.	Pachhunga University College	1958	Arts, Science and Commerce
2.	Lunglei Govt. College	1964	Arts, Science and Diploma
3.	Govt. Champhai College	1971	Arts, Science and BCA
4.	Govt. Serchhip College	1973	Arts and Commerce
5.	Govt. Aizawl College	1975	Ars and Commerce
6.	College of Teachers Education	1975	B.Ed.
7.	Govt. Saiha College	1978	Arts
8.	Govt. Kolasib College	1978	Arts, Science and BCA
9.	Govt. Hnahthial College	1979	Arts
10.	Govt. Hrangbana College	1980	Arts and Commerce
11.	Govt. Lawngtlai College	1980	Arts
12.	Govt. Zirtiri Res. Science College	1980	Science and BCA
13.	Mizoram College of Nursing	1980	BSc Nursing & GNM
14.	Govt. Mamit College	1983	Arts
15.	Govt. J. Buana College	1983	Arts
16.	Govt. Mizoram Law College	1983	LL.B
17.	Govt. Saitual College	1984	Arts
18.	Govt. Khawzawl College	1985	Arts
19.	Govt. Zawlnuam College	1986	Arts
20.	Govt. Aizawl North College	1988	Arts
21.	Govt. Aizawl West College	1990	Arts
22.	Govt. T. Romana College	1992	Arts
23.	Govt. J. Thankima College	1992	Arts
24.	Govt. Johnson College	1993	Arts
25.	Govt. Kamalanagar College	1993	Arts
26.	RIPAN (now RIPANS)	1994	B.Sc. in Nursing, Pharm., ML etc.
27.	NIELIT (formerly DOEACC)	2001	BCA and Dip. in Computer
28.	College of Vety. Sciences & AH	2006	BVSc & AH
29.	HATIM	2007	BCA, B.Com., BSW
30.	National Institute of Technology	2010	B.Tech, M.Tech, M.Sc., Ph.D

Source: Workout from *www.mzu.edu*, college website, and personal interview.

Distance Education Council. And IGNOU is the largest university in the world by having student's enrolment of approximately 3.5 million students across the globe.

Some institutions of India, such as the Indian Institutes of Technology (IITs), National Institute of Technology (NITs), Indian Institutes of Information Technology (IIITs), Indian Institutes of Management (IIMs), International Institute of Information Technology (IIIT), University of Mumbai and Jawaharlal Nehru University have been globally acclaimed for their standard of education. However, there is a great significant challenge to increase student enrolment in the country.

Table 12.6 is the GER of Indian students for higher studies in 2012-13. Accordingly, the GER of USA is 94.3 per cent, but India has only 24.8 per cent. Among the developing countries, Argentina has 78.6 per cent, Sweden 70 per cent and Canada 58.9 per cent, all their GERs are much better than India. Thus, the authority should try to increase the national GER by arranging policy matters to increase annual intakes of the institutes.

It is very essential to emphasis the focus of National Knowledge Commission on access, inclusion and excellence for improving the overall standards of higher education in India. Quality control and improvement of syllabus is unavoidable for development to coup with international standards. According to Table 12.7, none of Indian Universities are figured among the top 200 in QS World Universities Rankings in 2015. Even our

Table 12.6: Gross Enrolment Ratio (GER) of Selected Countries

Country	*GER in Higher Education* (in %)*	*Position in the World*
USA	94.3	3rd
Argentina	78.6	15th
Russia	76.1	19th
Sweden	70.0	27th
UK	61.9	36th
Canada	58.9	45th
China	26.7	85th
India	**24.8**	**87th**
South Africa	19.2	93rd

Source: www.mhrd.gov.in

Table 12.7: QS (Quacquarelli Symonds Ltd.) World University Rankings 2015

Year	*Institution*	*World Rank*
2010-14	None of the Indian Universities figured in top 200 while universities from other Asian countries such as Japan, Hong Kong, China, South Korea, Singapore and Taiwan were listed among top 100 universities of the world.	
2012	IIT Delhi IIT Bombay, IIT Kanpur	212th 227th, 278th
2014	IIT Delhi	235th

Source: QS Reports.

prestigious Institutes, like IIT Delhi and IIT Bombay stood at 212 and 227 in world rankings.

As shown in Table 12.8, the qualities of Indian Universities are far behind the world level. All our Universities are beyond 100 in world rankings, although some of our impressive institutes are within range of 1-100 among Asian Universities, we need to increase our institutes to top in world rankings.

The comparative Table 12.8 has depicted that among the BRICS countries, two institutes from India, viz. IIT Roorkee and IISc Bangalore fortunately occupies the 4th and 5th positions, but their rankings in Asia is only 92nd and 34th respectively. Moreover, some of our esteemed Universities, viz., University of Delhi and University of Calcutta were also very low in ranking at international levels.

Table 12.8: Comparisons of Top Ten Universities, 2015

Universities	*BRICS*	*Asia*	*World*
1. IISc, Bangalore	5th	34th	147th
2. IIT, Delhi	13th	42nd	179th
3. IIT, Bombay	16th	46th	202nd
4. IIT, Kanpur	18th	58th	271st
5. IIT, Madras	20th	56th	254th
6. IIT, Kharagpur	24th	92nd	67th
7. IIT, Roorkee	4th	92nd	67th
8. University of Delhi	46th	91st	286th
9. IIT, Guwahati	50th	98th	391st
10. University of Calcutta	52nd	149th	481-490

Source: QS Reports, 2015-16.

Thus, the authority and academicians need to take necessary steps to develop the qualities of Indian Universities, in one hand, and the qualities of technical institutes on the other. Table 12.9 is the latest University rankings of the world, prepared by *QS* and *The Times*. It is so challenging to be mentioned that no Indian university was inclusive in Top Ten Universities of the world.

Despite a dozen of backdrops in Indian higher education system, the Government lost no time to enhance the qualities of our Universities and Colleges. Many of our professional institutes have attracted international entrepreneurs. The most important component resides on the improvement of our educational vision. All these can be achieved through political will and administrative supports.

Table 12.9: QS-Top Universities in World University Rankings

Universities	*QS World University Rankings 2015-16*	*The Times HE World Univ. Rankings 2015-16*
Massachusetts IT (MIT), USA	1st	5th
Harvard University, USA	2nd	6th
Univ. of Cambridge, UK	3rd	4th
Stanford Univ., USA	4th	3rd
California IT, USA	5th	1st
University of Oxford, UK	6th	2nd
UCL (Univ. College, London), UK	7th	—
Imperial College, London	8th	8th
ETH Zurich-Swiss Federal IT, Switzerland	9th	9th
University of Chicago, USA	10th	10th
Princeton University, USA	11th	7th

Sources: Analyse from *QS* and *The Times* HE—World Univ. Rankings, 2015-16.

REFERENCES

Alok Chakrabarti, *Higher Education and Research in India: An Overview* (Sitra Report 74), ISBN : 978-951-563-600-3 & ISSN : 1457-5728 (www.sitra.fi).

Arnold, David (2004), *The New Cambridge History of India: Science, Technology and Medicine in Colonial India*, Cambridge University Press, ISBN : 0-521-56319-4.

Barbhuiya, Abdul Hannan (2014), *Cost and Finance of Higher Education in Mizoram*, Concept Publishing Company Pvt. Ltd., New Delhi-110059, ISBN : 13:978-93-5125-039-5.

Blackwell, Fritz (2004), India: *A Global Studies Handbook*, ABC-CLIO, Inc., ISBN : 1-57607-348-3.

Ellis, Catriona. (2009) "Education for All: Reassessing the Historiography of Education in Colonial India," *History Compass*, (March 2009).

Gale, Thompson *et al.*, *Encyclopaedia of India* (Vol. 2) (Edited 2006), "Educational Institutions and Philosophies, Traditional and Modern", ISBN : 0-684-31351 0.

Kumar, Deepak (2003), *"India", The Cambridge History of Science,* Vol. 4: *Eighteenth Century Science,* edited by Roy Porter, pp. 669–687, Cambridge University Press, ISBN : 0-521-57243-6.

Singh, Mahendra P. (2010), *Constitution of India* (11th Edition), Eastern Book Company, ISBN : 81-7012-891-9.

13

Status of Arabic Language in Higher Education in Jammu & Kashmir

Sayeeda Wajal

Holy *Qur'an* is written in Arabic and almost all Islamic Literature is in Arabic language. Millions of Muslims both Arabs and non-Arabs study this language. Arabic is an international language, it is spoken and understood in more than 30 Arab/African countries. This language is one of the ancient languages. With the oil boom in Middle East (Arab Countries) most countries of the world want to establish contacts with the Arab countries. Learning Arabic language is all the more important for seeking employment in Middle East. Arabic has been taught worldwide in many Elementary and Secondary Schools especially in Muslim Countries. Universities around the world have special classes for teaching Arabic as part of the foreign languages.

Advent of Islam in Kashmir

With special reference to Jammu & Kashmir, Islam is the major religion practiced in the valley of Kashmir, with maximum population identifying as Muslims in Kashmir. Islam came with the influx of Muslim Sufi preachers from Persia and Central Asia.[1] There is no doubt, however, that Islam in Kashmir received great impetus because of Sayyid al-Hamid and his followers. He is accompanied by his disciples travelled widely throughout the valley. He left his disciples at a number of places. These followers of Sayyid al-Hamid started preaching Islam[2], with these Sufis Arabic language came into existence in Kashmir and also introduced in

Islamic schools, colleges as well as universities.

The history of conversion to Islam in Kashmir as a mass movement is synonymous with the peaceful effort of various Sufis in the area beginning from the early fourteenth century after the establishment of the region's first Muslim dynasty (Bukhari, 1998:4). There is clear evidence of Islam having entered Kashmir considerably before that, however, but this did not assume the form of large scale of conversations. Yet, it was only from the Early Fourteenth Century that great masses of Kashmir began converting to Islam in large numbers, at that time many people accepted Islam with Quranic language "Arabic".[3]

Sufism in Kashmir

Sufism, the religious philosophy of Islam, is described in the oldest extant definition as "the apprehension of divine realities and Mohammedan mystics are fond of calling themselves *Ahl al-haqq*, the followers of the real."[4] The spread of Islam in Kashmir by the Sufis has been discussed by various scholars, academics and writers, but the lesser known aspects of various Sufi orders, role of Sufism in promoting pluralistic culture in Kashmir. Sufism as a channel of Inter-Faith Dialogue, lessons which Kashmiri Sufism has for the world to make it a peaceful place to dwell; such serious, and sensitive academic studies of Kashmir Sufism are rare, and even neglected. Yogesh Sikand, a writer, pointed out that "the conflict in Kashmir is understood as being but the latest stage in over a thousand-year history of unceasing, relentless conflict between Hindus and Muslims, whose religious beliefs are said to be so different from, and so contradictory to, each other as to make constant strife between them inevitable".[5]

The development of Sufism is a fascinating chapter in the religious history of Islam. In the beginning, Sufism was considered as an alien growth brought the impact of culture and traditions other than Islam.[6]

Arabic is the oldest living language in the world, but we cannot determine the date exactly when it arrived to India, however, it was believed to have been distributed in the form of Qur'an and Hadith language. And then the Muslim were interested in Indian culture and language began to propagate the language to the other part of the country like J & K. There emerged some eminent social scientist who generated utmost interest in the Arabic language in the state of J & K. Among the promoment scholars who shined bright in developing the Arabic language are Mir Syed Ali Hamdani & Sheikh Yaqoob Sarfi are worthy to the mentioned.

Mir Sayyid Ali Hamadani: Is the farewell, tourists, and a large woolly, blending between science and general knowledge advised people also preaches sultans, kings and khaleda left traces in the form of his works, the most important values is: Wird Afatthah. This booklet includes *Adhkaar* derived from the *Qur'an* and *Sunnah,* which tones unification of God Almighty be read by the people of Kashmir, just after dawn prayers voice modulators and learns adults and children.

Scholar Sheikh Yaqub morphological Kashmiri (928-1003): He approaches is renewed for a second Professor Sheikh Ahmed Abdul Ahad Aserhende and Oukrn Dad Flux bin Mubarak Nakovra. His interpretation "Soata inspiration" which is unprecedented because it neglected the semicolon characters.

He combines poetry and literature and modern interpretation and *Maghazi* and politics, most scientists Taiada to the right himself and was really a touch stone to say: Tell the truth even on you, the author of dozens of huge with TFM books about the interpretation of the demand of the students, languages merits and others.

Sheikhs Ahmed preacher: Sheikh Ahmed knows from the third century scientists in terms of scientific and doctrinal and literary productions, it has a leading role in the defence of Islam and Muslims. It became a reference for scholars and virtuous and mystics and students of the arts and science faculty in Srinagar delegation of him began Attash flag from each phage. Atiq Dhiravat and Ouhdana have received a flag from him and Bulgoh to people of different sects and their ways. Behind Sheikh superb raised, the most important are: "Eye to explain the ongoing continental forty" and "the most useful tools in the answer to five pm" and "masterpiece Asamadanah" and "Alhmdanih gift."[7]

Arabic studied in Islamic schools: The Islamic schools contributed to the promotion of the Arabic language and literature, including **Darul-Uloom-rahimiyah, Darul-Bilal-Srinagar, Islamic Darul-Uloom-Shopian, Darul-Uloom University Girls Srinagar girls, Ziaul-Uloom** etc. One of the most graduates of these religious schools who have published this language in the state of Jammu & Kashmir in the current era are the Director **Daralalom Rahimah Bandey Bora**, Maulana Rahmatullah Al-Qasimi, Deputy Prime Daralalom Rahimah Bandey Bora Maulana Mufti counterpart Ahmed-Al- Qasimi, Chairman Daralalom Bilal Srinagar Almolana Mufti Abdul Rashid and President of the Islamic Daralalom Shopian Almolana Mufti Ayoub, Al-Qasimi and chairman of Dar Al-Uloom University Girls, Srinagar Ghazi Moinuddin Nadwi.

Arabic Studied in the Colleges of Jammu & Kashmir: The

Government Modern Colleges under the higher education of Jammu & Kashmir focused on teaching the Arabic language at all levels of study are: Government College, Poonch, Government College, Thana Mandi, Government College, Rajouri, Government College, Srinagar, Government Degree College, Budhal, Government College, Shopian, Government College, Sopore and others. Arabic language is taught in these colleges and the number of students who are studying this language more than a thousand undergraduate level. The most important professors of these colleges have contributed great contribution to the Arabic language are: Dr. Muzaffar Hussain Nadwi, who has written several books, including "Omathl Kashmir" and "Contribution of Kashmir scientists in the Arabic language" and Dr. Abdurrah Manvar, who wrote about twenty books in Arabic some of them are included in the syllabus of higher education including **"logic bird, lettering cutters, innovation in intonation, recitation of the Qur'an.** "Dr. Merajuddin Nadwi, who wrote the book "Pioneering Test for the Success of the Righteous" and others.

Arabic studied in the Universities of Jammu & Kashmir: Arabic language is studied in the universities of Jammu & Kashmir. The master's programme at Kashmir University started from 1980 to impart knowledge of language and literature among the student. In the light of this objective and viewing Arabic as a language of global importance, great Islamic civilisation and rich Arab culture as well as a force and medium of interaction among various cross currents of social and cultural thoughts conveyed through its rich literature, courses in specific areas of study like classical literature, modern literature and Indo-Arabic literature and literary criticism were designed with the teaching approach of critical assessment and appreciation. Later on the research programme at M.Phil. and Ph.D. level was started to promote in-depth research in various domains of language, literature, history and culture. Arabic is a living language with rich literary heritage, it is the language of Qur'an, it is studied in BGSB University, Rajouri, the Department of Arabic in Baba Ghulam Shah Badshah University established in 2004. The university started Arabic language from that time. At that time Arabic studied at PG level, but now, it is studied in B.A., M.Phil. and Ph.D. level.

Besides conducting routine classroom teaching in the university, the department has regularly been organised national seminars, workshops, poetic symposia, exbition, Qirat-e-Qur'an and workshop etc. Arabic language is also studied in Islamic University of Science and Technology, Awantipora, Kashmir. Some of the subjects currently being taught in the Masters programme are History of Arabic Literature, Classical Poetry and Prose, Syntax and Morphology, Translation, Modern Arabic Poetry, Novel, Drama, Short Story, Rhetoric and Prosody, Literary Criticism and Research Methodology. Following are the Major Courses:

- Arabic Morphology and Syntax.
- Classical Poetry.
- Fundamentals of Literacy Criticism.
- History of Arabic Literature.
- Translation and Oral Expression.
- Modern Arabic Prose and Poetry.
- Contemporary Arab World.
- Research Methodology.
- Spoken Arabic (Offered as Core Course to MBA Students).

Conclusion

With the beginning of the twenty-first century, a revitalised Arabic language has emerged following a century of struggle and growth that introduced a number of changes and reforms. The debate concerning the viability of literary Arabic as the medium for education, technology, and mass communication has virtually come to a halt. Modern Standard Arabic has been accepted as a common and unifying bond among the Arabs, transcending their diversity in economic status, political realities, religious beliefs, and national aspirations.

Now-a-days, Arabic language is rapidly increasing its existence in different spheres such as at school, college and university levels.

Arabic language played an important role to eradicate the routes of Sufism and enrich the pure Islamic culture. There are so many prominent scholars who put their endeavours in the field of Arabic learning, teaching as well as in the field of research. On this behalf I can prove that this language is making its place as a wide and spacious room.

NOTES

1. Sufi GMD (2015). *Kashmir: Being A History of Kashmir from the Earliest Times to Our Wwn,* Gulshan Books, Kashmir, Srinagar.
2. Snedden, Christopher (2015). *Understanding Kashmir & Kashmiris,* Oxford University Press.
3. Rafiqi, A.Q. (2003). *Sufism in Kashmir* (14-16th Century), Srinagar, Kashmir: Crown Printing Press.

4. *The Valley of Kashmir—The Making and Unmaking of a Composite Culture*. Manohar Publishers, New Delhi.
5. Nicholson, Reynold A. (1963). *The Mystics of Islam*, London: Routledge & Keagan Paul.
6. M.D. Sadiq (2013). *Kashmir Sufism.*
7. Lings, Martin, (1995). *What is Sufism*. London: Goerge Allen & Unwin Ltd.
8. Translated from Arabic Book *Amatil E Kashmir*, Dr. Muzzafar Hussain Nadwi, Kashmir, J & K.

14
Indian Higher Educational System
Challenges and Suggestions

Rajiv Kumar Agarwal

Introduction

> Today, more than ever before in human history, the wealth—or poverty—of nations depends on the quality of higher education. Those with a larger repertoire of skills and a greater capacity for learning can look forward to life times of unprecedented economic fulfilment. But in the coming decades the poorly educated face little better than the dreary prospects of lives of quiet desperation.
>
> — *Malcolm Gillis, President of Rice University, 12 February, 1999.*

> Our university system is, in many parts, in a state of disrepair. In almost half the districts in the country, higher education enrolments are abysmally low, almost two-third of our universities and 90 per cent of our colleges are rated as below average on quality parameters. I am concerned that in many States university appointments, including that of Vice-chancellors, have been politicised and have become subject to caste and communal considerations, there are complaints of favouritism and corruption.
>
> —*Formr Prime Minister Manmohan Singh, 2007.*

Education is a lifelong process for development of an individual. It not only tries to develop the innate potentialities of the individual in a harmonious manner but also tries for harmonious development of all the powers of the human being, i.e. physical, social, intellectual, aesthetic and spiritual. So, education is intimately connected with the life as well as with experience of an individual. Hence, all these three, i.e. education, life and philosophy are closely interrelated. There are no antitheses between philosophy of life and philosophy of education. They may practically sail in the same boat.

Normally, 'Education' is utilised in three senses, i.e. Knowledge, Subject and a Process. Achievement of degree up to a certain level is generally not called education, e.g. if a person has secured Masters degree then we utilise education in a very narrower sense and call that the person has achieved education up to Masters Level. In the second sense, education is utilised in a sense of discipline, e.g. if a person had taken education as a paper or as a discipline during his study in any institution then we utilise education as a subject. In the third sense, education is utilised as a process. In fact when we talk about education, we normally talk in the third sense, i.e. education as a process. Thus, we talk what is education as a process? What are their importance etc.? By going through the text we may be able to know the process of education—

- To know the meaning and concept of higher education.
- To define the narrower as well as wider meaning of education.
- To explain the analytical meaning of higher education.
- To know the aims along with scope of education.

Meaning of Education

In English, the term "Education" has been derived from two Latin words Educare (Educere) and Educatum. The meaning of "Educare" is to train or mould. It again means to bring up or to lead out or to draw out, propulsion from inward to outward. The term "Educatum" defines the act of teaching and throws light on the principles and practice of teaching. The term "Educare" or "Educere" basically indicates development of the latent faculties of the child. But, child does not know these possibilities. It is either the educator or the teacher who can know these and take appropriate methods to develop the powers.

In Hindi, the term "Shiksha" has come from the Sanskrit word "Shash". The meaning of "Shash" is to discipline, to control, to order, to direct, to rule etc. In the traditional sense, Education means controlling or disciplining the behaviour of an individual. In Sanskrit "Shiksha" is a particular branch of the *Sutra* literature, having six branches, i.e. *Shiksh, Chhanda, Vyakarana, Nirukta, Jyotisha* and *Kalpa*, which was designed to learn the *Vedas*. *Shiksha* explain rules of pronunciation.

There is another term in Sanskrit, which highlights the nature of education. It is "Vidya" which may be known as knowledge. The term "Vidya" has been originated from "Bid" meaning knowledge. On mentioning certain definitions of education of great educators of the East and the West, we may be able to have a clear picture of the nature and meaning of the term education.

> "Education is the manifestation of perfection already in man. Like fire in a piece of flint, knowledge exists in the mind. Suggestion is the friction; which brings it out." —*Swami Vivekananda*

Aims of Education in Age-old India

The basic aim of education in India history was the ultimate outcome of the Indian theory of knowledge and the corresponding scheme of life and values. People in ancient India were greatly impressed and affected by the fact of death as the central fact of life. There was only one aim of life to solve the problem of death by achieving knowledge of the whole truth of which life and death are arts and phases. This aim was not only simply abstract and theoretical, but also practical and concrete aims too. The first was the acquisition of knowledge and is evident in the Vedic period. In those days, it was also regarded as an important aim of education to inculcation of social and civic duties in the minds of the students. There was another important aim, i.e. Education for occupation. Character training along with moral education was regarded as very important aim of ancient Indian education.

Aims of Education in Medieval India

During medieval age, mainly religion was the main guiding force in life and society. Medieval civilisation centred round religion. The Muslim rulers of India generally took a keen interest in education, and many of them founded schools, colleges and libraries in various places in their kingdoms. A centre of instruction and of literary activity was the mosque. Muslim education included those eternal teachings and values of the *Quran* and *Haditha*, which would have been able to promote moral and spiritual knowledge. Islamic education aimed not only physical, but also mental development of the students. Thus, it aimed at total development of personality of an individual.

Aims of Education in British India

The British uprooted the indigenous system of Indian education with predetermined intentions. The Indian educational system which established by the British, was colonial in character. It was designed to prepare Indian people only for taking certain subordinate positions in Government offices. It was not intended to develop among the people capacities to take leadership and initiative in different paths of life. The main educational objective can better be understood from the following declaration in the India educational policy of Lord Bentinck (1835): "We want a class of persons Indian in blood and colour, but English in taste, in opinion, in morals and intellect." The Wood's Despatch also declared almost the same policy. The aim of British education was to inculcate European knowledge in the minds of the Indian people.

Aims of Education in Independent India

After independence, the Indian leaders realised the inherent defects in the system of education introduced by the British. The need of the hour was Universalisation of Indian education. Education must be linked with national development in all directions. With these mentioned national goals in view the independent Indian Government set up different committees and commissions for educational reforms in the desired lines. These committees and commissions formulated educational aims as well as objectives.

There are not any great ideological battles or debates that are confronting the world anymore. The doctrine of liberal democracy has emerged as the most suitable and acceptable form of governance. Twentieth century has been broadly redefined the role of the state to provide education, healthcare, rule of law, and infrastructure development to enable every citizen to fulfil their potential, irrespective of their social position.

In Present knowledge economy, it is an indisputable fact that quality education is not only mandatory to fulfilling one's potential, but also is the key for vertical mobility and economic growth. Indeed, an educated population is the precondition for economic prosperity of any nation in present scenario. The main function of a higher education system is to add real value to human resources, and to produce wealth creators and leaders in all fields, i.e. business, professions, politics, administration, and creative pursuits.

Over the past seven decades, India has impressive strides in the field of higher education. Enrolment in higher education has been growing at a faster rate than population growth in the 18-23 age groups. A few elite institutions such as IITs and IIMs are recognised for their excellence, and we have a huge pool of technologically trained English speaking manpower in present independent India. Yet, there is much wrong so the higher education system is in deep crisis.

The quality of the bulk of our graduates is extremely bad because many university graduates do not have even rudimentary knowledge, or conceptual understanding, or problem-solving skills in their own discipline. Although, the students are doing their best—they are studious and disciplined; they cram, clear entrance tests, pass examinations, and obtain degrees. A bouquet of cultural rote learning, lack of application of knowledge, and a poor examination system have undermined Indian higher education. Mostly graduates are lack basic communication skills, and have no problem solving capacity. Educated unemployment is rising continuously, because most graduates cannot promote wealth creation and therefore unemployable.

This chapter not only tries to debunk some of the myths surrounding Indian higher education system, but also define the meaning of quality education and outlines the nature of crisis afflicting higher education, points out the key challenges, opportunities and highlights a few reform proposals to address the current morass.

Crisis in Higher Education

Hourglass Human Resources Structure

In any society of the world, the human resource structure may be represented by a pyramid. There will be the unskilled work force at the base of the pyramid. The semi-skilled (to suit a given society's requirements), having vocational trades such as electricians, plumbers, public health workers etc. occupy the middle layer. The apex of the pyramid usually consists of well-trained and qualified professionals such as engineers, doctors, lawyers, teachers, managers etc.

Unfortunately in Modern India, the structure of our human resources is in the form of an hourglass. Indeed, Indian society cannot be able to accommodate or put to productive use a huge number of mid and top level professionals such as doctors, engineers and lawyers of an indifferent quality. In spite of this, there is lack of professionally trained semi-skilled people such as electricians, plumbers and mechanics to fulfil the society's need. There are the millions of unskilled, illiterate workers eking out a precarious livelihood through back-breaking drudgery at the bottom. There are more electrical engineers in place of electricians, more civil engineers in place of masons, more super specialist doctors in place of general physicians, more mechanical engineers in place of mechanics.

There are more lawyers in place of teachers! There is a complete mismatch between the requirements of society and the kind of graduates which is being produced by our higher education system. It has been indicated in a WHO report itself that India had more doctors than it could accommodate, given its socio-economic status and ignoring this fact, we are continuously establishing more-and-more medical colleges to produce physicians and surgeons of indifferent quality, who may not be gainfully employed!

The past two-three decades witnessed mushrooming of so-called professional institutions offering courses in engineering, management, pharmacy, medicine, law etc. These institutions are producing thousands of graduates every year without having the skills which can be gainfully employed for producing the kind of goods and services that is needed in India. In spite of the impressive economic growth over the past decade or so, educated unemployment is on the rise, as these graduates are not equipped to become wealth creators. In the southern states of India, institutions which offer professional courses such as engineering etc., are not able to fili-up their quota of seats, in spite of this, new colleges are being allowed to be set up! On the other hand, there is a requirement for thousands of new teachers, which is not being met. There is also an unmet need for large number of public health professionals and general physicians.

Outdated Indian Examination System

The examination system for higher education is outdated and disgraceful. Normally, the stress is on testing the student's memory and rote learning. A careful memorising of answers to previous three years excluding the immediate past year questions posed in, will guarantee high grades! Analytical skills, application of knowledge, problem-solving capacity and innovation are rarely tested in the Indian higher education examination system. The student is only judged by his/her performance in a single final examination in absence of stress on continuous appraisal. There is an absolute mismatch between what is being taught in the class and what is being tested in the examination. Indeed, the teacher who teaches the course may be best suited to evaluate a student's performance in that course. But in the current system, there is a completely disconnected because evaluator sitting somewhere else grades the student's exam! In most Western universities of the world, the professor who teaches the course is allowed to evaluate the students throughout the duration of the course, administers tests or examinations and grades the test papers! Therefore, the student's final grade for the course is published within a week after the finals because there is a transparent mechanism for addressing any issues the student may have with the way his/her work is evaluated or graded. There is a tragedy with Indian students who are smart, ambitious, hard working and are just responding to what is being demanded by the system. The entire education infrastructure with extremely large number of coaching institutes is feeding this demand. If only the nature of demand is changed, the students and the associated infrastructure will be able to respond and to adapt the new conditions, and improve supply. There is a variety of models of examinations for evaluating the students skilfully, and creating demand for better education by redefining success.

Inflexible Curriculum without Electives

The higher education curriculum is extremely inflexible, centrally defined and leaving no room for individual choice or experimentation. It has resulted in creating a rigid and ridiculous academic atmosphere, with not only artificial divisions of various disciplines but also pre-determined combinations of courses on offer. Therefore, more and more students are ignoring humanities education and consequently lack broad perception, depth and communication skills. There is also an artificial differentiation and packaging of majors into various streams such as commerce, sciences etc. or into professional and non-professional courses. When a stream of study is selected, he/she has to take are pre-defined courses. Neither, he may be allowed to change the course of study in mid-stream, nor may he be allowed to take any courses which are not predefined and packaged for that major. It means, if any student starts within tent to sciences and wants to change track and wishes to major in humanities or commerce for whatever reason, the system does not allow for the same. An Indian student also does not have the opportunity to combine humanities with science and technology in today's world, in spite of this fact that most knowledge is not only inter-disciplinary but also barriers between various branches of learning are shrinking by the day. Therefore, many youngsters are bound to take up a specific stream of study more due to peer pressure, without understanding what they are getting into and the system unfortunately locks them into it. Contrast this with the Western education system with its system of core curriculum and electives.

Universities Exit from Undergraduate Education

Completely removal of Indian universities from undergraduate education is one of the worst peculiarities which crept into Indian higher education system. In fact, a high quality undergraduate education is the very essence of higher education so mostly public universities if having separate entities, must restrict themselves to graduate education and research. Without exception, all great Western universities having a world class reputation for research and graduate programmes, are also well-known for their rigorous undergraduate programmes. To fulfil this condition, it is mandatory to teach undergraduate courses in most Western universities for the finest researchers and world renowned faculty.

Poor Teaching Quality, Inbreeding, and Lack of Appraisal

The quality of mostly Indian colleges and university teachers is appallingly low. There is enormous in-breeding, with alumni being recruited to teach in the same institution where they have graduated from. Many times you may find someone pursue all his education in a specific university, not only have a chance to get recruitment to teach there but also have a chance of promotion in due course and end up as the Vice-Chancellor of the same university. All these without ever getting exposed to any other centres of higher learning! This incestuous practice has created an inflexible atmosphere in most Indian universities and has constipated academic freedom. There is lack of cross-fertilisation of ideas whatsoever, depriving the universities' new blood and rigorous intellectual discourse that accompanies it.

There is also shortage of qualified faculty due to the explosive growth in so-called professional colleges offering courses in Engineering, Sciences and even Medicine. In fact, most of them straightaway appoint a graduating student as a teaching assistant/lecturer in the same institute! For passing the MCI (Medical Council of India) inspection, mostly medical colleges are resorting to the disgraceful practice of renting faculty for a day or two.

There is no provision for appraising the quality of teaching or the performance of the teachers themselves due to absence of incentive for the teacher or faculty to perform well. Sometimes, without regard to either academic accomplishment or excellence, academic appointments are being made on the basis of caste, political patronage or other corrupt considerations. In most Western universities, the students themselves not only rate their teachers/faculty at the end of the course, but also the course as well as the faculty member who taught the course are evaluated by the respective academic departments on the basis of student rating. In fact there are a lot of instances where either a course is dropped, or a faculty member is denied tenure because of poor rating by the students. The input from students is considered very seriously not only for appraising the course and faculty, but also to redesign or restructure the course to meet their expectations.

Vested Interests

Among the various vested interests, the most powerful is the vested interests of politicians who normally assumed that the establishment of a college brings prestige, power and popularity, and is one of the surest means of securing the support of an electorate, and push for expansion. Since, a University and the State Government carry authority to grant final permission for the establishment of a new college so both are in a position to resist the establishment of new colleges if they are indoctrinated that expansion is likely to be detrimental. But, in practice, they have almost unfailingly been unable to withstand pressure exercised by the politicians.

Investment in colleges in present scenario in India as commercial propositions is the second major vested interest in the expansion of higher education. In the pre-Independence era, investment in the ownership and management of institutions for higher education in India was made by missionaries who considered this activity to be an instrument for the promotion of their religious philosophy and values, by caste and community organisations interested in providing their youth opportunities for advance, or by socially committed citizens and idealists who served higher education because they considered it their social responsibility to do so. The present investors in education are an altogether different category. Mostly starts colleges because of having a lucrative business.

There are many ways in which this category of college managers, known as education aristocrat, push growth, such as, the number of students a college is allowed to admit is set by the university to which the college is affiliated. Arrangements for the examinations to be conducted by the university are designed on the basis of numbers so determined. However, colleges not only admit students in excess of the assigned number, but also inform the university about excess numbers only at the point at which the students are required to be presented for examinations. In a three-year degree course this is as late as three years from the point of admission of the student. Technically, such admissions are irregular and, therefore, they should not only be declared invalid but also the university should refuse to accept these students for examinations because they are in excess of the number allocated to the college. But the universities are forced by the management of the colleges using political pressure. Students protest, and go on strike. And eventually, if and when the matter goes to a court of law, the court almost invariably asks the university to accept the students for examinations on the ground that students should not be made to suffer for a wrong that the management of the college has done.

Absence of Regulatory Framework

Normally, state opened the doors for private providers of education services without creating a regulatory framework for ensuring standards, quality and accountability. Much of the privatisation in higher education generally remained captive to the facultative powers of the state. In other words, the state controlled where and what kind of private institution will be established. This is mostly done through political patronage and rent seeking behaviour by the quasi-regulatory agencies such as AICTE (All India Council for Technical Education) and MCI (Medical Council of India). This resulted in an utterly chaotic scenario, and the higher education system is suspended between over-regulation and discretionary privatisation.

Normally, the education provided in the private sector is not only of an indifferent and poor quality, but also the students are bound to pay a sheer price for no mistake of theirs. In spite of ambitious, hard working and smart students and their parents are incurring significant expenditure (a few lakhs of rupees for a 4-year course), they do not have a solid skill set to productive use after completion of graduation. There is the absence of independent mechanism for evaluating the quality of education and the quality of output from both public and private educational institutions.

Lack of Leadership

In the early decades of 20th century and also during the initial years after independence, many Indian universities and centres of higher learning were fortunate to have visionary leaders, widely recognised for their professional accomplishment, integrity and commitment to excellence in higher education. Illustrious names such as Pandit Madan Mohan Malaviya, the founder of Benares Hindu University (BHU), Sri Ramaswamy Mudaliar (BHU), Sir C.R. Reddy (Andhra University), Sri S. Radhakrishnan (Andhra University), Prof. Zakir Hussain (Zamia Millia Islamia), Prof. C.V. Raman (IISc.), Prof. Kelkar (Founder Director of IIT Kanpur) stand out in the archives of higher education in India. These leaders had a vision of higher education and they not only shaped the institutions they led into centres of excellence, but have also influenced generations of students and faculty. The governments of the day gave them complete freedom and rarely intervened in the functioning of these institutions. More importantly these leaders were recognised public intellectuals who played a key role in shaping public policy in various spheres.

But, one will have to really anxiety to name a major public figure who led any institution of higher learning in the past few decades. Mostly public universities and institutes of higher learning have reduced to personal fiefdoms of leading politicians. Caste, regional origin, and political affiliation or plain ability to satisfy rent seekers emerged as the major considerations for academic appointments rather than competence and excellence. So on getting the appointment, individuals try have to satisfy their patrons by obliging their requests in appointments, promotions etc. It normally led to a natural decline of these institutions of higher learning.

The Gap between Country Needs and Provision of System

Within the limited time available to us, it is not possible to magnify this statement, to explain how and why there is a gap between the provision of higher education systems and the need of economy. But basically, this gap is the result of the fact, that the expansion of higher education in our country has been closely modelled after higher education in developed societies. It almost exclusively focuses on providing technical, technological and professional education appropriate to a fairly sophisticated level of industrialisation and technological advance. The decision to provide the country with higher education to an extent suited to a high level of technology and industrialisation has paid off.

Today, the country is not only self-sufficient for its needs for technologically trained personnel, but also the products of our universities—particularly of the new apex institutions, such as Institutes of Technology and Management—are able to compete successfully for jobs in the international market. However, even as we celebrate this success we are beginning to realise that we have made a mistake in not taking cognizance of the fact that the mass of people in our country continue to live by traditional occupations and use traditional knowledge, skills and technologies handed down through generations and that their needs, which are distinctive and different, must also be met.

Challenges

The challenges encountering India are manifold. In its quest for modernisation and pursuit of economic growth, aimed at lifting hundreds of millions of people out of poverty, providing high quality education and healthcare to its population are the greatest challenges that India has to address. The policy-makers and the political executive in India must address the following challenges in reforming the higher education system:

- How to create an equitable and accessible higher education system of high quality?
- How to cultivate competition in providing education services and offer choice to the students?
- How to popularise the importance of a true liberal education?
- How to enlarge and upgrade public financial provision for higher education?
- How to establish an independent regulatory framework to ensure high standards and quality?

Opportunities

While the challenges are manifold, there are following few opportunities and strengths that India should take advantage of:

- Young demographic profile (% of 18-24 age group).
- Hard working, ambitious, motivated teenagers.

- Enormous demand for quality education.
- Culture and society that values education and abundance scholarship.
- Parents willing to spend significant resources (1,10,000 students studying abroad spend approx $ 1 billion/year).
- Graduates no longer seek a comfy government job and are willing to compete in the market.
- Impressive infrastructure that can be redeployed.
- Non-monetary inputs that can make a difference 24 Reforming Higher Education in India.

Possible Measures and Reforms

It would be supercilious to try to offer solutions to this situation, particularly in view of the fact that the efforts that have been made so far have not been rewarded with much success. However, some steps should be taken. First and foremost step may be that there should be a concerted and massive move to delink jobs from degrees in situations where the content of the degree is not really relevant to the job for which the degree is required. Second the system should be freed from the dead wood and weight of constraining service conditions, administrative practices, procedures, rules and regulations and allowed space to creatively respond to the needs of society. Government controls on higher education, including well-intentioned supervision and monitoring by bodies such as the University Grants Commission have become counter-productive. They tend to drive away people with sound values and commitments to education and leave the field open for those who do not mind sacrificing quality and relevance as long as their vested interests are served.

To an extent, higher education should not only be liberated from government controls without any radical changes in the present framework but also should be carefully examined the relationship between the State and higher education, so as to make way for alternate, more independent structures. Even the basic requirement to establish universities by statute is needed to be reviewed and revised. Some of the key reform proposals are as under:

Non-monetary Inputs

While enhancing funding to suit the demographic realities of India and increased investment to create better infrastructure are absolutely essential, the real issue in reforming higher education in India is not only money. There are some other non-monetary inputs that may make a vital difference. Some of them are as under:

Encourage Unorthodox Education and Humanities

Any society needs a mixture of specialists and generalists to fulfil its unique requirements. While the need for science and technology, and vocational and other specialised forms of skill-based education is well recognised and appreciated, especially in a developing economy, the importance of broad, liberal education is not much appreciated. A true liberal education will go a long way in producing the kind of leaders and permissive citizens who will take-up a career in business, organisational management, government, politics and academia that are badly needed by the developing world. It is a manifestation to the maturity of a tremendously industrialised and developed nation such as the US, that the bulk of its university graduates major in liberal arts and humanities.

Creative Examination System along with Continuous Evaluation

The current examination system leaves little for imagination. The standard pattern should be to test the student's breadth of knowledge and the emphasis must be on one final all encompassing examination. There should be a fundamental and cardinal shift in the examination system to achieve the following:

- Test the deepness of student's knowledge, not breadth.
- Test expository skills, application of knowledge and problem solving capacity.
- Test should challenge the student's ability to be originative and innovative.
- Stress should on continuous evaluation and not one final test.
- Evaluation should be done by the course teaching faculty.

Faculty Recruitment and Appraisal

The quality of teaching and teachers among mostly Indian universities and centres of higher learning is appallingly low. Most Western universities go out of their way to recruit and retain top faculty. Even in India, in yester-years students used to select a university or college based on the quality of instruction and reputation of faculty. Not only recruitment but also appraisal of faculty in Indian universities and colleges must be changed on the basis of following principles:

- No conjugation at any cost, i.e. no recruitment of alumnus.
- Everlasting appraisal and rating by students.
- Effort to recruit contemporary thinkers and promote of new ideas.
- Encourage scrupulous intellectual discourse.
- Compulsory undergraduate teaching by all appointed faculty.
- Constant new blood.

Problem Solving Research

There is deficient in meaningful research of any kind among mostly Indian Universities. What passes off for research is normally a rephrase of existing material, and lacks in intellectual piquancy, insights, painstaking and thorough data gathering, intemperate analysis, and logical consistency. Mostly academics are inadequate in writing and communication skill. As a result academia have become increasingly marginalised in shaping public discourse and solving real problems in the societal, scientific and technological domains absence of academic rigour, poor communications, and lack of relevance. Innovative funding mechanisms as well as other incentives to promote high quality, problem-solving research in both technologies related fields and humanities need to be evolved. It is vital at school level to emphasis on reasoning and analysis and good writing skills so that productive research may be possible at university level.

Monetary Inputs

Indeed, Good quality education demands momentous resources. It will be naïve and short-sighted to think that providing top notch education infrastructure and attracting talented faculty will be possible without substantial resources.

Structural Reforms Differentiation of Indian Higher Education Institutions

The current system of higher education in India consists of 3 years college offering courses in humanities, commerce and pure sciences, 4 years colleges offering courses in engineering and related technical fields. In addition there are Medical colleges (5 years), Law Schools (3 years and 5 years) and Universities normally offer graduate (Master's and Doctoral) programmes in various disciplines. There are various research institutes offering doctoral programmes. This structure postulates that everyone needs a 3 or 4-years college degree in the Indian higher education system. There is no room for the majority of youngsters, who might be on the lookout for acquiring a skill that is readily marketable and which will get them gainful employment. This framework puts most of the students in a straight jacket without having any room for flexibility, choice or experimentation of any kind. So, there is need of the hour to bring about a qualitative differentiation in the structure of Indian higher education, with the following objectives:

- Offering flexibility and choice for students.
- Offering strong vocational as well as skill based courses (diploma) of shorter duration (2 years on average).
- Facilitate vertical mobility, i.e. people who with a 2-years diploma may use that credit to earn a 3 or 4 years college degree at a time of their choice.
- Couple the vocational courses with internships in partnership with industry.

Public, Private and Non-profit Providers

We need to recognise that there must not be monopoly of higher education. Really stating, excessive state regulation has only weakened our educational erection, and constipated innovation and excellence. Therefore, there should be minimal entry barriers in creation of private universities in any state key policy decision. There is a need to offer not only suitable tax incentives for all educational investments but also full tax benefits for all endowments in education. In order to provide uniform basis for appraisal of the candidates' scholastic level, there is a need to conduct a nation-wide examination on the pattern of SAT or ACT in the US, or 'A' levels in the UK in a creative way to assess the calibre of students who are seeking university admission. There should be a policy so that competition and choice should dictate admissions, and demand and supply should dictate the fee structure. The state can gratify primarily to the economically weaker sections, and offer admission at subsidised fees. Non-state institutions should be encouraged to adopt a differentiated fee structure as is adopted by a manufacturing concern, charging higher fee from those who can afford, and cross-subsidizing the education of those who need support. Such strategic and selective intervention, freedom of entry, autonomy in operation, complete transparency, competition, choice, cross subsidisation, and credible rating will together constitute the necessary conditions to create a first rate higher education system to meet the challenges of the future.

Politics, Governance and Education

It is necessary for individual growth and national advancement; there should be limited government and political and economic freedom to citizens. But liberty cannot be construed in a very narrow and negative sense of State not abridging individual freedoms. While State's role in business is now universally opposed, there are no realistic substitutes to State in school education, primary health care and the like. It is equally important that the state must create conditions not only for imparting good quality higher education and promotion of excellence, but also for meeting the challenges of a growing, modern economy and vibrant society. It does not mean that State alone should either pay for these services or necessarily deliver these services. Private and voluntary sectors should have a significant role, and nowhere in market economies is that role more pronounced than in India. Reforms in education cannot be isolated from reforms in governance and administration. In fact, Freedom is a glorious asset for growth instead of a liability. Sound politics is about making democracy and growth compatible, not finding excuses for non-performance.

No problem relating to governance is unmanageable. All these crises are amenable to simple, practical, effective, acceptable solutions. We need far reaching reforms of the great institutions of state to make our politics work for our people, to ensure decentralisation of power and citizen-centred governance, to provide speedy, efficient and accessible justice to all, and to hold our public servants—elected or appointed—to account by a variety of self-correcting mechanisms. Only when we accomplish these goals will our children fulfil their true potential, and India will be free from the great sin of avoidable suffering. In a fundamental sense, the future of India depends on what this generation of Indians will do. Through collective, informed assertion we can, and will, make a difference, and transform our governance. Really, no challenge may be greater, and no task may be nobler.

Indeed, India has the potential to be a great source of technological manpower. Our youngsters have the ambition along with our tradition worships knowledge. But there is a need of hard work and common sense to bridge the gulf between promise and fulfilment. Although education is a necessary, but it is not sufficient condition for high growth. There are various other conditions which guarantee prosperity, *e.g.* Infrastructure, free enterprise and rule of law. But, first of all, we must set-up our right educational system. Now, the people are ready and willing. Are governments and 'educationists' really prepared to accept the challenge?

Privatisation

Privatisation will inescapably figure definitely in any consideration of more independent structures. But the concepts of privatisation along with sharing the burden need to be advanced far ahead of where they stand at present. In modern scenario, privatisation and sharing are basically perceived interms of sharing costs or the financial burden. Privatisation in the sense of freedom from control over academic programmes, modes of organising teaching and research, and liberalisation in several other ways has not yet been accepted.

On the other hand, wherever privatisation has been allowed or even encouraged, it has been pinned down by rules and regulations that restrict creative advance and pin private bodies down to sharing the obligations of the State. For instance, private ventures in higher education are also required to share in the obligation to provide low cost higher education, i.e. "affordable to all" or the obligation to honour and serve the policy of reservations. Moves towards free and full privatisation may be haunted by fear of commercialisation. The possibility that privatisation may in fact help to fight the corrupt commercialisation that is flagrant today is not given adequate consideration. Really, there is time to take the risks involved and to liberalise higher education with full heartedly. It is also necessary to allow market forces to free play with the conviction that this will restore quality and excellence.

Extending and Legitimising the Contribution of Non-Formal Educators

Finally, NGOs who are already engaged in development related research and education to extend their activities, must be encouraged. Wherever convenient it would be useful to give full recognition to their research and to the courses they offer by according them parity with what the formal system provides. Simultaneously, universities could be firmly encouraged to draw upon the work that NGOs have done to develop courses. Therefore, there may be two challenging tasks, i.e. to develop courses that can be offered by the universities to their own students for graduate and post-graduate degrees on one hand and to get their different departments to develop courses that can be offered by schools as well as by non-formal education programmes at the primary school, middle school, high school and higher secondary school levels on the other hand. It may be able to give not only fresh lift but also needed substance to the country's efforts to vocationalize education at these levels. It will empower universities at the same time.

Not Impossible

The moves suggested above may be difficult, but not impossible. Under colonial rule we, as a people, moved firmly and determinedly to get the British to establish universities in India and to provide us with European education. We were successful in our effort to a large extent. Few other colonies British, American, Belgian or French were able to achieve the advances in higher education that India did as a British colony. Today, there is need to put in the same kind of pre-determined effort on behalf of higher education that we did then. The resolution of the crisis in higher education in our country normally depends on how soon and how effectively we move.

REFERENCES

Agarwal, V., Sharma, U.R. (2004) Privatisation *vs*. Commercialisation of Higher Education: Some Facts, Concerns and Suggestion. *University News*, 42(07), pp. 25-28 and 34.

Ahmad, N., Siddiqui, M.A. (2003) Privatisation of Higher Education: An Appraisal. *University News*, 41(07), February 17-23, pp. 4-12.

Centre for Higher Education Policy Studies (CHEPS) (2005), "The European Higher Education and Research Landscape 2020. Scenarios and Strategic Debates".

Dongaonkar, (2004) Higher Education in India: The Varied Dimension. *University News*, 42(21), pp. 17-23.

El-Khawas, E. (2002), "Developing an Academic Career in a Globalizing World", in J. Enders and O. Fulton (eds.), *Higher Education in a Globalizing World: International Trends and Mutual Observations, A Festschrift in Honour of*

Ulrich Teichler, Kluwer, Dordrecht, pp. 242-54.

Higher Education in Developing Countries, Peril and Promise, a World Bank Report.

Higher Education Reform in India (Ed. Suma Chitnis and Philip G. Altbach), Sage Publications, New Delhi, 1993.

http://www.education.nic.in/htmlweb/edusta.html, Ministry of Education, Government of India's Official Website

Higher Education: The Lessons of Experience—Development in Practice Series. The International Bank for Reconstruction and Development: The World Bank, Washington DC, 1994.

Indian Higher Education Reform: From Half-Baked Socialism to Half-Baked Capitalism, by Devesh Kapur and Pratap Bhanu Mehta.

Ischinger, B. (2006), "Higher Education for a Changing World", *OECD Observer*, June.

Jacobs, B. and R. van der Ploeg (2006), "Guide to Reform of Higher Education: A European Perspective", *Economic Policy*, Vol. 21, Issue 47, pp. 535-92.

Karuppayil, Mohan (2004) Privatisation and Access to Higher Education, *University News*, 42(07), pp. 62-64.

Madhusudanan, K.N. and Manjunath, B.R. (2003) Internationalisation of Higher Education: Indian Scenario, *University News*, 41(39), pp. 1-6.

OECD (2004a), *Internationalisation and Trade in Higher Education: Opportunities and Challenges*, OECD Publishing, Paris.

Sahni, R., Sumita, K. (2004) GATTS and Higher Education: Some Reflection, *Economic & Political Weekly*. May 22, 2004, pp. 2174-80.

Sant, Bharat R. (2004) Private Participation in Indian Higher Education: Towards Excellence in Teaching and Learning. *University News*, 42(07), pp. 55-61.

Singh, Amrik (2004) Challenges in Higher Education. *Economic & Political Weekly*, May 22, 2004, pp. 2155-58.

The Structure of Higher Education: A World View. Eric Ashby: International Council for Educational Development, New York, 1973, Occasional Paper Number 6.

Vincent-Lancrin, S. (2009), "What is Changing in Academic Research? Trends and Prospects", in *Higher Education* 2030, Volume 2: *Globalisation*, OECD Publishing, Paris.

Stakeholders' Responses", CHEPS/Universiteit Twente, accessed 22 June

Vught, F.A. van (2006), "Higher Education System Dynamics and Useful Knowledge Creation", in J. Duderstadt and L. Weber (eds.), *Universities and Business: Towards a Better Society*, Economica, New York.

15
Instructional Strategies for Creating a Positive Classroom Climate

Mona Mehta

Introduction

Teachers play various roles in a typical classroom, but surely one of the most important is that of classroom manager. Effective teaching and learning cannot take place in a poorly managed classroom. Effective teachers appear to be effective with students of all achievement levels regardless of the levels of heterogeneity in their classes. If the teacher is ineffective, students under that teacher's tutelage, will achieve inadequate progress academically, regardless of how similar or different they are regarding their academic achievement. Current research indicates that students in classes of teachers classified as most effective can be expected to gain about 52 per centile points in their achievement over a year's time. Students in classes of teachers classified as least effective can be expected to gain only about 14 per centile points over a year's time. This comparison is even more dramatic when one realises that some researchers have estimated that students will exhibit again in learning of about 6 per centile points simply from maturation from growing one year older and gleaning new knowledge and information through everyday life (*see* Hattie, 1992; Cahen & Davis, 1987).

The effective teacher performs many functions that can be organised into three major roles:

1. Making-wise choices about the most effective instruction strategies to employ.

2. Designing classroom curriculum to facilitate student learning, and
3. Making effective use of classroom management techniques (Marzano, Pickering, & Pollock, 2001). Therefore, effective teachers have a wide array of instructional strategies at their disposal, are skilled at identifying and articulating the proper sequence and pacing of their content, are skilled in classroom management techniques.

Organising Your Classroom and Supplies

Arranging the physical setting for teaching is a logical starting point for classroom management because it is a task that all teachers face before school begins. Many teachers find it easier to plan other aspects of classroom management once they know how the physical features of the classroom will be organised.

Four Keys to Good Room Arrangement

- Keep high-traffic areas free of congestion.
- Be sure students can be seen easily by the teacher.
- Keep frequently used teaching materials and student supplies readily accessible.
- Be certain students can easily see whole-class presentations and displays.

Arrangement of Student desks—Arrange desks so students are facing and can readily see the primary whole—group instructional area.

Small-Group Instruction Areas—Arrange this area so you can monitor the rest of the class from your seated teaching position.

Checklist Room Preparation

Floor Space

- Student desks/tables
- Small-group area
- Computer Workstations
- Teacher's desk and equipment
- Bookcases

- Centres
- Pets and plants area
- Traffic patterns
- Classroom library

Storage Space and Supplies

- Textbooks and trade books
- Student Work
- Portfolio Files
- Frequently used instructional material
- Teacher's supplies
- Classroom supplies
- Student belongings
- Equipment
- Seasonal or infrequently used items

Establishing Classroom Norms and Expectations

For students to have a successful year in your classroom, they must understand and practice the behaviours you expect from them.

What is an Effectively Managed Classroom?

An effectively managed classroom is one that runs smoothly, with minimal confusion and downtime, and maximizes opportunities for student learning.

- Goals are target aspirations not necessarily attained everyday. However, long-term goals determine our daily actions.
- Expectations are desired behaviours or outcomes. An effective teacher makes her expectations known to the students and consistently teaches and reinforces the expected behaviours.
- Rules and procedures refer to stated expectations regarding behaviour. A rule identifies general expectations or standards of behaviour. A procedure also communicates expectations for behaviour. They are usually applied in a specific activity, and they are directed at accomplishing something rather than prohibiting behaviour.
- Effective teachers generally involve students in the democratic

process of determining classroom rules, but generally the rules entail respect and courtesy towards all people, be prompt and prepared, listen quietly while others are speaking, and obey all school rules.

Checklist Norms, Expectations, Rules, and Procedures

- What are my short and long term goals for myself this year?
- What are my short and long term goals for my students this year?

Individual Work and Teacher-led Activities

- Attention during presentations
- Participation Talk among students
- Obtaining help
- When individual work has been completed?

Transition into and out of the Classroom

- Beginning the school day
- Leaving the room
- Returning to the room
- Ending the day

Procedures for Small-Group Instruction

- Getting the class ready
- Student movement
- Expected behaviour in the group
- Expected behaviour of students out of group
- Materials and supplies

Procedures for Cooperative Group Activities

- Roles of group members
- Expected behaviours
- Interaction to include every member
- Interaction to move towards instructional goals

General Procedures

- Distributing materials
- Classroom helpers (students)
- Interruptions or delays
- Restrooms
- Library, resource room, school office
- Cafeteria
- Playground
- Fire and disaster drills
- Classroom helpers (parents, aide etc.)

Fostering Student Accountability

Additional procedures are needed to encourage students to complete assignments and to engage in other learning activities. Ultimately, the goal of any accountability system is to help students develop into independent learners; thus, your procedures should give as much responsibility as possible to the students themselves, rather than having the student depend on either you or their parents to see that assignments are completed.

- Clear Communication of Assignments and Work Requirements
- Monitoring Progress on and Completion of Assignments
- Feedback to Students

Checklist Accountability Procedures

Communicating Assignments and Work Requirements

- Where and how will you post assignments?
- What will be your standards for form and neatness?
- How will absent students know what assignments to make up?
- What will be the consequences of late or incomplete work?

Monitoring Progress on Completion of Assignments

- What procedures will you use to monitor work in progress?
- When and how will you monitor projects or longer assignments?
- How will you determine whether students are completing

assignments?
- How will you collect completed assignments?
- What records of student work will you retain?
- How will you encourage students to monitor themselves?

Feedback

- What are your school's grading policies and procedures?
- What kinds of feedback will you provide, and when?
- How will you encourage students to reflect on their own progress?
- What will you do when a student stops doing assignments?
- What procedures will you follow to send materials home to parents?
- Where will you display student work?
- What records, if any, of their own work will the students maintain?
- Will students keep portfolios? If so, how will entries be selected, and how will students reflect on them?
- How will you handle grading disputes?

Getting Off to a Good Start

The beginning of the school year is an important time for classroom management because your student will learn attitudes, behaviour, and work habits that will affect the rest of the year. It is the first few weeks of school that students learn the behaviours expected of them and how to accomplish school tasks successfully.

Creating a Positive Climate in Your Classroom

Effective teachers create a positive learning environment through actions and deeds. The foundation of a positive climate is positive interaction between the teacher and students and among students. A positive environment encourages students to be excited about their school experience and about learning.

(1) *Speak courteously and calmly*—Say "please", "thank you" and "excuse me" for courtesies to become expected. A calm voice indicates acceptance and self-control.

(2) *Share information*—Learn names as soon as possible and engage in activities that help students learn more about each other. Speak personally with students and get to know them as individuals.

(3) *Use positive statements as often as possible—Accentuate the positive*—Not only do negative comments cause a student to feel negative; they also tend to create a negative environment that affects everyone.

(4) *Establish a feeling of community*—Teach students to work cooperatively and give them regular opportunities to learn in structured cooperative activities. Conduct class meetings on a regular basis for class-building, problem-solving, and content-related discussions.

Teaching Rules and Procedures

One of the surest ways to communicate your expectation for student behaviour is through a planned system of teaching classroom rules and procedures. The term 'teach' is purposely used because you will not communicate your expectations adequately if you only tell students about rules and procedures. Three important aspects include:

(1) *Describing and demonstrating the desired behaviour*—Use words and actions to convey what behaviour is acceptable or desirable. Be as specific as possible.

(2) *Rehearsal*—This means practicing the behaviours. Rehearsal serves two purposes:
    (*a*) It helps children learn the appropriate behaviour, and it provides you with an opportunity to determine whether they understand and can follow a procedure correctly.
    (*b*) It also affords the teacher the opportunity to explain why the rule or procedure is important.

(3) *Feedback*—Tell students how well they did. Even if improvement is needed, be positive.

Planning for a Good Beginning

Planning for a warm and friendly learning environment for your student is a positive first step in starting the school year. Some typical activities include:

- Greeting the students, introductions, room description, get-acquainted activities, presentation and discussion of rules, procedures, and consequences, content activities, time fillers, administrative activities (distributing textbooks etc.).

Communicating with Parents

Prepare a letter to send home explaining any essential information not already covered in school handouts. Typically, teachers at one grade level collaborate on the letter. A cheerful, friendly letter that is neat, legible, grammatically correct, and free of misspellings will create a good impression and communicate a professional image to the parents. The letter may include: Information about you, materials or supplies their child will need, class schedule with conference times and how parents may reach you, curriculum units or special field trips, and special events for parents.

Special Problems

Interruptions by office staff, parents, custodians, and others; late arrivals on the first day; one or more children are assigned to your class after the first day; child forgets lunch money or supplies; large amount of paperwork the first week of school; child forgets bus number or misses bus; insufficient number of textbooks or materials; student disability that interferes with understanding or following directions; crying; wetting; child becomes sick.

Preparing for a Substitute

Create a handbook for the substitute who may teach in your absence. Include the following: Class roll, seating chart, copy of classroom rule and consequences, daily schedule, list of medical alerts and medication times, emergency lesson plans, emergency procedures, names of teachers and students who can provide assistance, and map of school.

Planning and Conducting Instruction

Your classroom is organised, you have thought about the climate to be established and the expectations you want to communicate, you have developed and taught your rules and procedures, and you have systems in place to manage student learning. Now, that your students are attentive and ready to participate comes the point that management and instruction meet. Well-planned lessons with a variety of developmentally appropriate activities support the positive learning environment you have created.

Planning Instructional Activities

Types of planning include both long-range and short-range. Accomplishing the longer plan requires dividing the work into terms, the terms into units, and the units into weeks and days.

Types of instructional activities include:

- Content Development (Whole-Group Instruction),
- Grouped Basic Skill Instruction,
- Individual Work, and
- Feedback.

Planning for Clear Instruction:

- Presenting new concept,
- Checking for understanding, and
- Reteaching.

Kounin's Concepts for Managing Whole-Group Instruction

A central theme in managing teacher-led activities well is the idea of activity flow—the degree to which a lesson proceeds smoothly, without digressions, diversions, or interruptions. Lessons with good flow keep students' attention and prevent deviation because most of the cues for behaviour during the lesson are focused on behaviours appropriate for the lesson. Kounin's concepts include:

Preventing Misbehaviour

- With-it-ness is the degree to which the teacher corrects misbehaviour before it intensifies or spreads to more students and also targets the correct student when doing so.
- Overlapping refers to how the teacher handles two or more simultaneous events.

Managing Movement

- Whereas withitness and overlapping are accomplished by handling external interruptions and student intrusions into the flow of the lesson, movement management is accomplished by avoiding teacher-caused intrusions or delays.
- Momentum refers to pacing and is indicated by lessons that move along briskly.
- Smoothness is epitomised in lesson continuity. A smooth flowing lesson keeps student attention.

Maintaining Group Focus

- A teacher must be conscious of the group influence on the instruction. Group focus can be maintained through several techniques.
- Group alerting means taking action to engage the attention of the whole class while individuals are responding.
- Accountability occurs when the teacher lets students know that their performance will be observed and evaluated in some manner.
- High-participation formats are lessons that programme the behaviour of students when they are not directly involved in answering a teacher's question.

Managing Cooperative Learning Groups

Strategies and Routines that Support Cooperative Learning

Room arrangement, talk and movement procedures, group attention signals, promoting interdependence within the group, and individual accountability.

- Monitoring Student Work and Behaviour, and
- Effective Group Work Skills.

Social Skills/Explaining Skills/Leadership Skills

Active listening includes listening to others without interrupting, being able to summarize other's ideas, incorporating them into the discussion, and using them constructively in completing the group's assignment.

Beginning the Use of Cooperative Learning Groups

Room Arrangement/Procedures and Routines/Forming Groups/Initial Group Tasks/Teaching Group Skills/Student Goals and Participation/ Using Group and Individual rewards.

Checklist Planning for Cooperative Group Instruction

Room Arrangement

- How will student seating be arranged?
- How will individual and group materials and supplies be stored?

Routines and Expectations

- What are your expectations for student movement to, from, and during group work?
- What expectations about talking will you communicate to students?
- What group attention signals will be used?
- Will students have specific roles?
- Do any group skills have to be discussed, modelled, or practiced?

Monitoring, Accountability, and Feedback Procedures

- Will group work have individual products, group products, or both?
- How will individual or group work be assessed?
- How will you monitor student behaviour and work during group activities?
- How will students receive feedback about individual and group performance?
- How will students receive feedback about their behaviour in groups?

Group Skills that must be Discussed, Modelled, or Practiced

- Social skills?
- Explaining skills?
- Leadership skills?

Maintaining Appropriate Student Behaviour

- Monitoring Student Behaviour during whole group presentations, small group instruction, individual work, by moving around the room, during cooperative group work, and monitor completion of assignments.
  - Consistency
- *Management of Inappropriate Behaviour*—Make eye contact or move closer to student. Use a signal, such as finger to the lips or a head shake, to prompt the appropriate behaviour. Monitor until the student complies. Provide a simple reminder of the correct procedure by either stating the procedure or asking the student to recite the procedure. Redirect student to a task if he is off-task. Ask student to stop misbehaviour.
  - Building a Positive Climate-Use praise.
  - Improving Class Climate Through Incentives and Rewards.

Communication Skills for Teaching

- ***Constructive Assertiveness***—Describe your concerns clearly, insist that misbehaviour be corrected and resist being coerced or manipulated.
- ***Empathic Responding***—Listen to the student's perspective and react in ways that maintain a positive relationship and encourage further discussion.
- ***Problem Solving***—Includes several steps for reaching mutually satisfactory resolutions to problems; it requires working with the student to develop the plan.

Managing Problem Behaviours

Management Strategies

- ***Minor Interventions***—Use non-verbal cues, get the activity going, use proximity, use group focus, redirect behaviour, provide needed instruction, issue a brief desist, give the student choices.
- ***Moderate Interventions***—Withhold a privilege or desired activity, isoiate or remove student, use penalty, assign detention, use a school-based consequence.

- ***More Extensive Interventions***—Use problem solving, use five-step intervention procedure, use "think time" strategy, use the Reality Therapy Model, confer with parent, create an individual contract with the student.
- ***Special Problems***—Bullying, tattling, rudeness towards teacher, chronic avoidance of work, fighting, power struggles.
- ***Final Reminder***—Think and act positively, do not personalize.

Managing Special Groups

Strategies for Individual Differences

- *Team Teaching*—Coordination of schedules, transitional routines, reminding students what they are supposed to take with them, rules and procedures, maintaining responsibility for work.
- *Modifying Whole*—Class Instruction—Interactive instruction, seating arrangement, directions, and assignments.
- *Supplementary Instruction*—Coordinating times with other teachers, staying on schedule, having something for drop-in students to do while waiting for instruction, getting returning students involved again, activities when supplementary instruction is not held, in-class aides, content mastery classroom, and inclusion.
- *Individualized Instruction*—Cooperative groups, peer tutoring.

Creating a successful classroom climate with a supportive environment is one of the most important classroom management strategies teachers need to get right if they want to create a classroom where learning is highly valued. If your classroom climate is to be successful it has to be positive and motivate your students to want to be successful. As with many aspects of classroom management, the most important component of a positive classroom is the teacher, and this is where the process must start. The climate in the classroom is of course more than the physical classroom environment. It is a process that builds the psychological framework for all activity that happens in the classroom. The classroom climate is not just about motivation and student well being, it is a major ingredient of the context for successful learning. Real learning cannot take place in a negative classroom climate, in the same way that plants will not grow if the soil is not right.

How can Teachers Create a Positive Classroom Climate?

It seems that three particular features are present in all successful classrooms:

- The first key factor is the quality of the relationships, in other words how much everyone helps and supports each other. The relationship between teacher and students is clearly important, but a relationship between students is equally important in ensuring a successful classroom climate.
- The second key feature is the personal development of students, and how easy we make it for them to grow as learners and fulfil their potential.
- The third key factor is the smooth running of the classroom, characterised by an orderly environment where teacher expectations and standards of personal behaviour and achievement are high and clearly understood by everyone.

The three broad pillars mentioned above are solidly present in successful classrooms, but the components of good relationships, student personal development and the smooth running of the classroom are not discrete entities, but rather fluid elements skilfully managed by good teachers and brought together to make a warm, positive and successful classroom environment.

Although some teachers have a personality type that makes it easier for them than for other teachers to establish a successful classroom climate, all teachers can learn the skills and classroom management strategies that are the components of a successful classroom.

Common strategies that successful teachers use to build a positive classroom climate:

(1) They Create a Warm Classroom Environment

Research studies seem to suggest that students respond best to teachers who are at the warm end of the spectrum in terms of how they relate to their students. In other words, teachers who are approachable, friendly, helpful and supportive and who can control the class and impose themselves without appearing too strict or overbearing. The opposite side of this coin is that students seem to respond less well to teachers who are inconsistent, uncertain and who tend to criticise students frequently and draw attention to students' shortcomings. The key finding here is not just how well or badly students relate to their teachers' relative warmth or lack of it, but that the quality of learning outcomes is affected by how warm and approachable students perceive their teachers to be.

When teachers make it clear to students that they are concerned about their students' emotional needs, as well as their curriculum and learning needs, students seem to participate better in class, and in particular seem more prepared to ask for help when they are in difficulty. Research shows that it is often the least able students, who have the most need of help, who feel least able to ask for help, if they sense that their teacher is unaware of their emotional needs. The result is their need goes unanswered. To create a warm supportive classroom climate teachers can—

- show understanding and openness so students feel confident to speak openly about their needs and to talk about problems, in an atmosphere that is not confrontational;
- be approachable and let students see the teacher sees them as people and values them as individuals—students need to feel they can trust the teacher before they will open up about difficulties they may have, either personal problems or problems with understanding the learning;
- help students by making it clear that it is acceptable to make mistakes when learning, in fact making mistakes is important for true learning to take place. One of the posters in my classroom that I refer to often with students says "The only dumb question is the one you do not ask; and
- be principled by making sure you treat students fairly and justly, that you can tell the difference between the person and the behaviour they may display.

(2) They are Enthusiastic

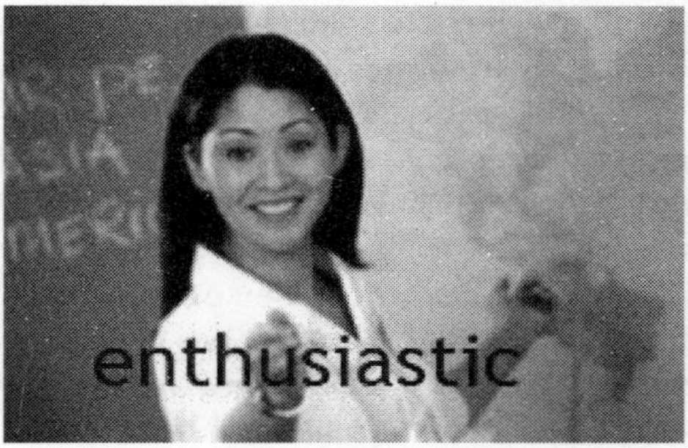

Another classroom management strategy that promotes a positive classroom climate is enthusiasm on the part of the teacher. The research shows that teachers who consistently send positive messages about the subject being studied do have an influence on how students respond, by motivating students more than teachers who are less enthusiastic. Students never get inspired by teachers who are not enthusiastic, or who create a negative classroom climate. Enthusiastic teachers often come across as confident specialists who really enjoy teaching their subject and can "wrap up" the learning in many different ways to make it interesting and accessible to all learners.

(3) They have High Expectations

One of the most consistent research findings is the effect on student performance of teacher expectations. In short, students do better when they believe their teachers expect them to do well and create a supportive academic climate. For example, a high teacher expectation is among the teacher interventions with the highest effect sizes that Hattie identifies in his book "*Visible Learning for Teachers*." By contrast, students who think their teacher does not have high expectations of them, are caught in a self-fulfilling prophecy and tend do less well. Teachers often communicate their own perceptions in subtle ways, and perhaps unintentionally. It is easy, for example, to believe we are praising students, but actually be undermining them by saying things such as: "Well done, I was surprised how good your answer was." The subliminal message picked-up by students here is that the teacher perception actually is that these students are of low ability.

Sometimes, there are other, possibly unintentional, behaviours that students interpret as negative perceptions. For example, it is easy for a teacher to ask more questions to students they perceive as being more able, and in so doing create fewer opportunities for students who are seen as not so able.

In the same way, low teacher expectations may result in some students being asked only to answer low order questions, which do not take learning forward in a meaningful way.

The real danger of basing teacher expectations on mistaken perceptions is that students realise what is going on and start to internalise these perceptions, with the result that everyone in the class starts to behave in ways the teacher expects them to behave. This can lead to a very positive cycle for those "high expectation" students, who may become high achievers. The opposite is also true for the "low expectation" students who sink further and further down their negative cycle. As principled educators we cannot accept this kind of "collateral damage".

Teachers with high expectations of students seem to have these things in common:

- They pay very close attention to the progress their students are making, and check against objective data that their perceptions or "gut feelings" about students are backed up by facts, and so avoid acting on mistaken perceptions of students' abilities.
- They take great care not to communicate low expectations: students may have limited abilities, but teachers need to communicate their faith that students will do the best they can within the limits of their abilities.
- Make sure students get useful feedback on their progress,

feedback that is honest but constructive and focused on continuous improvement, it is the "I wan't you to show me how well you can do" approach, not the "This is what you have shown me you can not do" approach.

- Take great care about how they ask questions in class—they ask high order questions, usually involving open questions [What/Where/When/Why/How [particularly How], that encourage deep rather than superficial answers. These questions are sometimes called "fat questions", and teachers need to allow students enough time to construct well thought out answers.
- They emphasise good presentation of student work as much as the content, and, crucially, expect all students to meet these high presentation demands, because they expect all students will take a real pride in their work.

Good teachers know how important it is to build and maintain a classroom climate that is positive and supportive, and are proactive in their approach because they want to take as much responsibility as they can for creating a classroom environment that:

1. helps to deliver a curriculum that promotes social and emotional learning as well as academic learning;
2. helps teachers to be effective with a wide range of students;
3. promotes good quality of life for learners and teachers; and
4. reinforces the central importance of student progress.

> "Expert teachers are proficient in creating optimal classroom climates for learning, particularly to increase the probability of feedback occurring (which often involves allowing for, and certainly tolerating, student errors). They build climates where error is welcomed, where student questioning is high, where engagement is the norm, and where students can gain reputations as effective learners."

They are Able to Help the Students to Identify Similarities and Differences

The ability to break a concept into its similar and dissimilar characteristics allows students to understand (and often solve) complex problems by analysing them in a more simple way. Teachers can either directly present similarities and differences, accompanied by deep discussion and inquiry, or simply ask students to identify similarities and differences on their own. Research also notes that graphic forms are a good way to represent similarities and differences.

Applications

- Use Venn diagrams or charts to compare and classify items.
- Engage students in comparing, classifying, and creating metaphors and analogies.
- Summarizing and Note Taking.
- These skills promote greater comprehension by asking students to analyse a Subject to expose what is essential and then put it in their own words.
- Provide a set of rules for creating a summary.
- When summarising, ask students to question what is unclear, clarify those questions, and then predict what will happen next in the text.
- Research shows that taking more notes is better than fewer notes, though verbatim note taking is ineffective because it does not allow time to process the information. Teachers should encourage and give time for review and revision of notes; notes can be the best study guides for tests.
- Use teacher-prepared notes.
- Stick to a consistent format for notes, although students can refine the notes as necessary.

(4) Reinforcing Effort and Providing Recognition

Nothing Worth Having Has Ever Achieved Without Effort

- Effort and recognition speak to the attitudes and beliefs of students, and teachers must show the connection between effort and achievement. Research shows that although not all students realise the importance of effort, they can learn to change their beliefs to emphasize effort.

Applications

- Share stories about people who succeeded by not giving-up.
- Have students keep a log of their weekly efforts and achievements, reflect on it periodically, and even mathematically analyse the data.
- Find ways to personalise recognition. Give awards for individual accomplishments.
- "Pause, Prompt, Praise." If a student is struggling, pause to discuss the problem, then prompt with specific suggestions to help her improve. If the student's performance improves as a result, offer praise.

(5) Homework and Practice

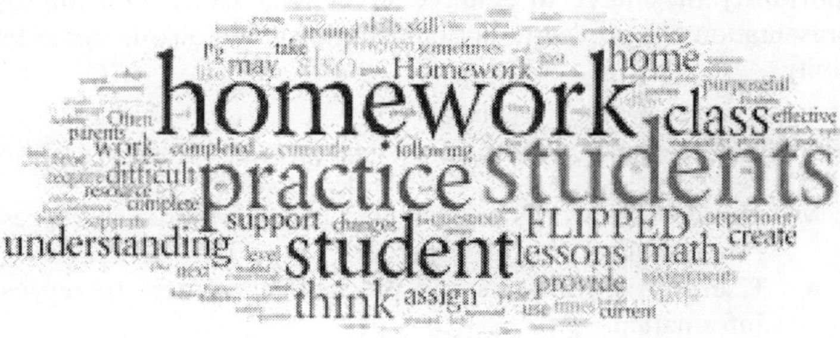

Homework provides students with the opportunity to extend their learning outside the classroom. However, research shows that the amount of homework assigned should vary by grade level and that parent involvement should be minimal. Teachers should explain the purpose of homework to both the student and the parent or guardian, and teachers should try to give feedback on all homework assigned.

Applications

- Establish a homework policy with advice—such as keeping a consistent schedule, setting, and time limit—that parents and students may not have considered.

- Tell students if homework is for practice or preparation for upcoming units.
- Maximise the effectiveness of feedback by varying the way it is delivered.
- Assign timed quizzes for homework and have students report on their speed and accuracy.
- Focus practice on difficult concepts and set aside time to accommodate practice periods.

(6) Non-linguistic Representations

> Learning results from what the student does and thinks and only from what the student does and thinks. The teacher can advance learning only by influencing the student does to learn.
>
> —*Herbert Simon*

According to research, knowledge is stored in two forms: linguistic and visual. The more students use both forms in the classroom, the more opportunity they have to achieve. Recently, use of non-linguistic representation has proven to not only stimulate but also increase brain activity.

Applications

- Incorporate words and images using symbols to represent relationships.
- Use physical models and physical movement to represent information.

(7) Setting Objectives and Providing Feedback

> Discipline is the Bridge between Goal and Accomplishment.
>
> — *Jim Rohn*

Setting objectives can provide students with a direction for their learning. Goals should not be too specific; they should be easily adaptable to students' own objectives.

Applications

- Set a core goal for a unit, and then encourage students to personalise that goal by identifying areas of interest to them. Questions like "I want to know" and "I want to know more about." get students thinking about their interests and actively involved in the goal-setting process.

- Use contracts to outline the specific goals that students must apply.

BIBLIOGRAPHY

Aldridge, J., Calhoun, C., and Aman, R. (2000). 15 *Misconceptions About Multicultural Education.* Retrieved May 5, 2007, from : *www.udel.edu/bateman/acei/misconceptions.html*

Banks, J.A. (1991a). *Teaching Strategies for Ethnic Studies* (5th ed.). Boston: Allyn & Bacon.

Banks, J.A. (1991b). A rationale for ethnic pluralism and multicultural education. In Curriculum guidelines for multicultural education, (ed.) *NCSS Task Force on Ethnic Studies Curriculum Guidelines*. Silver Spring, MD: National Council for Social Studies.

Banks, J.A. (1993). Multicultural education for young children: Racial and ethnic attitudes and their modification. In D. Spodek (ed.), *Handbook of Research on the Education of Young Children* (pp. 236-250). New York: MacMillan.

Banks, J.A. (1997) *Educating Citizens in a Multicultural Society*. New York: Teachers College Press.

Banks, J.A. (1999). *An Introduction to Multicultural Education.* Boston: Allyn & Bacon.

Banks, J.A., Cookson, P., Gay, G., Hawley, W. D., Irvine, J., Nieto, S., Schofield, J.W., and Stephan, W. G. (2001). Diversity within unity: Essential principles for teaching and learning in a multicultural society. *Phi Delta Kappan*, 83 (3) : 196-203.

Benett, C.I. (2003). *Comprehensive Multicultural Education: Theory and Practice* (5th ed.). Boston: Allyn & Bacon.

Bredekamp, S., and Copple, C. (1997). *Developmentally Appropriate Practice in Early Childhood Programmes.* (Rev. ed.) Washington, DC: National Association for the Education of Young Children.

Brown, C. and Marchant, C. (2002). *Play in Practice: Case Studies in Young Children's Play.* St. Paul, MN: Redleaf Press.

Bull, B.L., Fruehling, R.T., and Chattergy, V. (1992). *The Ethnics of Multicultural and Bilingual Education.* New York: Teachers College Press.

Castagno, A.E. (2006). Uncertain but always unthreatening: Multicultural education in two urban middle schools (Doctoral dissertation, The University of Wisconsin-Madison, 2006). *Digital Dissertations*, UMI Proquest, AAT 322855.

Coople, C., and Bredekamp, S. (2006). *Basics of Developmentally Appropriate Practice*. Washington, DC: National Association for the Education of Young Children.

Davidman, L., and Davidman, P. (1997). *Teaching with a Multicultural Perspective: A Practical Guide* (2nd ed.). New York: Longman.

Derman-sparks, L. (1989). *Anti-bias curriculum: Tools for Empowering Young Children*. Washington, DC: National Association for the Education of Young Children.

Garmon, M.A. (2004). Changing pre-service teachers' attitudes/beliefs about diversity. *Journal of Teacher Education*, 53 (3) : 214-226.

Gates, K.D. (2006). Multicultural education in public schools (Doctoral dissertation, University of Denver, 2006). Digital Dissertations, UMI Proquest, AAT 3218978.

Gay, G. (1988). Designing relevant curricula for diverse learners. *Education and Urban Society*, 20: 327-340.

Gorski, P.C. (2001). Mission and Purpose. St. Paul, MN: Ed Change Multicultural Pavilion. Available at: *www.edchange.org/multicultural/mission.html.*

Hall, N.S. (1999). *Creative Recourses for the Anti-bias Classroom*. Albany, NY: Delmar.

Jones, E., and Derman-Sparks, L. (1992). Meeting the challenge of diversity. *Young Children*, 47 (2) : 12-18.

Kendall, F.E. (1983). *Diversity in the Classroom: A Multicultural Approach to the Education of Young Children*. New York: Teachers College Press.

Ladson-billings, G. (1994). *The Dream Keepers*. San Francisco: Jossey-Bass Publishing Co.

Maxim, G.W. (2006) *Dynamic Social Studies for Constructivist Classrooms: Inspiring Tomorrow's Social Scientists*, (8th ed.). Columbus, OH: Pearson Merill Prentice Hall.

Meyer, C.F., and Rhoades, E.K. (2006). *Multiculturalism: Beyond Food, festival, Folklore, and Fashion*. Kappa Delta Pi Record, Winter 2006, pp. 82-87.

Ming, K., and Dukes, C. (2006). Fostering cultural competence through school-based routines. *Multicultural Education*, 11 (3) : 42-48.

Nieto, S. (2000). *Affirming Diversity: the Socio Political context of Multicultural Education*, (3rd ed.). New York: Longman.

Pattnaik, J. (2003). Learning about the other: Building a case for intercultural understanding among minority children, *Childhood Education*, 79, 4; Olney, MD: ACEI.

Pimentel, C.N. (2006). On becoming a multicultural teacher: Three case studies of white teachers in diverse classrooms (Doctoral dissertation, The University of Utah, 2006). *Digital Dissertations*, UMI Proquest, AAT 3239667.

Ramsey, P. (1982). Multicultural Education in Early Childhood. In J. Brown (ed.), *Curriculum Planning for Young Children* (pp. 131-142). Washington, DC: NAEYC.

Ramsey, P. (1987). *Teaching and Learning in a Diverse World: Multicultural Education for Young Children.* New York: Teachers College Press.

Seefelt, C. (1997). *Social Studies for the Pre-school-primary Child.* Columbus, OH: Merrill.

Sleeter, C.E., and Grant, C.A. (1987). An analysis of multicultural education in the U.S.A. *Harvard Educational Review*, 57 : 421-444.

Sleeter, C.E., and Grant, C.A. (1988). Making choices for multicultural education: Five approaches to race, class, and gender. Columbus, OH: Merrill Publishing Company. U.S. Bureau of the Census. (2003). *http://www.census.gov/prod/www/statistical-abstract.html*

Yin, R.K. (1984). *Case Study Research: Design and Methods*. Newbury Park, CA: Sage Publications.

16

Relevance of Higher Education in the Context of Women Empowerment

Sewali Borah

Introduction

Higher education is a powerful tool to build a society that leads to harmonious development of the nation. Higher education plays a multiple role to produce new knowledge, acquire capability, adopt knowledge produced elsewhere and create an intelligent human power, at all levels. Higher education plays a significant role and is an integral part of development in every sphere of human life. But, if half the nation remain absence from higher education the holistic development of the nation cannot be possible. All mothers are the best and first teacher of every human being. To be the best and first teacher of every human child women must be empowered with effective education. Without higher education of women it cannot be dreamed and realised.

Rationale of the Study

The NPE (1986) emphasized "Higher education provides people with an opportunity to reflect on the critical social, economic, cultural, moral and spiritual issues facing humanity. It contributes to national development through dissemination c. specialised knowledge skills." Higher education is most essential for superior growth and development especially in the context of shaping a nation as a super knowledge power. The empowerment of women is a critical issue in developing the status of women in the society. No society can achieve the progress without the whole-hearted contribution of the women of the society. It only can be possible through the process of women empowerment and higher education plays a vital role in the process of women empowerment. "Women empowerment is a process, which enables women to establish self-control, autonomy and confidence in a situation of oppressive society. Self-depending and economic liberty are the main resources for empowering women" (Thahuria, 2013). In reality women are suffering a lot in different ways in their social and family life. "It is a fact that higher education at present is mainly catering to the needs of women. Particularly in rural areas women are totally dependent on men, as they do not have economic power spend. The historical relationships with their husbands can be seen as influenced by historical factors that shape the social structures of how they are subordinate" (Murtaza, 2012). Higher education is the key factor in overcoming the barriers that women face in their different spheres of life. Khalid and Mujahid (2002) observed that "Education is a key to giving women more control over their lives. However, social norms continue to prevent women from having equal access to education." Dominance on women is everywhere. "The content of textbooks and curriculum design were seen as strong contributors to the perpetuation of gender discrimination in the education system" (Mattu and Hussain, 2004). Regarding gender bias Dean (2007) states that "Gender bias in textbooks is an important reason why existing curricula persistently fail to project women as full members of society." Women empowerment is a significant part of the holistic development of the nation. Women empowerment has dimensional focus and envisages greater access to knowledge, social and economic resources and greater autonomy in economic and political decision-making process (Kabeer, 2005). Empowerment of women refers to giving decision-making power to women in social, economic and political spheres of life. Higher education is the biggest liberating force and the rise in the levels of education, which nourishes progressive outlook. Education is regarded as the key factor in overcoming the barriers that women face and the basic tool for empowering women and bringing them into the main stream of development. Higher education plays a vital role in national development and this includes the advancement of women. Higher education helps women in different ways for their life upliftment. Higher education enables qualified women to become leaders in society and allows them to become role model for younger girls. UNESCO accords the greatest importance to the role of women graduates who, because of their training, constitute part of a country's skilled human resources and are, therefore, in a position to make a significant contribution to the process of sustainable human development. They contribute in various ways as professionals within their chosen domains of expertise, as decision-makers through their influence on policy issues related to social, economic and cultural development and through their participation in family and community life. Women play a vital part in the growth of a society. Their contribution has been very considerable throughout the rise and fall of civilisations. Theroles of women in social life are always vivid and highly valuable. Sharma and Afroz (2014) stated that, "Dependent women are not empowered women. If women think just that being highly educated and employed they are empowered, it is a myth. Women have to awake from deep slumber and understand the true meaning of empowerment. Everyone must understand that empowering women does not mean empowering in technical areas only. Women should remember that they are also rational, intelligent and thinking human beings." Considering the importance of higher education in the holistic development of the nation the investigators have selected the following topic for study can be stated as "Importance of higher education in the context of women empowerment."

Objectives of the Study

1. To study the attitude of parents regarding girls' higher education.
2. To study the problems of girls' higher education.

Methodology of the Study

This study is conducted on 100 sample parents of Naga on district of Assam which were selected randomly to meet all the two objectives of the study. The main intention of conducting this study is to know the attitude of the parents regarding girls' higher education; and the problems of girls' higher education. Present study is basically a survey-*cum*-quantitative type of research. For the present study the investigators collected data personally from the parents through the self-developed tools.

Tools Used

For meeting all the objectives two tools were used by the investigators.

These tools are self-developed. For developing the tools the investigators consulted with a few experts in this field. For meeting both the objectives two questionnaires, one consisting of 5 questions containing "yes or no" and other consisting of 10 questions containing "yes or no" were developed for collecting data to study the attitudes of the parents regarding girls' higher education and finding the problems related with girls' higher education.

Procedure of Analysis of Data

After obtaining the data from the participants, the investigators used quantitative methods for analysis and interpretation. Here, the collected data are tabulated and classified in the meaningful way for better interpretation. Simple statistics, i.e. per centage was used for quantitative description of the data.

Table 16.1: Attitude of the Parents Regarding Girls' Higher Education

(In per cent)

Sl. No.	*Nature of the attitude*	*Yes*	*No*
1.	Girls' higher education is only wastage of money	77	23
2.	No practical value of higher education	75	25
3.	Maximum hope on boys' for future life of the parents	80	20
4.	Girls' are suitable for only household activities	77	23
5.	Boys' are always given more preference than girls'	80	20

To meet the first objective, i.e. to study the attitude of parents regarding girls' higher education tool-I was administered and presented the result in Table 16.1. Table 16.1 indicates that 77 per cent of parents expressed that higher education for girls' is only wastage of time. Seventy five per cent of parents think that higher education for girls' has no practical value in their life. From Table 16.1, it has been observed that 80 per cent of parents show their maximum hope on boys' for their old-age life. In the study 77 per cent of parents expressed their view that girls' are suitable only in household activities than education.

To meet the second objective, i.e. to study the problems of girls' higher education, a questionnaire having 'yes' or 'no' containing 10 questions, was developed. After getting the scores, investigators analysed the data and following Table 16.2 is prepared which presents the findings of the data.

Table 16.2: The problems of girls' higher education

(In per cent)

Sl. No.	Status of the Problem	Yes	No
1.	Family attitude	62	38
2.	Cultural stereotyping	80	20
3.	Discrimination in classroom management	60	40
4.	Teachers attitude towards girls'	82	22
5.	Societal attitudes to women	60	40
6.	Defective design of curriculum	60	40
7.	Giving more preference on male child in the family	80	20
8.	Early marriage of girls'	50	50
9.	Girls' are forced to do their job only as girl	75	25
10.	Sexual harassment	80	20

Table 16.2 indicates the problems that are hindrances in the way of girls' higher education. Table 16.2 reveals that Sixty two per cent parents were in favour of the problem of family attitude towards girls' higher education. It is observed that 80 per cent of the parents express their views that cultural stereotyping is an obstacle in way of girls' higher education. Sixty per cent of the parents said that classroom management is also not in favour of girls' education that can inspire the girls' for higher education. Teachers' attitude towards girls' is a factor of hindrance of girls' higher education. Eighty two per cent of the parents said yes for the same. Sixty per cent of the parents admitted societal attitudes to women badly affected the girls' higher education. Sixty per cent of the parents agreed that defective design of curriculum is another problem of girls' higher education. Eighty per cent of the parents said in family life more preference has been shown to the boys' in case of higher education than girls'. Fifty per cent of the parents agreed that early marriage of the girls' is always affect the girls' higher education. Seventy five per cent of the parents observed that girls' are forced to do their job only as girl in home not encouraged for higher education by the parents. Eighty per cent of the parents admitted that sexual harassment is a problem due to which girls' are not allowed by the parents for their higher education.

Major Findings of the Study

- Seventy seven per cent of parents expressed that higher education for girls' is only wastage of time.
- Seventy five per cent of parents think that higher education for

girls' has no practical value in their life.

- Eighty per cent of parents show their maximum hope on boys' for their old-age life.
- Seventy seven per cent of parents expressed their view that girls' are suitable only in household activities than education.
- Sixty two per cent parents were in favour of the problem of family attitude towards girls' higher education.
- Eighty per cent of the parents express their views that cultural stereotyping is an obstacle in way of girls' higher education.
- Sixty per cent of the parents said that classroom management is also not in favour of girls' education that can inspire the girls' for higher education.
- Eighty two per cent of the parents said teachers' attitude towards girls' is a factor of hindrance of girls' higher education.
- Sixty per cent of the parents admitted societal attitudes to women badly affected the girls' higher education.
- Sixty per cent of the parents agreed that defective design of curriculum is another problem of girls' higher education.
- Eighty per cent of the parents said in family life more preference has been shown to the boys' in case of higher education than girls'.
- Fifty per cent of the parents agreed that early marriage of the girls' is always affect the girls' higher education.
- Seventy five per cent of the parents observed that girls' are forced to do their job only as girl in home not encouraged for higher education by the parents.
- Eighty per cent of the parents admitted that sexual harassment is a problem due to which girls' are not allowed by the parents for their higher education.

Conclusion

Education has a great role in developing any society. But the development of the future generation of the society only depends on women empowerment. Higher education for women is the foremost need for empowering women feels by every member of the knowledge society. The study reveals that many hindrances are still working in the path of progress of women empowerment, but policy and plan of higher education itself will be the strong weapon to removing all of these.

REFERENCES

Dean, B.L. (2007b). Creating subjects for gender apartheid: A critical study of an English language Pakistani textbook. In *Gender and Education in Pakistan,* (ed.) R. Qureshi and J.F.A. Rarieya, pp. 170-196. Karachi: Oxford University Press.

Kabeer, Naila (2005). Gender equality and women's empowerment: A critical analysis of the third millennium Development Goal. *Gender and Development,* 13(1) : 13-24.

Khalid, S.M. and Mujahid, M. (2002). The future of girls' education in Pakistan: A study on policy measures and other factors determining girls' education. Islamabad: UNESCO office.

Mattu, A. and Hussain, N. (2004). Class and gender in school texts. In *The Subtle Subversion: The State of Curricula and Textbooks in Pakistan* (ed.) A.H. Nayyar and A. Salim, pp. 91-10. Islamabaad: Sustainable Development Policy Institute.

Murtaza, K.F. (2012). Women empowerment through higher education in Gilgit-Baltistan. *International Journal of Academic Research in Business and Social Sciences,* 2(9) : 343-377.

Sharma, R. and Afroz, Z. (2014). Women empowerment through higher education. *International Journal of Interdisciplinary and Multidisciplinary Studies,* 1(5) : 18-22.

Thakuria, D. (2013). Women Empowerment and Human Eevelopment in the Context of Assam. *Janachintan.* Published by Department of Political Science, Vol. 1.

17
Quality in Teacher Education

Jahitha Begum, A.

Quality has a variety of contradictory meanings. As Naomi Pfeffer and Anna Coote have observed in their discussion of quality in the welfare services 'Quality' is a slippery concept. It implies different things to different people. Everyone is in favour of providing quality education. The arguments start because there is a lack of agreement as to what it means. It is, therefore, necessary to have a clear understanding of the various meanings of quality otherwise there is a danger that it becomes a mere catchphrase, a world with high moral tone but little practical value. Understanding of the diverse meanings of quality is a necessary starting point for the discussion of Total Quality Management (TQM).

A possible reason for the enigmatic nature of quality is that it is a dynamic idea. The emotional and moral force which quality possesses makes it a difficult idea to tie down. There is the danger that much of its vitality can be lost if it is subjected to too much academic analysis. Westley and Mintzberg make the point that this happens to many important concepts which are freely used in practical settings. A strange process seems to occur as concepts such as culture and charisma and we can add quality move from practice to academic research. Loosely used in practice, these concepts, as they enter academia become subjected to a concerted effort to force them properly scientific. In the process they seem to lose emotional resonance, no longer expressing the reality that practitioners tried to capture. Quality is a dynamic idea and exact definitions are not particularly helpful. However, its range of meanings does cause confusion. Important practical consequences flow from these different meanings. For this reason they need discussion. Good qualities teach education programme produces high quality students of education. Quality Education is fundamental to national development, become school supply the larget single human resources of the lower end of the human resources hierarchy. Further, school education feeds higher and professional education without quality education professional education cannot achieve quality (NCTE, 2009).

The issue of quality is an inalienable aspect of any educational policy discourse. However, the concept eludes a consensus definition, despite an agreement on the need to achieve it. The concept of quality is changing with developments in educational theory and practice, trying to keep pace with changing educational needs and aspirations of people. In the era of globalisation, as governments focus more and more on developing skills and capabilities of their human resources, there is a need to ascertain how different governments and educational providers understand 'quality' and attempt to attain it in their educational regimes. One also needs to know where they stand *vis-à-vis* one another so that policy lessons can be drawn. This calls for a comparative study of the quality of education in various countries. Such studies are few in number due to issues of time, finance and cross-country coordination involved in the enterprise.

The term "quality education" conveys multiple meanings due to its relative nature. Dhankar (2002) has examined the notion of "Child-centred MLL-Oriented" (CMO) notion of quality inherent in the District Primary Education Programme then run in India. Ruling out the CMO model which includes child-centred methods, multi-level/multi-grade teaching and Minimum Levels of Learning (MLL). Dhankar suggests an alternative framework which constitutes interconnected aspects like curriculum, pedagogy, school organisation and evaluation. Quality is related to the content and process of education, i.e. classroom processes, textbooks and materials used, and teacher training. Factors like community participation, monitoring, evaluation, school building are also important indicators of school quality, but are secondary.

A framework for quality can also be advocated in Kumar (2005) where goals of education are seen to be in direct link with the capacity of the system to reform itself with the coming of new practices. Quality in education as stated by Agarwal, *et al.,* (1995) depends on—

(i) *Reliability*: the ability to impart knowledge dependably and accurately;
(ii) *Responsiveness*: willingness to help students and provide prompt guidance;

(iii) *Tangibles*: physical facilities, laboratory equipment;
(iv) *Assurance*: knowledge and courtesy of faculty and their ability to convey trust Sand confidence; and
(v) *Empathy*: caring, individualized attention to students.

Power (2002) tells us that the notion of quality is a matter of location and perception.

While discussing quality, students may focus on facilities provided, teachers on the teaching-learning process, management and parents on the scores or grades achieved by pupils, and the prospective employers on the nature of output. According to UNESCO Chief, Koichiro Matsuura (2005), the way societies define the purpose of education illustrates what quality is. Two objectives must be fulfilled-cognitive development of learners and cultivating creative and emotional growth of learners which helps them imbibe values and attitudes for conscientious citizenship. Moreover, quality should provide for equity whereby there is no bias against any group in an education system.

Quality Movement in Indian Higher Education

Too many concepts of management as applied in business and industry cannot be applied as such in Higher Education. According to Pillai (2006) there are limitations in applying the market metaphor to education. According to him the products of education are not really finished products that can be bought off from the shelf. The student (customer) competes to get admission and the educational institution (provider) often chooses its customers. Though the customer pays the fees, the output (graduation) is not guaranteed. The student has to play an active role in the process; and behaves more like an entrepreneur (investing time, efforts and money) to produce (acquire) knowledge and skills that are useful in the job market. Thus, quality cannot be managed in the way it is done in business and the industry.

The University Grants Commission (UGC) with its statutory powers is expected to maintain quality in Indian Higher Education Institution. Section 12 of the UGC Act of 1956 requires UGC to be responsible for "the determination and maintenance of standards of teaching, examinations and research in universities." To fulfil this mandate, the UGC has been continuously developing mechanisms to monitor quality in colleges and Universities directly or indirectly. In order to improve quality, it has established National Research Facilities and Academic Staff

Colleges to re-orient teachers and provide research courses in subject areas. The UGC also conducts the National Eligibility Test (NET) for setting high standards of teaching (NAAC, June 2006).

When many higher education institutions are facing scarcity of resources, no one would disagree to better and improve quality of management of the non-academic activities leading to creation of an environment conducive for quality academic development.

Dimensions of Quality in Higher Education

Quality, as we know so far, was originally developed in the manufacturing industry. In the area of higher education, the adoption of quality control has been superficial and diluted by the exercise of academic freedom (Largosen *et al.*, 2004). Further, the prevailing culture of universities is often based on individual autonomy, which is zealously guarded (Colling and Harvey, 1995). Thus, it is usually difficult to apply the features of quality to higher education considering the fact that quality requires teamwork (Boaden and Dale, 1992). However, the quality of higher education is very important for its stakeholders such as students, staff and employers (Srikanthan and Dalrymple, 2003).

Service Dimensions of Quality

The service dimension of quality is probably more akin to the educational processes. We know that unlike physical goods, services are ephemeral to the extent that they can be consumed only as long as the activity or the process continues. Thus, there is inseparability of production and consumption. Thus, services cannot be stored and are perishable. The consumer is also an integral part of the service process. Thus, in higher education, this framework is more applicable as the teaching learning situations are more like a service. Parasuraman *et al.* (1985) identified the following dimensions of service:

1. *Reliability:* The service is carried out in the way it is promised.
2. *Responsiveness:* The service is carried out promptly according to the needs of the customers.
3. *Competence:* The staff of the service provider has the knowledge and skills required for delivering the service in a proper way.
4. *Access:* It concerns the location, opening hours etc.
5. *Courtesy:* How polite, friendly and respectful the employees are.

6. *Communication:* It is the process of keeping the customers informed in a language that they could understand and also listening to them.
7. *Credibility:* How trustworthy, believable and honest the service provider is?
8. *Security:* Freedom from danger, risks or doubt.
9. *Understanding the customer:* The effort of the service provider to understand the needs and wants of the individual customers.
10. *Tangibles:* Physical objects that are needed for carrying out the services such as facilities equipment etc.

Product Dimension of Quality

Garvin (1987) proposed the following eight dimensions for quality that, as he stated, can define both product and service:

1. *Performance*—It is concerned with the primary operating characteristics of a product. For example, for a TV, the performance comprises sound and picture quality. In higher education performance is the abilities expected from a graduate.

2. *Features*—Those characteristics that supplement the basic performance functions called features. In higher education, flexibility of course offering could be a feature.

3. *Reliability*—It is the probability of a product working fault-free within a specified time period. In higher education, it can be considered as to what extent the knowledge gained is correct and up-to-date.

4. *Conformance*—The extent to which a product meets the established specification/standard. For higher education, it can be defined as the extent of meeting the established educational standards and its own promises to the client.

5. *Durability*—The product's assumed life to perform satisfactorily is durability. In higher education it can be defined as the depth of learning.

6. *Serviceability*—It is concerned with the repair and field service of the product. In higher education it is concerned with handling of complaints from students, staff and industry. Some also emphasize the continuous updating of their alumni as evidenced by professionals like the Chartered Accountants through their magazines, newsletters and continuing education to provide after training service.

7. *Aesthetics*—In the context of product, it is concerned with the design, looks, colour and presentation and how the customer views it.

8. *Perceived quality*—This is yet again subjective like aesthetics and 'customers' opinion is more appropriate in service quality dimension. For a product too, through branding, the customer perceives a certain degree of confidence on quality.

Software Dimensions of Quality

The characteristics of software as an intangible product are more consistent with higher education. The software quality dimensions widely used in software engineering are: correctness, reliability, efficiency, integrity, usability, maintainability, testability, expandability, portability, reusability and interoperability (Watts, 1987). Owlia and Aspinwall (1996) apply these quality dimensions to higher education.

Importance of Teacher Education

(a) Education is the cradle of success. Its is the vital key of Nation. Administrators, educationalists and policy-makers across the country recognise that education system needs fundamental changes to keep pace with an increasingly complex global society. Education should not only reflect the needs of the society, but also excellence. Every effort should be made to adopt our educational system to days changing economical and social realities.

(b) Education is a never ending process, it is a growth, a progress and a development which never stops and goes on all through the life and even travels from one generation to another and ultimately inculcates in an individual the creative thinking, reasoning power and analytical ability which enables him to act and adapt to changing social scenario in the best possible way for the further enhancement and development of his personality. Education is the process of living through a common reconstruction of experience. It is the development of all these capacities in the individual which will enable him to control his environment and fulfil his possibilities. As a result of individual experience education is considered as a change or an adjustment.

In our increasingly complex and rapidly changing society, teacher's tasks are more demanding and changing than ever before. The teacher plays a vital role in educating the future generations and in contributing to national and international development and prosperity. Teacher

Education and appropriate pedagogy is thus very important as it enables them to discharge their responsibilities successfully. If you are a teacher in whatever capacity you have a very special role to play because more than anybody else it is who are shaping the future generation. Teacher Educators should update their content knowledge and develop competencies to meet the latest challenges in the society. They should a role model for teacher trainees who are the architects of our future citizens (A.P.J. Abdul Kalam, 2009).

The most important means for improving the quality of Education is improvement in the teaching. Teachers are the heart of the education system, they are the main players. Teaching and learning makes the institution. It is the teacher who makes it. Thus, their preparation, performance and accountability for educational task should relieve top priority. The most important input or capital for an educational institution is its teachers. Thus, emphasis on the caliber and qualification of teachers requires immediate attention.

Teachers are meant to teach the students. They should enable them to learn at the mastery level; at learning of course, they should be masters of what they teach the students and should be professionally trained teachers. It is wrong to think that teaching methods are meant only for school teaches. A mastery over the subject, knowledge of teaching strategies is necessary for teachers at all levels whether school, college or university. This will make them more effective teachers. The more skilled a teacher is the better will be his teaching and the use of different strategies make a teacher more skilled. The art of teaching is not constant but dynamic it is and lifelong learning.

Teachers should always try to reflect on their own training. There is need for self-assessment to be better teacher. Thus, there can be no question regarding the necessity of teacher education. Without education and knowledge of modern teaching techniques teachers would remain incomplete. They will not realise their own heritage. The need of the hour is re-engineering the teacher architects who are in the process of mankind. Educational and skilled teachers who are in the process of mankind. Educational and skilled teachers are required who will master a new approaches and technique.

Learning is a personal endeavour and a process of knowledge construction. Different students adopt different learning styles. Researchers in the field of cognitive neuropsychology proved that brain is the central contributor to learning. If the teachers know more about brain functioning they can adopt different instructional methods. An effective teacher should think about different ways of teaching to make the students remember better and to help students to find meaning in what they are learning (Begum Jahitha, 2010).

Quality in Teacher Education

Education is the cradle of success. It is the vital key of Nation. Administrators, educationalists and policy makers across the country are recognizing that education system needs fundamental changes to keep pace with an increasingly complex global society. Education should not only reflect the needs of the society but also excellence. Every effort should be made to adopt our educational system today's changing economical and social realities.

Education is a never ending process, it is a growth, a progress and a development which never stops and goes on all through the life and even travels from one generation to another and ultimately inculcates in an individual the creative thinking, reasoning power and analytical ability which enables him to act and adapt to changing social scenario in the best possible way for the further enhancement and development of his personality. Education is the process of living through a common reconstruction of experience. It is the development of all these capacities in the individual which will enable him to control his environment and fulfil his possibilities. As a result of individual experience education is considered as a change or an adjustment. Quality Indicators for Ten Criteria identified as applicable to Teacher Education programmes:

- Curricular aspects
- Academic activities
- Students equality
- Research programme
- Extension service
- Professional development of staff
- Infrastructure and learning resource
- Student support and progression
- Organisation and
- Health practices and Quality Indicators are reflect on teacher education.

In our increasingly complex and rapidly changing society, teacher's tasks are more demanding and changing than ever before. The teacher plays a vital role in educating the future generation and in contributing to national and international development and prosperity. Teacher Education and appropriate pedagogy is thus very important as it enables them to discharge their responsibilities successfully.

In order to make a teacher perfect or better, it is essential that course for teachers be re-oriented, re-shaped, and re-drafted to improve the overall status of a teacher. An adequately trained teacher will be able to deliver quality education, which will be reflected in providing better education to the future generation of the country. The findings of the study conducted by Fuller & Alexander (2004) indicated that students who were taught by educationally qualified teachers showed better results. Laczko-Kerr and Berliner (2002) also showed in another study that those students who were taught by untrained teachers performed substantially poor than those who were taught by new teachers, but who were qualified. Darling-Hammond (1999) in their study showed a substantial linkage between good results and qualified teachers. The study also showed a substantially negative linkage between results obtained by untrained teachers, who were comparatively new on the jobs. Fetler (1999) was of the view that teachers with short training did not perform well, when compared with those who were fully trained and had longer experience.

Balon (1990) is of the view that an effective teacher can be valuable for the students, the society, and the country. This is because of the fact, that such a teacher educates the future generation, on whom the future of the society and the nation depends. Such an education involves primarily an over all development of a person, to make him a complete individual of the society. The difference between a trained and an untrained teacher lies in methods adopted for teaching and development of children. There is great diversity in the type of training available to teachers and thus comparisons become difficult. Analyst have, therefore, tried to find effects of training for teachers and are of the opinion that pedagogical training is better than those who do not have this type of training (Hedges and Laine, 1996).

A joint study by Harvard University and the Academy of Education, indicated that level of training obtained by a teacher contributed to rise in obtaining marks in Math for grades four and five. The efforts to develop the abilities of teaching staff are aimed at helping the faculty to acquire learning skills and knowledge about subject matters, teaching techniques, related to learning (Main, 1985). The performance of a teacher before the class is dependent on training provided to him. To assess how effective is the teaching, one has to look at the performance of teacher in the class and the attitude of the instructor in teacher training establishments. The output of teacher is dependent on his knowledge and ability. The effective teaching process is thus dependent on professional training and learning (Glaser, 1989). According to Aggarwal (1993) the training of teacher is required for formulating a positive attitude and a purpose for the profession.

According to Schiefelben (1921), it has been usually assumed that the quality of teaching performance is directly influenced by the academic qualification and professional training of teachers. Effective teaching is determined by content, mastery and pedagogical skills.

REFERENCES

Abdul Kalam, A.P.J., *India 2020: A Vision of the New Millennium.*

Boaden, R.J and Dale, B. (1992). Team work in service. Quality circles by another name? *Institutional Journal of Service Industry Management,* 4(1) : 5-24.

Colling, C. and Harvey, L. (1995), Quality Control, Assurance and Assessment the Link to Continuous Improvement, *Quality Assurance in Education*, 3 (4) : pp. 30-34.

Crosby, Phillip B. (1984). *Quality without Teams,* Singapore.

Lagrosen, S., Seyyed-Hashemi, R., and Leitner, M. (2004). Examination of the dimensions of quality in higher education. *Quality Assurance in Education, 12*(2) : 61–69. *http://dx.doi.org/10.1108/09684880410536431*

Pillai C.R. (2006). *Understanding Quality in Higher Education*, Personal Communication to NAAC, Delhi: McGraw Hill.

NIST. (2005). *Education Criteria for performance Excellence.*

Srikanthan, G., and Dalrymple, J. (2003). Developing alternative perspectives for quality in higher education. *International Journal of Educational Management,* 17(3) : 126-136. *http://dx.doi.org/10.1108/09513540310467804*

Temponi, C. (2005). Continuous Important Framework Implication for Academic. *Quality Assurance in Education* 13(1) : 17-36.

Walts, R.A. (1987). *Measuring Software Quality*, Oxford : National Competing Centre.

18

Quality in Education for Higher Education in India

Haseena V.A.

Introduction

Universities and colleges are starved of funds as the support of Government is being reduced and grants are not being provided in time causing hardship to them. One of the easier options to overcome the financial crisis in the educational sector is to start self-financing courses. But this alternative is possible only for courses with high demand. Secondly, these courses further strengthen the numerous entry barriers to higher education existing already. Thirdly, the scope for self-financing educational institutions in Kerala is much more limited than for the country as a whole. Fourthly, these institutions cannot evolve as centres of excellence. But, however privatisation of higher-level education especially in the field of professional and technical education, like Medical, Engineering, Information Technology, Computer, Management, Teacher Education etc. has already commenced.

Quality in Higher Education

World over several definitions have been put forth on "quality in higher education". Quality is seen as a relative concept satisfying priorities of different interest groups of beneficiaries. These beneficiaries are students, teachers, technical and administrative staff, parents, would be employees, funding agencies and the society. In a manufacturing industry the input (the product) are pre-determined and the user needs to be assured of the quality of the product. However, in education, every element—the input, the process, and the output—is a human being and cannot, therefore, be dealt with such a simplistic approach. Ellis states that quality itself is a somewhat ambiguous term (in higher education) since, it have connotations of both standards and excellence. Most of the debates on quality and end with synonym between "Quality" and "Excellence". There is also a notion of quality as conformation to a standard o specification.

How to Improve Quality of Higher Education?

The next question, and the relevant one to be answered is, How to improve quality of higher education? One of the answers to this question is that concepts adopted in the profit-centred business and industrial organisations can be adopted improve the standard in educational institutions too. The debated whether the ideas and methods relating to business and industrial or other profit making organisations are relevant to educational institutions which are service-oriented and not profit-oriented, is no longer of serious importance, as in several countries, there is a transfer of three industry-based concepts to educational management. It is in this context that he TQM is suggested a way to improve the quality of education imparted in the centres of higher learning.

Higher education imparts in-depth knowledge and understanding so as to advance the students to new frontiers of knowledge in different walks of life (subject domains). It develops the student ability to question and seek truth and makes him/her competent to critique on contemporary issues. It broadens the intellectual powers of the individual within a narrow specialisation, but also gives him/her a wider perspective of the world around. According to Ronald Barnett (1992).

There are four predominant concepts of higher education :

(i) Higher education as the production of qualified human resources: In this view, Higher education is seen as a process in which students are counted as "products" absorbed in labour market. Thus, higher education becomes input to the growth and development of business and industry.

(ii) Higher education as training for a research career: In this view, higher education is Preparation for qualified scientists and researchers who would continuously develop the frontiers of knowledge. Quality within this view point is more about research publications and transmission of academic rigour to do quality research.

(iii) Higher education as the efficient management of teaching profession: Many strongly believe that teaching is the core of educational institutions. Thus, higher education institutions focus on efficient management of teaching-learning provisions by improving the quality of teaching, enabling a higher completion rate among the students.

(iv) Higher education as a matter of extending life chances: In this view, higher education is seen as an opportunity to participate in the development process of individual through a flexible, continuing education mode. Interestingly, all these four concepts of higher education are not exclusive; rather they are integrated and give an overall picture of higher education. If we look at the activities of colleges and universities, we will realise that teaching, research and extension form the three main functions of higher education.

Role of Higher Education in the Society

Higher education is generally understood to cover teaching, research and extension. Scientific and technological advancement and economic growth of a country are as dependent on higher education as they are on the working class. Development of indigenous technologies and capabilities in agriculture, food security and other industrial areas are possible because of our world-class higher education infrastructure. Higher education also provides opportunities for lifelong learning, allowing people to upgrade their knowledge and skills from time-to-time based on societal needs. The Kothari Commission (1966) listed the following roles of the universities (Higher education institutions in the modern society).

- To seek and cultivate new knowledge, to engage vigorously and fearlessly in the pursuit of truth, and to interpret old knowledge and beliefs in the light of new deeds and discoveries;
- To provide the right kind of leadership in all walks of life, to identify gifted youth and help them develop their potential full by cultivating physical fitness, developing the powers of the mind and cultivating right interests, attitudes and moral and intellectual values;
- To provide the society with competent men and women trained in agriculture, arts, medicine, science and technology and various other professions, who will also be cultivated individuals, imbibed with a sense of social purpose;
- To strive to promote quality and social justice, and to reduce social cultural differences through diffusion of education; and

- To foster in the teachers and students and through them in the society generally, the attitudes and values needed for developing the "good life" in individuals and society (GoI, 1966, pp. 497-98).

Quality has a few central ideas around which the whole concept revolves: Quality as absolute, Quality as relative, Quality as a process, and Quality as culture. When we consider quality as absolute, it is given and considered as the highest possible standard. The Egyptian Pyramids and the Taj Mahal are works of high standards and quality. In product terms, they are attached with high "brand" values, status and positional advantages. Educational institutions such as Oxford, Cambridge and Stanford in the West have this absolute quality standard, though in the case of education it might still be perceptual. Quality as relative suggests that the quality of a product or service can be described in relative terms. Quality here can be measured in terms of certain specifications. According to Mukhopadhyaya (2005) the adherence to "product specification is actually, the minimum condition for quality but not the sufficient condition. The sufficient condition is customer satisfaction and beyond."

Why Higher Education Institutions should Worry About Quality?

As teachers, principals, heads of the department and policy-makers in education we should worry about quality of teaching, programmes, and institution because of the reasons:

(1) **Competition:** We are entering a new regime, where competition among educational institutions for students and funds will be highly significant. With globalisation and GATS (Global Agreement on Trade in Services), the educational environment will be seized by increased competition. In order to survive in such situation, educational institutions need to worry about their quality.

(2) **Customer satisfaction:** Students, parents or sponsoring agencies as customers of the educational institutions are now highly conscious of their rights or getting value for their money and time spent. They are now demanding good quality teaching and receiving employable skill set and thus, we should constantly worry about the relevance of our courses and programmes to the needs of the market.

(3) **Maintaining standards:** As educational institutions, we should always concern about setting our own standard and maintaining it continuously year after year. In order to maintain the standard, we should continuously make efforts to improve quality of educational facilities.

(4) **Accountability:** Every institution is accountable to its own stake holder in terms of the funds (public or private) used on it. Concern for quality will ensure accountability of funds utilised and inform the stake holders about taking appropriate decisions. Thus, quality can be considered as a monitoring mechanism.

(5) **Improve employee morale and motivation:** Concern for quality as an institution will improve the morale and motivation of the staff in performing their duties and responsibilities. If quality system is in place, the internal process would be systematic making every department complementing each other's service domain and helping in developing internal customer satisfaction leading to high morale and motivation.

(6) **Credibility, prestige and status:** If institutions are concerned about quality, continuously and not once in a while. It will bring credibility to institutions and individuals because of consistency leading to practice, status and brand value.

(7) **Image and visibility:** Quality institutions have the capacity to attract better stake holder support, like getting merit students from far and near, increased donation/grants from funding agencies and higher employer interest for easy placement of graduates.

To sum up, TQM implies:

1. Serious concern for improving quality "at all levels".
2. Giving utmost importance for the customers' demands, treating the customer.
3. As sovereign and trying to satisfying customer fully.
4. Management's total commitment for enhancing the quality of the products.
5. Setting-up goals and planning in advance for upgrading quality.
6. Removing the defects in the process of production, and improving the process at all levels.

Is TQM Relevant for Education?

TQM is applied in business and industry; but it has been recently introduced and experienced in higher education. Many universities and colleges apply Total Quality Management as a tool to enhance the quality of higher education. The concept of quality is accepted by everyone. In a world of ever increasing competition, privatisation, and internationalisation of higher education, many educational institutions in India and abroad apply TQM principles in education.

Dimensions	*Characteristics*
Tangibles	Sufficient equipment/facilities Ease of access Visually appealing environment Support services (accommodation, sports...)
Competence	Sufficient staff (Academic) Theoretical and practical knowledge, qualifications Teaching experience, communication
Attitude	Understanding students needs Willingness to help Availability for guidance and advice Giving personal attention
Content	Relevance of curriculum to the future jobs of the students Communication skills and team work Flexibility of knowledge, being cross-disciplinary Containing primary knowledge/skills
Delivery	Effective presentation Sequencing, timeliness Consistency, fairness of examinations Feedback from students
Reliability	Trustworthiness Giving valid award Handling complaints, solving problems

Source: Owlia and Aspinwall (1996).

To suit the TQM principles to educational institutions, the following steps should be followed:

Creating quality consciousness, among all concerned with the educational institutions, namely, management, faculty, students, parents, and the society at large.

Total commitment of the management of the educational institutions, be it government, university, or a private body, for providing quality education.

Treating the students as the sovereign authority and creating a feeing amongst the faulty that he institution exist for the students and not for the staff. Students are not the only customers of an educational institution; the parents, employees, and the society at large are also coming under the purview. Since, students are the primary and direct customers of an educational institution, the students should get the best from them.

Setting-up short term and long term goals for improving the quality of education and preparing plan of action for achieving the goal.

Monitoring the quality improvement programme at frequent intervals and making suitable alternations whenever necessary in the programme.

1. Motivating the staff to work with enthusiasm and dedication to achieve the goals set.
2. Pay attention for improving the entire process of teaching-learning and the environment in the institution to bring out the best from the students. If the quality of education is to be improved, the entire process of learning-teaching and then educational environment in the organisation has to be improved.
3. Provide effective and dynamic leadership to be institution for successfully implementing the TQM programme.

The concept of the TQM is applicable to academics. Many educators believe that he Deming's concept of TQM provides guiding principles for needed educational reform.

Conclusion

The present system of higher education in India is not the result of a considered or organised set of the relevant ideas. Not is it the product of evolution, responsive, in its growth, to the changing needs of the society it serves. It was made elsewhere to meet the needs and aspirations not our own. It was modeled on the British curriculum of ancient times when kings and nobles had to be educated on the basis of the philosophy of liberal education. The absence of an appropriate philosophy of education is one of the lacunae of higher education in India. It lacks the touch of the wealth of our tradition, rich literature, art and culture. Our curricula and pedagogy do not represent them. Fossilized or irrelevant curricula, ineffectual pedagogy, absence of accountability among the constituents of the educational enterprise and non-performance on the whole are the ills of present day higher education in India. An educational philosophy addressing itself to such needs is yet to be evolved. We often look back nostalgically at he *Guru Kula* system of education Rabindranath Tagore attempted to capture such a vision of education at Shanthinikethan. Accepting spiritualism fully and leaving materialism wholly may not be suitable for the modern era. Jawaharlal Nehru, hence, advocates the integration of scientific temper with spirituality in devising a system of education for India, for 20th century.

REFERENCES

Bostingl, John Jay, (1992). The Article, *The Quality Revolution in Education*, November.

Crosh, Philip, (1989). *Zero Defects*, MIT, USA.

Deming, W. Edwards, (1986). *Out of the Crisis*, MIT Press, Cambridge, U.K.

Frazer, Malcom (1989). *Quality in Higher Education*, p. 139.

Garwi, David, (1999). *Managing Quality* Harvard University Press, Harvard, USA, p. 289.

Gilbert, G. (1992). "Quality Improvement in a Defense Organisation", *Public Productivity and Management Reviews*, 16(1): 65-75.

Ishikawa, K. (1985). *What is Total Quality Control? The Japanese Way*. Englewood Cliffs, New Jersey : Prentice-Hall.

Juran, Joseph, (1969). *Managerial Breakthrough: A New Concept of the Mangers' Job*, New York: McGraw Hill.

Perry, Baroness Pauline (2003). *What is Quality in Higher Education*, p. 99.

Ramsden, S. (1992). *Learning to Teach in Higher Education*, p. 13.

Subramanian, "TOM in Higher Studies", *The Hindu Daily*, January 29, 2003.

Sudha, T. (2013). "Total quality management in higher education institutions", *International Journal of Social Science and Interdisciplinary Research*, ISSN 2277 3630, *IJSSIR*, Vol. 2 (6), June.

The Conference Boucher: 2; "The Bangkok Conference on Higher Education", November 2000, Bangkok.

The Education Reform Act, 1988.

The Report on "Objectives of Higher Education" UNESCO, 2003, Paris.

Tribus, Myron (2004). *Total Quality Management in Education*, p. 169.

Venkataiah, S., "Quality Education", *Encyclopaedia of Education for 21st Century*. Vol. 34, p. 3, New Delhi : Anmol Publications Pvt. Ltd.

Zangwill, W., and Kantor, P. (1998). "Towards a Theory of Continuous Improvement and the learning Curve". *Management Science*, 44(7): 910-920.

Section-IV
Technology and Distance Learning

19
Distance Education in the 21st Century in Reference to Personal Contact Programme (PCP)

Sandhya Jain and *Sunita Shrivastava*

Introduction

In formal system of education, students meet their teachers throughout the academic session on the classroom and beyond the classroom which create confidence, motivation and satisfaction among the students and faculty. However, students in Distance Education (DE) System being geographically scattered cannot avail of this facility and advantage resulting in many social and psychological problems. What is the way to come out of this chaos? How to bridge this gap between the students and their faculty members? How to ensure their association though limited to remove their apprehensions and other academic problems? The answer is the institution of Personal Contact Programme (PCP) which is designed to narrow the gap between the aspirations of the students and the faculty and make them feel a sense of belongingness to the institution to which they belong.

Personal Contact Programmes, as is clear from the very nomenclature, are designed to meet the needs of the student of DE system for purposeful social contact and intellectual confrontation between the Faculty and the students of DE system.

UGC rightly mentions "The provision of personal contact programmes should be regarded as an essential feature of correspondence through lectures, tutorials, seminars and discussions. The personal contact programmes through intensive classroom instruction, individual guidance and counselling help in giving a proper orientation to the students, add to their motivation, encourage regular study habits and in still confidence in them."

The term "Personal Contact Programme (PCP)", as used in Indian context, denotes the assembly of distance students and representative teachers of the supporting institution or other teachers employed especially for the purpose at a predecided place for a specific period with the intention of teaching, motivating, creating a sense of belongingness and supplement distance learning material already sent.

The teaching at personal contact programmes has to be quite different from classroom teaching provided in the colleges or universities as these lectures aim at revision of syllabus already covered through lessons, supplementing. Material provided in the lessons and introducing students to the portions still to be covered so as to motivate them to read further. These programmes proved a good feedback from the students to the teachers and enable them to understand the requirement of students as also the shortcoming that may be there in the reading materials supplied by the institute. In case of science/commerce/professional courses both at PG and UG levels, attendance should be compulsory.

Merits of PCP

The following benefits result from personal contact programme:

(i) **Generates Harmonious Relationships between DE System and Students:** It creates a climate of understanding. This creation of awareness is integral to liberate the minds and potential of the DE students. Besides, the DE students also feel elated in the company of their fellow students which were earlier unknown. They develop many permutations and combinations among them keeping in view their nature, proximity and interest, which help them substantially later on, i.e. after the PCP. Such contacts generate many informal relationships which help them to come out of academic drudgery or mechanical life.

(ii) **Psychological Motivation:** The research theory in social and organisational psychology has suggested that participation in classrooms would enhance student's satisfaction and remove many of inherent and self-created tensions. PCP becomes a morale booster and generates a feeling in him like a student in a formal system.

(iii) **Better Understanding of DE Students:** PCP provides opportunities to understand the profile of DE students. This is a challenging and interesting task for the DE faculty. The DE students come with different aspirations, perceptions and attitudes. PCP provides the opportunity to fulfil their needs.

(iv) **Development of Loyalty to the DE System and Institutes:** DE students attending PCP are the messengers of DE System. They will carry the impression as of the PCP with them and later on exchange with the potential users. This chain reaction can generate good will and ultimately raise the status of DE institutes and system.

Procedure and Contents of PCP

In principle, as per the UGC guidelines, a PCP is required to be held at places wherever there is a concentration of more than 200 students. Most of the institutions reported that they do keep in mind this principle while deciding the venue for the PCPs. But they are often unable to stick to it.

The success of the PCP depends upon micro-planning so that the benefits can be optimised. We mention here important steps (Fig. 19.1).

Procedure and Contents

(a) **Advance Planning of Dates and Venue:** The DE faculty should decide in sufficient advance about the dates of the PCP keeping in view the needs of the students, availability of the faculty and dispatch of reading material. Venue should be the proximity of large number of students. Venue should have nice classrooms with blackboard and electric fittings for use of audio-visual aids. It is better if these dates are published in the prospectus to avoid expenditure on post later and also ensure the knowledge of PCP to students. It is advantageous to both. The DCS, Punjab University, Chandigarh adopted this practiced a decade ago.

(b) **Advance Planning of Contents to be Taught:** We should prepare in advance the topics to be covered during the PCP. We may select topics in which DE students can face difficulty in comprehending from the lessons or in the areas where more light can be thrown on the topic, books recommended in the topics must be checked from the Library so that the students if they want to consult then, these are available to them. It has been

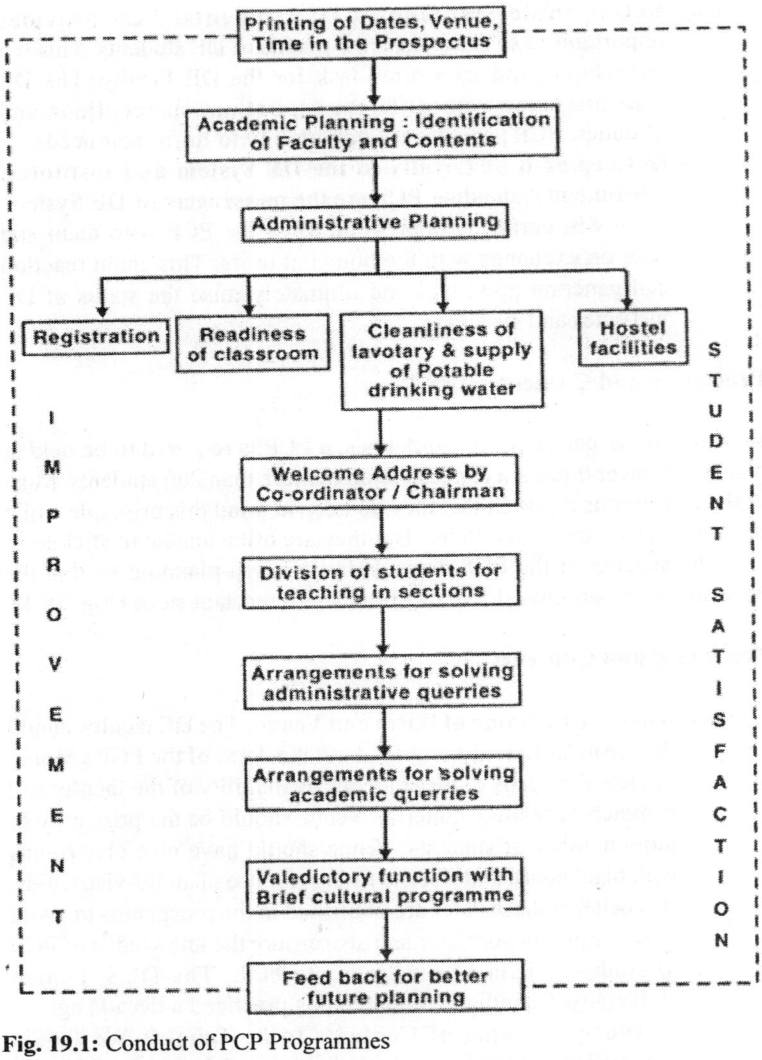

Fig. 19.1: Conduct of PCP Programmes

seen that faculty members teach the topics without telling in advance which make the students non-participative. Advance decision would make the students come prepared for better understanding and appreciation. This would also keep the faculty well prepared.

(c) Deciding about the Faculty keeping in view the Topics to be covered: We must decide as to who would teach, which topic so that he can prepare well in advance. While allocating the topic to an outside teacher we must be sure of his capability and competence.

(d) Keeping the Infrastructure Well Planned: The coordinator of the PCP must see that those persons who are to assist in the conduct of PCP are told in advance. The Audio-visual aids may also be booked in advance.

(e) Introductory Lecture: The coordinator may give introductory lecture to familiarise the students about the institute and the course. It would be better if he also introduces the faculty of the department to the students.

(f) Registration Counter: At the start of the PCP, students are registered to know the number and names. This creates and facilities harmonious relationships. This also keeps a check on outside element who tries to attend the classes or create problems.

(g) Clean Class Rooms: The classroom need be inspected. They must be kept neat and clean to give good image of the institute.

(h) Need of Effective Communication by the Teacher in Understanding the Essentials of Communication: The essentials of Communication are:

1. *Clarity of Thought:* The first *sine qua non* of good communication is that the idea to be transmitted must be absolutely clear in the mind of the communicator. It must spring out from a 'clear' head. It should be understood by the students so that it may be fully appreciated and acted upon.
2. *Importance to Action Rather than Words:* In all communication, actions are more significant than words. Example is better than precept.
3. *Participation:* In this connection it is essential that both the parties (the communicator and the recipient special check) should participate in the communication. It is the only way to make the communication effective.
4. *Transmission:* The communicator must plan carefully what to communicate and how to communicate. The success of this would depend upon the understanding of the students. According to Terry, eight factors are essential in making communication effective:

(a) Inform yourself fully;
(b) Establish a mutual trust in students;
(c) Find a common ground of experience and slowly raise their level;
(d) Use mutually known words already sent in lecture script;
(e) Have regard for context;
(f) Secure and hold the receiver's attention;
(g) Employ examples and visual aids; and
(f) Reinforce the main points.

According to Millet, seven factors make communication effective. It should be clear, consistent with the expectation of the recipient, adequate, timely, uniform, flexible and acceptable.

Need of study—PCP is very effective in distance education. To see the effectiveness and problems of PCP researcher conducted a research.

Problem—To study the effectiveness of PCP of B.Ed. students of distance education.

Objective of the Study

1. To study the problems of B.Ed. students of distance education.
2. To study the effectiveness of PCP in B.Ed. students of distance education.
3. To study the suggestions of B.Ed. students regarding the improvement in PCP.

Sample and Procedure

The sample of 50 students of B.Ed. of distance education selected from Mahesh Blind Institution, Navlakha, Indore, study centres of Bhoj Open University, Bhopal. This sample was purposive. Observation, Interview and Questionaire method was used to get data.

The study suggests that 85 per cent of respondents were aware of the dates of PCP. However, 60 per cent were aware of the topics to be covered in the PCP. Seventy per cent were satisfied with the regular conduct of classes. Eighty six per cent were satisfied with the coverage of the contents at the PCP. Eighty five per cent were satisfied with the duration. Forty per cent did not like the taking of the classes by outside teachers as they were not well versed with the style of teaching to Distance Education students. Ninety per cent were highly enthusiastic about the quality of teachers at PCP.

Student's Response to PCP

Sl. No.	*Activity*	*Yes*	*No*
1.	Did you get the information about the PCP well in advance?	85%	15%
2.	Did you know the topics to be covered during the first and second PCP?	60%	40%
3.	Were all the classes held regularly and punctually as per the time-table provided to you?	70%	30%
4.	Are you satisfied with the coverage of contents at the PCP?	86%	14%
5.	Do you approve the duration of PCP of 10 days to get sufficient exposure?	85%	15%
6.	Do you like the teaching by outside teachers who taught you at the PCP?	40%	60%
7.	Did your level of confidence increased after the PCP?	92%	8%
8.	Did you find your teachers effective and enthusiastic?	90%	10%
9.	Did your teachers and administrative staff help you in solving your personal problems?	87%	13%
10.	Does your friendship developed at the PCP help you in learning?	92%	8%
11.	Is the overall impact of the PCP positive in your mind?	100%	Nil

The study suggests that the students were happy about the programme. But they suggest some effective ideas which make their stay enjoyable and the PCP as fruitful. The study also unfolds some facts that can make PCP more successful.

Suggestions

The following are the facts and suggestions:

(a) **Need of Increase in Duration as well as Coverage of Course:** Most of the students wanted that number of days and frequency for holding PCPs should be increased. This is a demand from those who are not employed. However, there are others who are too busy and feel happy with the existing arrangements.

(b) **Need of Deciding Convenient Time and Place of PCP:** The time and place of PCPs should be decided in a way that these are within easy reach of students. We can also arrange PCP during Sundays or other holidays.

(c) **Need of Allocating Time for Discussion as Well:** Subject specialists/experts be deputed to conduct PCPs and they should give more time for discussion than teaching alone. Time at the disposal of the students is very short which need be utilised profitably.

(d) **PCP Need be Held Sufficiently Advance of Examinations:** All PCPs should be completed atleast two months before the commencement of the examinations and students should not be disturbed by asking them to participate in the PCPs just before the examinations. This would provide sufficient time at their disposal for the preparation of the examination.

(e) **Need of Small Sections:** More number of teachers should be involved and students should be divided into small groups according to their needs and assigned to teachers separately, so that individualised tutoring is possible. The number of students in some classes is very large and the students feel like sitting in a crowd and not in a class room. There should not be more than 50 students in a class.

(f) **Need of Hostel Facilities:** Necessary accommodation for out-station students be arranged and if possible at subsidised rates. Accommodation should be such where they feel comfortable.

(g) **Need of Despatch of Lessons:** Before the conduct of PCP necessary steps be taken to ensure that all the lessons are mailed to the students before the PCP so that the students should come fully prepared for the PCP.

(h) **Preference for Teachers from Parent Institution for Teaching at PCP:** The institution of part-time tutors engaged to teach at the PCP should be abolished and of the faculty members of the parent institution should share the full responsibility of running the PCP among themselves.

(i) **Need of Advance Planning of Contents to be covered at PCP and Communicating the same to Students:** The faculty members of each department would identify at least one month in advance of the commencement of the PCP at a particular station, the topics that they would be covered in the course at the PCP and would communicate the same to the students so that the latter may also be able to spell out their difficulties in writing to their teachers (the students may in fact be encouraged to do so). When both the teachers and the students go adequately prepared to the PCP, the Instructional content of the PCP would get strengthen considerable which in its turn would make the PCP much more effective and popular.

(j) **Need of more Emphasis on Discussion on Examination Related Topics:** During the PCP emphasis should be on the preparation of the students for the examination and not merely academic orientation.

(k) **PCP Need be Held Sufficiently in Advance of Examinations:** When the DE Institutes find convenient efforts may be made to extend its coverage to a larger number of stations, so that more and more students may be able to get benefit from this programme.

(l) **The home page should be up-to-date:** The home page should be on going part of course development. Make sure that you add or change information as necessary. Periodically verify whether other home pages to which you are linking still exist.

Library Services

Distance education has been described more attuned to learning than teaching. Library and other information technology have a central place in the process of Distance Education.

Networking

Networking means pooling of resources and sharing of benefits by Distance Education system. This would improve the quality of services as an individual institution cannot afford the quality required to implement distance education programmes. IGNOU has already established more than 400 study centres which can be further strengthened to provide services to the institutes of other distance education system.

Prompt Reply to the Quarries of the Students

Students develop many problems relating to Distance Education Programme. It is very difficult for them to approach the Distance Education Institutes. It is suggested that teachers in Distance Education System can be allocated students according to enrolment numbers. Students may be asked to approach that teacher or correspond with the person whose name may be mentioned to the students in advance.

Need of Review of Structure of DE System

It is the duty of personnel in Distance Education system to review the structure for quality with specific quality indicators to meet the requirements of 21st century. They should encourage thinking and innovation. Cost and benefit of the quality process must be kept in view.

Use of WWW for Distance Education

The WWW and Web browsers have made the Internet a more user-friendly environment. The ability to integrate graphics, text, and sound into a single tool means that novice users do not have to struggle with such a steep learning curve. In addition, organisations and individuals can create home pages independently and link to other home pages on their own computers or to pages created by others on different computer systems. For educators, the WWW provides an exciting new opportunity for distance teaching and learning the WWW can be used by the distance educator to build a classroom home page.

The home page can cover information about the class including the syllabus, exercises, literature reference and instructor's biography. The instructors can also provide links to information on the WWW that would be useful to students in the class (e.g., research data on agricultural markets, global climate change, or space missions). Other links can access library cataloges or each student's individual home page. In addition, the home page can link students to a discussion list that set-up for student communication. It is also a relatively simple matter to use the homepage to create forms that students can fill out and that will end-up being sent to you as an e-mail message.

Training for Instructors and Students Functions

It is important that an instructor be taught how to use all features of the equipment. A short session (30 minutes) should be sufficient to give the instructor a "hands-on" overview of the equipment features. It would also be helpful to provide the instructore with a quick reference sheet outlining major functions.

Conclusion

PCP is the most important aspect of a Distance Education system to bring together students and faculty face to face. A well organised PCP has tremendous potentialities for a comfortable, and motivated to learn and move ahead. Based students who took keen interest have performed will in examination as well.

REFERENCES

Goel, Aruna and Goel, S.L. (2000): *Distance Education in the 21st Century*, New Delhi: Deep & Deep Publications Pvt. Ltd., pp. 119-36.

Prasad, D.C. (2007): *Distance Education,* New Delhi: KSK Publishers and Distributors, pp. 91-102.

Rao, V.K. (2007): *Distance Education*, New Delhi: A.P.H. Publishing Corporation.

Siddiqui, M.H. (2007): *Distance Education : Theory and Research*, New Delhi: A.P.H. Publishing Corporation, p. 76.

20

ICT in Higher Education

A Switch Over to Learner-Centric-Learning

V.S.V. Laxmi Ramana

Introduction

The Department of Higher Education, MHRD, is responsible for the overall development of the basic infrastructure of Higher Education sector, both in terms of policy and planning. Under a planned development process, the Department looks after expansion of access and qualitative improvement in the Higher Education, through world class Universities, Colleges and other Institutions. The National Mission on Education through Information and Communication Technology (NMEICT) has been envisaged as a Centrally Sponsored Scheme to leverage the potential of ICT, in teaching and learning process for the benefit of all the learners in Higher Education Institutions in any time an where mode.

The Education System has been witnessing a dramatic change since then. The EduSAT has provided a new idea for the teachers to change their teaching style. Across the world the Information Technology is altering the style of teaching and learning. Smart phones usage, Internet availability are revolutionising the student life. Teachers too feel it convenient, because the explanation has become very easy especially when they have to concentrate on the diagrammatical explanation. In some educational institutions, smart classes have been introduced. The information is open equally to the teacher and the taught. The ICT has changed the traditional paradigm of teaching and learning process.

Profile of Higher Education at a Glance

The Indian Higher Education system, which includes Technical Education, is one of the largest of the world, just after the United States and China. Being at the apex of the educational pyramid, it plays a key role in producing quality teachers for the country's education.

According to the Annual Report 2014-15, the Higher Education as follows :

Name of Institutions	*Enrolments*		
	2010-11	*2011-12*	*2012-13 (P)*
Universities	621	642	665
Colleges Stand alone	32,974	34,852	35,829
Institutions	11095	11126	11443
Enrolment (in lakhs)	275.00	291.84	296.29
Enrolment in Distance Mode	33.14	34.15	296.29

Source: All India Surveys on Higher Education, MHRD.

It is evident that there is a constant growth. The enrolment shows the phenomenal growth of Higher Education.

Grass Enrolment Ratio (GER) in Higher Education

The following table indicates Higher Education for 2010-11 and 2012-13:

Category	*2010-11*	*2012-13*
Male	20.8	22.3
Female	17.9	19.8
Total	**19.4**	**21.1**

It is observed that there is a marginal growth in Women education and is a healthy sign for Indian society.

The Ministry of Human Resource Development, formerly Ministry of Education (until 25 September, 1985), is responsible for the development of human resources in India. The Ministry is divided into two departments—the Department of School Education and Literacy, which deals with primary, secondary and higher secondary education, adult education and literacy, and the Department of Higher Education which deals with university education, technical education, scholarship etc. The erstwhile Ministry of Education now functions under these two departments, as of 26 September, 1985. The University Grants Commission (UGC) came into existence on 28th December, 1953 and became a statutory body of Government of India by an Act of Parliament in 1956, for the coordination, determination, and maintenance of standards of university education. Higher education is the chief instrument for ensuring the upward mobility of the people and the advancement of the country. The Indian higher education system is being supported by Plan assistance. The University Grants Commission sponsored a number of studies on various dimensions of higher education in the country in order to develop necessary information base as a source material to prepare a report on approach and strategy for the Twelfth Five Year Plan. One of the main objectives of the Plan is to promote "quality and excellence".

National Mission in Education through ICT

The National Mission on Education through Information and Communication Technology (NMEICT) has been envisaged as a Centrally Sponsored Scheme to leverage the potential of ICT, in teaching and learning process for the benefit of all the learners in Higher Education Institutions in any time any where mode. This was expected to be a major intervention in enhancing the Gross Enrolment Ratio (GER) in Higher Education by 5 per centage points during the Eleventh Five Year Plan period.

The three cardinal principles of Education Policy, viz. access, equity and quality could be served well by providing connectivity to all colleges and universities, providing low cost and affordable access-*cum*-computing devices to students and teachers and providing high quality e-content free of cost to all learners in the country. NMEICT encompasses all the three elements. The Mission has two major components:

- Providing connectivity, along with provision for access devices, to institutions and learners; and
- Content generation.

It seeks to bridge the digital divide, i.e. the gap in the skills to use computing devices for the purpose of teaching and learning among urban and rural teachers/learners in Higher Education domain and empower those, who have hitherto remained untouched by the digital revolution and have not been able to join the mainstream of the knowledge economy. It plans to focus on appropriate pedagogy for e-learning, providing facility of performing experiments through virtual laboratories, on-line testing and certification, on-line availability of teachers to guide and mentor learners, utilisation of available Education Satellite (EduSAT) and Direct to Home platforms, training and empowerment of teachers to effectively use the new method of teaching learning etc. (Last Updated by admin on Tue, 04/19/2016-12:26).

The UGC initiated scheme called "ICT for teaching and learning process" for achieving quality and excellence in higher education. Network facilities with the help of ERNET, Ministry of Information and Technology, Government of India, were installed at UGC office to promote a healthy work culture. Along with this UGC launched a mega programme namely, 'UGC INFONET', a network of Indian Universities and Colleges, by integrating Information and Communication Technology (ICT) in the process of teaching, learning and education management. The network is managed by ERNET India and almost all the universities are its members. Information for Library Network (INFLIBNET), an autonomous Inter-University Centre of UGC is the nodal agency for coordination and facilitation of the linkage between ERNET and Universities. Training programmes for the manpower were conducted to manage the ERNET facilities and other aspects of systems including electronic subscriptions. In addition, UGC is encouraging creation of e-content/learning material for teaching learning process and management of education in colleges and universities.

The introduction of ICT into classrooms has changed the teaching learning system. At the initial stages, teachers in various universities and technical institutions used e-content provided by the UGC. Later on, the teaching community has started using the web sources for their teaching and then the students have been introduced to browse various resources to enhance their knowledge. The students started to browse the net resources and began to enhance their knowledge in the subject. Virtual class rooms, podcast, webinars, MOOCS etc. have been introduced and changed the classroom environment.

The age old traditional or conventional teaching and learning processes have undergone a paradigm shift. The focus of instruction is promotes, competence and performance. All over the world, Internet has become handy to get solutions for many challenges. Having to be connected to the world is the demand of the day. Technology has changed the learning environment. Teachers have become facilitators. In the new paradigm of the teaching-learning process, the students' role is very important. New approaches like Flip classrooms, Blended learning, Problem-based teaching, Project-based teaching etc., have been introduced. Teachers have been trained in these approaches and new methods.

The Role of ICT in Higher Education

The e-Education Policy States that every Indian manager, teacher and learner in the general and further education and training bands will be ICT capable (that is, use ICTs confidently and creatively to help develop the skills and knowledge they need as lifelong learners to achieve personal goals and to be full participants in the global community) by 2013 (Department of Education India, 2004: 17).

The Four Rationales for Introducing ICT in Education

Rationale	*Basis*
Social	Perceived role that technology now plays in society and the need for familiarising students with technology.
Vocational	Preparing students for jobs that require skills in technology.
Catalytic	Utility of technology to improve performance and effectiveness in teaching, management and many other social activities.
Pedagogical	To utilise technology in enhancing learning, flexibility and efficiency in curriculum delivery.

Source: Cross and Adam (2007).

In view of ICT, education can be classified in three main categories:

- E-learning,
- Blended Learning, and
- Distance Learning.

India's higher education system is the third largest in the world with respect to student enrolment, after China and the United States. Higher education is significant in its relevance that it equips people with specialised skills and that the majority of the population in India is below 25 years of age given its demographic structure. In a technology savvy environment, online capability has become a core part of the modern day educational institution.

The online courses have come into vogue. E-learning is emerging as an important strategy to provide widespread and easy access to quality higher education. E-learning is a generic term referring to different uses and intensities of uses of ICTs, from entirely online education to campus-based education and through other forms of distance education supplemented with ICTs in some way. Although, presently the initiatives for development of e-learning in India are continuing in a periodic manner, UGC is advocating and making efforts to enhance the quality of higher education by framing policy guidelines for their integration in classroom and other activities.

Education is a very socially oriented activity and quality education has been traditionally been associated with highly qualified teachers who have been assumed as knowledge providers. Hence, it used to be teacher-centred teaching. The quality of the students is decided based on their retention power of the content. But the change of Education system introduced the teachers to put student-focused teaching process. The students' involvement has been made mandatory. The accreditation process started examining the educational institutions based on certain criteria. Hence, every institution today is in need of getting approval of NAAC and other accreditation certificates. The perception of the students' changed and they started selecting only those colleges who have been accredited. Therefore, the responsibility of the educational institutions has been enhanced. They need to produce quality students who are competent enough to face the challenges in the work front. This will not be happened unless; the student is involved in the learning process. ICT has opened new arenas to the students to confront and learn something on their own. Slowly, the students understand that the classroom alone is not the abode of learning, beyond that knowledge can be perceived. In the process, along with his basic education, he started exploring new knowledge by joining various online courses according to his wish and time. Thus, the innovative use of ICT removes the barriers that are causing problems of low level education. Use of ICT improved the higher order skills such as analysing, evaluating and creating. It improves the perception and understanding of the world of the student. It involves the student in learning process where he learns by doing.

Objectives of ICT in Academics

Generally, three objectives are distinguished for the use of ICT in education:

(i) The use of ICT as object of study refers to learning about ICT, which enables students to use ICT in their daily life.

(ii) The use of ICT as aspect of discipline or profession; refers to the development of ICT skills for professional or vocational purposes.

(iii) The use of ICT as medium for teaching and learning; focuses on the use of ICT for the enhancement of the teaching and learning process.

Experiential Learning

Experiential Learning implies learning from experience. This is a learning process, where knowledge is created through the transformation of experience. The internet facility helps the students to browse instructional material without wasting much of their time. It enhances the students' motivation through the effective use of the familiar technology. ICT-based support works very well with English students—taking advantage of their usual and favourite hobbies—working on the computer, surfing the Internet, chatting, watching videos. At the same time, ICT respects their individual learning styles and needs as well as learners' own pace. A variety of skills and activities can be mixed and blended effectively via technological applications.

The technology roles for experiential learning should—

- provide tools to support knowledge construction;
- be the information driver to explore knowledge to support learning by constructing;
- be the basis of learning by doing;
- be the social medium to support learning by conversing; and
- support learning by reflecting.

Teachers can guide the students in experiential teaching with the help of technology are:

- Incorporate social learning and interaction into online learning.
- Make students complete specific assignments using technology.
- Use technology that employs sensory input.
- Facilitate collaboration.

E-learning : E-learning is the use of Internet technologies to enrich knowledge and performance. E-learning technologies provide learners control over content, learning sequence, place of learning, time, and allowing them to fit their experiences to meet their personal learning objectives. E-learning is synonymous to web-based learning, online learning, computer-assisted learning. Distance learning and Computer-aided instruction are the two collective modes in E-learning. The learners from different locations can make use of the instruction which is passed on through information technologies. Blended learning is a new approach which will help the teachers to combine web information and the content that they prepared to deliver in one go. The teachers can update the content time-to-time very easily and the learners, on the other hand, can feel free to learn the content conveniently. For teachers, however, the opportunities and merits of e-learning rather hoop the changes of expectations of learning in the 21st Century, offering us the chance to review and adapt learning and teaching practices, familiarising ourselves for the decades of change that lie ahead of us as we adapt to globalisation and all it means for our societies and cultures, communities and institutions.

Blended Learning

Blended learning is an education programme (formal or informal) that combines online digital media with traditional classroom methods. It requires the physical presence of both teacher and student, with some element of student control over time, place, path, or pace. It reassures the acquisition of knowledge combined with traditional information-gained, skills-development learning. It is a thoughtful integration of traditional learning experiences with online learning experience. A continuum of E-learning is the combination of Enhanced+blended+online.

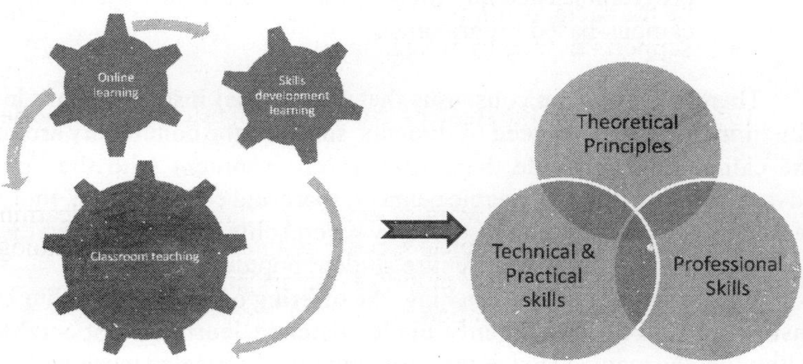

Fig. 20.1: Blended Learning Methodology

Distance Learning

Distance learning is a way of learning remotely without being in regular face-to-face contact with a teacher in the classroom. In recent years the advent of the internet and widespread use of the computer has led to a huge growth in distantly delivered tuition and study. At undergraduate level distance learning usually means students engaging with learning materials at home or work.

- These materials are produced by the university, college or learning provider and are either sent directly to the student or more usually today accessed via the internet.
- Tutorial support is provided via a virtual learning environment, telephone, e-mail or other electronic means.
- There may be occasional face-to-face encounters with tutors and attendance at week-long summer schools.
- The main advantage of distance learning is that it allows you to fit your learning around your work and home life.
- One can usually also set your own pace of study.
- It is the decision of the student as to when and where he wants to study.
- It does not matter where he lives—he can gain a degree from anywhere in the world.
- As with a full-time degree, students may find that they gain useful, transferable skills, such as planning and research.
- A distance learning course often costs less than a full-time degree.
- Universities and colleges ensure that their distance learning programmes and qualifications are of the same high quality as campus-based programmes.

There is a common consensus that educational institutions are in a situation to cater to the need of students, staff and the community around the campus and provide them with an environment with the latest advancements in the way people connect, share and communicate. India's massive open online courses, started by several elite research universities, collectively enrol the world's entire student population.

With respect to online teaching, the offering of MOOCs by elite US institutions in 2012 suddenly made distance learning respectable. Although, the many distance-teaching universities created worldwide on the model of the UK Open University from 1970 onwards gave access to higher learning to millions, they had little impact on the way that existing universities operated. Distance learning still suffered from the poor image of correspondence education. But once Harvard, MIT, and Stanford went online the established universities sat up and took notice. Online enrolments in regular programmes had been growing steadily since 2000 in a somewhat haphazard manner, but following the MOOCs frenzy in 2012 a survey in 2015 could declare that "online learning in higher education now mainstream." (See more at: *http://blog.oup.com/*2016/04/moocs-higher-education/#sthash.DaRzK9Rr.dpuf).

Flipped Classroom

Flipped classroom is an instructional strategy and a type of Blended learning that reverses the traditional learning environment by delivering instructional content, often online, outside of the classroom. It moves activities, including those that may have traditionally been considered homework, into the classroom. In a flipped classroom, students watch online lectures, collaborate in online discussions, or carry out research at home and engage in concepts in the classroom with the guidance of a mentor.

In the traditional classroom, teacher is the primary source to deliver the subject knowledge. It is dine basically in lecture mode. The students' interaction used to be very limited. They become passive listeners. Their involvement is almost nil in the learning process. The flipped classroom purposefully shifts the instruction into learner-centred model, which creates meaningful learning opportunities. A teacher's interaction with students in a flipped classroom can be more personalized and less didactic, and students are actively involved in knowledge acquisition and construction as they participate in and evaluate their learning.

Potential Drawbacks-*cum*-Challenges in Using ICT in Education

In the traditional method of teaching the teacher has to bear the responsibility of teaching and the results of the students. The institutions blame the teachers if thestudents do not pass. The teachers are glad with the emergence of the ICT in to the education system. They used to have limited sources and lot of responsibilities to deliver the knowledge. A question arises, do all the educational institutions use the modern technology to enhance the better learning environment? An authentic

Benefits of ICT in Education to the Main Stakeholders

Stakeholder	*Benefits*
Students	■ Increased access. ■ Flexibility of content and delivery. ■ Combination of work and education. ■ Learner-centred approach.
Employers	■ Higher-quality of education and new-ways of interaction. ■ High quality, cost effective professional development in the workplace. ■ Upgrading of employee skills, increased productivity. ■ Developing of a new learning culture. ■ Sharing of costs and of training time with the employees. ■ Increased portability of training. ■ Increase the capacity and cost effectiveness of education and training systems.
Governments	■ To ensure the connection of educational institutions and curricula to the emerging networks and information resources ■ To promote innovation and opportunities for lifelong learning.

answer cannot be expected. Still there are certain educational institutions which do not allow the teachers to use new approaches and trends. However, with the help of the ICT the students can manage their learning. It helps to develop their organisational skills, presentation skills and communication skills. The student enhances his learning through ICT. The web sources are readily available for him to teach and clarify his doubts. It also boosts the confidence levels of the students. They are enrolling themselves in various distance e-learning programmes to get diplomas and degrees for their future endeavours. The globalisation process has also created a large market of offshore students. To reach them, information technology is the only convenient medium, which can offer education as a service (Bhattacharya and Sharma, 2007). It increases education provision substantially and can contribute to mass education. It also creates competition among the institutions for providing education and hence improves the quality (Cross and Adam, 2007).

Initiatives of Use of ICT in Education

India is making use of powerful combination of ICTs such as open source software, satellite technology, local language interfaces, easy to use human-computer interfaces, digital libraries etc. with a long-term plan to reach the remotest of the villages. Community service centres have been started to promote e-learning throughout the country (Bhattacharya and Sharma, 2007). Notable initiatives of use of ICT in education in India include:

- Indira Gandhi National Open University (IGNOU) uses radio, television and internet technologies.
- National Programme on Technology Enhanced Learning: A concept similar to the open courseware initiative of MIT. It uses internet and television technologies.
- Eklavya initiative: Uses internet and television to promote distance learning.
- IIT-Kanpur has developed 'Brihaspati', an open source e-learning platform (Virtual Class Room).

Premier institutions like Calcutta University have entered into a strategic alliance with NIIT for providing programmes through virtual classrooms. Jadavpur University is using a mobile-learning centre. IIT-Bombay has started the programme of CDEEP (Centre for Distance Engineering Education Programme) as emulated classroom interaction through the use of real time interactive satellite technology.

Higher Education in India: Vision 2030, FICCI Higher Education Summit 2013

"Higher Education in India: Vision 2030", FICCI Higher Education Summit 2013, states that curricula are outdated and institutions face a severe shortage of well-trained quality faculty. While enrolment in higher education has grown six times in the last 30 years, faculty strength has only grown four times. Around 35 per cent of faculty positions in state universities and 40 per cent in central universities are lying vacant.

E-Learning Market Trends and Forecast 2014-2016 Report by DOCEBO, March 2014 E-learning market in India was valued at INR 18.41 in 2010-11 and is expected to grow at a CAGR of 20 per cent. The global market size for e-Learning is predicted to grow more than double by 2017 at CAGR of 23 per cent. By mid-2030s physical schools will have been replaced by studios and virtual teaching. These "Virtual/ Physical Studios" rely on technology to provide a hybrid version of education that optimizes the process by, "Bridging the online-offline gap, offering a potential future where embodiment is secondary to information access". (Courtesy: Meenakshi Thanji, *et al.*, *American International Journal of Research in Humanities, Arts and Social Sciences*, 9(2), December 2014-February 2015, pp. 143-147).

Challenges or Limitation to ICT

The drawbacks-*cum*-challenges to using ICT in education and concludes ICT enabled education will ultimately lead to the democratisation of education:

1. There is a possibility of shifting attention from the primary goal.
2. It may divide the teacher and the taught for various reasons.
3. Many teachers are not computer savvy, they cannot update information or content time to time, as these are not trained periodically.
4. Students instead of learning feel happy to copy.

It is important that teachers or trainers should be made to adopt technology in their teaching styles to provide pedagogical and educational gains to the learners. Successful implementation of ICT to lead change is more about influencing and empowering teachers and supporting them in their engagement with students in learning rather than acquiring computer skills and obtaining software and equipment. ICT enabled education will ultimately lead to the democratisation of education.

ICT, no doubt, improves the quality of education by facilitating learning by doing, real time conversations, self-learning, problem solving, critical thinking skills. Critical thinking and, research and evaluation skills are growing importance as students have been increasing the volumes of information from web sources to start through (New Media Consortium, 2007). ICTs changing processes of teaching and learning by adding elements of vitality to learning environments including virtual environments.

REFERENCES

Al Ansari, H. (2006). Internet Use by the Faculty members of Kuwait University, *The Electronic Library*. Vol. 24, No. (6).

Bhattacharya, I. and Sharma, K. (2007). India in the knowledge economy—An electronic paradigm, *International Journal of Educational Management*, Vol. 21, No. 6, pp. 543-68.

Cross, M. and Adam, F. (2007). "ICT Policies and Strategies in Higher Education in South Africa: National and Institutional Pathways", *Higher Education Policy,* 20(1) : 73–95.

Mishra, S. and R.C. Sharma (2005). Development of e-Learning in India. *University News*, 43(11), March 14-20, 2005.

Meenakshi Thanji *et al.*, *American International Journal of Research in Humanities, Arts and Social Sciences*, 9(2), December 2014–February 2015, pp. 143-147.

New Media Consortium (2007). *Horizon Report, www.nmc.org/pdf/2007*

21
E-learning

A Disruptive Approach in Higher Education System

Swaleha Zubair

Introduction

Novel communication technologies, particularly the Internet, appear to offer exciting avenues for overcoming geographical access and cost barriers in learning. It is hard to comprehend that these technologies can have a positive influence on the education of children and adults who lack basic living resources and live with an under-developed educational infrastructure in the environment of political instability. This chapter explores the advances in open and distance learning in developing nations, and questions if these advances are addressing the educational gaps. The discussion highlights the challenges created by poverty, lack of social and educational infrastructures, and cultural issues that restrict educational progress in developing countries. This chapter explores the conundrum that learning technologies on one hand (i.e., print-material, radio, television, video, audio, telephone, computers, and the Internet) are seen as an answer to the limitations and rigidities of conventional education because they reach a larger number of learners (Sutaria, 1990); while on the other hand, where these technologies are being used, the difficulty of accessing them and the digital divide between privileged and deprived groups continues to widen the educational gap.

During the last decade, higher education has gained importance in India's changing policy landscape as the government realises that India's strength lies in education. The gap between demand and supply of higher education has necessitated the governments and institutions to formulate the policies for the better use of ICT. And, in order to bridge the gap, it is necessary to evolve the cooperation between the public and private sectors for the successful implementation of ICT in higher education (R. Nayak, *Indian Express*, 2011).

The evolution of ICT into universities clearly changes the way education is conducted. It is possible to work with distance learning and achieve a closer collaboration between different universities, but also paving the way for a new pedagogical approach where there is unparallel ability to spread knowledge and disseminate information. The pace of change brought about by new technologies has had a significant effect on the way people live, work and play worldwide (Rev. Dr. Obiora Nwosu).

Why e-learning?

Economists have identified India and China, the world's two most populated and diverse nations, as the fastest growing economies in the world (*New World Economy*, 2005). India, as a global leader in the outsourcing of IT services is, unlike most developing countries, contributing to the technological revolution (Sharma, 2005). The growth of China's manufacturing industry now means that most products used by people around the world are manufactured in China. The Indian and Chinese open and distance learning case studies above, combined with their economic success, paint a picture of success in education and opportunity for their people. Do all Indian and Chinese citizens share these successes?

Per capita incomes for India and China are rising, but this may be happening at the expense of the poorer citizens in these populous nations. A closer look at the critical literature on distance education exposes the poverty challenges that persist despite the economic growth and technological developments of these two nations (Carr-Chellman, 2005). According to Abdul Waheed Khan of the Indira Gandhi National Open University (Sharma, 2005), despite the Indian NOS raising the aspirations of the poorer classes, "only 6.5 per cent of school graduates pursue higher education degrees in India as compared to 30 per cent in developed countries" (p. 54). This highlights the educational divide in India, which dates back to the policies proposed after Independence in 1947.

While NOS has reached some individuals and helped to raise their living standards by enabling them to gain employment in different government sectors, overall there has been limited funding to address the growing demands of primary education sectors. Unlike China, which made primary education compulsory in 1960s, since Independence in 1947 India has concentrated investment in university education (Sharma, 2005). As a result India now has a large number of uneducated adults (Dhanrajan 1997, cited in Sharma), and a small number of middle-class, educated adults and their children, who continue to benefit from private and public investments. This middle-class, white-collar workers are now leading the information technology revolution in India, making the elite wealthier whilst ignoring the needs of the non-elite (Sharma, 2005).

The Indian Constitution (Article 24) identifies the need to protect children from forced labour, but it was not until 1994 that the government called for elimination of child labour altogether. Yet there is no evidence that this proposal is being enforced. Only recently has the Indian government sought to make free and compulsory education a fundamental right for all children between 6 and 14 years of age (UNESCO, 2004). Badiwala (1998) discusses the successes of Sri Lanka and the Indian State of Kerela, which have enforced compulsory education, and by spending more on mass primary and secondary education than on higher education. This enforced compulsory education, combined with the changing attitudes and aspirations of the people, has reduced child labour in Sri Lanka and Kerala, but the remainder of the Indian subcontinent lags behind in basic education.

What can new information and communication technologies (ICTs) do to raise the status and actual and perceived quality of distance education status in developing countries? And what can they do to influence the status of those who engage in distance learning? Can ICTs benefit those who are resource poor and have limited or no access to chapter-based modes of distance education delivery? The 1998 Working Conference on *Capacity Building for IT in Education in Developing Countries* demonstrated the importance those developing countries' governments place on computer education (Marshall & Ruohonen, 1998). The Conference representatives identified the need to provide computers to enable students to first develop computer skills, and second to use computers to learn at a distance.

As an example, Botswanan policies identify computer education as necessary for the people of Botswana to compete in a modern, IT-driven, global economy (Ojo & Awuah, 1998). Their goal is not to create computer experts, but to give citizens basic computer skills and to enable them to use computers for learning. Despite the government's efforts to supply computers to primary and secondary schools, there are significant challenges, including a shortage of teachers who know how to use computers and teach IT skills. The rural-urban infrastructure disparities indicate that while urban areas can boast about electricity and telecommunications, rural areas remain unconnected and hence disadvantaged. There is a high dependency on expatriate teachers and learning materials developed in the West to support teaching in subjects such as science and technology. Limited internal human resource capacity means learning is not specific to the local populations and their learning needs. The critical challenge in Botswana is the need to balance investment in computer education against more pressing needs of basic living resources, particularly in rural and deprived areas (Ojo & Awuah, 1998).

Likewise, efforts of the Namibian government to offer computer education in schools since 1995 have resulted in only the most privileged private schools connected, with 0.5 per cent to 2.6 per cent of students enrolled in computer courses at any one level (Kiangi, 1998). While the number of Internet cafés in urban areas is growing in Namibia, the telecommunications infrastructure and human resources to provide computer education in rural areas remains under-developed to meet the educational demands of the poor majority. Kiangi also points out that these challenges mean, "Namibia is mainly a consumer rather than developer of IT" (p. 46).

Similar findings were confirmed in a survey of IT used in education in the Philippines. Philippine educators have used combinations of radio, print, audio, and video recordings for distance education of learners scattered around the Filipino islands since 1952 (dela Peña-Bandalaria, 2007). Yet the country faces typical infrastructural and digital divide challenges between rural-urban populations when it comes to using computers and associated technologies for learning. The proliferation of mobile phones in developing countries like the Philippines may enhance the development of mobile learning (m-learning), to educate the masses. The University of the Philippines' Open University launched an m-learning programme in 2004 that offered print and mobile materials for simple and universally relevant health, literacy, and numeracy education. Such mobile learning programmes may have potential for growth, but the limited capacity of mobile devices, the cost of synchronous interactions, and the rural-urban divide may hinder further developments (dela Peña-Bandalaria, 2007).

Other developing countries that have large populations and a rural-urban divide also have less than 1 per cent of their populations accessing the Internet (Mutonyi & Norton, 2007). China, for example, has 70,000 schools with computers and more than 10 million students who have mastered basic computer skills, but most of these schools are in cities, not in poorer, rural areas (Zhang, 2005). Despite the availability of technologies in urban regions, rural and poor people continue to be deprived of investment, infrastructure, and skilled teachers. Thus far, the introduction of computers into education in developing countries seems to have done little to widen educational access to the rural poor, who also do not have easy access to conventional schools and colleges. A small per centage of individuals are gaining access to computers in developing countries; however, this minority is not yet ready to contribute independently to the world's digital content. They remain the consumers rather than producers of this content.

Is e-learning working?

A review of 150 distance education programmes in sub-Saharan Africa has concluded that traditional, chapter-based means of distance learning continues to be more reliable, sustainable, and widely used than online and Web-based methods of learning (Leary & Berge, 2006). Does this imply that developing countries with limited infrastructures should not use online learning methods? There have been reported advances in e-learning in developing countries, and there are several determinants that may influence e-learning success in these countries, as exemplified in the case studies below.

First, Internet access at home is an obvious determinant of who has access to online learning and who benefits from these e-learning initiatives. According to UNESCO (1999, as cited in Mackintosh, 2005) 42 per cent of the inhabitants of developed countries have telephone connections in contrast with 4.5 per cent in developing countries, and only a mere 1.4 per cent in sub-Saharan Africa. In addition, most single telephone connections in rural areas in developing countries are typically shared among communities, rather than owned by individual households (Mackintosh, 2005). The cost of Internet connections remains high for those who cannot afford such basic educational necessities. For instance, in Turkey, a middle-income country, the cost of an Internet connection (available only in cities) is US $50 per month, a substantial proportion of the average monthly income of between US $300 and $500 (Gursoy, 2005). This basic lack of infrastructure in telecommunications continues to define the online learning experience of different groups of learners in developing countries.

A survey of 387 students in their final undergraduate year at the Virtual University of Pakistan (established in 2002) concluded that the majority of students (over 90%) found learning over the Internet and *via* satellite TV beneficial (Hussain, 2007). As of 2004, however, Pakistan had only five internet cafés for every 10,000 people, and most students rely on these locations for access (Syed, 2004). The result is that Pakistani students in this study reported difficulties in accessing computers, libraries, friendly learning environments, and efficient mentors. The majority also reported on electricity failures, computer vision syndrome, finger joint pain, backaches, headaches, and dizziness due to occasional long periods of computer use to compensate for limited access (Hussain, 2007).

At Indonesia's Open University, the University of Terbuka, 320,000 students reported similar limitations in online infrastructure and access (Belawati & Zuhairi, 2007). Distance education systems and students continue to rely heavily on post, courier services, and telephones (Belawati & Zuhairi, 2007). The widespread use of print, audio cassettes, face-to-face tutorials, and intermittent, government-controlled radio and television broadcasts supports over 600,000 urban, sub-urban, and rural learners attached to the Bangladesh Open University (Islam, Rahman & Rahman, 2006). These traditional methods may be more reliable, but they are often one-way and lack teacher-student and student-student interactivity.

Second, the underlying intentions and goals of investment and educational developments determine whether deprived and poorer groups are able to participate in the information society. The Former Prime Minister of India, Atal Behari Vajpayee (1998, cited in Sharma, 2005) recognised the potential of information technology to enable the Indian citizen to "overcome historical disabilities and once again become the master of [his or her] own destiny" and to "enable India to achieve the goal of becoming a strong, prosperous and self-confident nation" (Sharma 2005 : 56). The recent announcement by the Indian Government that it will invest in providing free broadband to all residents by 2009 is ambitious and a step in the right direction (Broadband Initiatives, 2007). India's technology and distance learning institutions, including the Indira Gandhi National Open University (IGNOU), the Indian Institute of Technology, the Birla Institute of Technology, and the School of Education Technology at Jadavpur University, have led the way in online degree courses and modules (Sharma, 2005). A government supported project called Vidyakash aimed to develop support and training for teachers and provide an infrastructure for Indian institutions to use Internet technologies for education. As a consequence, India now has 4 million technology workers, 700,000 software professionals, and 1,700 technical institutes (Sharma, 2005). These initiatives, however, have arguably been supported by courses demanding high fees and therefore remain the privilege of the elite, educated, and wealthy. Moreover, they fail to consider the need to provide basic literacy and computer skills and access to computers to poorer groups before they can begin to engage in higher online learning.

Third, there are issues surrounding the practice of buying offshore courses with the aim of meeting the learning needs of diverse population groups. The World Bank-supported African Virtual University Project is being launched in African universities to provide online access to undergraduate and remedial academic courses, including calculus, differential equations, physics, chemistry, statistics, computers, and engineering. Academics, administrators, and technologists in Western countries including Australia, United States, Canada, and Belgium have led the task force, seminars, and courses. For example, for mounting on the system, "Universities in Belgium and Canada are developing French-language seminars in business management, environment, teacher training, and computer and Internet literacy. Recently, a curriculum task force was formed to structure a four-year undergraduate degree programme in computer science, computer engineering, and electrical engineering (World Bank, 1998 : 2). Mackintosh (2005) argues that for sub-Saharan African countries, the offshore courses provided by Western countries may result in university education becoming even more elitist. Zhang (2005) also criticizes the courses available from U.S. universities in China, and argues that these courses are not culturally grounded, have language barriers, and exhibit limited awareness of students' backgrounds and experiences in the field of study.

Fourth, the types of courses and learning methods influence who has a greater opportunity to contribute to global, digital content and developments. For example, in India and China, computer-supported courses and computer skills courses available for the less privileged are focused on developing vocational skills to perform an identified task. These tasks are typically repetitive and often require working for long hours for a subcontract firm, which, in turn, is contracted by larger software companies or service providers. This is in contrast with the computer education programmes developed by collaboration between the government and foreign investors to train software engineers (Sharma, 2005). Entry into the latter programmes is extremely competitive and targeted at upper middle-class professionals, who gain the opportunity to contribute to the digital content. In the information society, this division between which computer courses are available to whom further contributes to the digital divide and widens inequalities between 'haves' and 'have-nots.'

The above discussion of e-learning determinants suggest that e-learning does have the potential to meet the educational needs of masses of poor people in developing countries; however, this potential has yet to be recognised. The present IT provisions in developing countries is limited to the elite. Existing infrastructures allow only a few to develop communication and interaction skills and to become part of the new social networking paradigm. Education for the masses continues to be didactic and devoid of interaction and critique. And while e-learning may offer the opportunity to shift the distance learning paradigm from delivery of content towards learner-centred and discussion-led learning, continuing reliance on print material and broadcast technologies dominates in developing countries (Islam, Rahman & Rahman, 2006). The IT access gap is contributing to the widening digital divide between 'haves' and 'haves-not' in developing countries.

Developing countries, wherein only a small proportion of the population has Internet access, need to realise the disparities between rural and urban communities, male and female students, and elite and non-elite groups. They need to consider how to adapt global software and hardware to benefit all of their citizens. Distance learning quality frameworks need to take into account the actual needs of their target populations, not just the learning content (Belawati & Zuhairi, 2007). Belawati (2005) identifies this as the critical challenge for developing countries—to educate students and teachers to use computers and develop accessible infrastructures so that they may benefit from the interactivity offered by online learning.

With growing number of internet users, India's potential as a huge market for e-learning is enormous. A large number of new users are accessing the internet for the first time from their smart-phones, which is emerging as an ideal, personalised and commerce-enabled platform for e-learning adoption.

As per the Docebo Report issued in July 2014, the worldwide market for self-paced e-learning reached \$35.6 billion in 2011. The five-year CAGR is estimated to be 7.6 per cent, so revenues should reach \$51.5 billion in next few years. While the aggregate growth rate is 7.6 per cent, several world regions have higher growth rates. At present, the highest rate is in Asia at 17.3 per cent, followed by Eastern Europe (16.9%), Africa (15.2%) and Latin America (14.6%).

According to another report, India's online education market size is set to grow to $40 billion by 2017 from the current $20 billion. Because of its enormous population; India has one of the largest education systems in the world with a network of more than 1 million schools and 18,000 higher education institutions. More than half of the country's 1.2 billion population falls in the target market for education and related services.

e-learning brings unique advantages, the prominent being the ability to provide personalised attention to all students. In a conventional set-up, this is only possible when a highly skilled tutor offers one-to-one tutorials. However, considering that most institutions have a classroom-based set-up, such attention becomes difficult. It can also facilitate links between the people living in smaller towns and cities can get access to the best possible learning resources from across the world, at a very affordable price. In fact, the face of education has experienced massive changes over the decades. Once characterised by the traditional classroom model, education has metamorphosed into learning that is instant, online, self-driven and on the go. The journey of education in India, too, has been dotted with numerous milestones—the most modern among these is e-learning.

1. **The reform push:** The government policies efficiently support e-learning, for instance the Department of Electronics and Information Technology (DeitY) has been actively indulged in budding tools and technologies for desired encouragement. DeitY supports e-learning-focused R & D projects at various academic educational institutes. These comprises content development, R & D technology initiatives, HRD projects and faculty guidance initiatives to advance literacy through distance education.
2. **Live instruction:** Knowledge can be disseminated employing electronic gadgets. Experts can deliver lecture on specific topics that can be broadcasted for wide audience sitting in remote areas. This will facilitate dissemination of knowledge from one place to the students sitting in other locations.
3. **Video content delivery:** The teaching and information delivered on a specific topic can be recorded in the form of lectures, documentaries and other video content. The pre-recorded matter may be stored and delivered as and when needed.
4. Student-to-student interaction *via* internet tools. Video-conferencing can be used in interaction of students with the

teacher. The learning process can be made effective by encouraging interaction among themselves.

5. **Remote test administration:** It is customary to conduct standardised tests to evaluate students on a level-playing field. However, testing schedule to conduct these test are important as all the participants are ought to get equal opportunity while attempting the test. The dissemination should be prompt and displayed securely.
6. **Up-to-date materials:** Timely update in the text is important while retaining the basic knowledge texture. This is important to cope-up with the advancement made in the knowledge on the routine basis. Digital delivery solves this issue when coupled with e-readers.
7. **Self-learning:** Computer-based training or self-paced learning is common in higher education than trade-oriented learning. However, authentication of information is quite important in such type of knowledge gain.
8. **The VSAT advantage:** Satellite broadband, typically VSAT (very-small-aperture terminal), offers sincere efforts in bridging gap between source and learners. During the early advancement days, satellite connectivity was too expensive, sluggish and often non-reliable. With the advent of high through put satellites (HTS) and advances in radio technology, the cost and reliability of satellite connectivity has improved a lot. Satellite broadband offers distinct advantages such as competitive cost; multicast capability; universal coverage; and low cost and simple installation. Further, specialised equipment such as digital white-boards, video-conferencing systems, multimedia systems and even 3D learning experiences may be connected to take advantage of the broadband connectivity.
9. **A business opportunity:** E-learning raises the level of education, literacy and economic development in developing countries. This is especially true for countries where technical education is expensive and lot of economic disparities exist. On the positive note, the incurred expenses have come down so significantly that students at the level of school, university and even medical/ engineering science may do a rotation in a remote area—can take full advantage of bandwidth provided by broadband satellite systems.

Technologies for e-learning Revolution

1. Big Data

Big Data is the data produced by learners interacting with the learning content and collected through tools such as Learning Management System (LMS), Content Management Systems (CMS) and other media. The access to Big Data help us in learning well-informed knowledge about the learning programmes that we develop. However, the real strength of Big Data lies in its power to help forecast or predict scenarios and take preventive actions (such as learners' performance and outcomes before they start a training programme). The Big Data based technology is set to revolutionize various components of e-learning.

A more detailed article is available at:

- *http://learnnovators.com/big-data-a-game-changer-for-e-learning/*
- *https://www.coursera.org/course/bigdata-edu*

2. Application Programming Interfaces (API)

Application Programming Interfaces or APIs is one of the most promising technological possibilities that hold a great promise for education and learning.

An API is basically a web-based application's interface. It helps other applications to interact and provide improved or added functionality at the user end. APIs are useful for extending the data or functionalities of one application and create other applications.

APIs offer incredible possibilities in learning systems and tools. They help in gaining knowledge, sharing of data and also help in learning resources, ideas, and much more. This technology, we believe, is going to play a crucial role in the learning scenario of the future.

Some of the most popular APIs related to education and learning available on the Internet include APIs such as The Deadline API, Khan Academy API, Blackboard Collaborate API, Knewton API etc. For more enhance and comprehensive details one can glance at the following searchable API/mash up repositories:

- Programmable Web: *http://www.programmableweb.com*
- APIHub: *http://www.apihub.com/*

3. Tin Can API

Tin Can API is a new and evolving learning technology specification (from ADL—the SCORM people). It addresses many of the limitations of SCORM such as the following:

- SCORM needs a web browser (no support for apps).
- It requires a constant Internet connection.
- It requires an LMS to initiate learning.
- It could track only formal learning activities (and not informal learning experiences).
- It does not support platform transitions (such as computer to mobile).
- It has limitations in sequencing, interoperability, and ensuring security of the learning content.

Tin Can API (also known as the Experience API) can be defined as the next generation of SCORM. It has removed all the barriers (listed above) that existed with the previous standards. In addition, it offers lot more features opening up the door to a whole lot of possibilities that make learning professionals excited. It allows track informal learning experiences such as playing games and simulations, and also real-world activities (such as visiting websites, attending conferences etc.) and not just digital ones!

With progression in the field, more disruptive changes incurred and eventually help us in performance improvement to the next level. Last but not the least, combined with the power of Big Data, Tin Can API could help us turn learning to more personalised and adaptive experiences. Tin Can API has already started creating an impact on the tools in the e-learning industry with more and more companies adopting this new standard.

If you would like to experience a few interesting prototypes using Tin Can API, check this link (below):

- *http://tincanapi.com/prototypes/*

4. HTML5

HTML5 is a new version of the Hyper Text Markup Language (HTML) from the Web Hypertext Application Technology Working Group

(WHATWG) and the World Wide Web Consortium (W3C). It is an evolving programming language that could lead the future of mobile web. Its potential is so huge that it is fast becoming the standard for e-learning delivery. The most important features of this disruptive technology are its support for:

- Mobile devices and platforms that do not support Flash.
- More accurate formatting.
- More interactive experiences.
- Greater Flexibility (than Flash).
- Better Performance.
- Takes less processing power and (hence battery life).
- No plug-in required.

Authoring tools such as Articulate Presenter, Storyline, Captivate, Lectora, Raptivity etc. are HTML5 compatible. It is interesting to note that even the desktop browsers are moving towards standardising on HTML5 in the near future.

More detailed knowledge can be achieved by course from the American Society for Training and Development (ASTD) that is specifically designed for e-learning professionals:

- *http://www.astd.org/Education/Programs/HTML5*

5. Responsive e-Learning Design

In general learners spend most of their time in front of multiple screens—a computer, laptop, smart phone, tablet etc. to learn or to perform other learning-related our tasks/activities. They move between these different types of devices in sequence (called 'Sequential Screening') or use them simultaneously (called 'Simultaneous Screening'). As per Google's Report "The New Multi-screen World", 90 per cent of our media interactions are screen based.

This scenario makes it very challenging for learning designers to ensure that the learning solutions they design work on all these devices with different screen sizes, shapes, resolutions, or Operating Systems (OSs). Responsive e-Learning Design (RED) is the solution to address this challenge. It is the technology that helps us design and deliver learning solutions that work across a broad range of devices smoothly. It follows and adapts the standards laid out by Responsive Web Design (RWD).

Like other technologies that we have discussed, Responsive Web Design is also in its early stages and is evolving with a potential to reshape the learning landscape.

If you would like to check a sample website that supports responsive design, check the link below:

- *http://www.thesearethings.com/*

6. Wearable Technology

Wearable digital devices with an electronic performance support system provide continuous learning to mobile workers. Though wearable devices such as Google Glass are raising privacy concerns presently, it promises a multitude of new learning opportunities for future learners. Though this technology is in the very early stages, the possibilities are enormous and could help transform learning.

Following is URL to have better understanding about the subject:

- *http://www.youtube.com/watch?v=yRrdeFh5-io*

7. VIDEO Conferencing

This is considered as one of the best mediums for effective learning. It helps in bridging the challenge with respect to different screen sizes and multiple platforms. With more and more video learning solutions and platforms emerging in the market, there are going to be radical changes in how we manage (conceive, design, develop, deliver and track) video-based learning solutions. The advancement of certain communication platforms such as Skype, Google hangout and Go meeting, have revolutionised the way a group of people communicate for these platforms provide features such as screen sharing, document sharing and general/ private communication options that can be used to set up a conducive online environment for education. Some learning management systems have already integrated these communication systems on to their platforms. Due to the convergence (TV with Internet) that is happening with the emergence of devices and services like Google TV and Apple TV, the demand for highly interactive video-based learning solutions is going to grow significantly in the future.

8. Digital Textbooks

Many schools and universities around the world have started using this new technology as an effective learning tool. Moreover, schools and colleges are getting more excited about the cost advantage these offer. Digital Textbooks, wired for Big Data Analytics, is likely to revolutionise the learning landscape by bringing in personalisation and adaptation to the learners.

9. 3D Printing

3D Printing is another attractive technology that holds promise in revolutionising many aspects of our life. It is a technology that helps turn a digital design (a 3-dimentional file) into an actual three dimensional physical product just with the click of a button! This technology is already creating waves in the market with the innovative and immense possibilities it offers for developing consumer models.

3D Printing technology is likely to create a big leap in the learning and education landscape 3D Printers offer learners greater opportunities for powerful practical experiences and also promote their creative thinking. In short, this technology is going to help educationists and learning professionals adopt a much larger experiential approach that provides a truly productive experience for learners. It is powerful enough to change the learning dynamics of future learners.

10. Mobile Learning

As more and more people purchase smart devices and use them as their primary device for receiving information, the use of only physical text as a form of sending across information has dwindled, as can be seen from the sales drop of newschapters experienced by major News vendors—Time, Daily Mail etc. This trend is slowly but surely creeping into educational circles as more educators now develop teaching materials in soft copy formats and simply share them to their students. The multi-facet sharing and storage options provided by smart devices will certainly reduce student's dependency on plain text as well as the clutter in their rooms. Smart Phones and tablets are poised to take a greater role in the following types of learning in organisations:

- *Smart Phones*: Just-in time learning/performance support.

- *Tablets*: Extended learning.

In short, this is another disruptive technology that is all set to re-shape the learning and education landscape.

Here is an interesting infographic (from Interactive Services) that depicts the future of mobile learning:

- *http://www.interactiveservices.com/wp- content/uploads/2013/06/Mobile_Learning_That_Works_Infographic_2013.pdf*

11. Cloud Computing

Cloud computing has been considered as one of the tech raves of the 21st century, it has imbibed itself into the teaching procedures available in today's modern society. Coursera—which has been dubbed as the Amazon of e-learning—can serve as a perfect example of how cloud education has been accepted into mainstream educational spaces for educators, universities and students from all works of life, now makes use of this Massive Open Online Course platform to pass and receive educational information. Cloud Computing is a technology that has started revolutionising the way we deliver learning. The concepts of Cloud Learning, Cloud Classrooms, and Cloud Campuses are catching up like wild fire today. More and more universities and institutions are gearing up to move on to embrace this innovative technological opportunity that promises many fascinating features and benefits over the traditional brick and mortar model that they had been following.

Cloud Learning refers to learning in a virtual world that is interconnected through the web or mobile networks. Many universities and higher education institutions are moving towards Cloud Campuses—virtual campuses through which they could deliver learning programmes in a highly efficient way. Cloud Learning Systems, with the combined power of Big Data, could transform education and learning to the most personalised and adaptive levels. Cloud technology offers a powerful and smart system that could help mould our learners into highly productive citizens of today in the most cost effective way.

Massive Open Online Course (MOOC) is a recent development that is powered by Cloud Computing technology. MOOC promoters (such as 'Coursera' which is known as 'the Amazon of education') offer a wide range of educational programmes from leading universities online for free. Though there are questions being raised regarding their pedagogical qualities and effectiveness, this surely is going to evolve as one of the most effective delivery models for education, if properly planned and designed by including engaging e-learning components. In fact, MOOCs have started threatening the rigid and inflexible model that the higher education institutions follow presently. Many predict that the future of learning delivery lie entirely within the cloud. We believe that Cloud Technology is one of the most disruptive technologies that is set to transform education and learning.

If you would like to take a quick look at the possibilities that cloud technology throws open for training, check the link below:

- *http://www.walkme.com/*

Conclusion

This chapter provides an insight into the challenges faced by policy-makers, educational institutions, course developers, and learners dealing with issues of access to education in developing countries. The analysis of open and distance learning developments in developing countries concludes that although these developments aim for equitable and extended educational opportunities that extend to disadvantaged and poor populations, the lack of educational and technology infrastructures, lack of trained teachers, negative attitudes towards distance learning, social and cultural restrictions imposed on girls and women, and inappropriate policy and funding decisions, have all resulted in furthering the gap between the rich and poor, rural and urban, and between genders.

The chapter identifies significant challenges faced in developing countries attempting to make learning more accessible by using Internet technologies for mass. The literature shows that while distance learning and e-learning are advocated as easily accessible, for the rural poor in the developing world, books, teachers, classrooms, money, and time, continue to be significant issues. The availability of new technologies may have opened-up developing economies to the world market, but they have done little to help deprived groups gain access to educational opportunities. There remain high per centages of people from lower social classes, females, and rural areas, who continue to be marginalised due to their lack of access to adequate learning resources and basic education.

In circumstances that are marred by limited IT infrastructure, traditional technologies such as printed material, radio, and television remain more effective and accessible for rural and disadvantaged groups.

Existing attempts to improve IT has limited scope. The incepted technology should focus general public and the developed should offer better opportunity at the grassroots level.

REFERENCES

Badiwala, M. (1998). Child Labour in India: Causes, Governmental policies and the Role of education. *The Child Labour Inquiry, 1.* Retrieved from: *http://www.geocities.com/CollegePark/Library/9175/inquiry1.html*

Belawati, T. (2005). The impact of online tutorials on course completion rates and student achievement. *Learning, Media and Technology*, 30(1) : 15-25.

Belawati, T., and Zuhairi, A. (2007). The Practice of a Quality Assurance System in Open and Distance Learning: A case study at Universitas Terbuka Indonesia (The Indonesia Open University). *International Review of Research in Open and Distance Learning,* 8(1). Retrieved from: *http://www.irrodl.org/index.php/irrodl/article/view/334/792*

Bof, A.M. (2004). Distance learning for teaching training in Brazil. *International Review of Research in Open and Distance Learning, 5*(1). Retrieved from: *http://www.irrodl.org/index.php/irrodl/article/view/172/387*

dela Peña-Bandalaria, M. (2007). Impact of ICTs on open and distance learning in a developing country setting: the Philippine experience. *International Review of Research in Open and Distance Learning,* 8(1). Retrieved from: http://www.irrodl.org/index.php/irrodl/article/view/340/774

Hussain, I. (2007). A study of student's attitude towards virtual education in Pakistan. *Turkish Journal of Distance Learning*, 8(2). Retrieved from: *http://tojde.anadolu.edu.tr/*

Kiangi, G. (1998). Computer education and human capacity for information technology in Namibia. In G. Marshall and M. Ruohonen (Eds.), *Capacity Building for IT in Education in Developing Countries* (pp. 39-48). London: Chapman & Hall.

Mutonyi, H., and Norton, B. (2007). ICT on the Margins: Lessons from Ugandan Education. *Language and Education*, 21(3) : 264-270.

Ojo, S. and Awuah, B. (1998). Building resource capacity for IT education and training in schools—The case of Botswana. In G. Marshall and M. Ruohonen (Eds.), *Capacity Building for IT in Education in Developing Countries* (pp. 27-38). London: Chapman & Hall.

Sharma, P. (2005). The distance in education and online technologies in India. In A. Carr-Chellman (Ed.), *Global Perspectives on E-learning: Rhetoric and reality* (pp. 52-66). London: Sage Publications.

Slam, M.T., Rahman, M. M., and Rahman, K.M.R. (2006). Quality and processes of Bangladesh Open University course material development. *Turkish Journal of Distance Learning, 7*(2). Retrieved from: *http://tojde.anadolu.edu.tr/*

Sutaria, M.C. (1990). Teaching for Maximum Learning: The Philippine experience. *International Review of Education,* 36(2) : 243-250. Retrieved from: *http://www.jstor.org/view/00208566/sp060144/06x2602b/0*

Web References

http://learnnovators.com/blog/top-11-disruptive-e-learning-technologies-for-2013

http://www.financialexpress.com/industry/jobs/why-e-learning-has-a-promising-future-in-india/19204/

https://elearningindustry.com/disruptive-technology-mlearning-2015

22
Institutional Benefits of E-Governance in Higher Education

Ismail Thamarasseri

Introduction

Administration is very important to the realisation of the educational institution's objectives—indeed, the success of the school system depends largely on the administration of the school it handled. The teachers, students, non-teaching staff and resources must be efficiently arranged, monitored and controlled, so that, they would work harmoniously according to the educational plan. Even the National Policy on Education emphasizes the success of the entire educational system on proper planning, efficient administration and adequate funding. School administration is the process by which principles, methods and practices of administration are applied in educational institutions to establish, maintain and develop such institutions in line with the goals of the institutions. Educational Administration as the scientific organisation of human and material resources and programmes available for education and using them systematically and meticulously to achieve educational goals. Educational administration implies the arrangement of the human and material resources and programme available for education and carefully using them systematically for the achievement of educational objectives.

Thus Educational administrator, whether in the Ministry of Education, the schools board, or in a school is essentially the organiser, the implementer of plans, policies and programme meant for achieving specific educational objectives. The Educational Administrator may contribute, one way or the other, in planning, policy-making and programme designing, yet his/her major role rests with the effective and efficient implementation of such plans, policies and programme for the benefit of education. Viewed from this angle, Educational Administration is concerned with organisation and implementation. The administrator is concerned with formulating general plans and policies for education.

Necessity of e-Governance in Higher Education

If the quality of our higher education system has to be improved to make institutions really world class, then there is no alternative to the introduction of e-governance in this sphere at the fastest possible pace. Implementation of e-governance in technical and vocational institutes will enable their effective and real time monitoring by Government/the regulatory bodies and other stakeholders their own managements, parents of the students and the society, thereby forcing them to maintain quality and become more responsible. E-governance process brings transparency in the system, so e-governance initiatives in the field of higher education will help reduce the corruption up to a large extent. The introduction of e-governance in higher education is one such concept that can empower the governing bodies to administer the progress of the education plan in the whole country and serves various stakeholders in a much better ways. E-governance is becoming a global phenomenon that is increasingly attracting the attention of community citizens including politicians, economists, decision and policy-makers amongst others (Naheed, 2009).

According Info Dev Report (2002) an effective e-governance satisfies these following needs:

- Providing greater access to government information;
- Promoting public engagement by enabling the public to interact with government officials;
- Making government more accountable by making its operations more obvious and thus reducing the opportunities for corruption;
- Providing development opportunities, especially benefiting rural and traditionally underserved communities.

E-governance in higher education system will enable various stakeholders to control the improved operational efficiency in various key processes like grants, utilisation certificates, approval processes, feedback mechanism etc. With deeper visibility and increased operational efficiency the Indian higher education system would be implemented not only to satisfy the needs of students by making them more employable but also combat possible competition from foreign universities.

Benefits of e-Governance in Higher Education

The benefits of e-governance in an educational sector are improved efficiency, increase in transparency and accountability of educational administrative activities convenient and faster access to services, and lower costs for administrative services. The multi-faceted benefits of e-governance can be described as under:

- Centralised information access from anywhere.
- Increase in student enrolment ratio.
- Provide quality e-services, e-participation.
- Increase clearness.
- Inventive teaching tools.
- Improved decision-making.
- Public Private Participation (PPP).
- Less paper work.

A good higher education system is required for overall development of a nation. A remarkable growth in the higher education sector had made the administration of higher education institutions intricate. E-Governance is understood as a set of activities involving the effective contribution of ICTs for strengthening administration and management in higher education system in India has declined somewhat over the past due to several reasons. It has become very important for the government to keep track of their functioning. Educational institutions may have various requirements that include computerisation and management of processes such as registration, admission, student information, classes, time-table, transport, attendance, library, salary and expenses, examinations, performance, grades, hostels, security and reports. Many of the software providers allow their clients to choose from the available modules to suit their needs to monitoring of these aspects (Shrivastava, 2014).

The National e-Governance Plan

The National e-Governance Plan (NeGP) which is the flagship

e-governance programme of the Central Government was approved by the Government of India in May 2006 comprising 27 Mission Mode Projects (MMPs) at the Central, State and Local Governments level. Under the NeGP, the state "Mission Mode Projects" are Land Records, Road Transport, Property Registration, Agriculture, Treasuries, Municipalities, Gaon Panchayat, Commercial Taxes, Police, Employment Exchanges, WCD & SW, Cooperation. By inclusion of education in the State-level MMPs of NeGP, the concept of effective governance of education sector is thoroughly innovated; for effective handling of new challenges confronting the education sector. Educational e-governance can facilitate in improving transparency, providing speedy information dissemination, improving administrative efficiency and public services in all aspects of the education. It is beyond doubt that for the quantity and quality of output of our education system to substantially improve, there is no option but to introduce e-governance in this sphere. The application of ICT for governance is somewhat poor because of which the NeGP is set-up, but it is further more poor in the education sector which is one of the key pillars for the rapid growth of economy of the country. The challenge is, therefore, to bring e-governance into educational sector. This research aims at bringing ICT for e-governance of the education sector (Suklabaidya, 2013).

Some e-Governance Solutions Suitable to Higher Education Institutions Biometric and Digital Signature System

It is an authentication method that uses the dynamics of a person's handwritten signature. The pen pressure and duration of the signing process, which is done with a stylus on a touch screen or digital-based pen tablet, is recorded as analgorithm that is compared against future signatures. The unique pattern of a physical feature such as a fingerprint, iris, or voice as recorded in a database for future attempts to determine or recognise a person's identity when these features are detected by a reading device. A digital signature is a mathematical scheme for demonstrating the authenticity of a digital message or document. A valid digital signature gives a recipient reason to believe that the message was created by a known sender, such that the sender cannot deny having sent the message (authentication and non-repudiation) and that the message was not altered in transit (integrity). Digital signatures are commonly used for software distribution, financial transactions, and in other cases where it is important to detect forgery or tampering.

Digital signatures are often used to implement electronic signatures, a broader term that refers to any electronic data that carries the intent of a signature, but not all electronic signatures use digital signatures. In some countries, including the United States, India, Brazil, and members of the European Union, electronic signatures have legal significance.

Digital signatures employ a type of asymmetric cryptography. For messages sent through a non-secure channel, a properly implemented digital signature gives the receiver reason to believe the message was sent by the claimed sender. In many instances, common with Engineering companies for example, digital seals are also required for another layer of validation and security. Digital seals and signatures are equivalent to handwritten signatures and stamped seals. Digital signatures are equivalent to traditional handwritten signatures in many respects, but properly implemented digital signatures are more difficult to forge than the handwritten type. Digital signature schemes, in the sense used here, are cryptographically based, and must be implemented properly to be effective. Digital signatures can also provide non-repudiation, meaning that the signer cannot successfully claim they did not sign a message, while also claiming their private key remains secret; further, some non-repudiation schemes offer a time stamp for the digital signature, so that even if the private key is exposed, the signature is valid. Digitally signed messages may be anything representable as a bit-string: examples include electronic mail, contracts, or a message sent *via* some other cryptographic protocol.

The Government of India's Aadhaar-based Biometric Attendance System (BAS) for Central Government employees also operational now. The Department of Electronics and IT (DeitY) has started the trial run of the website earlier and it will track the attendance of the employees. The system will start with tracking attendance of Central Government employees stationed in the national capital. The website is expected to bring more transparency as it would provide and update information about Central Government employees on real-time basis. The portal will use information entered in the biometric devices and will act as a centralised management information system (MIS) for attendance.

Under the new attendance system, the employees would be able to mark their attendance using biometric reading devices in various Government offices. It will facilitate employees mark their attendance at other Central offices also which would help the government to track their movements. According to the information available on the attendance web portal, as many as 148 Central Government Organisations have registered themselves for the same.

Bar Code Scanners for Everyday Library Applications

Barcodes were being developed and in the 1970s, they started to replace manual checkout programmes, taking the complexity out of those different filing systems. Today we find unique barcodes regularly used in library automation programmes for cataloguing and tracking books and reference materials. By tying to special library software, these systems not only help locate items, but they can also validate library card, assigned due dates, and check to see if the book has been requested by someone else. A wide variety of bar code scanners to handle everyday library applications. Bar code scanners save time and reduce errors. These scanners are great for libraries, schools, offices and warehouses.

Skype for Interviews

Conducting interview for recruiting right candidates is a headache for institutions. Similarly, attending an interview at far places is a tedious task for candidates too. Up to an end, interview *via* video conferencing is a remedy for these troubles. Video conferencing/interviews are a present trend in the job process. On the one hand, they help recruiters and organisations filter candidates at an early stage, but because they are different, there is potential to cause intimidation among job seekers. Some of the benefits of video conferencing *via skype* are enlisted below:

- Cheaper than international flights, *Skype* avoids having to fly people.
- Easy to set up as a user.
- Can enable a shorter-notice interview.
- Donot need a visa to video-visit.
- Video enables you to check you are interviewing the right person.
- Gives visual clues more useful than just voice.
- But not as much as physical presence.

Digital filing is another means of e-governance, that ensures paper-less/eco-friendly offices.

Benefits and Uses of Surveillance Systems in Educational Institutions

There are a variety of situations in which CCTV cameras are used to provide surveillance, especially schools. Sometimes, in larger institutions, providing security guards is not enough. It is not uncommon for some schools to install CCTV security systems in their premises to monitor and keep track of all the activities that take place. Sometimes, in larger schools, providing security guards is not enough for school security. This is usually done with complete awareness on the student's, parent's and teacher's parts. CCTV security systems help in preventing or identifying unauthorised intruders who enter the premises, thereby promoting school security. CCTV surveillance systems in schools are a way of ensuring a safe, secure and healthy learning environment for children.

When we installing CCTV cameras in educational institutions, must ensure that their use is appropriate and justified. It is must to display signage prominently and close to the cameras. This should inform members of the public that their images are being recorded and the reasons for doing so. It may only use CCTV for monitoring the movement and behaviour of pupils and staff in justifiable circumstances. No camera be placed where privacy is expected, for instance a toilet or changing room. It must not be used for recording conversations. Before installing CCTV for these purposes, it is needed to carefully assess all alternative solutions.

Human *vs.* Mechanical Relationships

There are several criticisms are arising towards the implementing of e-governance in educational institutions. One of the main observation is that, human being are the higher level creatures, educational institutions are sacred places, how the machine can monitor an individual? The objective of educational institutions is much more difficult to define than the purpose of commercial organisation. There are clear-cut educational equivalents to such major private sector objectives as profit maximisation of product diversification. Schools and colleges are to develop personal abilities of the individuals, to inculcate the accepted values and beliefs to prepare pupils for the next stage of education or for employment. In this industry give and take or teach and learn is the main maxim of administration, where at both ends human beings are involved giver as well as taker, i.e. human beings. This way approach to the management of educational institutions markedly depends upon human relationship.

Conclusion

In educational scenario pupils are clients or outputs of school and colleges.

They are not processed or programmed or manipulated. The learning programme or process is purely built on personal relationships between managers, teachers, pupils, parents, community members, organisers and administrators. Even leaders, politicians, officers, inspectors and local bodies have their access to the educational administration. All human beings responsible at their own positions and places have cordial relationships with each other. It gives an effective and efficient impetus to the better educational process.

REFERENCES

Bhantil, P., *et al.* (2012), E-Governance: An Approach towards the Integration of Higher Education System in India. *International Journal of Emerging Technology and Advanced Engineering*. Vol. 2, No. 8, August.

Bhatnagar, H., (2013), E-Governance in Higher Education: A Case Study of IGNOU, New Delhi. *International Journal of Scientific and Engineering Research*. Vol. 4, No. 5, May.

Kumar, A., (2012), E-Governance in Education Sector. *Gian Jyoti E-Journal*, Vol. 1, No. 2, January-March.

Library Book Labels, retrieved from : *http://www.barcode-labels.com/solutions/asset- labels/library#sthash.X5t1DREH.dpuf*

Shrivastava, R.K., *et al.*, (2014), Role of E-Governance to strengthen higher education system in India. *IOSR Journal of Research and Method in Education*. Vol. 4, No. 2. March-April. retrieved from : *http://www.iosrjournals.org/iosr-jrme/ papers/Vol-4%20Issue-2/ Version-1/ J04215762. pdf*

Suklabaidya, S. and Sen, A.M., (2013), Challenges and Prospects of E-Governance in Education. *International Journal of Emerging Trends and Technology in Computer Science*. Vol. 2, No. 3, May-June, retrieved from : *http://www.ijettcs.org/ Volume2Issue3/ IJETTCS-2013-06-24-124.pdf*

Suresh, S., *Benefits and uses of CCTV cameras in schools*., retrieved from : *http://officeneeds.sulekha.com/benefits-and-uses-of-cctv-cameras-in-schools_111131_blog*

Tiwari, S.K., *et al.* (2013), Promoting E-Governance Culture in Higher Education Institutions. *IOSR Journal of Research and Method in Education*. Vol. 2, No. 3, July-August.

When to use CCTV in your school, retrieved from *https://czone.eastsussex.gov.uk/schoolmanagement/schoolpolicies/dataprotection/cctv/pages/whentouse.aspx*

23
Information Communication Technology in Teacher Education

Afshan Anees

Introduction

Today's age of 21st Century and it is also the age of information and technology (IT). Every aspects of life are related to science and technology. Huge flow of information is emerging in all fields throughout the world. Now information and technology is popularly using in educational field for making teaching learning process successful and interesting for students and teacher both. In 1998, UNESCO World Education report refers about student and teachers must have sufficient access to improve digital technology and the internet in their classroom, schools, teacher educational institutions. Teachers must have the knowledge and skills to use new digital tools to help all students achieve high academic standard. The quality of professional development of teacher education depends on the extent of ICT integration in teacher education programme. According to UNESCO (2002) "ICT is a scientific, technological and engineering discipline and management technique used in handling information, its application and association with social, economic and cultural matters." Teachers are at the core of any living society. Technologies play an important role in training programme of teachers. Students' accesses knowledge and information through TV, digital media, cable network, internet and social media, i.e. Facebook, Twitter, Whatsapp, Linkedinn, Igo, Line, Wechat etc. ICT is very important for Preservice teacher education programme in the 21st Century. Without proper knowledge of ICT teacher cannot perform in his/her class room and it could not be said to be a complete one. Information and Communication Technology (ICT) is a diverse set of technological tools and resources used to communicate and to create, disseminate, store and manage information. ICT has become part of everyday life and all sectors from banking to tourism now depend heavily on ICT for carrying out their transactions.

Information and communication technologies in education refer to teaching and learning the subject matter that enables understanding the functions and effective use of information and communication technologies (ICTs). As of 2004, a review and contextualisation of the literature on teaching ICT as a subject implied that there was limited, systematically-derived, quality information.

Concept of Information Technology

Today's world is a world of information explosion. This information explosion is taking place in such a fast speed that even a literate person is feeling as if he or she is illiterate being not able to cope up with such an information explosion Information Technology (IT) is the acquisition, processing, storage and dissemination of vocal, pictorial, textual and numerical information by a micro-electronics-based combination of computing and telecommunication. The term in its modern sense first appeared in a 1958 article published in the Harvard Business Review, in which authors Leavitt and whisler commented that — the new technology does not yet have a single established name.

Information Technology consists of two words Information and Technology. If you know the two words you can understand the word information technology together. The term — Information refers to — any communication or representation of knowledge such as facts, data or opinions in any medium or for, including textual, numerical, graphic, cartographic, narrative or audio-visual forms. Technology is the practical form of scientific knowledge or the science of application of knowledge to practical.

Teacher Education in Present Scenario

As our society changes due to the implementation of new technologies. Teacher education is a part of our society, so, it also undergoes some changes. It is natural that teacher education must include new technology.

Teachers should also know the right attitudes and values, besides being proficient in skills related to teaching. As we know the minimum requirement of any training programme is that it should help the trainee to acquire the basic skills and competencies of a good teacher. Now-a-days, new trends in teacher education are Inter-disciplinary Approach, Correspondence courses, orientation courses etc. Simulated Teaching, Micro-Teaching, Programmed Instruction, Team Teaching are also used in teacher education. Now-a-days, Action Research also implemented in Teacher Education. ICT acts as the gateway to the world of information and helps teachers to be updated. It creates awareness of innovative trends in instructional methodologies, evaluation mechanism etc. for professional development. Different Strategies for applying ICT in Teacher Education:—(i) Providing adequate infrastructure and technical support. (ii) Applying ICT in all subjects. (iii) Applying new Pre-service teacher Education curriculum; and (iv) By using application software, using multimedia, Internet, e-mail, communities, understanding system software. Baishakhi Bhattacharjee and Kamal Deb Role of ICT in 21st Century's Teacher Education—ICT helps teachers in both pre-service and in-Service teachers training. ICT helps teachers to interact with students. It helps them in preparation their teaching, provide feedback. ICT also helps teachers to access with institutions and Universities, NCERT, NAAC, NCTE, UGC etc. It also helps in effective use of ICT software and hardware for teaching-learning process. It helps in improve Teaching skill, helps in innovative Teaching. It helps in effectiveness of classroom. It also helps in improving professional Development and Educational management as well as enhances Active Learning of Teacher Trainees. It is now replacing the ancient technology. As we know now-a-days, students are always have competitive mind. So, teacher must have the knowledge of the subject. This can be done through ICT. ICT helps teachers in preparation for teaching. In order to introduce ICT in pre-service teacher education different methods and strategies are applied. Different tools are used such as word processing, Database, Spreadsheet etc. Various technology based plans are used to help the teachers for their practice teaching. ICT prepares teacher for the use of their skills in the real classroom situation and also make students for their future occupation and social life. ICT used as an "assisting tool" for example while making assignments, communicating, collecting data and documentation, and conducting research. Typically, ICT is used independently from the subject matter. ICT as a medium for teaching and learning. It is a tool for teaching and learning itself, the medium through which teachers can teach and learners can learn. It appears in many different forms, such as drill and practice exercises, in simulations and educational networks. ICT as a popular tool for organisation and management in Institutions. Teachers must provide technological support to learn using motion picture, animation, simulation training which helped student teachers to give model presentation. If the teacher is highly equipped with technology, the student will also be equipped with technology. It removes the traditional method of teaching and prepare teacher to apply modern method of teaching. ICT is plays an important role in student evaluation. ICT is store house of educational institution because all educational information can safely store through ICT. ICT helps Teacher to communicate properly with their students. So, ICT bridge the gap between teacher and students. ICT helps Teacher to pass information to students within a very little time. ICT helps Teacher to design educational environment. ICT helps Teacher to identify creative child in educational institute.

Role of ICT in 21st Century's Teacher Education

ICT helps Teacher to motivate students and growing interest in learning. ICT helps Teacher for organisational preconditions (vision, policy and culture). It is also helps Teacher for their personnel support (knowledge, attitude, skills). ICT helpful for technical preconditions (infrastructure). ICT helpful for designed learning situations which are needed for both vocational education and the training of future teachers (in the teacher training institutes). Teacher training institutes can develop their curriculum using ICT. With the help of ICT Teacher training institutes can develop communication network. Teachers learn most from their own networks (learning from others) with the help of ICT.

ICT in education is any hardware and software technology that contribute in the educational information processing. In the context of present era, ICT mainly comprises Computer technology with its hardware, like, Personal computer machine, infrastructure required for setting-up Internet facility and also Software like, CD ROM including various programme packages, E-learning strategies etc. ICT in education is any Information Technology that focuses on the acquisition, storage, manipulation, management, transmission or reception of data required for the educational purpose. For example, the information about students' records, their admissions, updates of their auricular and co-curricular activities. ICT in education is any technology that deals with the exchange of information or in other words communication in the teaching learning process. Uses of Electronic learning technology like, Teleconferencing, power point presentations, CD ROM are Communication Technology which is the part of ICT.

ICT in education is any educational technology that is applied in the educational process. It encompasses Hardware approach like use of machines and materials, Software approach like use of methodologies and strategies of teaching learning and Systems approach that uses the management technology that deals with the systematic organisation of the hardware and the software. Different software packages for the use in different department of education; e.g. library software, administration software, software related to managing the entire teaching learning process.

Advantages of the Use of ICT in Education

ICT encompasses all those gadgets that deal with the processing of information for better and effective communication. In education, communication process takes place between teachers, students, management and administrative personnel which requires plenty of data to be stored for retrieval as and when required, to be disseminated or transmitted in the desired format. The hardware and software like OHP, Television, Radio, Computers and related software are used in the educational process.

However, ICT today is mostly focused on the use of Computer technology for processing the data. In this context, advantages of ICT in education can be listed down as follows:

(i) Quick access to information,
(ii) Easy availability of updated data,
(iii) Connecting Geographically dispersed regions,
(iv) Catering to the Individual differences,
(v) Wider range of communication media, and
(vi) Wider learning opportunities for pupils.

Role of Teacher in Multimedia Approach

The Teacher has to make a lot of modifications and adjustment if he has to adopt multimedia approach. His role would have a different connotation compared to the traditional role. He would have to make these changes.

- The teacher has to be aware of the different available media and their availability. The teacher should be physically competent to use and demonstrate the use of different media.
- The teacher should be skilful enough to make a judicious choice of media and be competent enough to mix them sequentially and in an orderly manner.
- The teacher's role is that of a facilitator or manager of activities. He has to lead his students for independent, individualised learning.

Impact of ICT on Teaching-Learning

ICT is a discipline in itself and it is usually taught in computer labs. At the same time it helps in the teaching-learning of the current curricular subjects. The large proportion of school subject such as mathematics, social science, science, communication and language, use computer. Consider the reaching area of mathematics, which has tended to be very abstract while most learners tend to operate on a concrete-level. The use of concrete, the computer can provide experiences with virtual concrete materials. Computer simulation offers a replica of real environment of object that fools our senses into perceiving the simulation as real. Computer simulations are built from models of real world situations.

Computer simulations are very much useful in teaching science. The learner can manipulate the size, shape, orientation and dimensions of any diagrammatic illustrations through simulation.

Robert Bracewell and Therese Laferriere (1996) give the following fourteen observations relating to the changes in learner behaviour attributed to ICT:

(i) ICT has the power to stimulate the development of various intellectual skills such as reasoning and problem-solving ability, learning how to learn, and creativity.
(ii) Learners show greater spontaneous interest in a learning activity that uses ICT in class.
(iii) ICT has the power to stimulate to access more extensive information on a subject and develops the research spirit.
(iv) It promotes broader cooperation among learners within and beyond school.
(v) Teachers gain information on new instructional resources and availability of support for their use much more readily with ICT.

(vi) The orientation of planning is more towards learners performing real work in co-operation with other learners.

(vii) Relationships between teaches and learners are more interactive and guiding, rather than transferring information from teacher to learner. The teacher interacts with learners in classroom, as a facilitator a mentor, a guide to the discovery and gradual mastery of knowledge, skills and attitudes.

(viii) ICT helps teachers to view teaching and learning as a process of continuous research in which they share the difficulties and results with their learners.

(ix) ICT fosters a positive, close association of learners with the assessment of their own learning and uses and manages much more demanding assessment methods.

(x) It facilitates effective diagnosing of learner's strong points as well as the specific learning difficulties he/she encounters.

So, it is important that ICT support to learning in schools is not wasted and therefore, care is to be taken in choosing to use ICT to support learning.

Changing Technology

The pace of technological change has accelerated to the point that almost any personal technology currently being explored is likely to be not only commercially available within ten years, but also available cheaply enough for mass publicly-funded use by students. The rule of thumb over the nineties that the power of a PC doubles every 18 months without any increase in real cost is starting to break down it is too conservative.

New and experienced teachers will regularly come in contact with new technology they have no experience with. They will thus need to learn how to approach and master new technologies, as well as existing technologies already in the classroom. Teacher education programmes should not simply prepare students to use the technology currently in schools, they should anticipate future developments and help students cultivate strategies for learning and using new technology as it becomes available.

Pre-service teachers should be aware of numerous forms of teaching and learning including "teacher-centred" or direct instruction, as well as the many forms of student-centred instruction. And they should understand how technology can support these forms of instruction. Improving education depends, not on teaching teachers to apply better axle grease more often, but on transforming teaching and learning into something quite different than it is today.

Critical Technology Integration Across the Curriculum

Most teacher education programmes have operated as loose collections of programme elements: foundations, methods, student teaching, liberal arts core, and content area courses. In this process, technology has often been treated as a separate element, often represented in a single course taught by the 'technology' faculty. That will not work but it is a commonplace approach to technology in teacher education. The Office of Technology Assessment (OTA, 1995) report, *Teachers and Technology: Making the Connection,* concluded that "technology is not central to the teacher preparation experience" (p. 165) and that teacher education programmes tend to treat technology as an add-on to the curriculum that is not integrated across the entire teacher education curriculum.

Technology should be integrated across the entire curriculum, and participants in all areas of teacher education should help to develop and implement an integrated plan that provides students with the models, mentors, content, practice, and experiences needed. If teacher education students are to graduate with strong skills, positive attitudes, including the idea of lifelong learning, and a thoughtful approach to using technology in their classrooms, it will be necessary for them to experience technology at all levels of their preparation. Teaching pre-service student's basic computer literacy "the traditional topics of operating system, word processor, spreadsheet, database, and telecommunication topics" is not enough.

> "To what degree are higher education institutions meeting their responsibility for preparing tomorrow's classroom teachers? Bluntly, a majority of teacher preparation programmes are falling far short of what needs to be done. Not using technology much in their own research and teaching, teacher education faculty has insufficient understanding of the demands on classroom teachers to incorporate technology into their teaching. Many do not fully appreciate the impact technology is having on the way work is accomplished. They undervalue the significance of technology and treat it as merely another topic about which teachers should be informed. As a result, colleges and universities are making

> the same mistake that was made by K-12 schools; they treat "technology" as a special addition to the teacher education curriculum "requiring specially prepared faculty and specially equipped classrooms", but not a topic that needs to be incorporated across the entire teacher education programme. Consequently, teachers-in-training are provided instruction in "computer literacy" and are shown examples of computer software, but they rarely are required to apply technology in their courses and are denied role models of faculty employing technology in their own work" (NCATE, 1997).

Pre-service teachers should be aware of numerous forms of teaching and learning including "teacher-centred" or direct instruction, as well as the many forms of student-centred instruction. And they should understand how technology can support these forms of instruction. Improving education depends, not on teaching teachers to apply better axle grease more often, but on transforming teaching and learning into something quite different than it is today.

Critical Technology Integration Across the Curriculum

Most teacher education programmes have operated as loose collections of programme elements: foundations, methods, student teaching, liberal arts core, and content area courses. In this process, technology has often been treated as a separate element, often represented in a single course taught by the 'technology' faculty. That will not work but it is a commonplace approach to technology in teacher education. The Office of Technology Assessment (OTA, 1995) report, *Teachers and Technology: Making the Connection,* concluded that "technology is not central to the teacher preparation experience" (p. 165) and that teacher education programmes tend to treat technology as an add-on to the curriculum that is not integrated across the entire teacher education curriculum.

> "To what degree are higher education institutions meeting their responsibility for preparing tomorrow's classroom teachers? Bluntly, a majority of teacher preparation programmes are falling far short of what needs to be done. Not using technology much in their own research and teaching, teacher education faculty has insufficient understanding of the demands on classroom teachers to incorporate technology into their teaching. Many do not fully

> appreciate the impact technology is having on the way work is accomplished. They undervalue the significance of technology and treat it as merely another topic about which teachers should be informed. As a result, colleges and universities are making the same mistake that was made by K-12 schools; they treat "technology" as a special addition to the teacher education curriculum "requiring specially prepared faculty and specially equipped classrooms", but not a topic that needs to be incorporated across the entire teacher education programme."

As with any profession, there is a level of literacy beyond general computer literacy. In education this more specific or professional literacy involves learning to use technology to foster the educational growth of students. To develop that professional expertise students will have to see instructors model appropriate uses; have opportunities to learn how to use technology to support learning; see technology used appropriately in schools; and have many opportunities to develop and teach technology-supported lessons themselves under circumstances that support professional growth.

ICT in education is any hardware and software technology that contribute in the educational information processing. In the context of present era, ICT mainly comprises Computer technology with its hardware, like Personal computer machine, infrastructure required for setting up Internet facility and also Software, like CD-ROM including various programme packages, E-learning strategies etc. ICT in education is any Information Technology that focuses on the acquisition, storage, manipulation, management, transmission or reception of data required for the educational purpose. For example, the information about students' records, their admissions, updates of their auricular and co-curricular activities. ICT in education is any technology that deals with the exchange of information or in other words communication in the teaching learning process. Uses of Electronic learning technology like, Teleconferencing, power point presentations, CD-ROM are Communication Technology which is the part of ICT.

ICT in education is any educational technology that is applied in the educational process. It encompasses Hardware approach like use of machines and materials, Software approach like use of methodologies and strategies of teaching learning and Systems approach that uses the management technology that deals with the systematic organisation of the hardware and the software. Different software packages for the use in different department of education; e.g. library software, administration software, software related to managing the entire teaching learning process.

REFERENCES

Alexis Leon and Mathews Leon (1999). *Fundamentals of Information Technology, Leon Tech World,* New Delhi : Vikas Publishing House Pvt. Ltd.

Anonymous. (1993). *What should pre-service education look like? An Atlas community's answer.* Horace: Coalition of Essential Schools, 10(1).

Apple, M.W. (1992). Computers in schools: Salvation or Social disaster? *Education Digest,* 57 (6) : 47-52.

Aslam Mehdi (2001). Printed Media and Electronic Era, "Challenges Before the Librarians", *University News*, 39 (38) September, New Delhi.

Dick, B., and Dalmau, T. (1999). *Values in Action: Applying the Ideas of Argyris and Schon,* (2nd ed.). Brisbane: Interchange.

Fullan, M. (1991). *The New Meaning of Educational Change* (2nd ed.). New York: Teachers College Press.

Fullan, M. (1992). *Successful School Improvement.* Philadelphia: Open University Press.

Fullan, M. (2001). *Leading in a Culture of Change.* New York: John Wiley.

Section-V
Problems and Challenges Ahead

24

Problems and Challenges of Higher Education in India for 21st Century

Amrutajyoti Mohanty

Present Scenario of Higher Education

India's higher education has managed by the University Grants Commission (UGC) and the various councils. The UGC set-up under UGC Act, 1956, has been empowered to promote and coordinate university education in India and also approve grants to them. The UGC is responsible for coordination, determination, and maintenance of standards and release of grants to universities and research organisations. The National Assessment and Accreditation Council (NAAC) is an organisation that assess and accredits institution of higher education in the country. In the last sixty decades, the higher education sector in India has witnessed exponential growth, both in terms of the numbers of institutions and the rate of enrolment.

While talking about the growth in student enrolment, the recent UGC report states that in 1950-51, when there were only 3,97,000 students enrolled in all disciplines in 750 colleges affiliated to 30 universities. Now, the growth of higher education in India has been phenomenal. In 2015, India had 740 universities, over 38,056 colleges and about 13,000 stand alone institutions. Education System in India currently represents a great contradiction. On the one hand we have IIMs and IITs that rank among the best institutes in the world and on the other hand there are numbers of schools and colleges in the country that do not even have the basic infrastructure. Even more than 70 years after Independence we are far away from the goal of universal literacy. But on a positive note, Indian professionals are considered among the best in the world are in great demand. With about 50 per cent of the Indian population below the average of 25 years, and an estimated 150 million people in the age group of 18-23 years. It is expected that India will have the largest population in the world, in the higher education age bracket by 2013. More than 85 per cent of students are enrolled in bachelor's degree programmes with majority enrolling in three-year B.A., B.Com. and B.Sc. degrees. One-sixth of all Indian students are enrolled in Engineering/Technology degrees. India still lacks in terms of well qualified faculty, appropriate infrastructure, meaningful research and development projects and equal access to higher education.

The Former President of India, Pranab Mukharjee called for concrete steps to create a "culture of excellence" in higher education. The National Knowledge Commission, a high level advisery body to the Prime Minister, has projected a requirement of 1500 universities and 45,000 colleges to achieve this target. Higher education has given ample proof of its viability over the centuries and of its ability to change and to induce change and progress in society.

Problems and Challenges of Higher Education

The state of Indian higher education has always been in question, more specially for its quality. When it is compared with the required skill set and with the higher education system of others developed countries, our higher education system seems to fall short of quality, up-to-date course structure and the way education is imparted. The aim of higher education is to prepare a person to play his part well, as an enlightened member of society. Rabindranath Tagore rightly said, "The higher education is that which does not merely give us information, but makes life in harmony with all existence." It has significant advantages in the 21st century knowledge race. But, the severity of challenges that the system faces is exceedingly high. The challenges confronting the Indian higher education system are also challenging, complex and have different hues. One the fundamental weaknesses of the system are lack of transparency and recommendations has been made to mandate high standards of data disclosures by institutions on performance.

The higher education system in India has grown in a remarkable way after independence, to become one of the largest systems of its kind of the world. The system has many issues of concern at present, like financing and management, adequate infrastructure, technology and research, access and equality, safeguarding of national academic standards, ethical relevance, improve and enhancement of quality of higher education together with the assessment of institutions and their accreditation. About 62 per cent of universities and 90 per cent of colleges were average or below average of their NAAC accreditation. Unattractive compensation packages, lengthy recruitment procedure, and working environment is not conducive to retain are some other problems faced by higher education institutes. As a result, a substantial proportion is high-ranking students who could fill-up such assignments prefer to work elsewhere or go abroad. Under-investment in libraries, laboratories and classrooms makes it very difficult to provide top class instruction or engage in cutting-edge era. These issues are important for the country, as it is now engaged in the use of higher education as a powerful tool to build knowledge based information society of the 21st century.

Now, there is an urgent need to work for the development of the educational sector to meet the need of the emerging opportunities, increasing younger generation population and challenges of the 21st century. A new strategy for this challenge needs to be evolved with complete policy commitment on the part of the Government because service sector export requires a steady supply of highly skilled manpower which can only be supported by a robust Higher Education System.

Some Measures for Promotion of Excellence in Higher Education

All-round development of personality is the purpose of education. But the present day education is neither imparting true knowledge of life and nor improving the talent of a student by which one can achieve laurels in the field one is interest. There are some possible measures for improving quality in higher education:

- A well-planned and structured interaction should be developed between Centres of Academic Excellence and other Universities/ Institutions. Industry and Academia connect necessary to ensure curriculum and skills in line with requirements. Skill building is really very crucial to ensure employability of academia to understand and make sure good jobs (keeping in view knowledge + skills + global professional skills = good jobs). To remain competitive, India must grow its pool of skilled worker by improving and expanding access to higher education.

- Imparting quality education, India must encourage a reverse brain drain and attract overseas scholars to transmit ideas. They will help the higher education system of India by explaining and implementing new techniques of teaching and research. Emphasis should be laid on not just increasing the number of higher education institutes but Centre of excellence. Great stress must be laid on good infrastructure and facilities. Achievers in very field should be rewarded adequately.
- India is a promising market and itself has to step up its efforts to create investor confidence and build an enabling investment climate. The first step towards improvement should be taken at school level with aptitude tests being introduced to know where the interest of the student lies. These students should then be encouraged to join those fields of interest.
- Public Private Partnership (PPP) is most essential to bring in quality in the higher education system. University Grants Commission and Ministry of HRD should play a major role in developing a purposeful interface between the Universities, Industries and National Research Laboratories (NRLs) as a step towards PPP. To achieve excellence, we thus need to create a real partnership between Government, Educators and Industry Partnerships that can provide our higher-tech industries with skilled workers who meet the standards of their industry.
- The RUSA and State Higher Education Councils should play key role to undertake the process of planning, execution and evaluation, in addition to other monitoring and capacity building functions.
- Recommendation of National Knowledge Commission (NKC) should be implemented fro establishing an Independent Regulatory Authority for Higher Education (IRAHE) to monitor the quality of overall higher education in India.
- Indian Government should take steps to give more students access to a college education. The goal now is to more than one and half the number of 18-23 year olds who enroll in higher education, from the current estimated 20 per cent to 30 per cent. According to the HRD Ministry, to achieve this goal, India will need to add more than1,500 universities and 45,000 new collages in the coming decade.
- There must be better mechanisms to evaluate the quality of teaching. Each higher education institution should define its

mission according to the present and future needs of the society to reach the necessary level of sustainable and environmentally sound economic and social development.

- At present NAAC is assessing and accrediting Universities and Colleges. This may not truly reflect the programmes/activities at the Departmental level. With a view to encourage this NAAC could move a step further by starting the practice of assessing and accrediting Teaching and Research Departments within Universities/Colleges.
- E-learning appears to be a fast emerging mode of global entry at the present time. The universities and other institutions of higher education can design their web sites for offering online education worldwide.
- Libraries should be fully equipped with the latest books, journals and periodicals. A library must be online and conducive for serious study. Make available high quality e-textbooks, e-reference books, e-research paper and e-content in different language free of cost to genuine learners.
- Laboratories should be updated and obsolescence in equipment/facilities should be removed on regular basis. Innovative practices related to examination reforms should be empirically tested and institutionalised. All the examination processes should be computerised and recent advances in ICT should be exploited to make the process automated and efficient.
- Teachers should also be encouraged to attend various conventions, conference, seminar and workshops in their disciplines to update their professional knowledge and skills.
- There should be regular monitoring and evaluation of teaching and research in the Universities and other Institutions of higher learning. There is a need to create a dozen or more universities that can compete internationally to fully participate in the new world economy.
- Excellence depends on its all functions and activities: teaching and academic programmes research and scholarship, staffing, student, building, facilities, equipments, services to the community and the academic environment. It also requires that higher education should be characterised by its international dimensions: exchange of knowledge, interactive networking, mobility of teachers and students and international research projects, whiles taking into account the national cultural values and circumstances.

Strategic Planning for Development of Colleges Through RUSA

Union Minister of Human Resource Development has launched its ambitions programme to revamp the higher education sector in the country, Rashtriya Uchchatar Shiksha Abhiyan (RUSA). Through RUSA its aim to cover 316 states public universities and 13,024 colleges across the country. RUSA is a holistic scheme of development for higher education in India. It provides equal development to all higher institution and rectifies its weakness. RUSA is a final tier of centrally sponsored schemes of the Minister of Human Resource Development.

It is centrally sponsored scheme with matching contribution from the State Government and Union Territories. It is proposed to set eligibility criteria for state to achieve a high and sustained impact of the project through monitoring and evaluation. The primary responsibility of monitoring will be institutions themselves. The State Government and the Centre through the project appraisal board will monitor the project existing autonomous colleges to universities. The other attempt will be to convert colleges to cluster universities and set-up new model colleges. The strategy of RUSA will also include converting existing degree colleges to model colleges.

The view of Government reform and improve quality of higher education sector through RUSA and as per RUSA document, emphasis will be laid on improvement of quality of teaching learning process, provide greater autonomy to universities as well as colleges and have a sharper focus on equity based development and improvement in research sector in order to produce employable and competitive graduate, post-graduate and Ph.D's.

Key Objectives of RUSA

The main objectives of RUSA are to improve access, equity, excellence and quality in higher education through planned development at State-level. The planning at State-level emphasis on creating new institution, expanding and upgrading institutions and strengthening self-reliant institutions. The institutional strengthening employability improvement and learning outcomes are the specific objectives.

Setting-up of Higher Education Institution in Remote Areas

The institutional development proposal include improving employability of graduates, increased learning outcomes of the students, obtaining autonomous states within 2 years, achieving the target of 60 per cent of the eligibility UG and PG programmes accredited with two years of joining the project, 100 per cent accreditation obtained and applied for the end of the project of the eligible UG and PG programmes, improving interaction with industry and enhancement of research and consultancy activities.

Ensure adequate availability of quality faculty in all higher educational institutions and ensure capacity building at all levels.

The finishing studies plan involves organising a finishing studies/ school/for improving the academic performance of SC/ST/OBC/ academically weak area through innovative methods such as remedial and skill development classes for increasing the transition rate and pass rate with the objective of improving their employability.

Planning and Funding Approach

With respect to planning and funding approach, some key changes are as under—

(a) Funding will be more impact and result oriented. It means funding will be performance based funding. Incentives will be offer to well performing institutions. The flow of funds is based on outcomes and achievements, physical outputs as well as intended outcomes, decision-making through clearly defined norms.
(b) Various equity related schemes will be integrated for a higher impact.
(c) Instead of unplanned expansion, there will be focus on consolidating and developing existing system adding capacities.

There are three broad categories of higher education institutions in India, Centrally funded institutions, State funded institutions and private institutions. Centrally funded institutions receive generous funding from Centre Government, while they have a limited coverage in terms of enrolment. About 94 per cent students enrolled in State funded or State control private institutions which come under the State higher education system. Thus, any efforts for development in this sector must recognise the importance of State higher education institutions and strive to improve their states.

UGC is also not allowed to channelise funds through State Government or through any entity other than an education institution, which makes it impossible for the UGC to fund any planning, expansion activity through State higher education. This creates unawareness of funding to the State institutions and makes difficulties on planning and funding for the State. Under RUSA the Centre Government aims at an optimum solution to create an alternate way of providing funding to a larger number of institutions and channelise fund through a body that ensures cohesive and integrated planning at State level.

Strategic Focus

The strategic focus of RUSA for development of colleges are as under:

(a) Spatial and regional planning and mapping,
(b) Programme and discipline planning,
(c) Mandatory accreditation and quality improvement,
(d) Reforms: Governance and Academic,
(e) Infrastructure,
(f) Review of affiliating system,
(g) Transparent and norm based funding,
(h) Outcome based reimbursement,
(i) Faculty planning,
(j) Equity intervention, and
(k) Focus on Research and Innovation.

Planning and Equity Intervention

Other related points that came-up are expanding the institutional base by creating additional capacity in existing institutions and establishing new institution in order to achieve enrolment targets, correcting regional imbalances in access to higher education by facilitating access to high quality institution in urban and semi-urban areas creating opportunities for student from rural areas to get better access to better quality institutions and improving equity in higher education by providing adequate opportunities of higher education to SCs/STs and socially/educationally backward classes.

Infrastructure

Under RUSA, the Centre Government will provide 90 per cent for infrastructural development of college, faculty recruitment, support, faculty improvement, vocationalisation of higher education, institutional reform and restricting, capacity building and planning support, while state will provide 10 per cent remaining. In insurgency infested scenario, RUSA is focusing on instant need for improvement both infrastructure faculty support and expansion and providing better education to outgoing student.

Transparent and Norm based Funding

Once eligible for funding under RUSA, after meeting the prerequisite commitments, the states will receive funds on the basis of achievements and outcomes. The yardstick for deciding the quantum of funds for the States and institution comprise the norms that reflect the performance in the key result rears (access, equity and excellence). The State plans will capture the current position areas of the states and institutions with respect to these indicators as well as target that need to be achieved. The State Higher Education Council will undertake this process of planning, execution and evaluation in addition to other monitoring and capacity building factors.

Review of Affiliating System

In order to raise funds, most universities rely heavily on affiliation fees that receive from affiliated institutions and one self-financing courses. Treating affiliation fees as source of income and starting courses for revenue generation have led to further dilution of quality and perpetuation of inequity. Except few institutions, most affiliated institutions depend heavily upon the University Administration, examination related and curricular matter. This adds to the burden of the university as it is reduced to an adistrative and exation conducting unit rather than institution focused on promoting teaching, research and faculty development of associated colleges.

The system also takes away the autonomy of affiliated institutions in teaching and conducing examinations. Instead of increasing access in a positive way, the affiliation system creates highly centralise and inefficient institutional structure which does not allow its constituent any room for creativity in teaching, learning, curriculum development of research. In such structure quality enhancement can only be brought by reducing the burden at the university level and giving greater autonomy and accountability to the constituent through affiliation reform.

Conclusion

According to the view of this author there is a lack of vision and planning for the development of institution in the higher education sector at the state level. Given the complexities of managing the access and equity issues within and among states as well as the large number of institutions that already come under the state university system, there is a crying need for planning in higher education focusing on the state as the basic unit. This planning should be done by an autonomous body that can raise and allocate funds from the State as well as Central Government.

However, on the other hand higher education can play an instrumental role in the achievement of these outcomes through the creation of knowledge networks, research and innovation centres, corporate backed institutions, and support for faculty development. Problems faced by the Indian Higher Education System have been noticed by the Government and the Twelfth Five Year Plan (2012-2017) has proposed many schemes in this regard with its core focus on "Excellence and Quality of Education". Society as a whole must support education at all levels, including higher education, given its role in promoting sustainable economic, social and cultural development. Recognizing the above and the basic fact, that the Universities has to perform multiple roles, like creating new knowledge, acquiring new capabilities and producing an intelligence human resource pool, through challenging teaching, research and extension activities so as to balance both the need and the demand. In conclusion, it may be said, the Higher Education System in India while critical for the development of the economy is afflicted with some serious concerns. It is a long way from a transformational change which is envisaged by various committees. Finally, this is the time to consider steps to make India in to the world's major hub for quality higher education in the 21st century.

REFERENCES

Agarwal, P. (2006): "Higher Education in India: The Need for Change". Working Paper No. 180, Indian Council for Research on International Economic Relations.

Anandkrishnan, M. (2004): "Higher Education in Regional Development: Some Key Pointers", Indo-UK Seminar on Regional Development, organised by UGC.

Anandkrishnan, M. (2006): "Privatisation of Higher Education: Opportunities and Anomalies", Paper presented in the National Seminar on Privatisation and Commercialisation of Higher Education, organised by NIEPA, New Delhi on May 2, 2006, *mimeo.*

Bhargava, P. (2006): "Knowledge and National Development", paper presented in the National Seminar on the Education Commission organised by NIEPA, New Delhi from December 26-28. 2006, *mimeo.*

CABE (2005): "Financing of Higher and Technical Education", Report of the CABE Committee, NIEPA, New Delhi.

CABE (2005a): "CABE Committee Report on Autonomy of Higher Education Institutions", June.

Carnoy, Martin (2006): "Higher Education and Economic Development: India and China and the 21st Century", Working Paper No. 297, Stanford Centre for International Development.

GoI (1966): "Education and National Development", Report of the National Commission on Education (1964-66), New Delhi.

GoI (various years): Analysis of Budgeted Expenditure on Education, MHRD, New Delhi.

GoI (various years): "Selected Educational Statistics", Ministry of Human Resource Development, Government of India, New Delhi.

Gupta, Asha (2005): "International Trends in Higher Education and the Indian Scenario", Centre for Studies in Higher Education. CSHE-11-05, available at : http://*repositories.cdlib.org/cshe/CSHE-1-05.*

Khemani, Tulika and Narayan, Jayaprakash (2006): "Higher Education Sector in India: Opportunities and Reforms", Foundation for Democratic Reforms, Hyderabad.

Kumar, Krishna (2003): "Judicial Ambivalence and New Politics of Education", *Economic & Political Weekly*, December 6.

NIEPA (2005): "Report of the Committee on National Common Minimum Programme's Commitment of Six per cent of GDP to Education", NIEPA, New Delhi.

Patel, I.G. (2003): "Higher Education and Economic Development" in J.B.G. Tilak (ed.), *Education, Society and Development: National and International Perspectives*, APH for NIEPA, New Delhi.

Tilak, Jandhyala B.G. (2005): "Post-Elementary Education, Poverty and Development in India", Post-Basic Education and Training, Working Paper Series No. 6, Centre for African Studies, University of Edinburgh.

——(2006): "Private Higher Education: Philanthropy to Profits" in Higher Education in the World 2006: The Financing of Universities, GUNI Series on the Social Commitment of Universities 1, Palgrave, New York and GUNI.

University Grants Commission (UGC) (various years): *Annual Reports*, UGC. New Delhi.

UNESCO (2006): *Global Monitoring Report*, UNESCO.

25
Students Unrest on Higher Education

Annie Kavitha, L.

Introduction

The ship of progress of any country floats on the hard work and dedication of its young generation and its innovative thought. But now widespread frustration has been found in the youth of society which is decreasing their work efficiency. So, the present chapter is to study the unrest among students. Students are an integral part of our society. Individually as a body, they represent the younger generation and constitute more fortunate stratum of society. Naturally, they cannot be viewed in isolation. We can say that the problem attracted the attention of hundreds of scholars and the leaders for drawing references about the patterns of behaviour and the critical relationships. The society has been witnessing frequent strikes, mass demonstrations and occasionally even violent agitation by the students. Yet this problem of students is usually described in very general terms and relevant issues are seldom discussed in specific details, therefore, real understanding is rarely achieved (SI LAW, 1968).

Unrest

Unrest is a state of dissatisfaction, disturbance, and agitation, typically involving public demonstrations or disorder. Growing unrest and indiscipline among students is a matter of great concern. In recent years they have assumed alarming proportions. Student unrest is not confined to India alone. It is a worldwide problem. There are agitations, strikes, boycotts of classes etc., in colleges, universities and other educational and training institutions now and then. Student unrest is a great threat to our system of education, training programmes and development. The students indulge in violence, arson, destruction of property. They use unfair means to get through the tests and examinations, insult their teachers, threat their invigilators and abuse the staff on any pretext. They want more freedom, rights, both legitimate and illegitimate. If these undesirable activities and indiscipline are allowed to go on unchecked, the whole education and training system would soon be paralysed. It would eat into the very vitals of our national ethos and development. This unrest among the students reflects the prevailing dissatisfaction, disillusionment, frustration, dejection and hopelessness. The students are now a frustrated lot; they lack orientation and proper guidance. They feel insecure as far as proper employment opportunities are concerned. They are afflicted with aimlessness, indecision and crisis of character. They do not have role models to follow on national or regional levels.

According to UNESCO (2009) students unrest and violence is not a new problem. It occurs between two or more individuals as interpersonal violence, or it involves identifiable groups in the society and erupts as intergroup violence between two or more different religions or ethnic groups. For centuries, violence has been a commonplace feature of school life with its causes embedded in the social, cultural, historical and economic contexts of its time (Leach, 2003; Achoka, 2009). The focus of unrest that leads to violence can be individuals, objects or the school itself, and the nature of the damage can be psychological, physical or material. Since the middle of the 20th century, violence against children has increasingly been viewed as a violation of their fundamental human rights, in particular of their right to physical safety and psychological security and well-being (Rukundo, 2009; UNICEF, 2011).

Students' Unrest in India

India is facing the trouble of rising indiscipline among the students. Student unrest in India has assumed frightening magnitude. This is a danger to our traditions and our national entity. The frequency reluctance among the students is nothing, but a manifestation of universal frustration and disapproval prevailing among them. Why students in India are resorting to the acts of violence need to be understood. We have noticed of that students go wild, throwing stones etc. Their meaningless action results in the brutal suppression by the police officers who make them the targets of their gun and sticks. We have seen closure of schools and universities, *gheraos* of Principals and beating of teachers by the students. All this is truly an unhappy state of affairs. The reason behind this unrest among Indian Students is a plethora of frustration, grievances and anxiety of the students. The inability of the authorities resolve to the grievances and demands of the students results in the indulgence of the students in the acts of violence, strikes and demonstrations.

There has been student unrest all over India. The unrest has not been confined within educational institutions. There have been student strikes. There have been student demonstrations in the streets. Many valuable properties of the universities, colleges and schools have been destroyed. Even railway properties and other Government properties have been damaged or destroyed. Students have resorted to violence. Considering it a problem of law and order, police have come to stop it. They have opened fire. There have been case of death as a result of firing. But the police interference has not been able to stop the agitation of the students. Rather, the disturbance has spread over new areas.

Nature of Students' Unrest

Student unrest is a world-wide phenomenon. There is hardly a country free from it. There are many socio-economic factors causing this. The unrest among students is an outward expression of the resentment that the community feels towards the government, the society and the institutions that they study in. It is human nature that when a person, especially the youth, is alienated or his problems are not heeded to, or if he is unable to face the realities of life, he resorts to violent means to focus public attention. When the number of such students grows large, they unite on a common platform and together tread on the path of violence.

Role of Education in Students' Unrest

Actually education plays a vital role in molding one's behaviour and in preparing a child to the world at large. This role, it seems, is not carried out satisfactorily by most institutions now-a-days. When a student steps into the world of reality, he is baffled to find himself a misfit. In this fast-changing society, he cannot perhaps keep pace. Hence, there is unrest among the youth. The youth get frustrated when they see a great deal of disparity between the theory and its application. This causes them to wonder whether all that they ever learnt would ever come in use or would go waste. Added to this is their economic dissatisfaction. All these factors blend together and give rise to a cult of violence. It is only a beneficial educational policy and a better social order that can bring about a sobering effect on them. It is hence the duty of the sensible and responsible citizens of the society and the authorities that they should do all that they can to remove the irritants that cause such unrest. The students should never be neglected. They are impatient, hasty and full of new ideas and vision. Their dreams have to be materialised and they like to see this happening as a result of their hard work and sometimes by force. However, they often lead the country to new horizons; because, out of unrest emerges and a better society.

Main Causes of Student Unrest in India

Defective Education System: The present education system does not fulfil its proposed aims and nor does it give the students any practical skill which can make them capable of taking-up any job after their education. As a result, the students do not find themselves capable of fending for themselves. Passing of examination has become the sole aim of present education.

Aimless Life and Uncertain Future: The present education does not give the student any such qualifications which may assure to them a certain future. Now-a-days, there is great unemployment in our country. The report of the Employment Directorate tells that the number of unemployed persons has doubled. This situation makes it clear that unemployment in the country is on the increase. The young generation is the victim of this unemployment. Consequently, student unrest and indiscipline has touched it peak.

Economic Difficulties: Our economic difficulties have become so complex, that we do not know as to what will be the economic situation in the future. Most of our students come from families that are economically poor. Such families cannot easily give higher education to their children. Sixty per cent of our students generally do not get higher education. Out of the remaining, 20 per cent students who go to colleges or university, come from middle class families and 20 per cent from upper class families. The present higher education has become so expensive that the students find it difficult to bear this burden. So, it is natural for students to agitate.

Excessive Number of Students in the Class: Generally, the number of students in every class is so high that the students and teachers are unable to establish contact with each other, that is, the teachers are unable to understand the difficulties of individual students. Likewise, the personality of the teacher has no impact on the student. There are several colleges and universities where class-rooms, laboratories, libraries and teachers are not available for several departments. In such a situation, unrest and indiscipline amongst students is not surprising.

Defective Teaching Methods: The teaching methods in colleges and universities have become defective. They do not arouse curiosity in the students for new knowledge nor do they increase knowledge. The result is that the students do not find the classes interesting nor are feeling of respect generated towards most of the teachers who have an indifferent attitude. Consequently, students pass the examination by hook or by crook, such as, cramming or on the basis of guess papers sold freely in the market or on the basis of copying in the examination-hall by terrorizing the invigilators.

Indifference of the Family-Members: The influence of the family members on the students is negligible today. Parents, elder brothers or sisters pretend to be so busy that they do not hesitate to say that they have no time to attend to the studies of their wards. The result is that the students wander about unbridled and they ruin the conduct find character of others also and thus bring dishonour and anguish to themselves and their family by their indisciplined behaviour. Needless to say that so long as the responsible members of the family do not fulfil their responsibility towards their wards, the indiscipline prevailing amongst students will not end and nor will the unrest and discontent calm down.

Unsuitable Teachers: Today in schools, colleges and universities, we find many such teachers who have no interest in their teaching work. All concerned persons know it well that in every department of colleges and universities, there are some teachers who do not go to teach in the classes even for a day. Such teachers present a wrong example by their behaviour and conduct. As such, the students coming in contact with such teachers learn nothing but roguery. Besides, many teachers suffer from different types of inferiority complexes. Due to this, some undesirable elements remain inherent in their behaviour and many students who come under their influence are inclined to follow suit.

Student Union: In various educational centres, the students naturally are eager to organise unions and generally they are provided adequate facilities to do so. But in the process of organisation and elections of these unions, various political parties and teacher-politicians try to serve their vested interests. The interference of the political elements vitiates the nature of the student unions in various ways and generates a sense of indiscipline in the students.

Lack of Cocurricular and Creative Activities: The function of an educational centre is not simply to prepare the students for examinations. In fact, the aim of education is to develop the entire personality of the individual harmoniously. This development is not possible only through the curricular teaching. For this, various cocurricular activities such as games, sports, contests, competitions, dramas, music, magazines, collective social service etc., are necessary because through them the different aspects of the personality of a person manifest themselves and attain the high state of development.

Defective Examination System: The examination system is such that the teaching process has become dependent on it. The passing of examination has become the sole aim of education. Due to this examination system, the students have begun to think that there is no need of studying throughout the year and only a little study near the examination time will be sufficient. So, rest of the time may be spent recklessly. As a result of this tendency, the students are left with a lot of unoccupied time which they spend in indiscipline activities of various types.

Elements of Indiscipline and Anarchy Prevailing in the Society: The elements of indiscipline and anarchy prevailing in the society, in fact are reflected in the indiscipline behaviour of students. Generally, the students may be divided in three categories. The first category consists of those students who are interested in studies and after finishing the studies they become engineers, doctors, administrators and other Civil Servants. The second category is of those students who take admission in colleges and universities simply as a matter of fashion. Such students mostly come from traders, contractors and other business class families. Their aim is not to imbibe the cultural or real nature of learning. They consider the classes as picnic spots. The third category is of the student politicians. They are connected with different political parties and at their instance they indulge in various kinds of indiscipline activities.

Under such a situation there is little wonder that our younger generation is standing on a cross-road, little knowing in which direction to move. As a result, it is aimless, dissatisfied and misguided. So long as we are not successful in giving it a right direction, it will continue to remain discontented and indisciplined.

Students Unrest—A Reflection of Society

It is true that social situation breeds frustration. It is also true that there is no national goal beckoning the spirit of the youth. It is a fact that the present education has failed to give any direction or purpose to the life of the student. The student is always asked to behave without any guidance as to how he should behave. He has tremendous energy but there is no consciousness as to his rights and responsibilities. By and large, he is apathetic, drawn in struggle only when mass frenzy grips his mind. There is no connection between his struggle for survival and the education which is supposed to help him in the matter. He is not interested in knowledge in the abstract. He goes to the college because he has no alternative. He must get a degree if he has to 'make it'. He has no options. "Therefore, his only aim is to get in, get out and get on with it." The university is no more an isolated community of scholars but is more community of young people. The reality of the world today involves serious problems and the universities just are not doing much about it.

Conclusion

It is imperative to recognise the issues that are likely to generate students unrest, especially in the subsequent decades of the millennium: student higher education life issues; poor funding by the government. In appreciation of the potential issues that would generate student protests in the near future, student services professional would be challenged to evolve strategies that would help to bring the incidents of student unrest in higher education to the barest minimum.

REFERENCES

*http://www.shareyouressays.com/*115497/11-main-causes-of-student-unrest-in-india

*http://www.importantindia.com/*6511/student-unrest-in-india/

*http://nonpartisaneducation.org/*Review/Essays/v4n2.html

*http://ijepr.org/*doc/V2-IS1_Jan13/ij5.pdf

*http://www.preservearticles.com/*201104155468/unrest-among-students-essay.html

*http://www.shareyouressays.com/*2375/946-words-essay-on-student-unrest-sample-essay

http://erepository.uonbi.ac.ke/xmlui/bitstream/handle/11295/90835/Mathai_Influence%20of%20 schoolbased%20factors%20on%20students%20unrest%20in%20public%20secondary%20school s.pdf?sequence=1 & isAllowed=y

http://krepublishers.com/02-Journals/JSS/JSS-10-0-000-000-2005-Web/JSS-10-1-001-076-2005- Abst-PDF/JSS-10-1-017-022-2005-169-Aluede-O/JSS-10-1-017-022-2005-169-Aluede-O.pdf

26

Challenges and New Trends in Higher Education

Mujibul Hasan Siddiqui and *Zaffar Ahmad Nadaf*

Introduction

The university as the home of higher education has always faced challenges in history. We would like to discover the challenges in our time. Since the university is a part of the general education, in order to discover these challenges we must try to understand the nature of education, which can broadly be understood as a "process of acquiring knowledge." For in the actual sense education consists of learning and teaching. The former is acquiring knowledge and the latter is imparting knowledge. In that case, both teaching and learning are processes of knowledge. But since the aim of education is learning then our attention must be on this aspect. Therefore, if we analyse the nature of learning as the process of acquiring knowledge, we must discover the real nature of education. This way I am hoping at the same time to develop more effective methods of teaching in education.

The process of acquiring knowledge has two aspects: one is external the other is internal. What we mean by the internal aspect of the process of acquiring knowledge is the operations of our faculties, which we employ while acquiring knowledge. As such, the analysis of this process is a theory of knowledge investigated in the branch of philosophy known as epistemology. The external process of acquiring knowledge is on the other hand what we call "learning". This is the process which is the subject of examination here as "education". Of course, in this external process there are many external factors, such as instructor, teaching methods and other means utilised in teaching and learning, all of which will be briefly discussed in this context.

Learning

Learning as an external process of acquiring knowledge can be in two ways: one is natural learning, which is attaining knowledge mainly by the use of our faculties of learning and senses. The most effective method in this kind of learning is trial and error. The other kind of learning is systematic knowledge acquisition. It is this second kind of learning that we should consider as real education. Now, we come to a point where we have to recognise the role of epistemology in education because education as systematic learning is an external process acquiring knowledge, which is based on the internal process of acquiring knowledge. For, the internal process of acquiring knowledge as learning is mainly the operations of our mind and other faculties of learning while we try to acquire knowledge. This means if we know how our faculties of learning operate then obviously we can teach the students more effectively. In that case, the internal process of acquiring knowledge can give us more effective methods of teaching and thus we need to utilise it. However, this aspect is discussed in epistemology, so I will try only to assume a theory of knowledge on the basis of which I shall attempt to develop a theory of education that may guide us in determining the challenges we face today in higher education.

Our explanation so far reveals that a theory of education consists of the internal process of acquiring knowledge on the one hand, and the learning subject (the human being), which represents the external process including teaching on the other. The former includes an analysis of the internal processes, which take place in the mind and learning faculties of the learning subject (the human being). The latter includes the efforts of systematic learning and teaching. Let us then try to analyse these structures in order to pinpoint the place of higher learning in education so that we can discover our challenges and new prospects. The internal process of learning is the operation of our faculties, which we use in order to acquire knowledge. These operations begin at the level of objects of knowledge and ends at the level where their complete concepts, ideas and knowledge are transferred to the mind. This process can be natural or systematic. We shall try to understand the processes that will give us an effective method of teaching to be utilised in any education.

Natural Learning

The natural process of learning or of acquisition of knowledge is the personal trial of an individual in acquiring knowledge. Usually, we first begin to learn things when we arrive to this world. The main method of natural learning is trial and error. Because of this process, a worldview is formed in the mind of the learning subject. Initially, this worldview is simple and as such has only two structures: Life Structure and World Structure. The former starts to be formed as soon as we are born. In this first experience of life, it is extremely hard to determine what will be the first that we learn. In other words, what is our first experience that is converted into a piece of knowledge? We can, on the other hand, identify more or less what kind of knowledge this mental content is; for example, it cannot be an abstract idea, or a philosophical notion and the like. It will be a kind of knowledge that pertains to our life at that time. Since we are naturally inclined to preserve our life, most of our experiences will be related to the preservation of life, such as finding and choosing certain food and developing habits of how to attract the attention of others to make food available and so on. Therefore, in our early ages, we *naturally* have such experiences available to our mental consciousness and it is these experiences that are converted into knowledge. What we call Life Structure is the knowledge that is available for us in this way and is primarily related to our biological and daily life. In that case, Life Structure in our worldview includes most of our daily habits related to the preservation of our life. This Life Structure becomes more refined and sophisticated as we add to it what we learn from our social environment. In this way, it begins to include many of our cultural habits as well, such as habits of eating, our social culture, and the ways of daily behaviour, manners and customs. We call it 'structure' because our mind forms it according to its natural rules and principles explained in such disciplines as logic and epistemology. For this reason, knowledge gathered in this structure is not a hodge-podge gathering of experience in our mind; it is rather an orderly unity according to certain rules and principles. Life Structure is, therefore, such a coherent mental unity which makes up the total contents of our mind in our earliest life onwards enriching itself until adulthood according to the natural rules and principles of the mind through its social and physical surrounding. We call this internal process natural. When there is interference from either our surroundings or us then learning becomes systematic.

I would like to illustrate the natural internal process of learning with a concrete representation. We have a digestive system, which is biological. Yet, if our capacity to attain knowledge is called "knowledge system" following our naming of the "digestive system", then it actually resembles our "knowledge system". Our digestive system, too, has internal and external processes, both of which also have "natural" and "systematic" ways, although they may not be called as such in anatomy. The former is the process, which takes place after the food, is put into the mouth; and the latter is the process, which takes place during the gathering and preparing the food before it is eaten. Hence, the internal process of digestion is like the internal process of learning or of acquiring knowledge, namely the process that takes place after the "information" received from the objects of knowledge is put into the *mind.* The external process of digestion is a good illustration to the external process of learning or of acquiring knowledge, namely the process that takes place before the "information" received from the objects of knowledge is put into the *mind.* It is clear that in all processes there are natural and systematic procedures. We have explained so far the natural internal process of acquiring knowledge. Now, let us see the systematic learning or acquiring knowledge.

Systematic Learning

As far as the internal process of learning is concerned, there is no difference in natural or systematic learning. Here, the difference comes because of the external applications of our learning faculties and as a result, in the mind a more systematic worldview is formed. This makes a significant change in learning. For, as soon as we begin to form a mental conception of a natural experience, which we had from babyhood onwards, we will begin to act no longer out of the natural instincts alone, but also out of the mental content that we have acquired which we have called "Life Structure". The more sophisticated the Life Structure is the more conceptual becomes the experience and thus the more we act out of our mental frameworks. This means we are now acting on our knowledge, which we have thus far acquired, and hence knowledge formed thereupon is more systematic. In such a conceptual Life Structure, we may be able to distinguish certain elements, which we call 'mentality'. A mentality is actually an understanding or conception of certain things, living types, and facts of life and of the world. As we grow these mentalities are developed according to our personality, mental abilities and the kind of education we receive. Each mentality begins to develop through the education we receive into a structure and thus can be termed 'sub-structure'. These mentalities are so coherently related to each other that together they form the totality of the Life Structure. Then, we begin to arrange our lives according to our own Life Structure, which is the totality of the contents of our mind thus far. Since, as a total unity, the mind reflects all the ideas we have thus far formed in our mind, its contents as the Life Structure will also reflect our attitude for life and understanding the universe in general. Our worldview at this stage has only a Life Structure, which reflects our conception of the universe, such as the meaning of life, the origin of existence, human destiny and so on.

As we grow-up certain conceptions concerning the world we live in gradually develop in our worldview; first, certain fundamental questions arise in the mind, such as the meaning of life, from where we have come and where we are going. As we try to answer, or find answers to these fundamental questions, a conception concerning the world and things around us is formed. As this conception begins to be more sophisticated through our education, it gradually forms a clearly discernible structure in the mind, which can be distinguished from the Life Structure. This new structure first forms a mentality within the Life Structure. However, if it can be fully developed, it provides well-formed ideas, doctrines and even scientific opinion concerning the world we live in; hence, it is apt to call it "World Structure". As soon as this new structure is established within the worldview, it begins to function in conjunction with the life-structure and *vice versa.*

If, there is a good education in the community then the worldview in our mind develops further. Usually, there are certain concepts in our worldview that dominate our lives. It is possible to reduce these concepts into only five fundamental ones: life, world, knowledge, human and value. A fundamental concept is one, which forms a complicated understanding and a mentality in our mind, which directs us to a certain behaviour in life and society. As such, these concepts can be characterised as "doctrinal concepts" because each one of them may constitute a specific well-developed doctrine, which determines our worldview. The development of these concepts depends upon the type of education a person receives. This brings forth the importance of education, which will be evaluated as the external process of acquiring knowledge. We should be able to see here that at least two doctrinal concepts grow into structures in our worldview as a natural internal process of learning; Life and World Structures. But if the education is scientific then the concept of knowledge can also acquire a doctrinal characteristic and as such formed into a "Knowledge Structure". In the same way both human and value concepts can also develop into doctrinal concepts and as a result form the structures of Man and Value. What is important for an educational philosophy is the process in this development. Two structures, namely Life and World Structures, develop as a result of the natural internal process of learning or of acquiring knowledge. We must, however, realise that no structure is perfect in relation to knowledge unless it is developed through systematic process of learning. That is why the other three structures, Knowledge, Human and Value, can develop only if there is a systematic process of learning. Therefore, we shall build our educational philosophy on the system of the development of a worldview. Before we do this, however, it is important to clarify further our concepts of structures and the way they lead us to certain behaviour in life. In fact, we need to prove that it is these concepts in our worldview that guide us in our actions.

First, we need to show what other concepts are restored in these structures. The Knowledge Structure includes within itself the key scientific terminology and all other concepts of technology that may be derived from these concepts. The network of the key scientific terminology may be called "Scientific Conceptual Scheme", which will be dealt with briefly below. In the Value Structure, we may find moral concepts, ideas, doctrines, and depending on the kind of worldview, we may have our religious and legal conceptions. In the Human Structure, on the other hand, we have our conceptions of ourselves, as well as of the society and the societal organisation. All structures of a worldview operate in relation to each other. None of them can operate independently; hence, our treatment of them independently is only a logical analysis of a worldview. Otherwise, it is not intended to establish each structure independently.

Secondly, we may give a concrete example in order to illustrate the structures of a worldview on the basis of the Islamic worldview. Since the Life Structure is grounded in human biology, it will have the most common elements with all other worldviews, and as such, the Life Structure of the Islamic worldview is its aspect that is most dominant in the Muslim local cultural activities. The World Structure is that aspect of the Islamic worldview which includes the most fundamental elements, such as the idea of *tawhid* (God's Being and Oneness), Prophet-hood, resurrection and the ideas of religion and hereafter, *Akhirah.* We do not mean that these are the only fundamental concepts of the Islamic worldview because each structure by itself represents a doctrinal element, which includes within itself many other fundamental Islamic key terminologies. Nevertheless, the extensions of these key concepts and terminology constitute substructures; hence, there lie many substructures within the basic structures of the Islamic worldview, which may not be so fundamental, and as a result, differences of opinion in those sub-structural elements can be allowed. As an extension of the World Structure, Knowledge Structure is also a fundamental doctrinal element, which is represented by the umbrella term '*Ilm*'. This structure includes within itself the key scientific terminology of Islamic science, which may be called "Islamic scientific conceptual scheme". The Value Structure in the Islamic worldview, on the other hand, includes moral, ethical and legal practices. But since the concept of law; namely *al-fiqh*, in the early Islamic worldview is closely linked with the World Structure; it naturally included religious law, which cannot be devoid of moral content. Hence, law, religion and morality are manifested as an integral part of one structure. This conceptual understanding of law, religion and morality never brought about a sharp distinction between these three sub-structures. Finally, the Human Structure is represented within the Islamic worldview by the concepts of *Khalîfah* and *Ummah*. As such, this structure manifests the Islamic understanding of man and society, which is totally grounded in the World Structure, because, again, even these conceptions themselves are derived from the concepts of *Tawhid*, Prophet-hood, religion and *Akhirah*.

Thirdly, each structure in a worldview has a specific function in life and in human activities. This point can be explained from another perspective as well; let us assume a worldview in which the Knowledge Structure is not discernible as a manifest mentality. In such a case, no scientific activity will ensue from the individual having such a worldview. There will not be in that worldview any scientific concepts that can form a scientific framework for the mind to work in. As a result, there will be no scientific attitude or any scientific tradition, which can support such activities. In fact, if there is no Knowledge Structure within a worldview, then that worldview can only be analysed into its Life and World Structures. For it is the scientific activity which manifests other structures as analysable units of a worldview; if there is no such activity those structures cannot be developed to such an extent that they become manifest in their respective worldviews. This does not mean that a worldview without a manifest Knowledge Structure lacks a value system, or a Human Structure that acts as the ground of social and political activities; on the contrary, all these activities will be carried out and regulated by a World Structure, which may acquire a degree of sophistication within its respective worldview. But, it cannot acquire the level of sophistication manifested in such scientific worldviews that can adequately be analysed into their Knowledge, Value and Human Structures. This is where the significance of what I am inclined to call "scientific worldviews" lies. For, it is only these worldviews that can clearly be analysed into their manifest structures.

The Operations of the Internal Process of Learning and the Faculties

The operations of the internal process in education constitute a full-fledged epistemological theory. The operation itself depends on our faculties of knowledge. Therefore, we need to analyse this process as an epistemological function of our mental faculties, which shall reveal both the internal learning process, and the faculties at the same time. In the first place, this process begins at the level where our faculties of external experience somehow get in touch with an object of knowledge. Here we may ask, which faculty is it that gets in touch with such an object? This depends on the object; if it is a material object then it is received into the mind by way of one or more of the five senses called external senses. If the object of knowledge is non-material then it is received into the mind through one or more internal faculties. There may be objects whose nature is such that we can never get in touch because we lack the faculty to get in touch with it. Such objects may exist but remain unknown to us and therefore, it is futile to attempt to acquire their knowledge and to convey such knowledge. This tells us also where education may begin and where it should end.

When an object of knowledge is thus received into the mind, the impression we form is called "mental representation", which is the result of an object's undergoing through the process of experience. Since, there are only two categories of objects for knowledge, there are also two kinds of experience, external and internal, both of which take place differently. The latter depends on the former; therefore, external experience develops in us first, and thus, it is in the first place, the beginning of the process of experience, and in the second place, the beginning of the whole process of knowing. Any philosophy of education must pay attention to these processes in order to form a theory of education.

The awareness of an object of knowledge produced in us is perception. If this awareness is received through one or more of the five senses, then it is a *sensible perception*; this means that whatever is received through the five senses can be qualified as 'sensible', and everything that is received in this way can also be termed "sense datum". All the data of the sensible perception are what we call "external" or "outer experience". Since, we have no senses other than the five senses to be in contact directly with the material reality, the ultimate beginning point of the process of acquiring knowledge concerning the physical universe is sensible perception, which originates from the five senses. The process of outer experience begins at one or more sense organ(s) and ends at the *physical consciousness*. Since this process as a whole is very physical, it needs mental consciousness to be conceptualised. If a sensible perception, which is yielded at the physical consciousness, is not conceptualised, it cannot be utilised as an object of knowledge. Therefore, such a perception needs to be perceived by the mind as well so that it can be a proper object of human knowledge. This leads us to posit the existence of a mental perception on the one hand, and of a mental awareness on the other. So far, the internal process of knowledge has been explained to the point of the faculty of physical consciousness where all sensible perceptions are produced. These perceptions then are utilised in two ways: they are directly perceived by the mind and thus are on the way to be conceptualised; and/or they are taken by the faculties of internal experience to be utilised, to use Kant's term, as raw-material in their functions. This means that the process of acquiring knowledge after the physical consciousness will continue to two directions: to the direction of the internal experience; and/or to the direction of the mind. But since the product of the internal experience is also utilised by the mind in the process of knowing, we shall first try to first analyse the direction of the internal experience, and then continue to the analysis of the mind. The *inner* perception of an object of knowledge is an emotion. The fact that emotions play a role in the process of acquiring knowledge cannot be denied. Therefore, the role of emotions cannot be denied in education either. For, an emotion moves us, excites us or makes us feel miserable, but how can it contribute to the process of acquiring knowledge.

We may answer this question by illustrating with the example of a lion. Suppose we do not have any feeling of fear, would we still run away from the lion even if we knew that a lion is a formidable and dangerous animal? I am not saying that we still have the emotion but we simply do not fear anything; on the contrary, I mean we have no such emotion at all. I think it is the emotion and not the sensible perception of the lion that is mentally evaluated and then decided whether to run away from the lion. For sometimes, we think that we have seen a lion, although there is no lion and we are immediately activated to find a shelter.

Similarly, the idea of a lion by itself is not sufficient to make us look for a shelter, even if it is sufficient by itself, it will not prompt us immediately to move. Hence, the decision to look for a shelter is considerably influenced by fear. We would like to formulate this conclusion in the epistemological sense as "the internal perception of an object of knowledge is given to the mind as raw-material" just like the sensible perception of an object of knowledge. In other words, our mental faculties of knowledge cannot function without our faculty of outer experience, nor can they work in isolation from the faculties of inner experience. The internal experience which is nearest to the sensible perception is the *sensible intuition* which may perceive an object without physically perceiving it, because no physical object can directly affect our faculties of internal experience. Therefore, if an object is intuited as existing this is the result of the function of the sensible intuition. We call this faculty "sensible intuition" because it intuits its object the way our mind intuits the conclusion of a deductive argument, and yet the intuition of an object is not mental intuition; since, though a sensible perception is absent, yet it is assumed as mediating between the faculty and its object, it is apt to call it "sensible intuition". It is the faculty of sensible intuition that produces our instincts, which are direct and immediate; and as such, they can play a significant role in the manifestation of an emotion. Because of this function, the sensible intuition may interfere to mediate between the sensible perception and the other faculties of inner experience. In a sense, it senses the data of the sensible perception and makes them available for the other inner faculties. When such a sensible intuition of a sensible perception is made available for an emotional state, the corresponding emotion may be yielded. Another important function of the sensible intuition is that it retains the copies of our emotions through which we instinctively recognise such emotive experiences, because it is the centre of our instincts. The central faculty of our inner experience is heart, which assesses our emotions in the sense that it renders them meaningful for the ethical and religious life. The function of the heart in the epistemological process is to provide our mind with representations of ethical and fundamental concepts of life and death in an experiential way. Heart is not a faculty of outer experience and as such, it cannot perceive external objects, but it can perceive what we may call "emotive objects of knowledge" which transcend our external experience. The sphere of knowledge comprehensive of all things that may be subjected to the emotive process may be identified as the "Experiential Realm", which is transcendent to the external experience. With this conclusion, it is clear that we are distinguishing two comprehensive realms of knowledge: the Realm of External Experience and the Realm of Internal Experience, which we have identified as Experiential Realm. All these realms are to be taken into consideration in educational curricula as well. On the other hand, the Experiential Realm has also two further spheres; one moral, the other religious. The former is clear in the sense that its limits can be quite easily drawn, but the latter needs further clarification. In the theological sense, both realms involve the same subject but different aspects of it; whereas the experiential realm, for instance, encompasses God as an existent Being, the Transcendent Realm has God in the Absolute sense, namely as He is in Himself. Therefore, the experiential representation of God's existence is an inner experience, but His Essence is an Absolute behind "seventy thousand veils" as expressed in a tradition of the Prophet. Moreover, our mind also needs the guidance of the Revelation in attaining the theological experiential realm. For as we shall see, our intellect operates with causality in order to infer a Maker for the whole existence; it may thus discover a *Cause* for the universe, but it still needs another argument to prove that that *Cause* is God as defined in the Revealed Texts. Does the heart sufficient to make such an inference provide the experiential perception? This is the greatest dilemma of philosophy and it seems that it is still not sufficient and therefore, we need a *guidance*, which is provided by the Revelation. This epistemological principle guides us as to which method is to be used in education of these subjects. Experiential inquiries belong directly to the inquirer, though they are not perceived directly. What I mean by this is that our inner faculty of representation needs an awakening by the mediation of Revelation. Just as our faculty of outer experience sometimes needs the mediation of a device to see or hear things afar, though they are perceivable directly; in the same manner the inner faculty needs a finer and more subtle mediation. Again, this mediation is guidance, which is reflected in the mental states of the inquirer, and these states represent the terms of the internal experience. Since as such it is primarily our emotions that yield such a mental state, we would like to call it "subjective mood". As a mental state, the subjective mood is very important for the faculties of inner experience to perceive the truths of the experiential realm. Our analysis of the process of knowledge has brought us to the faculty of ethical feelings, called 'conscience'. Therefore, heart does not represent all our internal faculties, although, it is the most fundamental one, because it is through the heart that most of our moral and religious experiential representations of entities as objects of knowledge originate.

This approach solves an issue that remains inadequately answered in the Critical Philosophy of Kant.

This process of knowledge through internal experience converges into and culminates at a unity, which makes us to be aware of our 'self', and as such, it functions as a faculty, which we term "the faculty of consciousness" or "faculty of the self". Through, this faculty one experientially becomes aware of his/her existence which is very similar to the external experience through which one becomes aware of an object around him; just as this external awareness is different from the mental awareness, in the same way this internal awareness of the *subject* is different from the mental awareness of the *self*. Hence, in addition to the external and internal awareness, we must have a mental awareness. The first process of consciousness yields the awareness of things and the world around us. Whereas the second one, through the aid of our internal faculties and the experience resulting from them, yields the awareness of our inner world which revolves around the consciousness of our *self* (ego). The third one, namely the mental awareness, yields a conception of both the external and internal awareness. Therefore, in order to grasp these experiences in the way a human conceives them, the mental awareness is essential.

All the representations of objects of knowledge are thus transferred to the mind to undergo mental operations. We use the term 'mind' in general to mean the "faculty of conceptual experience". In this sense 'mind' refers to the totality of our mental activities that are mainly conceptual. Such a conceptual understanding, as we have seen, begins at the level of mental consciousness, which is thus the lowest faculty of the mind. In order to discover all mental faculties we need to examine the functions of our mind. Let us try to show the internal process of learning thus far outlined on a Fig. 26.1.

First, the mind must somehow retain all conceptual activities so that it can utilise them in all its functions and this leads us to the faculty of *memory*. Second, objects of knowledge must be presented to the mind in a conceptually concrete way, which means the reproduction of representations as images and this poses a *faculty of imagination* (*Khayal*). Third, the mind must think the objects of knowledge, which leads us to postulate a *faculty of thinking* which we call 'intellect' (*Aql*). Fourth, since the mind as a result of thinking must decide in order to know its objects, and that deciding is actually an act of 'choice', the mind must need a *faculty of judgement*, which is already known as the 'will' (*Iradah*). Finally, the mind functions to formulate arguments and reach conclusions

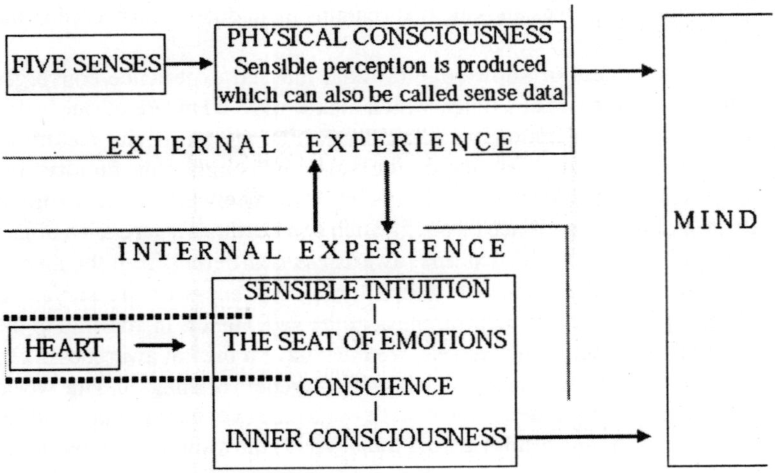

Fig. 26.1: Internal Process of Learning

out of these arguments, which means that it must somehow possess a faculty, which enables it to deduce the implications and entailments of organised propositions, and this is the faculty of inference which we would like to call "(mental) intuition".

We already know all these mental activities; they are not new discoveries that must be studied now. In fact, we apply them all in our daily life without thinking that this process, which has been taking place in our mind, can be analysed in this way. We do not have to know the process of knowledge in order to acquire knowledge; just as we do not need to know how our stomach functions in order to digest the food we eat. For all the functions of the mind are already provided for the process of knowledge, which is, therefore, a natural process but we may interfere at certain levels of this process, which makes it different in this sense from digestion. Hence, we do not need to know this process in order to acquire knowledge; but we need to know it for scientific reasons; for instance, if someone argues that science is a universal and absolute activity, which cannot change from culture to culture, then, in order to show that this is not the case we must explain how we acquire knowledge in general and then scientific knowledge in particular. Hence, in this case we need a theory, which explains how we acquire knowledge.

For educational purposes also a theory of knowledge would be very useful, because if we know how humans acquire knowledge then we can teach them with more effective methods, since teaching primarily consists of "making the student acquire knowledge", i.e., "to learn". These mental operations can be illustrated in Fig. 26.2.

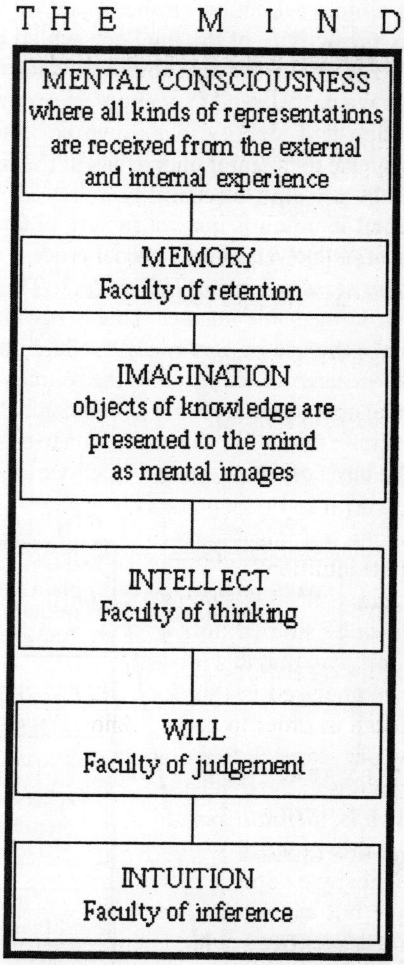

Fig. 26.2: Mental Operations

That activity of the mind, which holds the object of knowledge in abstraction, is called 'thought'; the faculty through which thought is actualised is the intellect. Thought or the activity of thinking itself does not necessarily include judging and inferring, although ordinarily we refer to all these activities as 'thinking'. In our analysis of the process of acquiring knowledge, we would like to distinguish the thinking activity of the mind, which involves judgement and inference from the kind of thinking which is a mere reflection on the object of knowledge and as such requires only the activity of the intellect, which can thus be called also 'intellection'. The intellect is also able to develop certain principles. This is done in two ways: the mind may apply its own natural principles, such as contradiction and identity to its own content and derive new principles, or it may use the natural operations of the intellect to derive a principle; such as the principle of causality.

Since the mental intuition is the last faculty in the process, we may confidently say that our analysis of the internal process of learning ends in this faculty. We may show our result in Fig. 26.3. This process does not always repeat itself in the same manner. This is because our faculties of knowledge can make the use of previously available data, whether from external or internal experience, or yet from the sources of our mind itself. Therefore, the actual operations are more complicated than this systematic exposition. However, we may utilise this exposition to establish a philosophy of education on the basis of which we can erect our theory of education.

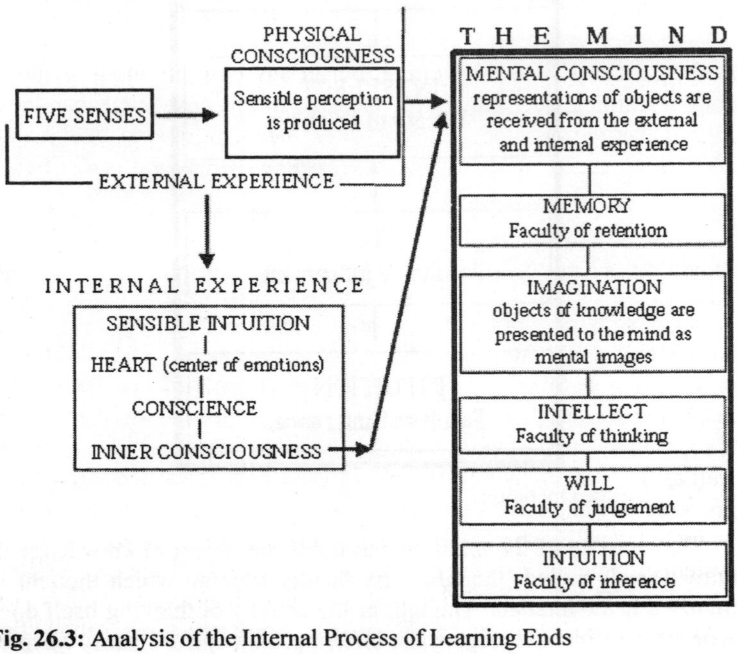

Fig. 26.3: Analysis of the Internal Process of Learning Ends

The External Process of Learning: Philosophy of Education

The external process of learning is all the activities taking place outside the learning subject when someone is engaged in learning and hence, it is education in the real sense. If we fully outline this process it will be in the true sense our philosophy of education on the basis of which our educational theory will be developed. We are not in a position to fully outline it in this context because there are more concepts involved in it, such as the purpose of education and the nature of the subjects to be educated. We shall, therefore, concentrate on the main problems that will guide us through the challenges of higher education. Since, the internal and external processes do not work independently of each, other during the actual activity of learning it should also take place at two planes; natural and systematic.

Natural Learning

As we have pointed out, the natural process of learning or of acquiring knowledge is the personal trial of an individual in acquiring knowledge. Usually this is the way, we first begin to learn things when we arrive in this world but it continues after even we begin to learn systematically through our regular school education. Everyone can develop his/her own method for this kind of learning, but in any case the main method of natural learning is trial and error. Because of this individual character of natural learning, no educational theory can be established for it. The actual education evolves when systematic learning begins in a scientific way and we shall now examine this.

Systematic Learning

We have so far developed the basis of a philosophy of education. Now, we need to eradicate our philosophy on this basis. First of all, two processes of learning, namely internal and external processes are parallel to each other and therefore cannot be totally independent of each other. If so, then the natural internal and external processes are also parallel as well as the systematic internal and external processes. Since the natural processes are excluded from the educational philosophy, though they can be included within the theory of education itself, then we need to use the systematic internal process to develop the skeleton of our philosophy of education. The systematic internal process of learning as we have seen gave us the concept of worldview with its basic structures. Among these structures as we have seen the Life Structure is developed within the natural process and thus cannot be included in the systematic process. This does not mean that it should not be discussed in an educational philosophy. On the contrary, the epistemological process at this stage through which a worldview emerges should be discussed here. Nevertheless, it is not significantly relevant for the challenges facing higher education today. Hence, we suffice by indicating that this is the initial process through which worldview begins to be formed in the mind of an individual. If we thus exclude this structure then we are left with two fundamental groups of structures: in the first group, we have the World Structure, as the fundamental outlook representing the individual's identity as well as his perception of the whole world. In the second group, we have the Knowledge structure as representing the rest of the structures. We argue here that in the philosophy of education we need to include the rest of the structures in the Knowledge Structure because they are developed on the basis of knowledge and indeed through the scientific knowledge acquired through one's education. With this analysis, we are left with three structures: Life, World and Knowledge. As we have excluded the Life Structure from the philosophy of education, we are to utilise only World and Knowledge Structures.

Since the Knowledge Structure regulates our scientific activities, it also includes within itself the network of our scientific terminology, which we have called "Scientific Conceptual Scheme". As this is a developed mentality, it must be included in the higher stages of education. It is, therefore, inevitable to include the Scientific Conceptual Scheme in our philosophy of education. This outline gives us three stages in education:

1. The Stage of the World Structure and as such it constitutes the earliest systematic learning process. Since at this stage the worldview of the individual is not fully developed to be distinguished from his/her World Structure, it is more apt to call this the "Stage of Worldview".
2. The Stage of the Knowledge Structure, which constitutes the middle stage and as such the basic terminology of sciences are given and the Knowledge Structure of the worldview is fully inculcated into the minds of individuals.
3. The Scientific Stage where attention is paid to develop in the worldview of the individuals a scientific mentality. Since this represents the final stage of education, it must be the stage of higher education.

We can add another stage to this philosophy of education, which is the Stage of Specialisation. This stage develops a more specific network of concepts in the minds of individuals called the "Specific Scientific Conceptual Scheme" in which the nomenclature of individual disciplines is harmonised.

It is possible to dwell upon these stages in more detail. But, because of space and time limitations I would like to skip this detail and rather concentrate on deriving an educational theory from this philosophy of education. Our educational theory, as based on this philosophy of education, reveals five stages of learning:

1. The early education, which has the Life Structure as the most important component and starts from the birth of an individual before the formal schooling starts. But we must add that this education should continue throughout one's life because it concerns the Life Structure, which is also the initial worldview.
2. Elementary Education, which is concerned with the worldview of the individual.
3. Middle Education is concerned with the Knowledge Structure within the worldview of the individual.
4. Higher Education is concerned with developing the Scientific Conceptual Scheme within the Knowledge Structure; and finally
5. Graduate Education aims at developing the Specific Scientific Conceptual Scheme and as such, it is the stage where more attention is paid to the specialisation.

The last two stages concern us here as they deal with higher education. But we need to elaborate all the stages in order to clarify how one comes to this stage. In the early education, the individual is prepared for the early education and taught the cultural elements in which knowledge should occupy a special place. This way every person knows that learning is significant. At this stage, the home environment and what the parents do is very important. An individual with a good Life Structure in mind means one who has a worldview that backs up knowledge tendency. I believe that it is at this stage that the person is motivated to do what he/she wants to do later in life and as such it determines for the most part the person's tendency to develop though somewhat unconsciously and naturally his/her leaning for a career in life. It may play a role to develop the person's inherent ability for whatever it may be.

Secondly, the individual is ready for the Elementary Education when he/she has a solid Life Structure in mind. Since this corresponds to the Stage of Worldview at this stage of education only elements that make up the basic structure of the individual's worldview must be given. Special techniques should be developed to the teaching of his/her worldview. The curriculum should also be developed on the basis of that worldview. There is no need to teach basic sciences at this stage as is done today in the Muslim world.

In the Third Stage the Knowledge Structure of the individual's worldview is given. We need to elaborate this because it is crucial for an educational theory. In addition, this stage prepares the student for higher education. In the Knowledge Structure of a worldview, there are concepts that provide a mentality to the individual. These concepts are held in unity under the umbrella concept "knowledge" which thus acquires a doctrinal character. Other related concepts in this unity are science, truth, falsehood, opinion, belief, certainty, method, theory, understanding, doubt and so on. All these concepts are well formed and harmonised together so well that their unity projects an understanding called "knowledge mentality". As such, it projects one's understanding of knowledge, method and truth together with their significance. The student learns with this mentality that knowledge is valuable and that one needs knowledge in life. In addition, the student finds out that knowledge acquired with special method is called "science". The application of science is technology and so on. Of course, the way these propositions are put here may be expressed in different ways in every worldview. There is just one common characteristic in all worldviews here; they all have a specific Knowledge Structure of their own. When this structure is well developed in the minds of the students then they find out what to do with knowledge. Those who are still interested in the same type of systematic knowledge will continue for higher education where they will begin to learn all sciences in a general way. Hence, we arrive at the Fourth Stage, which is the stage of Higher Education. The approach at this stage should be interdisciplinary so, that, the student learns about all the sciences in a general way but in later years of this stage, they drift to a more particular area, which will eventually become their area of expertise.

After the student graduates from this level which corresponds to what we call today the bachelors degree he/she continues for deeper specialisation in graduate studies which represents the Fifth and final stage of our educational theory. We may now summarize the completely educational process in Fig. 26.4.

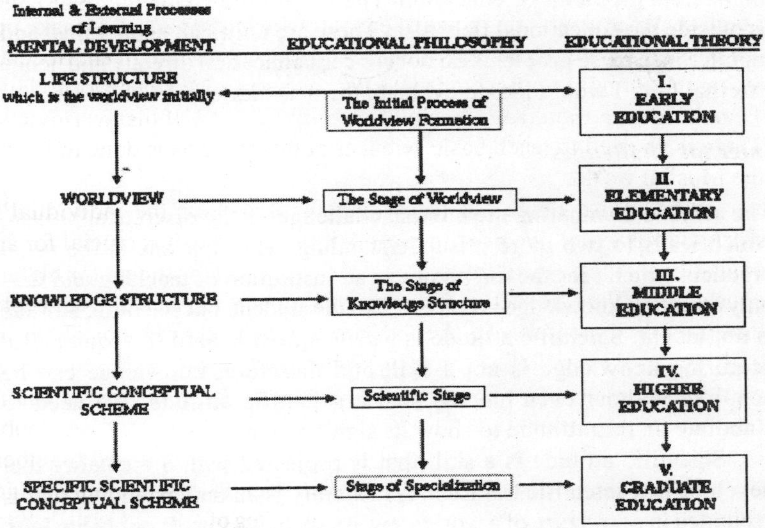

Fig. 26.4: Educational Process

Challenges for Higher Education

Based on our exposition above the most crucial challenge facing the university in the Muslim world is what I call the *discrete approach.* This approach takes higher education as a separate entity from the early education and does not consider it as integral and complimentary to it. In the past the *madrasah* education was not taken discretely, but as a whole from the beginning to the end of one's educational training. But, today the university is not seen any more a part of this general education but rather the training sanctuary for either practitioners of science or for those who seek to get a job for livelihood. As a result of this wrong understanding, most students come to the university not to acquire the scientific mentality of the age. They rather come with a wrong attitude thinking that they need to acquire the contemporary scientific knowledge. Above all most students think that acquiring this knowledge will give them a better chance to get a good job. They never think about how to be more successful after getting the job. As I see these problems more related to the internal process, I would like to evaluate them as "Internal Challenges".

Challenges that face our higher education today are not limited to the internal problems of education. There are more challenges that face us outside the educational field also. These are political, economical and moral. Since these problems do not concern education directly and hence external to it, I would like to evaluate them as "External Challenges".

Internal Challenges

The attitude dominating the internal challenges is the discrete approach, which leads to two more misunderstanding. The first one is the usual practice, which sees the university as an institution of teaching and thus only scientific knowledge is conveyed to the student, but scientific attitude is not taught. Scientific attitude is a *skill, which* is hard to acquire. But acquiring knowledge is not a skill and therefore, knowledge can be acquired without even having such a scientific attitude. We need to elaborate on this attitude to show its significance.

Scientific attitude is a skill that is projected with a mentality that develops in a scientific tradition. A mentality is an understanding that is grounded in a structure of a worldview. As such, it controls our behaviour. It is in a sense the mental framework or perspective out of which *naturally* and/or *actively* follows a human activity. Knowledge proceeds from a mental framework *naturally*, if it arises purely out of the capacities of our knowledge faculties. Therefore, if an activity springs only naturally from a mentality, then it depends totally on the internal process of knowledge, which we have outlined above. But, usually humans are not subjects that acquire knowledge passively; they are rather active agents who contribute to the process of knowing and learning. In this way, knowledge will proceed from the knowledge acquired through both our education and using the natural capacities of the mind. It is this kind of a knowledge acquisition process that we call 'active'. It is clear that mentalities are more important in the active knowledge processes because it is the mentality that controls the active participation in knowledge.

After this brief outline of mentalities, we may show how important it is to develop a scientific mentality. For, without such a mentality it is not possible to be actively engaged in scientific activities. In order to clarify this, we may give the following analogy: a student who cheats may be said to be cheating because he is selfish, dishonest, and because of the circumstances which led him to that undesirable action. We consider all these and similar motives or circumstances underlying the act to be the *external factors*, because they are not factors to be found directly in the actor and hence can be observed either directly or indirectly within the action itself. Yet, there are also certain other mental conditions that lead the student in question to his action. Such as his conception of cheating and the placement of that concept within his worldview. This is indeed the mentality, which the student has in his worldview. Upon analysing that action, therefore, it is possible to distinguish three elements constituting the performance of it:

1. The mental framework within which the action is conceptualised prior to its performance.
2. Certain physiological and environmental conditions leading to the action, and we would like to broaden the scope of these elements by not limiting them just to the environmental and physiological conditions.
3. The performance of the action itself.

As it is seen in our analogy, the development of these *factors* in the individual's life must take place in different ways, but in relation to each other. The mentality, for instance, does not develop instantly, though the action itself is performed in an instant. Even the environmental and physiological conditions may develop instantly, yet in relation to the mentality and the performance of the action. In fact, the mentality is the framework, which includes the totality of concepts and aspirations developed by the individual throughout his life, and as such, it constitutes a structural characteristic within a worldview. Since every related concept and event is evaluated within a certain mentality before a decision is taken to perform the action, then it must be considered as the *direct* factor of an action. Since we take worldview to be the *foundation* of mentalities then the worldview itself is the *prior most foundation* of any action. We conclude from this that every human action, including scientific activity, is ultimately traceable to its mentality through its worldview; and as such it is reducible directly to that scientific mentality and ultimately to that worldview. But unfortunately this foundation of human conduct cannot be perceived by observation directly and as a result, it can be overviewed easily; in order to emphasize this fact we may call a worldview the "non-observable foundation", or the "(conceptual) environment" of human actions. Our exposition of the concept of worldview thus brings us to the conclusion that science arises within certain worldviews only. This conclusion has other implications as well, besides clearly pointing to the fact that in certain worldviews no science can arise.

The proper environment for the rise of sciences means only the adequate worldview within which there is a possibility for the flourishing of sciences. Such a worldview is the one in which, a sophisticated Knowledge Structure has emerged. Then, as a result of this, the early scholars of that society in which that worldview predominates establish a sophisticated network of key scientific terms, which we call "scientific conceptual scheme". This leads us to conclude that although our scientific activities ultimately derive from our worldview, they do not directly follow out of it. For, there is a need for another framework, which directly supports such activities. It is this framework, which we may term "scientific mentality". This mentality leads to the development of a skill that is reflected on the scientific activities. Skills are developed through constant practice under the guidance of masters. This can be given only in the university. Therefore, this should be the aim of university education and it must have no other concern. We should not worry whether the student does not get the sufficient knowledge, which he will need after graduation when he starts working in his area of concern. For, since he has acquired the scientific mentality he will know how to develop himself and complete his knowledge wherever needed.

The second misunderstanding is seeing the university as an institution of teaching and thus it is believed that the aim of the university is primarily to teach the student contemporary scientific knowledge. This eventually leads to arrange the university not according to an educational philosophy and a theory. As a result, no thinker attempts to develop such a theory. We must understand that *theory* is the plan of an achievement. If there is no plan then the whole institution is simply copied from an existing model. This is why most developing nations copy a model of the university from a Western country and try to develop it in their own culture. They cannot develop because the university model in the West is developed because of an educational philosophy, which is foreign to the indigenous culture. Since they do not know that philosophy they do not know how to cope with its problems either. I would like to point out that this second problem is mainly dependent on the first one and thus can be solved because of scientific mentality only.

External Challenges

There are many external challenges facing higher education today in the Muslim world. There is first the economic challenge because the budget reserved for education is very low in most of these countries. There is a political problem also in the sense that there is hardly any scientific freedom, let alone freedom of thought and expression. Obviously, no scientific mentality is possible under these circumstances. But there is one more challenge, which over shadows all these external challenges and that is the moral challenge. Human determination can overcome all economic and political and even social problems with struggle, but the moral challenge can be faced effectively only with the proper moral attitude. Because, if its importance I would like to evaluate this challenge by way of concluding remarks and new prospects in higher education.

Concluding Remarks and New Prospects

I consider the moral challenge to be the most outstanding danger facing higher education today. We may deal with other challenges as we can easily recognise them since they are internal to education. But the moral problems facing us are not directly related to education and as a result cannot easily be diagnosed. Therefore, I would like to evaluate the moral challenge as the most conspicuous challenge facing the university today. I would like to illustrate this in the process of the emergence of scientific traditions. For, the moral element is almost totally neglected in analysis of scientific traditions. Therefore, if I evaluate how scientific traditions emerge in history we will be able to see the function of the moral element. Since, the university as an institution represents scientific tradition, then the moral challenge for higher education can also be obtained within the analysis of the emergence of scientific traditions. In this way, I am hoping to introduce at the same time scientific attitude embedded in scientific traditions as the new trend in higher education. I emphasize this point because unfortunately it is neglected in so many new universities especially in the Muslim world.

We have already clarified our point that there is a Knowledge Structure in a worldview, which directly acts as the ground of all scientific activities. But in this Knowledge Structure, there is a need for another conceptual basis to support these activities directly and that has been identified as "Scientific Conceptual Scheme". The emergence of a Scientific Conceptual Scheme within a given society leads to a scientific tradition. Therefore, the very concept of scientific tradition involves the assumption of a scientific community because the rise of a scientific tradition necessarily assumes the existence of a society. In this sense, the idea of scientific tradition, which is primarily a cognitive scheme, includes the achievements of generations of scientists within which scientific education is carried out and thus supplies a foundation for their further scientific practices. Therefore, this whole process can be analysed in order to reveal its basic factors and phases.

Obviously, there must be certain conditions in a society so that science and learning will flourish. However, these conditions cannot so easily be ascertained. That is why we deem it necessary to study them in this context in order to show that there must have been some conditions at the social level, with all its aspects, for the rise of learning and education in a given society. Since, these conditions are the causes for the rise of learning within a certain social and cultural context, I would like to call them "contextual causes" for the rise of scientific tradition. It is possible to distinguish certain contextual causes as more rudimentary and hence necessary for the emergence of any kind of scientific activity; we shall refer to such necessary elements leading to the rise of a scientific tradition as "nucleus contextual causes". All other peripheral elements that contribute to the rise of the nucleus contextual causes leading to the emergence of science and a scientific tradition can be termed "marginal contextual causes".

A nucleus contextual cause is a dynamism, which manifests itself at two levels. The first is at the social level, which causes certain unrest and stirring within the society as if the whole structure of the society is re-shaping itself and thus every social institution is affected by this dynamism, but most importantly, the political and educational institutions are re-organised because of this unrest. Second is at the level of learning (education) and it is this dynamism which causes a lively exchange of ideas on scientific and intellectual subjects among the learned of the community.

For instance, in the case of Islam it was internally generated by the thought of the Qur'ān through its dissemination within the first Muslim community. But here what we are trying to look for is whether there is any universal rule (or rules) governing the generation of that dynamism. At the social level two phenomena may be distinguished as corresponding to the nucleus contextual causes for the emergence of a scientific tradition: the first is moral dynamism; and the second is intellectual dynamism. Therefore, there are primarily two nucleus contextual causes: one is moral in character, the other is intellectual, both of which refer to a dynamism in a given society. With respect to moral dynamism, it is possible to divide the members of a given society into three groups:

1. Morally sensitive people;
2. The common mass; and
3. The selfish or morally insensitive people.

Among these three classes only the moral and the selfish are dynamic. For the former class struggles to restore morality and good order in society, whereas the selfish remain indifferent to this end by spending their dynamism to their own ends. The masses, on the other hand, are driven to either side, which may lead to a struggle on behalf of both sides to defend their goals that mayor may not result in intellectual dynamism. This is because the nucleus contextual cause is not the only cause of intellectual dynamism; for this development can be attained only when all other conditions are also present. But, if the morally sensitive class becomes victorious and draws the masses towards that end, then intellectual progress can take place once the second phenomenon of the nucleus contextual cause, i.e. intellectual dynamism, is present.

We would like to posit here a feature of scientific attitude, namely originality, which also encompasses dynamism inherently. We may illustrate this point with the Greek scientific tradition. We claim that if there were not in each case a new and fresh outlook, the intellectual dynamism would not have flourished and thus the flair of Greek intellectualism would have died out long before Plato. Moreover, just because there is hardly any original theory and doctrine after Aristotle, Greek intellectualism began to decline after his era. The same is also true for both the Islamic and Western scientific traditions, but the way this intellectual dynamism is manifested in all these societies varies. The "dynamism inherent within originality and novelty" (of ideas and doctrines) is what we call "intellectual dynamism". We consider this also as a natural element in human constitution. What we are showing here is the idea that originality inherently possessing dynamism contributes essentially to the rise of scientific traditions. In fact, originality is invigorating, fascinating and enlivening, it is just like the re-awakening of a land from the demise of winter, and this dynamism is reflected thereby in the society, which is then set into a process of scientific advancement provided that there are no impediments in the way of mutual companionship between science system and its community. Thus, without intellectual dynamism no intellectual development is ever possible. But, this does not mean that, as we have already stated, once there are original theories and philosophical systems, then such progress will necessarily take place. The reason for this is the other condition of the society, namely moral dynamism, which must conform to the originality of intellectualism and thus enable it to flourish. Otherwise, intellectual progress will soon die out, which was the case of Greek intellectualism after Aristotle, who is the most original Greek philosopher. But his originality was not sufficient to provide continuity to the apex of Greek thought. In history this has somehow been the ill-fate of all civilisations; a community or nation at the apex of its civilisation becomes 'worn out', being burdened by the tremendous weight of its history it begins to decline. Although we do not think that this is a necessary development of a civilisation, *viz.* born out-progress-apex-decline and fall, this seems to have been the course of all past-civilisations. If our view here concerning the course that intellectual progress and a civilisation takes at its rise, is granted then the opposite course will be the natural process of decline, which means that as long as the contextual causes are kept alive the civilisation carrying the scientific tradition will continue to live and progress.

One should be reminded that these contextual causes cannot exhaustively be enumerated for all societies. There may be, for example, ten such causes needed in the case of Greek civilisation, but this number may be eighteen for another society. Hence, although the number of the nucleus contextual causes as necessary elements may be precise for all societies, the general number of contextual causes, namely the nucleus and the marginal contextual causes taken together cannot be determined in a decisive manner. In fact, we can give examples from the Western scientific tradition that there were thinkers with original ideas and even with novel philosophical systems which did not lead to intellectual progress. Two famous examples are Boethius (d. ca. 524 or 525) and John Scotus Erigena (d. ca. 877). In both of these cases we do not find any continuity of ideas or doctrines after their death, although they both put forward original theories with sufficient vigour. This is because other elements required for intellectual dynamism were not present then and, as a result, we do not see any other scientists furthering their scientific endeavour to lead to a scientific tradition. They will thus remain "isolated cases" within the history of Western science.

It is possible now for us to elucidate how moral and intellectual dynamism may take place as social phenomena. The moral unrest within a particular society demonstrates a struggle mainly between two classes of people; the morally sensitive and the selfish class. The masses remain as the middle class between the two. When the struggle is taking place, although, it is only between the morally sensitive and the selfish, it is immediately passed on to the masses, who become the battle ground of the good and evil forces. Some of the masses are thus won to the moral side, and yet others to the selfish front we may apply here a term from the Islamic civilisation, which expresses this social fact: *Sunnatullah.* This moral struggle is a *Sunnatullah* and thus there is no human society in which this struggle cannot be found in one form or another. When the morally sensitive people exhort sufficient vigour, dynamism and energy, they win to their side an adequate number of the masses and thereby produce intellectual and social dynamism. When the moral struggle between the two groups continues with a victory of the moral class (for this struggle never ends with a victory, but always continues in different forms as long as the society exists). Either, the morally sensitive individuals, are themselves intellectuals who produce intellectuals and formulate original ideas, doctrines and systems by introducing fresh and novel definitions of key concepts that are moral and scientific or knowledge related. This way a lively exchange of ideas and alternative views come into existence within the society; a phenomenon which is necessary to produce intellectual dynamism.

The moral struggle, which is essentially a strife between the good and evil, may either give rise directly to social dynamism, or to intellectual dynamism first, which, then, in turn produces social dynamism. Hence, although in certain cases social dynamism may precede the intellectual one, it does not mean that social dynamism is a nucleus contextual cause for the emergence of a scientific tradition. For the activity in question is of a cognitive nature, namely science. Therefore, it is still a secondary contextual cause with regard to the nature of the activity in question. But, the social dynamism usually leads to an overall activity within the society, which we call "institutional dynamism". Hence, there are primarily two marginal dynamisms, which we shall now investigate, *social dynamism* and *institutional dynamism*.

The nucleus contextual causes, i.e. moral and intellectual dynamism, must necessarily produce social dynamism once they are adequately successful. But social dynamism is necessarily preceded by moral dynamism, which we have described quite simply as a moral struggle between the morally sensitive and the selfish; but it is not necessarily preceded by intellectual dynamism. On the other hand, all these various dynamisms are required for intellectual progress that eventually leads to the emergence of a scientific tradition. Yet we distinguish only the moral and intellectual struggles to be the nucleus contextual causes. Since, social dynamism is not found at this foundational level, it cannot be included among the nucleus causes. But it must be recognised as a marginal contextual cause. When the nucleus contextual forces are at work, a tremendous social mobility and dynamism begins. It is the dynamism of individuals working together to lead the society as a whole to a morally better situation that we call "social dynamism", which in turn leads to the re-organisation and betterment of social institutions including the political and economic ones as well. It is this reformative and enlightened effort at the organisational level that we call "institutional dynamism". When all these contextual causes come together, then they lead the society to intellectual progress. But besides contextual causes different societies may exhibit some other different causes of intellectual progress; such is the case with Western scientific tradition which has Islamic influences also as a cause for the rise of Western intellectualism. Whereas in the Islamic case, the causes are found only within the society, although after the development of Islamic intellectualism in the first century of Islam (i.e. the 7th century A.D.) it came under foreign influences, especially that of the Greek philosophy and science, which did help improve its intellectualism further.

Since institutional dynamism takes place at the level of social institutions, we must cite them here because of the crucial role they play in the rise of scientific traditions. The most significant of these is the educational institutions; a great reform and re-organisation in accordance with the knowledge produced by the intellectual dynamism is required of all the educational institutions, if the society is to produce intellectual progress. Usually, there seems to be a relation, although not a necessary one, between the political body and the educational reform. Either the political body brings about the educational reform at the request and direction of the intellectuals, or intellectuals themselves take the initiative and produce educational dynamism, which may in turn lead to a re-organisation of the political body and thus produce a great political mobility within the political institutions. These activities, which also include the legal undertakings, can be called "political dynamism". Among these institutional dynamisms, we must mention also economic activities. Similar reformations take place in the economic institutions yielding thereby to improve the prosperity of that society and this activity can be called "economic dynamism". All these institutional dynamisms do not necessarily develop together within the same period of time and thus helping each other become dynamic reciprocally; or following a different pattern of sequence in every civilisation. The educational, political, legal and economic dynamisms include within themselves, with a varying degree of intensity, all the nucleus contextual dynamisms explained above, and as such, they are the ones that produce culture. A scientific tradition is born in such a culture only.

We may, therefore, reduce the factors leading to the rise of a scientific tradition to the following seven factors: moral, intellectual, educational, social, legal and economic. The first two are necessary elements and the last three depend on the educational system. Since higher education represents the scientific attitude reflected in a scientific tradition then obviously the university ought to assume this task. If we see that all these factors are reduced to the moral struggle (ethical *jihad*), then the scientists in the higher educational institutions must realise where to start. It is for this reason that I am positing the scientific attitude as the most indispensable trend for universities in the Muslim world today.

REFERENCES

Agarwal, Pawan (2006) *Higher Education in India: The Need for Change* (ICIER Working Paper No. 180). New Delhi: Indian Council for Research on International Economic Relations, (*http://www.icrier.org*/publication/working_papers_180.html)

Altbach, Philip G. (2006) The Private Higher Education Revolution: An Introduction. *University News*. January 2-8. Vol. 44, No. 1.

Anandakrishnan, M. (2006) *Privatization of Higher Education: Opportunities and Anomalies*. "Privatization and commercialization of higher education" organised by NIEPA, May 2, New Delhi.

Carl Dahlman and Anuja Utz, (2005) *India and the Knowledge Economy: Leveraging Strengths and Opportunities* (World Bank Report No. 31267-IN), Washington DC: World Bank, (*http://wwwwds.worldbank.org*/servlet/WDSContentServer/IB/312670IN.txt)

Chronicle of Higher Education, various issues (cited as CHE) (*http://chronicle.com/*)

Delors, Jacques (1996) Learning the treasure within. *Report to UNESCO of the International Commission on Education for the Twenty-first Century*. Paris : UNSECO Publishing.

MHRD (2006) *Annual Report*. Ministry of Human Resource Development, Department of Secondary and Higher education. New Delhi : Government of India.

Mishra, Sharda, (2006). *UGC and Higher Education System in India*. Jaipur : Book Enclave.

Planning Commission (1999) *Approach Paper to the Tenth Five-year Plan* (2002-2007). New Delhi : Planning Commission.

Powar, K.B. (2002). *Indian Higher Education: A Conglomerate of Concept, Facts, and Practices*. New Delhi : Concept Publishing Company.

Sharma, Sharda, *UGC and Higher Education System in India*.

Stella, Antony (2002) *External Quality Assurance in Indian Higher Education: Case study of the National Assessment and Accreditation Council* (NAAC). Paris : International Institute for Educational Planning.

•

UGC (2005) *Research Handbook: Towards nurturing research culture in higher education institutions in India.* New Delhi : University Grants Commission.

University News, December 26, 2005, January 1, 2006.

University News, Vol. 49. No. 31, August 11, 2011.

University News, Vol. 49. No. 35, August 29, September 4, 2011.

World Bank (2004) "*Measuring Trade in Services Liberalization and its Impact on Economic Growth*: *An Illustration*", World Bank Group Working Paper, downloadable from *http://econ.worldbank.org*/files/2373_wps2655.pdf

Index